# Unifying political methodology

# Unifying political methodology

The likelihood theory of statistical inference

GARY KING

*Department of Government, Harvard University*

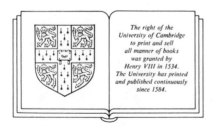

*The right of the
University of Cambridge
to print and sell
all manner of books
was granted by
Henry VIII in 1534.
The University has printed
and published continuously
since 1584.*

## CAMBRIDGE UNIVERSITY PRESS

*Cambridge*
*New York   Port Chester   Melbourne   Sydney*

Published by the Press Syndicate of the University of Cambridge
The Pitt Building, Trumpington Street, Cambridge CB2 1RP
32 East 57th Street, New York, NY 10022, USA
10 Stamford Road, Oakleigh, Melbourne 3166, Australia

First published 1989

Printed in the United States of America

*Library of Congress Cataloging-in-Publication Data*
King, Gary.
Unifying political methodology : the likelihood theory of
statistical inference / Gary King.
p.    cm.
Bibliography: p.
Includes index.
ISBN 0-521-36622-4. – ISBN 0-521-36697-6 (pbk.)
1. Political science – Methodology.    2. Political statistics.
3. Probabilities.    I. Title.
JA71.K563        1989
320′.018–dc19                                                          88-27025
                                                                              CIP

*British Library Cataloging in Publication Data*
King, Gary
Unifying political methodology: the
likelihood theory of statistical inference
1. Political science.    Research.    Quantitative
methods
I. Title
320.′072

ISBN 0-521-36622-4 hard covers
ISBN 0-521-36697-7 paperback

**For Elizabeth**

# Contents

**II  Methods**

x        **Contents**

# Preface

This book is about methodology in political science. Its purpose is to unify existing methods and formulate some new methods, under a general theory of statistical inference. As explained in Section 1.1, it is also intended to stimulate and centralize methodological debate in political science. From this, I hope a new and much needed subfield of political methodology will eventually emerge.

I address this work principally to political scientists. However, insofar as I write about the foundations of statistical methodology, and because the vast majority of methods currently being used in the discipline were created elsewhere, some scholars from other social science disciplines may also find it of interest.

Political methodology is a fledgling subfield. As such, quantitative researchers in political science generally do not have as extensive a background in algebra, matrix algebra, calculus, and probability theory as their counterparts in some other social science disciplines. However, most have a fairly good understanding of regression analysis and some exposure to, but usually no formal courses in, these other areas. I address *Unifying Political Methodology* to researchers with about this level of preparation. Readers willing to consult a college algebra (or occasionally calculus) text when necessary should have little difficulty.

I have been extremely fortunate to be able to confer with some of the best methodologists and empirical researchers in the discipline about this book. Neal Beck's suggestions, and our nearly continuous communications via electronic mail, were invaluable. My thanks go to Chris Achen, Larry Bartels, John Jackson, and Doug Rivers for detailed comments on earlier versions of this manuscript. Henry Brady has been a great resource, and Jim Alt provided important advice at many stages. The annual Political Science Methodology Group meetings provided an unparalleled forum in which to try out many of these ideas. My appreciation goes out to Jo Andrews, Stephen Ansolabehere, Nancy Burns, Keisuke Iida, Walter Mattli, Elizabeth Rosenthal, and Paul Zarowin for very useful discussions and helpful comments. Nancy also provided superb research assistance. I especially thank Elizabeth for encourage-

xi

ment and support. Thanks go to the National Science Foundation for research support (NSF#SES-87-22715) and to Emily Loose and Louise Calabro Gruendel at Cambridge University Press for editorial assistance. Finally, I am grateful to the many colleagues and students at Harvard and around the country who, in asking for statistical advice, enabled me to explore a wide spectrum of substantive questions and methodological issues.

*Cambridge, Massachusetts*                                        Gary King

# PART I

# Theory

CHAPTER 1

# Introduction

## 1.1 Toward a new political methodology

Since the emergence of the discipline, political scientists have focused their methodological efforts on creating new data sources. Scholars have polled millions of citizens in personal interviews, recorded exhaustive lists of cooperative and conflictual international events, collected enormous quantities of aggregate data, and preserved the formal and informal decisions of numerous elected officials. These new data sources have enabled political scientists to consider myriad new empirical questions and unexplored theories.

In data collection, political science outdistances most other social sciences. However, in developing and adapting statistical methods to accommodate theoretical requirements and the special data that is collected, political methodology lags far behind the methodological subfields of virtually every other discipline. *This imbalance in political science research between state-of-the-art data collection and weak methods means that future statistical innovations are likely to have disproportionate impact on scholarly research.*[1]

This is not to say that political scientists have shied away from quantitative analyses. To the contrary, quantitative methods have gained widespread acceptance over the past decade. However, the overwhelming majority of statistical methods currently in use have been imported into political science directly from almost every other scientific discipline. Since these tools are generally imported intact and without adaptation, many are ill-suited to the particular needs of political science data and theory. In addition, most political scientists learn only a few of these methods and methodological perspectives, often with unfortunate consequences. For example, many observed political variables are fundamentally discrete; voter preferences, international event counts, and political party identifications are cases in point. The problem is that the application of techniques such as linear regression analysis forces researchers to define naturally discrete concepts as continuous or to try

---

[1] Since data in political science do not permit a standard set of statistical assumptions, some argue that we should use only very simple quantitative methods. But this is precisely incorrect. Indeed, sophisticated methods are required only when data are problematic; extremely reliable data with sensational relationships require little if any statistical analysis.

3

to elicit a continuous survey response about a discrete concept. The result is measurement error, bias, and the loss of a significant amount of information.

Given this practice of borrowing from diverse disciplines, political scientists have amassed considerable expertise in using methods created by others. Unfortunately, with a few notable exceptions, expertise in evaluating and adapting existing methods, and in creating new methodologies, is severely lacking. Paradoxically, political scientists make excellent applied econometricans, sociometricans, and psychometricians but often poor political methodologists.

The absence of a coherent field of political methodology has at least three important consequences: the lack of methodological standards, communication, and cumulation.

First, political science has few, if any, established methodological standards. Some researchers abide by statisticians' standards; some have adopted those of economists; others adhere to the statistical norms of sociological research. In short, the discipline of political science has nearly as many methodological standards as there are statistical methods. Unfortunately, this mosaic of largely incompatible standards and traditions has not coalesced into a consistent whole. If progress is to be made in substantive research, we must work toward some uniform, discipline-wide methodological standards. Pluralism and diversity in methods are welcome features; however, diversity in standards to evaluate the merits of these different methods is equivalent to the absence of standards. The frequency of statistical fads is a consequence of this undesirable state of affairs. The scholarly journals are littered with the surge, decline, and, in too few cases, eventual reasoned incorporation of numerous new techniques. Factor analysis, log-linear models for contingency tables, Box-Jenkins time series analysis, and vector autoregression are but a few examples of what were once statistical fads.

Second, institutional mechanisms to disseminate methodological developments, when they occur, are rudimentary at best. This compounds the discipline's methodological shortcomings in several ways. The absence of communication leads to frequent replication of the same statistical mistakes and repeated attempts to address methodological problems that have already been solved (King, 1986a). Moreover, scholars are slow to recognize that methodological developments in one field of political science may be applicable to similar problems in other fields.

Finally, the absence of cumulative progress in political methodology reduces the potential for methodology to influence substantive research in political science in positive ways. "Whatever else may be uncertain in methodology, there is ample evidence that the shaky foundation it provides has weakened intellectual structures across the discipline" (Achen, 1983: 71).

What political science needs, then, is a more highly developed and unified field of political methodology. From this should come a set of standards for evaluating quantitative research, more flexible and powerful statistical techniques able to extract significant amounts of new information from our wealth of quantitative data, new methodological perspectives that provide novel ways of looking at the political world, and the potential for cumulative progress in political science research.

This book is intended to take political methodology some way down this path. I have sought to unify the diverse statistical methods existing in political science under a general theory of scientific inference. Indeed, since "a theory is the creation of unity in what is diverse by the discovery of unexpected likenesses" (Bronowski, 1958: 8), unifying political methodology and articulating a general theory of inference are compatible, if not equivalent, goals. With the likelihood theory of statistical inference, one can go a very long way toward extracting the essential features of these methods while leaving behind the peculiar conventions and practices more appropriate in other disciplines. Likelihood is neither the only theory of statistical inference nor the best theory for every political science problem, but it generates, by far, the most widely applicable methods for data analysis.

I omit several aspects of ongoing research in political methodology from this book. First, with a few exceptions, I do not talk about how to derive statistical models from economic theory. Although several excellent examples exist in the discipline (see Enelow and Hinich, 1984), most areas of political science do not have fully developed formal theories. Second, political science contributions to other disciplines are not discussed except tangentially (e.g., Brady, 1985; Hildebrand, Laing, and Rosenthal, 1977; Rivers and Vuong, 1988). Finally, neither political statistics and data collection (see Tufte, 1977) nor descriptive statistics (Alker, 1975) and methods of graphical presentation (Tufte, 1983) are discussed in any detail. Each of these topics is of considerable importance, but I have tried to keep my focus on the theory of inference and creating statistical models for research in political science.

The remainder of this chapter defines terms, symbols, and the elementary ideas to be used throughout the book. Part I (Chapters 1–4) contains a comprehensive analysis of *uncertainty* and *inference,* the two key concepts underlying empirical research in political science. The basic concepts are introduced in Chapter 2. Then, the probability model of uncertainty is presented in Chapter 3 and the likelihood model of scientific inference in Chapter 4. The likelihood model is based on the probability model, but it is far more useful as a theory of inference, providing a more fundamental basis for statistical analysis. The chapters comprising Part II draw on the theory of inference developed in Part I. In each chapter, I present a different set of statistical models applicable to a different type of data and theory. A variety of discrete regression models is presented in Chapter 5. Chapter 6 reviews models based on cross-classified tabular data, and Chapter 7 demonstrates how to model time series processes. An introduction to multiple equation models appears in Chapter 8. Models for nonrandom selection are in Chapter 9, and general classes of multiple equation models are derived in Chapter 10.

Thus, this book explores a very broad set of statistical models. However, the subject of this book is a new perspective on the unity inherent in what are and should be the methods of political methodology, not a comprehensive guide to every possible method or even an exhaustive analysis of any one. My subject is the trunk of the tree and some of its branches, not the detail in the leaves. In addition, in many places, I have gone beyond the list of techniques commonly used in political science research and have described models that could profitably be used but have not been. Whereas some of these statistical methods are new just to political science, others were derived here for the first time.

## 1.2     A language of inference

In order to begin from a common frame of reference, I briefly develop a language to describe key features of the enterprise. The terms, phrases, and mathematical symbols in this language are not sacrosanct, but they do differ from more standard treatments for specific theoretical reasons (for a discussion and criticism of statistical language, see Bross, 1971). This is meant only as a brief general overview; each of the concepts mentioned here is more fully explained in later chapters.

*Social system:* The largest component of social scientific inference is the social system – the object under study. A social system may be a neighborhood, a government, an election, a war, a stock market, or anything else a researcher wants to know about. The social system usually contains certain *features* that are either known or estimable, but important elements remain unobserved and indeed unobservable.

*Explanatory variables:* Explanatory variables are measures of the features of a social system, symbolized as $X$. Unless otherwise stated, I assume that $X$ is *known* a priori. $X$ contains measures of each of these features for all $n$ observations $(x_1, \ldots, x_i, \ldots, x_n)$. If only one feature is known and relevant, $x_i$ is a scalar variable. If several known features are relevant, $x_i$ is a vector of variables.

*Output (dependent variable):* Every interesting social system generates some type of output. Outputs are consequences of the social system that can be observed and measured. For example, an election produces a victorious candidate, a coup d'etat in a developing nation could produce changes in policies toward the industrialized world, and a stock market may generate competitive prices for existing firms.

When parts of the social system are under control of the researcher, the process of producing output is called an *experiment*. In experiments, the researcher can manipulate the explanatory variables (the known features of the social system) and make it produce output as needed. Although true experiments are only infrequently possible in the social sciences, I will use the term generally where an experiment could be conducted, if only in theory. For example, a presidential election cannot be controlled by political scientists, but one can imagine the same election being "run" multiple times under essentially identical conditions. Let $Y$ stand for a vector of $n$ outputs of the social system. $Y_i$, one of the $n$ outputs, is generated in theory by setting the known features of the social system ($x_i$) to particular values and running the experiment. Even under identical conditions (i.e., values of the explanatory variables), the social system outputs different results for each experiment; this is because output is produced in a probabilistic instead of deterministic manner.

*Random variables:* Operationally, a random variable is the assignment of numbers to events (Democratic President = 1, Republican President = 0; income = number of dollars, etc.) with a probability assigned to each number. One should not confuse "random" with "haphazard." Random processes adhere to very specific probabilistic rules defined below. $Y_i$ is a *random* variable since the actual data are randomly produced from the social system's outputs according to each event's probability. The key idea behind a random variable is that $Y_i$ varies across an infinite number of hypothetical experiments. If the actual experiment were "run" again under essentially the same conditions, the observed values of the dependent variable (the "realizations" of the random variables) would differ but the nature of the experiment and the social system would remain constant.

*The data:* The data, $y$, are $n$ observed realizations of the *random variables Y*. They are a set of numbers, each $y_i$ being a random draw from a corresponding random dependent variable, $Y_i$. The process by which portions of output are chosen and measured is called *sampling,* and the data themselves are sometimes called "the sample." Survey sampling is one general category of examples, but many others exist. The specific sampling method used is central to both modeling and estimation. (Only occasionally will I use "the data" to refer to both $y$ and $X$.)

*Models:* A model is a mathematical simplification of, and approximation to, a more complex concept or social system. Models are never literally "true," although one often proceeds as if they were. Indeed, the idea that a model *is* a social system or that parameters exist in nature is certainly odd. Within this definition, many types of models exist. The next paragraph introduces a general *statistical model,* from which many even more specific statistical models are derived. In the next chapter, I also discuss *probability* as a general model of uncertainty and *likelihood* as a general model for statistical inference. Indeed, modeling is the core concept of this volume: Models provide precise views to the world; they contribute new ways of approaching old problems; and they provide a means of inferring from observed data to unobserved phenomena of interest (see Bender, 1978).

*Statistical models:* A statistical model is a formal representation of the *process* by which a social system produces output. The essential goal is to learn about the underlying process that generates output and hence the observed data. Since no interesting social systems generate outcomes deterministically, statistical models are assumed to have both *systematic* and *stochastic* components.

The most common way of writing a complete linear-Normal regression model, for example, is to express the random dependent variable ($Y_i$) as the sum of a systematic ($x_i\beta$) and a stochastic ($\epsilon_i$) component:

$$Y_i = x_i\beta + \epsilon_i, \tag{1.1}$$

$$\epsilon_i \sim f_n(e_i|0,\sigma^2),$$

where $f_n$ refers to the Normal distribution with mean zero and constant variance $\sigma^2$. This representation is very convenient for linear-Normal models, but quite burdensome in the more general case. Fortunately, these equations can be equivalently expressed as follows:

$$Y_i \sim f_n(y_i|\mu_i,\sigma^2), \tag{1.2}$$

$$\mu_i = x_i\beta.$$

In this format, the randomness in the dependent variable $Y_i$ is modeled directly, and the systematic component models variation in one of its parameters (the mean, $\mu_i$) over the observations. Since $Y_i$ itself is random, this formulation requires no artificial analytical construct for the random error ($\epsilon_i$).

In Equation (1.1), we generally assume that $x_i$ and $\epsilon_i$ are independent. We have become used to thinking in these terms, but conceptualizing $\epsilon_i$ and what it correlates with is not as easy to explain in terms close to one's data and theory. Fortunately, an equivalent assumption in Equation (1.2) is considerably easier to theorize about: All one needs to assume is that $Y_i$ depends on $x_i$ only through its mean, $E(Y_i) \equiv \mu_i$. In other words, $x_i$ and $Y_i$ are *parametrically* related but, conditional on this parametric relationship, are not *stochastically* related.[2] This is much easier to understand in more complicated cases because this parametric relationship is expressed explicitly in the second line of Equation (1.2).

The general form of the complete statistical model, for the linear-Normal or almost any other model, may then be written in two equations as follows:

$$Y \sim f(y|\theta, \alpha), \tag{1.3}$$

$$\theta = g(X, \beta). \tag{1.4}$$

I now proceed to more precisely define each of these equations and the symbols contained therein.

*Stochastic component:* The stochastic component is not a technical annoyance, as it is sometimes treated, but is instead a critical part of the theoretical model: "The fundamental intellectual breakthrough that has accompanied the development of the modern science of statistical inference is the recognition that the random component has its own tenuous regularities that may be regarded as part of the underlying structure of the phenomenon" (Pollock, 1979: 1).[3] The stochastic component may be written, in general, as Equation (1.3) and, for random variable $i$, as $Y_i \sim f_i(y_i|\theta_i, \alpha_i)$. Equation (1.3) is read: "$Y$ is distributed as $f$ of $y$ given $\theta$ and $\alpha$." $f$ is a probability distribution, an explicit model of the form of uncertainty in the random variable $Y$ across repeated experiments (see Chapter 3). $\theta$ and $\alpha$ are both parameter vectors. The distinction between the two is conceptual rather than mathematical or statistical. In general, $\theta$ is of more interest. In the linear regression special case, $\theta$ is $E(Y_i) \equiv \mu_i$, the expected value of the dependent random variable, $Y$. In another case, $\theta$ might be $\pi$, the probability of observing one of the two

---

[2] Still another way to think about this assumption is that the variation across hypothetical experiments in $Y_i$ and over observations in $\mu_i$ ($i = 1, \ldots, n$) is orthogonal.

[3] At one time, scientists had as their goal the complete systematic modeling of $Y$, with no stochastic component. Indeed, "18th century French mathematician Pierre Simon de LaPlace once boasted that given the position and velocity of every particle in the universe, he could predict the future for the rest of time. Although there are several practical difficulties to achieving LaPlace's goal, for more than 100 years there seemed to be no reason for his not being right at least in principle" (Crunchfield et al., 1986: 47). An example demonstrating the modern understanding of this phenomenon is "a game of billiards, somewhat idealized so that the balls move across the table and cross with a negligible loss of energy." In predicting the consequences of one shot, "if the player ignored an effect even as minuscule as the gravitational attraction of an electron at the edge of the galaxy, the prediction would become wrong after one minute!" (Crunchfield et al., 1986: 49). The combined effects of many small random processes in social science research would seem considerably more substantial than in this simple physical example. See also Suppes (1984).

outcomes of a dichotomous variable. $\alpha$ is a vector of parameters that is present in only some models. $\alpha$ contains subsidiary, but potentially important information about the process that drives the observed data. In the linear regression model, for example, $\sigma^2$ is often considered ancillary.

*Systematic component:* The systematic component of the statistical model is a statement of how $\theta_i$ varies over observations as a function of a vector of explanatory variables. This may be written generally as Equation (1.4) for the entire parameter vector and $\theta_i = g(x_i, \beta)$ for the $i$th element of $\theta$. We have already seen that in linear regression, the systematic component is a linear function of the expected value of the output of the social system $Y$:

$$E(Y) \equiv \mu = X\beta$$

for all $n$ random observations, and $\mu_i = x_i\beta$ for observation $i$. Chapter 5 introduces the logit specification which lets the parameter $\pi \equiv \Pr(Y = 1)$ vary over observations in a particular way:

$$\pi = \frac{1}{1 + \exp(-X\beta)}.$$

In a different specialized model, we might not want $\sigma^2$ to be constant over observations, as in the homoscedastic linear regression model. Instead, $\sigma^2$ might vary as a particular function of a set of explanatory variables,

$$\sigma^2 = \exp(X\beta),$$

so that the variance of some observations would be predicted to be larger than others. Subsequent chapters describe how to formulate and interpret these alternative *functional forms,* written more generally as $g(\cdot, \cdot)$. Functional forms are precise statements of how a particular characteristic ($\theta$) of the random dependent variable ($Y$) is generated by certain features of the social system ($X$). Although Equation (1.4) need not be a causal model, the elements of the vector $\beta$ are called the *effect parameters,* representing the degree and direction of dependence of $\theta$ on the explanatory variables $X$. The specific interpretation of $\beta$ depends on the functional form (see Section 5.2). In general, leaving $\beta$ as a symbol rather than assigning it a number enables one to estimate it by empirical analysis and thus to effectively choose a particular model from the family of models in Equation (1.4).

The systematic component of the statistical model is a statement of how different known features of the social system (the explanatory variables) generate various characteristics of the random output (the parameter values), such as the average output $\mu$. The particular function of the known features involves the functional form and the effect parameters, each of which may or may not be known in advance of any data analysis. In general, since $g$ and $\beta$

are restricted in only very limited ways, Equation (1.4) is an extremely flexible form for the systematic component of a model.

Statistical models exist that do not fit into the framework of Equations (1.3) and (1.4), but nearly all of those used in actual research situations are either formally special cases or simple generalizations. This formulation at least conceptually encompasses linear regression, Poisson regression, probit and logit, models for tabular data, time series, nonrandom selection, factor analysis, structural equations, switching regressions, variance functions, and hundreds of others. The list includes the vast majority of statistical techniques used in political science and those of other social sciences as well.

One form that does not *appear* to fit into the general model of Equations (1.3) and (1.4) is when $y$ is "transformed" (such as by taking the logarithm) and a linear regression is run on the transformed variable. However, transformation is merely a way of "tricking" a linear regression computer program into running a nonlinear regression. If we concentrate on what process drives our data, represented in its most substantively natural form, we are likely to retain an emphasis on theory rather than computing and technical issues.

For example, most people find it more natural to theorize about income than the log of income. If the functional form of the relationship between income and the explanatory variables is log-linear, then $g$ can be appropriately specified [rather than trying to conceptualize and model $\ln(y)$], and we can continue to theorize directly about the variable in its most interesting form – in this case, dollars.

For those schooled in the "tricks" of linear regression programs, the formulation in Equations (1.3) and (1.4) does encompass models that authors of econometrics textbooks call "nonlinear in the variables" (i.e., those models one can trick into a regression program) and "nonlinear in the parameters" (those models one cannot get into a linear regression). Though this distinction is useful for computational purposes, it is irrelevant to substantive theory. It should have no place in theoretical discussions of research methodology or empirical analyses of particular substantive problems.

*Statistics:* The word "statistics" derives from the meaning (but not etymology) of the phrase "sample characteristics." Statistics have many purposes, but, by definition, they are no more than functions of the data. The general form of a statistic $h$ is

$$h = h(y) = h(y_1, \ldots, y_n).$$

Statistics generally are of "lower dimension" than the data. For example, the sample mean $[\bar{y} = (1/n)\Sigma_{i=1}^{n} y_i]$ is one number ($\bar{y}$), whereas the data include $n$ observations ($y_1, \ldots, y_n$). A sample mean and sample variance together are probably a better description than just the mean. However, there is a tradeoff between concise and complete description: Interpreting a statistic is generally easier than the entire data set, but one necessarily loses information by describing a large set of numbers with only a few. "The fundamental idea of statistics is that useful information can be accrued from individual small bits of data" (Efron, 1982: 341). By carefully reducing dimensionality through statistics, useful information can be extracted from these many small bits of data.

*Descriptive statistics:* Descriptive statistics are statistics used for no other purpose than to describe the observed data. Since the goal of this enterprise is to model the process by which some social system produces output, it is often of use to begin with a simple description of the general features of the data. "Description in economics, as in other sciences, plays a key role in bringing to the fore what is to be explained by theory" (Zellner, 1984: 29). Descriptive statistics make no reference to any part of the statistical model or social system and, as used, cannot be part of a theory of statistical inference.

*Estimation:* Whereas *inference* is the general process by which one uses observed data to learn about the social system and its outputs, *estimation* is the specific procedure by which one obtains numerical estimates of features (usually parameters) of the statistical model. To calculate estimates, one uses statistics (functions of the data). These statistics may even be the same as are used for descriptive purposes. The use to which they are put, and the theory behind their calculation, distinguish statistics as estimators from statistics as mere descriptive tools.

Whereas *point estimation* produces a single number as a "best guess" for each parameter, *interval estimation* gives a range of plausible values. Both point and interval estimation reduce the dimensionality of the data considerably. By moving from all the data to a number or range of numbers, much interpretability is gained, but some information is lost. In contrast, *summary estimation* reduces the data as much as possible but without losing any information that could be useful for inference or testing alternative hypotheses under a single model. Summary estimators are usually too unwieldy to use directly for inference purposes, but they are often an excellent first step in reducing the data for analysis. Indeed, point and interval estimators can be easily determined once a summary estimator is available. A more precise mathematical definition of these concepts is given in the next chapter.[4]

---

[4] See Efron (1982: 343–4) for different definitions of similar concepts.

## 1.3 Concluding remarks

In contrast to the usual presentation of these concepts in introductory statistics and research methods texts, the language presented here focuses on social science theory rather than on technique: For example, introductory texts usually define the previous concepts more narrowly in terms of populations and samples, along with all the apparatus of designing sample surveys. Although surveys are an important part of political science, relatively few researchers actually design their own. Instead, they either use surveys others have conducted or, even more commonly, other types of data generated by someone or something else. Hence, the language presented above is more general than survey sampling, having the latter as a special case.

In addition, even survey researchers are not primarily concerned with "simple random sampling" or other technical methods of drawing samples from populations. Instead, what generates data in the context of individual survey interviews is more critical. For example, consider modeling the process by which an interviewer asks for the respondent's opinion on a subject about which the respondent is only vaguely aware. Will the respondent guess, report not knowing, terminate the interview, or create an opinion on the spot? Problems of nonresponse bias, self-selection, censoring, truncation, nonopinions, and other interesting theoretical problems should be the focus of statistical modeling efforts in many survey research problems.

My general approach is to focus on the underlying process that generates social science data. This is distinct from the much more narrow and usual focus on simple random sampling from fixed populations. Although understanding how to create reliable data can be important, the process of generating most social science data is not influenced by most data analysts. Indeed, in those cases when political scientists generate their own data, understanding how to derive models of these processes leads one to create considerably more interesting and useful data sets. The important question for political science research, then, is the underlying process that gives rise to the observed data. What are the characteristics of the social system that produced these data? What changes in known features of the social system might have produced data with different characteristics? What is the specific stochastic process driving one's results? By posing questions such as these, statistical modeling will be more theoretically relevant and empirically fruitful.

# CHAPTER 2

# Conceptualizing uncertainty and inference

The goal of this chapter is to define the *concepts* of probability and likelihood as models of uncertainty and inference, respectively. A more complete exposition of the *methods* of probability and likelihood appears in Chapters 3 and 4, respectively. The application of likelihood to inference in the linear regression model also appears in Chapter 4 and in Part II for more sophisticated models.

## 2.1  Probability as a model of uncertainty

To fully explain the concept of likelihood, I begin with the classical concept of probability in the particular context of a statistical model. Probability theory is a fundamentally important part of most theories of statistical inference, but it has many unrelated purposes as well. Traditional probabilities are usually written in this form:

$$\Pr(y|\mathcal{M}) \equiv \Pr(\text{data}|\text{model}), \tag{2.1}$$

where $y$ is observed or hypothetical data and $\mathcal{M}$ summarizes all the features of the statistical model defined in Equations (1.3) and (1.4). Thus, $\mathcal{M}$ includes the random outputs $Y$, the stochastic component $f$, the parameters of interest $\theta$, and the ancillary parameters $\alpha$, if any. In turn, $\theta$ includes the functional form $g$, the explanatory variables $X$, and the effect parameters $\beta$. One reads this equation as "the probability of the data $y$ given the model $\mathcal{M}$."

This equation corresponds to situations in elementary probability theory where one wants to know, for example, the probability of getting a heads given that the coin is fair. If we had observed ten heads in a row, we might want to know the probability of getting this result given a fair coin. Many people are interested in the probability of winning a fair lottery.

More generally, these statements are *conditional probabilities*, describing the uncertainty of an observed or hypothetical event given a set of assumptions about the world. We proceed to probabilistic calculation as if this set of assumptions were known for certain. Conditional probability is an enormously successful model for measuring uncertainty in situations such as these.[1]

---

[1] Fuzzy logic, belief functions, probability bounds, and other alternative models of uncertainty exist, but none have yet proved as generally useful as probability. See,

With a set of assumptions about the world ($\mathcal{M}$) fixed, one can assess the degree of uncertainty of any number of hypothetical statements. The variable $y$ is set to a particular observed or hypothetical value, and, by the rules and axioms of probability theory (see Chapter 3), a number between 0 and 1 is produced: the probability of a fair coin turning up heads is 0.5. The probability of drawing the Ace of Spades from a fair deck of playing cards is 1/52. The probability that I will finish writing this sentence is 1.0.

Most people have a sense of how to interpret these numbers. The closer the number gets to one, the more certain we are of the event in question occurring; the closer to zero, the more certain we are that it will not occur. However, except at the values 0 and 1, we are uncertain to varying degrees. The calculated probability – the number between zero and one – is a measure of uncertainty. Attaching measures to length (feet, centimeters), temperature (Kelvin, Centigrade), or income (dollars, rubles) might be more precise, but it is not a fundamentally different task. The primary superficial difference is that probability has no "natural units," like a centimeter or dollar. The importance of units is that they presumably allow comparison across contexts. Though the lack of natural units might make probability more difficult to interpret, it pays to remember that even units like "dollars" often take on different meanings and values in unrelated contexts.

One further distinction in the definition of probability will be relevant below. Some see probability as the limit of a *relative frequency* in the context of an "experiment" that is repeatable, at least in theory. For example, "the probability that the next flip of a fair coin will come up heads is 0.5" means that as the number of flips gets very large, the average number of heads that turned up approaches 1/2. According to this view, statements such as "the probability that Reagan will win the election is 0.6" can be understood and objectively compared only because the election can in theory be repeated an infinite number of times under essentially the same conditions. Although this definition does not establish natural units for probability, it does gives somewhat more of an objective referent for assessing and comparing probability statements in different contexts.

Others argue that the only reasonable definition of probability is *subjective* – inherently different for each person. For example, subjective probability implies that a statement such as "The probability of war between the United States and the Soviet Union is 0.05" has a different meaning from person to person. In this view, referents exist only when a single individual makes several probability statements in a single context. But without some external referent, objective probability statements are impossible.

for example, Lindley (1987, with comments and rejoinders) who believes that *"the only satisfactory description of uncertainty is probability,"* and that the interpretation of uncertainty as probability is fundamentally "inevitable."

In the discipline of statistics, a philosophical debate rages over the relative frequency and subjective interpretations of probability. The distinctions being fought over are deep and have important implications for the way statisticians and empirical researchers *conceptualize* their role. However, the *practice* of modeling uncertainty and inference is usually (but not always) unaffected by these subtle distinctions. Indeed, the beauty of probability as a model of uncertainty is that its axioms and rules are almost completely uncontroversial. Essentially the same model of probability can be applied whatever one's finely tuned interpretation may be.[2]

## 2.2    Inverse probability as a failed model of inference

Probability as described in the previous section provides a superior description of absolute uncertainty. It is formal and thus very precise; the rules and axioms of probability allow exact calculations and deductive reasoning; and many substantively different interpretations can be handled by the same model. Indeed, probability is one of the most successful models of any kind.

Nevertheless, the description of uncertainty is not a model of inference. Indeed, for inference purposes, $\Pr(y|\mathcal{M})$ is quite inadequate. In this probability statement, the model is assumed known and the data random. The problem is that the social system has already produced output, we have already taken the sample of the output, and the observed data already exist. Hence, the data are not random; they are known and must be treated as given. The opposite problem exists in the way the model ($\mathcal{M}$) is treated in Equation (2.1). That $\mathcal{M}$ is treated as given is a problem because uncertainty in inference lies with the model, not the data.

Ideally, social scientists would prefer to reverse the probability $\Pr(y|\mathcal{M})$ and, instead, attempt to evaluate $\Pr(\mathcal{M}|y)$. In this *inverse probability* statement, the data are taken as given, and the probability is a measurement of the absolute uncertainty of various hypothetical models. Were it possible to de-

---

[2] A third important position in the fight to define probability is an extension of formal *logic:* instead of "A implying B," this form of probability considers a "degree of belief" in this situation. Many more subtle distinctions also exist [See Barnett (1982: Chapter 3) for an excellent survey of most positions]. In turn, each of these definitions of probability leads to equally "religious" positions about the proper definitions and methods of statistical inference. As important as these debates are, the varying positions have yet to have profound impact on the way statistics is usually practiced in political science and elsewhere. Furthermore, although different authors might prefer the framework to be developed here to be taken in fundamentally different directions, the view of inference presented in this book cuts across and encompasses large portions of each of these positions. "The concept of *likelihood,* or the *likelihood function,* plays a crucial role in all three of the basic approaches to inference and decision making" (Barnett, 1982: 282).

rive a calculus of this inverse probability, one could determine the exact probability that alternative hypothetical models were true, given the characteristics of the observed data. We might even use this magic tool to search across all the models in the world (''the model space'') and choose the model with the highest probability as a single guess of the true, unobserved model.

As attractive as it may seem, three centuries of scholars have been unable to derive a method of measuring the *absolute uncertainty* of an inference using concepts like inverse probability (see Stigler, 1986). Indeed, inverse probability appears inherently unmeasurable. Fortunately, the concept of *likelihood* is a worthy substitute for inverse probability.[3] However, whereas inverse probability would be a measure of absolute uncertainty (at least with the relative frequency interpretation of probability), likelihood is a measure of *relative uncertainty*. This means that likelihood permits researchers to assess the relative uncertainty one may have about various statistical models given a particular data set. In two steps, the remainder of this section demonstrates precisely how inverse probability fails as a model of inference, and the next introduces likelihood.

First, the exact goal of inference must be more narrow and hence more reasonable. As is, the goal is to determine the probability of an entire model of the world, $\mathcal{M}$. An example demonstrates the unreasonableness of this goal: we might want to know the unobserved probability of a coin being fair, given that ten flips all produced heads. The uncertainty here is about the coin: Is it fair or weighted in some way? Most observers are willing to take as given the randomness of the flip and the usual effects of the forces of gravity, wind currents, electromagnetic fields, and even the stability of the space-time continuum. Indeed, most parts of the world ($\mathcal{M}$) are reasonably taken as given. Therefore, the specific goal of inference really does not involve all of $\mathcal{M}$, only parts.

In general, I divide $\mathcal{M}$ into two components: Let $\theta$ be the focus of uncertainty about which one would like to make an inference and $\mathcal{M}^*$ be that part of the model assumed given. $\theta$ can include any or all components of the model ($\mathcal{M} \equiv \{Y,g,X,\beta,f,\alpha\}$), but the first object of inference is usually the effect $\beta$ and ancillary $\alpha$ parameters. Thus, one can think of $\theta$ as being the effect pa-

---

[3] Although no longer the case, the doctrine of inverse probability was once widely believed to be true. Fisher (1930: 528) wrote: ''I know of only one case in mathematics of a doctrine which has been accepted and developed by the most eminent men of their time, and is now perhaps accepted by men now living, which at the same time has appeared to a succession of sound writers to be fundamentally false and devoid of foundation. Yet that is quite exactly the position in respect of inverse probability.'' Sir Ronald A. Fisher (1922, 1925) is almost solely responsible for the remarkable breakthrough of likelihood (but see Pratt, 1976). See also Edwards (1972) for an overview of the concept of likelihood, Norden (1972, 1973) for a survey of maximum likelihood, and Efron (1982) on maximum likelihood and decision theory.

rameters in the following discussion, as long as one remembers that $\theta$ can be more broadly defined. The range of possible values for $\theta$ is called its *parameter space* and is denoted as $\Theta$. Given the data ($y$) and part of the statistical model ($\mathcal{M}^*$), the goal of inverse probability is a measure of the absolute uncertainty of any hypothetical value of $\theta$ in its parameter space. These ideas can be expressed formally as follows:

$$\Pr(\theta|y,\mathcal{M}^*) \equiv \Pr(\theta|y). \tag{2.2}$$

For simplicity, the right hand side of this equivalence suppresses $\mathcal{M}^*$, since these parts of the world are assumed given in all subsequent calculations.

Second, consider how close one can come to inverse probability as an absolute measure of uncertainty. To begin, recall from elementary probability theory that a conditional probability is defined as the ratio of the joint to the marginal probability. With this rule, I define the inverse probability (of $\theta$) in terms of the traditional probability (of $y$):

$$\begin{aligned}
\Pr(\theta|y) &= \frac{\Pr(\theta,y)}{\Pr(y)} \\
&= \frac{\Pr(\theta)\Pr(y|\theta)}{\Pr(y)}.
\end{aligned} \tag{2.3}$$

Given the traditional probability $\Pr(y|\theta)$, which we already know how to calculate, the goal is to determine the inverse probability $\Pr(\theta|y)$. Equation (2.3), also called *Bayes theorem,* indicates that in order to do this we must determine the values of $\Pr(\theta)$ and $\Pr(y)$.

$\Pr(y)$ can be dispensed with easily since it is a function of the other two probabilities on the right hand side of Equation (2.3):

$$\begin{aligned}
\Pr(y) &= \int_{\Theta} \Pr(\theta,y)\,d\theta \\
&= \int_{\Theta} \Pr(\theta)\,\Pr(y|\theta)\,d\theta,
\end{aligned}$$

where the symbols $\int_{\Theta}$ and $d\theta$ mean that the joint probability distribution $\Pr(\theta,y)$ is to be collapsed over the $\theta$ dimension to leave only $\Pr(y)$.[4]

Hence, to determine the inverse probability in Equation (2.3), we only need to know $\Pr(y|\theta)$, which is straightforward, and $\Pr(\theta)$. Precisely how $\Pr(\theta)$ is to be interpreted is an object of considerable debate in the statistical literature. Those who have used this probability most are adherents of *Bayesian statistics,* a method I discuss later that seeks to use prior information in combination with the data to make inferences about $\theta$. $\Pr(\theta)$ is interpreted as a proba-

---

[4] Technically, $\Theta$ is the parameter space and the multiple integral is over all of $\theta$'s dimensions.

bilistic representation of one's subjective prior belief about $\theta$. For example, one might have a prior belief that a coin to be flipped is fair ($\theta = 0.5$), since most coins are. How many heads in a row would need to turn up in order for one's posterior belief to change? Prior beliefs will certainly influence the answer to this question. Although Bayesian statistics are of use in certain situations, $\Pr(\theta)$ is of little help in determining inverse probabilities as absolute measures of uncertainty. To demonstrate this, I consider in turn (1) the cases where we have no prior information about $\theta$ and (2) the cases where we have some.

An old concept called the *principle of indifference* is the primary means by which some attempt to represent ignorance about $\Pr(\theta)$ with a probability statement. The procedure assumes that events with unknown probabilities are equally likely. Thus, for $N$ events, one assigns each a probability of $1/N$. For example, in guessing about the probability of an undecided senator's vote, we assign "yes" a probability of 1/2 and "no" 1/2. In the absence of knowledge, 0.5 is assumed by the principle of indifference to be a reasonable representation of ignorance.

Is the principle of indifference a reasonable method of turning ignorance into probability statements? I show that it is not by means of a simple example. Consider the situation of ignorance about $\Pr(\theta)$ in the context of a coin flip. Here, $\theta$ is the parameter of a Bernoulli distribution, taking on the value 0.5 if the coin is fair. In general, $\theta$ can take on any value between 0 and 1, and a probability distribution used to represent subjective prior beliefs about it must be defined on that interval. In this case, the principle of indifference suggests applying a uniform probability density, which is written as follows:

$$f(\theta) = \begin{cases} 1 & \text{for } 0 \le \theta \le 1, \\ 0 & \text{otherwise.} \end{cases} \tag{2.4}$$

The simple form of this distribution is portrayed in Figure 2.1. The distribution implies that the probability of $\theta$ being in an interval of one length between 0 and 1 is the same as it being in any other interval of the same length. Thus, for example, $\Pr(0 < \theta < 0.25) = \Pr(0.25 < \theta < 0.5)$.

Now suppose that instead of $\theta$, we found $\alpha \equiv \theta^2$ to be particularly intuitive for some reason. Under this parameterization, a fair coin would have $\alpha = 0.25$ [because $(0.5)^2 = 0.25$], but valid values of $\alpha$ would still range between 0 and 1. Using methods explained in Chapter 3, the complete probability distribution for $\alpha$ can be derived by making no additional assumptions, directly from Equation (2.4). The result is as follows:

$$f(\alpha) = \begin{cases} \dfrac{1}{2\sqrt{\alpha}} & \text{for } 0 \le \alpha \le 1, \\ 0 & \text{otherwise.} \end{cases}$$

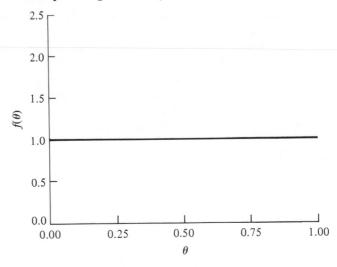

Figure 2.1. Uniform distribution for $\theta$.

This distribution is portrayed in Figure 2.2, and it clearly demonstrates the main problem with the principle of indifference: whereas we supposedly began the uniform distribution in Figure 2.1 as a representation of ignorance, simply squaring the parameter led to a nonuniform distribution – something to be interpreted as knowledge according to the principle of indifference. thus, the principle of indifference is invalid because it is internally inconsistent; it implies that we can extract knowledge from ignorance.

In the Bayesian literature, uniform or improper uniform prior distributions are often used to represent ignorance in actual research situations. Though this argument indicates that some of these priors are unwarranted, many are plausible because the researchers are not completely ignorant. For a practical example, in late September 1987, during the confirmation hearings of U.S. Supreme Court Justice nominee Robert Bork, Senator Alan Cranston announced that he had counted 41 senators for Bork, 49 against, and 10 undecided. Since the probability of each undecided senator voting for Bork could have been 0.99 as easily as 0.5, Cranston would not have concluded that the nomination would fail, as he did, if his prior were one of complete ignorance. Cranston probably had an *informative* prior near 0.5.

The general problem is that setting $f(\theta)$ to any value is a precise statement of knowledge possessing considerable meaning; it is hardly an adequate representation of ignorance. Hence, one cannot derive an inverse probability statement as an absolute measure of uncertainty from a traditional probability when $\Pr(\theta)$ is unknown.

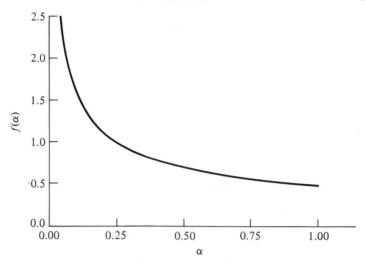

Figure 2.2. Distribution for $\alpha$.

What about when prior information about $\theta$ does exist? The problem here has to do with alternative definitions of probability discussed in the previous section. One conceivably could use a relative frequency interpretation of $\Pr(y|\theta)$ in Equation (2.3). This would provide an objective referent for interpretation and the possibility of measuring the *absolute* uncertainty of an inference. However, a relative frequency interpretation is impossible for $\Pr(\theta)$. By definition, it uses the subjective meaning of probability. As a result of this probability having no objective referent, the left hand side of Equation (2.3) cannot be an absolute measure of uncertainty.

Inverse probability as an absolute measure of uncertainty thus fails when prior beliefs are nonexistent, because the right hand side of Equation (2.3) cannot be fully specified. For in this latter instance at least part of the right hand side of Equation (2.3) becomes subjective without absolute referents. Hence $\Pr(\theta|y)$ either cannot be calculated or it can but is only good as a relative measure of uncertainty. I therefore drop the goal of inverse probability as a measure of absolute uncertainty in the context of statistical inference. In the next two sections, I describe likelihood and Bayesian statistics as two different measures of the *relative* uncertainty of an inference.

## 2.3 Likelihood as a model of inference

In traditional probability, $\theta$ is the single "true" value of the parameter. In likelihood, however, $\theta$ refers to one of many hypothetical models. In order to distinguish between these two cases, I refer to the hypothetical parameter value as $\tilde{\theta}$ and the single unobserved true value as $\theta$. In the next chapter, I will introduce $\hat{\theta}$ as a point estimator for $\theta$, based on the maximum of the likelihood with respect to $\tilde{\theta}$. $\hat{\theta}$ is a number in a single experiment, but a random variable across hypothetical experiments.

The *likelihood* that a hypothetical model (summarized by the hypothetical parameter value $\tilde{\theta}$) produced the data we observe, given $\mathcal{M}^*$, is denoted $L(\tilde{\theta}|y,\mathcal{M}^*)$, where $\mathcal{M}^*$ may again be suppressed since it appears in all subsequent expressions. The *likelihood axiom* then defines this concept as follows:

$$L(\tilde{\theta}|y, \mathcal{M}^*) \equiv L(\tilde{\theta}|y) \qquad (2.5)$$
$$= k(y)\Pr(y|\tilde{\theta})$$
$$\propto \Pr(y|\tilde{\theta}).$$

In the second line of this equation, $k(y)$ is an unknown function of the data; since it is not a function of $\tilde{\theta}$, it is treated as an unknown positive constant. In the third line, "$\propto$" means "is proportional to." The third line is only a more convenient way of writing the second without the constant. For a given set of observed data, $k(y)$ remains the same over all possible hypothetical values of $\tilde{\theta}$. However, $k(y)$ is a function of $y$ and therefore may change as $y$ changes. The likelihood $L(\tilde{\theta}|y)$ is similar to the concept of inverse probability in that it permits one to measure and compare the uncertainty one has about alternative hypothetical values of $\tilde{\theta}$. However, the unknown value $k(y)$ ensures that likelihood is a relative rather than an absolute measure of uncertainty. This likelihood axiom is but one way to make the measure explicitly relative. Indeed, one could use any monotonic function of $\Pr(y|\tilde{\theta})$.[5] The choice represented in Equation (2.5) is arbitrary, just as is the choice of making the scale of probability range between 0 and 1. The advantage of likelihood is that it can be calculated from a traditional probability, whereas inverse probability cannot be calculated in any way.

If the data are continuous rather than discrete, the likelihood is calculated in the same way, except that the underlying probability distribution is now a density. Hence, a more general way to write the formula is as follows:

$$L(\tilde{\theta}|y,\mathcal{M}^*) \equiv L(\tilde{\theta}|y) = k(y)f(y|\tilde{\theta}) \qquad (2.6)$$
$$\propto f(y|\tilde{\theta}),$$

where $f$ is a probability distribution that may be continuous or discrete.

The complete *likelihood function* is a summary estimator of $\theta$. With it, one can test any number of alternative hypotheses. One can even plot values of $\tilde{\theta}$ by the likelihood of each to get a feel for the support the data gives to the whole range of reasonable statistical models.

---

[5] A monotonic transformation is a function which does not change the ordering of the items: if $a > b$, then a transformation $q(\cdot)$ is monotonic if $q(a) > q(b)$.

We interpret the numerical value of $L(\tilde{\theta}|y)$ as the likelihood of a hypothetical model having generated the data (assuming $\mathcal{M}^*$). However, whereas a probability ranges from 0 to 1, the range of the likelihood depends on the observed data through the unknown constant $k(y)$. The numbers may range from 0 to 1, $-597$ to $-200$, $-900$ to $79600$, $5.9$ to $6.2$, or any other range. The ranges depend on the value of $k$, which in turn depends on the data. Again, we are led to the conclusion that a single value of likelihood has no absolute referent. The likelihoods of two alternative models may be compared, but only if they were calculated from the same data. In addition, the likelihoods of the same model applied to independent data sets may be combined by taking their product. The likelihood theory of inference thus explicitly allows for science to be cumulative.[6] The person most responsible for the modern development of the concept of likelihood, Ronald A. Fisher, made this point very clearly:

> There is therefore an absolute measure of probability in that the unit is chosen so as to make all the elementary probabilities add up to unity. There is no such absolute measure of likelihood. It may be convenient to assign the value unity to the maximum value, and to measure other likelihoods by comparison, but there will be an infinite number of values whose likelihoods is greater than one half. The sum of the likelihoods of admissible values will always be infinite. (Fisher, 1922: 327.)

Fisher also suggests in this quotation and elsewhere that a useful interpretation of the likelihood is to norm the values relative to the maximum, thus giving it some known range (0 to 1 or other) across different sets of data. He even seems to imply that likelihoods can be compared across data sets. Edwards (1972), while more emphatic about the relative nature of likelihood, also recommends norming. However, norming does not change the essential *relative* nature of likelihood. Thus, norming can have no real effect on substantive interpretation. Indeed, since norming can make it easier to forget that likelihoods are incomparable across data sets, it is a dangerous practice and should be avoided. In fact, it gives one the same false security that norming goodness-of-fit statistics does.

For example, in linear regression analysis, the standard error of the regression ($\hat{\sigma}^2$) gives both an estimate of an ancillary parameter ($\sigma^2$) and a measure of the goodness of fit of the regression. Unlike the raw likelihood, the units of $\hat{\sigma}^2$ are quite interpretable, as they are on the same scale as the dependent variable. No one would try to compare $\hat{\sigma}^2$ for different dependent variables. Suppose, however, one put $\hat{\sigma}^2$ on the scale from 0 to 1, which is essentially the more popular $R^2$ statistic. Since it is normed in this way and has no natural units, $R^2$ is far less interpretable than $\hat{\sigma}^2$. The 0 to 1 scale does not make it

---

[6] Of course, if political scientists always apply different models to unrelated data sets, we would lose all leverage for comparison or cumulation in any reasonable theory of inference.

possible to reliably compare $R^2$ across equations with different dependent variables, although researchers repeatedly make this mistake.[7] Norming a statistic that has no absolute interpretation to begin with, as does likelihood, can only be more alluring and dangerous to interpret.

One feature of the likelihood function does have a natural interpretation: the maximum value gives the specific statistical model (value of $\hat{\theta}$) with the maximum relative likelihood of having generated the data. Indeed, *maximum likelihood estimation* is a theory of point estimation that derives in this direct way from the likelihood function. The maximum is not always a very good summary of the entire likelihood function, but it is very convenient and often useful. The likelihood function can also be used to derive interval estimates around the maximum likelihood estimates, as well as standard errors and test statistics for each of these estimators.

I demonstrate specific methods of calculating the likelihood for various statistical models in Chapter 4 and the chapters that follow. In these chapters, I also detail the many other features of the function that are of use in statistical inference. For now, consider a very simple example that demonstrates these basic concepts as well as introduces a procedure for interpreting differences in likelihood.

A relatively simple notion of democratic representation is descriptive (Pitkin, 1967). The basic idea is that the demographic characteristics of public officials should reflect the citizenry they represent. Although concepts of representation are virtually always developed for and applied to legislatures, many are also relevant for executives. The particular example of this concept I will use here is presidential appointments to the Department of Education. More specifically, do these appointments reflect the gender division of American citizens (about 50%)? In other words, the goal is inference about $\pi$, the probability of a president choosing a woman for a post in the Department of Education. I use this particular department since presidents usually appoint more women in this area than in any other. I use two data sets to analyze this question, one from the Carter Administration and one from the first term of the Reagan administration. These data are easy to summarize without losing any information relevant to the substantive question: Eight of the eighteen

---

[7] $R^2$ is typically understood as the percentage of variance in $y$ (not $Y$) explained by the systematic component. But some of the variation in $y$ is systematic and some results from the random variation across experiments as governed by the stochastic component. Intuitively, one wants $R^2$ to measure only the proportion of systematic variation explained. To explain too little of the systematic part or too much of the random part are equally undesirable alternatives. Unfortunately, whether 58%, 5%, or 99% is all, less than all, or an over-fitting of the systematic component is not knowable in the context of one regression. The concept of an $R^2$ that is "good" in an absolute way is nonsensical. Hence, like likelihood, $R^2$ and other goodness-of-fit statistics are *relative* measures only.

appointments made by President Carter and three of the twenty-six Reagan appointees were women (see King and Ragsdale, 1988: Table 4.20). I will use $y_c$ to refer to the Carter data and $y_r$ for the Reagan appointments.

By assuming that each of the decisions made by each president is independent, and has the same underlying probability of choosing a woman, the random variables from which $y_c$ and $y_r$ were drawn ($Y_c$ and $Y_r$) can be shown to follow binomial distributions [see Equation (3.5) on page 45]. From this distribution, the probability of any particular outcome can be calculated for a particular value of the parameter. For example, imagine a president who intended to accurately reflect the gender distribution of the American public: $\pi$ would equal 0.5. From the binomial distribution, the probability of a president selecting eight of eighteen women if $\pi$ were really 0.5 is $\Pr(Y = 8|\pi) = 0.167$. The probability of selecting only six of eighteen under the same conditions is 0.071, and the probability of selecting eight of eighteen if $\pi$ were only 0.4 is 0.173.

These probabilities are of some interest, but they really miss the point of the analysis. For each of the two administrations, the data ($y_c$ and $y_r$) are given. Hence, the traditional probability of $y_c$ and $y_r$ occurring does not answer the question about whether the president is following a strategy of descriptive representation.[8] The relevant question, then, is about the unknown value $\pi$, the probability of the president choosing a woman. Is this value close to 0.5 or some distance from 0.5? To make an inference like this about $\theta$, the traditional probability is of no use. $\Pr(y|\pi)$ is also of no use in determining the inverse probability, $\Pr(\pi|y)$, which cannot be calculated by any means.

The solution is to use the likelihood, $L(\tilde{\pi}|y)$, defined as values *proportional* to the traditional probabilities for different hypothetical values of $\tilde{\pi}$. To further analyze this problem, I have calculated the likelihood of 1000 values of $\tilde{\pi}$ equally spaced from zero to one for each administration. These values are plotted in Figure 2.3 (for Carter) and 2.4 (for Reagan). Note first that the vertical axes report numbers (values of the traditional probability) multiplied by unobserved positive constants [$k(y_c)$ and $k(y_r)$]. Neither $k(y_c)$ and $k(y_r)$ nor the relationship between the two is known. Since these unobserved positive constants depend on the data, values of the likelihoods may be compared within, but not across, data sets.[9]

With Figures 2.3 and 2.4, one can assess the relative likelihood of any value of $\tilde{\pi}$. Since both likelihood functions are unimodal, a particularly inter-

---

[8] Indeed, the probability of $y_c$ and $y_r$ occurring as they did is 1.0.

[9] Aside from graphs, one could report these numerical values in a large number of ways. Indeed, any two monotonic transformations of them is also a reasonable representation. I show below that a particularly convenient monotonic transformation in the case of the likelihood is the natural logarithm, and the log-likelihood, $\ln[L(\tilde{\pi}|y)]$, is most frequently used.

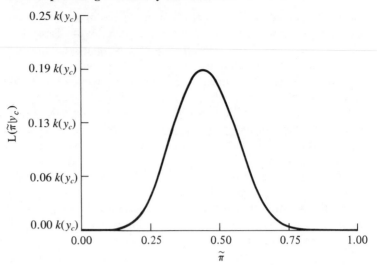

Figure 2.3.  Carter's appointments.

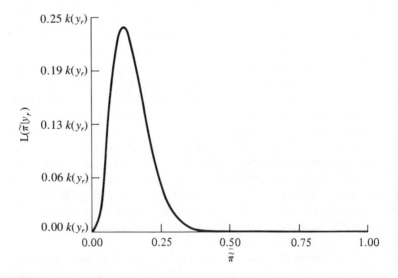

Figure 2.4.  Reagan's appointments.

esting feature of each is the value of $\bar{\pi}$ for which the likelihoods are maximized. The two presidents' likelihoods are maximized at $\bar{\pi}=0.44$ and $\bar{\pi}=0.12$, respectively, maximum likelihood (ML) estimates which I denote $\hat{\pi}_c=0.44$ and $\hat{\pi}_r=0.12$. This simple example also gives a quite intuitive result: the ML estimates in this case are merely the average proportion of women selected ($\hat{\pi}_c = 8/18 = 0.44$ and $\hat{\pi}_r = 3/26 = 0.12$). Indeed, since both curves fall sharply to either side of the maximum, the farther $\tilde{\pi}$ is from the maximum the lower the relative likelihood.

The only remaining problem is to determine exactly how far these maximum values are from the hypothesis of gender reflection, $\pi = 0.5$. Without natural units, the difference in likelihood values seems uninterpretable. For example, the maximum likelihood for Carter is $L(\tilde{\pi} = 0.44 | y_c) = 0.187 k(y_c)$, whereas the likelihood of $\tilde{\pi} = 0.5$ is only $0.167 k(y_c)$. One is obviously less than the other, but, without knowing $k(y_c)$, the extent of the difference is unknown.

To address this problem, one can exploit the fact that the unobserved constant in Equation (2.6) remains the same for different hypothetical models if the data $y$ and the assumed parts of the model $\mathcal{M}^*$ are unchanged. The *likelihood ratio* thus has a natural interpretation because the unobserved constants cancel out. In general, if $\tilde{\theta}_1$ and $\tilde{\theta}_2$ represent two different hypothetical values of the parameters in the context of a single data set,

$$\frac{L(\tilde{\theta}_1 | y)}{L(\tilde{\theta}_2 | y)} = \frac{k(y)\mathrm{Pr}(y | \tilde{\theta}_1)}{k(y)\mathrm{Pr}(y | \tilde{\theta}_2)} \tag{2.7}$$

$$= \frac{\mathrm{Pr}(y | \tilde{\theta}_1)}{\mathrm{Pr}(y | \tilde{\theta}_2)}.$$

We can therefore interpret the likelihood ratio with the same units as the ratio of the two corresponding traditional probabilities. Except for interpreting likelihood ratios, these probabilities have no other application in making inferences. Note that if a comparison were being done across data sets, the constants would not cancel out and the likelihood ratio would not be very useful.

For example, for President Carter, the two alternative hypotheses might be that $\pi$ is 0.5 (reflection) or 0.44 (the maximum likelihood estimate). How close is one likelihood to the other? The answer can be found by calculating the likelihood ratio:

$$\frac{L(\tilde{\pi} = 0.5 | y_c)}{L(\tilde{\pi} = 0.44 | y_c)} = \frac{0.167}{0.187} = 0.893.$$

Thus, the likelihood of gender reflection is 89.3 percent of the maximum. For President Reagan, the corresponding figure is only 0.02 percent. It therefore seems quite likely that the unobserved probability of President Carter selecting a woman was quite near that required for reflection ($\pi = 0.5$). On the other hand, the appointment strategy with regard to the Department of Education in the Reagan administration is almost certainly not one of reflection.

Estimated results such as these can always be due to true features of the underlying model or merely to random error. Hypothesis tests are designed to provide evidence about which of these is driving the result. For example, did $\hat{\pi}$ differ from 0.5 due to random error or because $\pi$ is really not 0.5? The likelihood ratio provides an intuitive interpretation of the relative probabilities of these two hypotheses. Using the background information introduced in Chapter 3, Chapter 4 demonstrates how the likelihood ratio, and other popular procedures, forms the core of more formal methods of hypothesis testing.

Several additional caveats: These ML estimates $\hat{\pi}$ should not be mistaken for the true values of $\pi$, which remain unknown, or the hypothetical values $\tilde{\pi}$. One should also not confuse likelihoods with inverse probabilities: Although the *likelihood* of $\tilde{\pi} = 0.44$ is higher than for any other value of $\tilde{\pi}$, for the Carter data, determining the *absolute probability* that $\pi$ is truly 0.44 is not possible. This is particularly clear in the temptation some have to compare the maximum likelihoods for the two data sets: The numerical value of the likelihood is $0.187k(y_c)$ for Carter and $0.238k(y_r)$ for Reagan, but making any statement about which is larger ignores the unknown positive constants. Since the data sets differ, one cannot determine which maximum has a higher absolute likelihood of being true. Of course, one can still make comparative statements about the two maximums and about other relative features of the two likelihoods. For example, since the Reagan curve is more sharply peaked at the maximum than the Carter curve, we should be somewhat more confident in using the maximum as a summary for the Reagan data.

## 2.4    The Bayesian model of inference

Another approach to a relative measure of the uncertainty of inference is the Bayesian model of inference. As with likelihood, Bayesian methods do not result in inverse probability statements (i.e., measures of absolute uncertainty), but they represent straightforward generalizations of the likelihood method incorporating prior information according to the tenets of rational decision making.[10] The result is a posterior probability distribution used to represent the relative (or subjective) uncertainty of any hypothetical parameter value. I introduce this model of inference here primarily for comparative purposes and do not discuss it subsequently.

---

[10] Statistical decision theory is a more general method of incorporating prior information, but it reduces to Bayesian statistics when decisions are governed by rational decision making (see Berkson, 1980; Ferguson, 1967). Adherents of game theory and rational choice theory will find much in common with the theory of inference underlying statistical decision theory. However, they will not necessarily find convenient methods of testing their theoretical models. Indeed, I believe likelihood is a considerably more natural concept for these purposes.

Instead of defining the likelihood as $L(\bar{\theta}|y) \propto f(y|\bar{\theta})$, a Bayesian *posterior density* is defined more generally as

$$f(\bar{\theta}|y) = \frac{\Pr(\bar{\theta})f(y|\bar{\theta})}{f(y)}$$
$$\propto f(\bar{\theta})f(y|\bar{\theta}),$$

where $f(\bar{\theta})$ is a probability distribution representing one's prior beliefs about the value of $\theta$. No adequate procedure exists when one is ignorant about $\theta$, so this does not represent a complete generalization of standard likelihood.[11]

The Bayesian approach can be quite useful for applying rational decision making to empirical questions. For example, social science statistical advice to the U.S. courts may benefit from Bayesian analysis. In making decisions, judges often try to combine judicial precedence and witnesses' credibility with the social science analysis offered to the court for a particular case. As a result, informal legal arguments sometimes resemble, or aspire to the equivalent of, formal Bayesian decision making (see DeGroot, Fienberg, and Kadane, 1986). Another example where Bayesian analysis might be of some use is when most of a discipline has an extremely strong prior about a particular relationship, but data are inadequate for precise estimation. For example, in financial economics, a fundamental theoretical result is that risky investments should demand a higher return; in empirical analyses, estimates of risk parameters ought to be positive. Unfortunately, since stock data are very noisy and have a stochastic component much larger in variance than the systematic component, empirical studies of the systematic component produce unsatisfactory results. In an attempt to improve the estimation by including as much information as possible, Robert Merton (1980) used a positive Bayesian prior on the risk parameter. Since any Bayesian analysis is dependent on the subjective beliefs of the investigator, Merton reported results using the standard likelihood as well as results with his Bayesian prior.

Another area where Bayesian priors are quite useful is when some parameters are unidentified or the likelihood function is unbounded (see Sections 4.5 and 8.1). In these cases, a more restrictive version of the model can be formulated by putting priors on some or all of the parameters. For example, in models based on a Normal-mixture, prior distributions can avoid these problems with probabilistic, rather than the usual deterministic, restrictions (see King and Gelman, 1988).

If one accepts the Bayesian paradigm, estimators can be derived with very

---

[11] See Chapter 3, Footnote 4, for an analysis that may be interpreted from a Bayesian viewpoint. On Bayesian analysis, in general, see, for example, Lindley (1965) and Zellner (1971). Leamer's (1978) book on specification searches may well be the most useful contribution to statistics from an informal Bayesian perspective.

attractive properties. In large samples, the posterior distribution is approximately normal with a mean equal to the maximum likelihood estimate. Even estimators based on small samples have good properties.

Bayesian statistics remain an excellent method of incorporating prior subjective information and making formally rational decisions about empirical questions. In addition, the concepts of a likelihood function and a posterior density are closely related concepts; both are relative measures of uncertainty and both must be used only within the context of a single data set. Both also have small sample interpretations. Unfortunately, Bayesian analysis also tends to be more difficult to apply in most practical research situations and is a very often intractible (see Efron, 1986). For these reasons, I do not treat the Bayesian approach in detail in this work. Nevertheless, since the likelihood approach is fundamental to a Bayesian interpretation, this book should be of interest even to those who will subsequently go on to adopt a fully Bayesian or decision theoretic approach to empirical research.

Frameworks other than likelihood, such as Bayesian statistics, can be used to present other approaches to statistical inference. In specific instances, these approaches may be more useful. However, none is as generally useful or as theoretically general. None is as central to all existing and competing forms of statistical inference. And, none is accepted by such a large proportion of the statistical community.

## 2.5    Restrictive versus unrestrictive statistical models

A fundamental issue in statistical modeling is how to divide a model of the world ($\mathcal{M}$) into the part that is left for estimation ($\theta$) and the part that is assumed ($\mathcal{M}^*$). Models can be seen as falling along a continuum from *restrictive,* where all assumptions are completely specified and nothing is left to estimation, to *unrestrictive,* where no assumptions are specified and everything is estimated. On the one hand, the ultimate theoretical goal is to make inferences about $\mathcal{M}$ and not $\theta$, or, in other words, to make the parameter space of $\theta$ "large" relative to $\mathcal{M}^*$. On the other hand, inferences require data: broader inferences require stronger data.

The difficulty is that in many political science problems data already exist and thus represent a finite good. In others, data are relatively expensive to collect. Narrower definitions of $\theta$ allow the data to be applied in concentrated form, resulting in more precise, statistically efficient, estimates. However, this restrictive definition of $\theta$ may require unrealistic assumptions about $\mathcal{M}^*$. A broader definition of $\theta$ avoids some of the restrictive assumptions about $\mathcal{M}^*$, but it puts more demands on one's data. A finite amount of data spread

---

[12] Specifying $\mathcal{M}^*$ requires prior information, just as does Bayesian analysis. The difference between the two is that Bayesian analysis is geared to rational decision

thinly in this way results in imprecise inferences and statistically inefficient estimates.[12]

What happens when political scientists expend time and money to improve measurement and data collection? In general, one can use the new data to estimate additional parameters *or* to improve the estimation of existing ones. Whenever new or better data are created or discovered, reestimation of existing statistical models leads to more precise estimates and reliable inferences. However, researchers using these better data sources are also able to reliably estimate progressively more unrestrictive statistical models. The consequence in political science is that researchers usually choose to forgo the increased precision in answering old questions to gain wider inferences into new ones.[13] As a result, new or better data relieve old tradeoffs but create new ones.

Consider, for example, a series of simple cross-sectional statistical models of presidential popularity. Let $Y_i$ be a random variable representing the degree to which individual $i$ supports the way the current president is handling his job. I begin with a Normal stochastic component for $Y_i$:

$$Y_i \sim f_n(y_i|\mu_i,\sigma^2).$$

The first and simplest, model assumes that the parameter for the mean is a constant:

$$E(Y_i) \equiv \mu_i = \beta. \tag{2.8}$$

$\beta$ is then the degree to which the typical survey respondent approves of the way the current president is handling the job. It may be interpreted as the degree of support for the president from each individual $i(i = 1, \ldots, n)$. Only $\beta$ needs to be estimated in this model, and one has all the data to apply to the problem. With a reasonable size sample, $\beta$ can be estimated with considerable precision.

However, the model is quite unrealistic because included in $\mathcal{M}^*$ is the assumption that each individual ($i$) has the same propensity to support the president. The absence of a subscript $i$ on the right hand side of Equation (2.8) means that the model assumes no variation in mean approval across individ-

making. The sort of prior information used to specify $\mathcal{M}^*$ is in a sense less realistic, since it is deterministic, rather than stochastic. However, this information is also required in the Bayesian context. In fact, even the choice of a prior distribution is in the end deterministic. Within the Bayesian framework, one could think about putting probabilistic priors on one's priors, but this approach quickly leads to problems of infinite regress. For discussions of attempts to formalize many other types of uncertainty in statistical inference, see DeFinetti (1974, 1975), Hodges (1987), and Leamer (1978).

[13] Technically, since the number of parameters to be estimated increases with the sample size, all social science estimators are statistically inconsistent. However, Koenker (1988) argues that in practice the number of parameters tends to increase at about the rate of $n^{\frac{1}{4}}$. He also reviews alternative asymptotic arguments that enable one to still prove consistency in these circumstances.

uals. However, this equation is unrealistic because Republicans and Democrats are likely to support the president at different rates. This less restrictive alternative hypothesis can be modeled by slightly complicating the systematic component in Equation (2.8):

$$\mu_i = \beta_0 + \beta_1 P_i. \tag{2.9}$$

Here, mean support for the president depends on the political party of individual $i$. Party is symbolized as $P_i$, where $P_i = 0$ if individual $i$ is Republican and $P_i = 1$ if $i$ is Democratic. As a result, the mean support among Republicans, $E(Y_i|P_i = 0)$, is $\beta_0$, and mean support for the president among Democrats, $E(Y_i|P_i = 1)$, is $\beta_0 + \beta_1$. If $\beta_1 = 0$, Equation (2.9) reduces to Equation (2.8). In general, this model is more interesting than Equation (2.8), as more information is included in $\theta$ (both $\beta_0$ and $\beta_1$). However, inferences about these two parameters based on the same data $y$ will be somewhat less precise than inferences about the single parameter in Equation (2.8), the more restrictive model.

Upon reflection, modeling the differences between the political parties ($\beta_1$) as identical for Northerners and Southerners also seems unrealistic. A less restrictive three parameter model can account for these differences:

$$\mu_i = \beta_0 + \beta_{1i} P_i, \tag{2.10}$$

where

$$\beta_{1i} = \gamma_0 + \gamma_1 R_i.$$

In Equation (2.10), $R_i$ stands for individual $i$'s region, where $R_i = 0$ for Southerners and $R_i = 1$ for Northerners. Substituting the second equation into the first, yielding the reduced form, makes the number of independent parameters more obvious:

$$\mu_i = \beta_0 + \gamma_0 P_i + \gamma_0 (P_i R_i).$$

The three parameters of this reduced form model can also be estimated from the same data as the other two, although inferences into these three will be correspondingly less precise and reliable.

One can proceed to complicate the model by increasing the number of parameters to be estimated and thus expanding $\theta$. This results in fewer unrealistic assumptions in $\mathcal{M}^*$. However, it also puts more demands on existing data, $y$. Equation (2.8) is at the most restrictive extreme. At the least restrictive extreme, one might prefer to model each individual $i$ with a separate propensity to support the president:

$$\mu_i = \beta_i. \tag{2.11}$$

The problem, of course, is that with $n$ observations ($y_1, \ldots, y_n$) and $n$ parameters ($\beta_1, \ldots, \beta_n$), Equation (2.11) provides no summary of the data at all. Although one can estimate this model, essentially by setting $\hat{\beta}_i = y_i$, this provides very little information beyond the data in original form. Furthermore, $\hat{\beta}_i$ are extremely imprecise and unreliable estimators.[14] In principle, one can even go beyond this extreme by attempting to use the data to estimate the outputs $Y$, the known features of the social system $X$, the functional form of the relationship $g$, the ancillary parameters $\alpha$ ($\sigma^2$ in this example), and the general form of the stochastic component $f$. Since estimating Equation (2.11) already uses up all available data, this particular example could not be extended further. With more or better data, one could move more elements from $\mathcal{M}^*$ to $\theta$, but even the best data cannot empty $\mathcal{M}^*$ entirely. Data, of even the best quality or largest quantity, will never be adequate for scientific inference without some theoretical structure.

What criteria should be used to select a model on the continuum from Equation (2.8) to Equation (2.11)? Three seem most relevant: First, an empirical modeler should begin by sticking close to the critical theoretical questions. Anyone who has sat down to analyze one of the ICPSR[15] sample surveys with more than a thousand questions, or the Conflict and Peace Data Bank (COPDAB) with international events coded by actor, target, issue area, and degree of hostility for each day since 1945, understands the value of maintaining a strong sense of what one wants to find out. Even if survey data were created by a random number generator, sufficient data mining will reveal any number of apparently strong "relationships." Of course, most of these "relationships" would probably not be apparent if another survey were taken under essentially the same conditions.[16] Second, researchers must also keep in mind the quality and extent of their data. "Over fitting" a legitimate data set by estimating too many parameters can be as dangerous as omitting theoretically important questions from the analysis (see Footnote 7).

Attention to the quality of data and theory helps to narrow down the possibilities somewhat, but a considerable range of models still remains. A third rule to guide analysis beyond this is to emphasize *simplicity*. Zellner (1984: 31) makes this point best:

> A leading econometrician has stated in public that economic reality is complex and therefore econometric models must be complex. This view of "economic reality" as well as the conclusion drawn from it are, to say the least, debatable. Economic reality, whatever that is, may seem to be complicated because it is not understood. Understanding in my view involves simplification not complication. There are many examples of sophisticatedly simple models that provide understanding and predictions that have been found to be useful. . . . On the other hand, it is difficult to find complicated

---

[14] They are also statistically inconsistent.

[15] The Interuniversity Consortium for Political and Social Research at the University of Michigan.

[16] One of every twenty regression coefficients will be "significant" at the 0.05 level even in a set of independent random numbers.

models that explain past variation well and also predict accurately. Thus when a speaker asserts that a "true model" is a complicated model with an infinite number of parameters, I usually stop him (or her) and request evidence and justification for this view. The Jeffreys-Wrinch simplicity postulate, Occam's razor, and the principle of parsimony all point in the direction of developing sophisticatedly simple models and evaluating predictions derived from them.

Thus, within the range of models one would theoretically like to estimate, some are eliminated because they require data of higher quality or more quantity than is available. The remaining choice in model selection ought to be to derive simple explanations of social science phenomenon. Whether or not one accepts Zellner's metaphysical assumption that nature is simple, it still pays to look for simpler explanations – for theoretical as well as aesthetic reasons.

A relatively new trend in statistical research, particularly in econometrics, is to find ways to weaken every possible assumption through what are called *robust* statistics: methods are being developed to estimate parameters and standard errors even when other parts of the model are misspecified (Hampel et al., 1986; Huber, 1967; White, 1980, 1982). With other techniques, the functional form (Box and Draper, 1987), the stochastic component (Silverman, 1986, on density estimation), and the explanatory and dependent variables (Jöreskog and Sörbom, 1979) can be estimated rather than assumed known. A methodology even exists to allow one to avoid structural models completely and concentrate on a single reduced form, presumably generated by the unknown structural model (see Sims, 1980; and Freeman, Williams, and Lin, 1986, on vector autoregression).

This new trend in statistical research addresses a valid concern about making incorrect theoretical assumptions. Having a set of available techniques for appropriate situations is clearly important. However, researchers are often too quick to claim ignorance about many parts of their models and revert back to the automatic linear and Normal assumptions. The wealth of knowledge most empirical researchers have about their subject matter should be mined as much as traditional data sources to improve estimation. In addition, we ought to be concerned that these new methods put too many demands on generally weak social science data. With a fixed set of data, one can avoid making all sorts of assumptions, but only by either losing precision or by narrowing the range of hypotheses one is investigating. In other words, these methods are valuable because they allow the researcher to move more parts of the statistical model from $\mathcal{M}^*$ to $\theta$, but any move of this sort will almost invariably reduce the precision and reliability of empirical estimators of everything in $\theta$.[17]

---

[17] An additional problem with some of these methods is that "In view of the potential importance of unusual and surprising data, it is troubling to see how often outlying observations are discarded without thought or averaged with usual observations by means of 'robust' techniques" (Zellner, 1984: 8).

As a consequence, the primary goal of this work will not be to weaken every possible assumption. I will demonstrate how to build and estimate a rich variety of statistical models. Weakening assumptions will be mentioned occasionally, but a full treatment of these new developments would require a separate volume, a new theory of statistical inference, and set of statistical methods none of which are as yet fully developed. For present purposes, the more critical task is to demonstrate how likelihood inference and statistical modeling form a theoretical unity underlying the diversity of available statistical methods. Through this approach I will also be able to identify which types of assumptions one might subsequently want to weaken. If one is willing to make the requisite assumptions, inferences better than those made with the concepts presented here are usually impossible.

## 2.6    Specification tests

Given that one must always choose how to divide one's model of the world $\mathcal{M}$ into a part to be estimated $\theta$ and a part to be assumed $\mathcal{M}^*$, a natural question to ask is whether the general guidelines in Section 2.5 can be formalized in some way. Can a test be constructed to determine whether one has the correct model? Under the likelihood theory of inference, it is the value of the likelihood that helps to estimate values of $\theta$. Could likelihood be used to help verify the rest of the specified model, $\mathcal{M}^*$?

Since the theory of inference explicated here is based intentionally on *relative* concepts only, one can never derive an *absolute* measure to assess the correctness of any part or all of a particular specification. This may seem like an obvious point, but the very popular $R^2$ statistic used in linear regression is frequently, albeit incorrectly, interpreted as an absolute measure of whether the model is correct. Its only proper interpretation is in comparing two models of the same data, just as with the value of the likelihood. Indeed, $R^2$ is a function of the likelihood and as such can only be used for *relative* inferences. $R^2$ may be the most popular, but many other specification tests have been proposed. For example, Judge et al. (1985) list eight popular tests. Every one of these, and all other specification tests, is a different type of *relative* measure. Nearly every one is a direct function of the value of the likelihood. Although many others are likely to be proposed and to be of use in the future, every specification test of this sort is a relative measure and is only valid for comparisons within the context of a single data set. By developing a better understanding of the fundamental theory of inference underlying empirical analyses, political science scholars are less likely to repeat these classic fallacies.

Once we move from the impossible goal of absolute measures of the validity of a particular specification to relative measures, we also quickly realize that one can never test the entire specification ($\mathcal{M}$) simultaneously. All the data in the world will get us nowhere without some theoretical structure. Indeed, the *only* way one could test the entire specification is if one happened to know the "correct" model. In the latter case, one could easily calculate a likelihood ratio to compare how well the current specification compares to the correct one. Of course, one never knows the correct model, so this approach is not generally useful.

A compromise might be to test part of the specification. The most common procedure of this sort is to compare the current specification to one with several additional explanatory variables through a likelihood ratio or similar test. Indeed, the meaning of the phrase "specification test" is often narrowed to a test of only the choice of explanatory variables. Other tests exist to check assumptions about the functional form, the stochastic component, and various other features of the specification, $\mathcal{M}$. As long as one is comfortable with the rest of the specification ($\mathcal{M}^*$), any one of these tests is a valid and useful tool. However, a sequential test of each assumption in turn is *not* appropriate since each test assumes that the rest of the model is correct. As we have already discovered, no test exists or could be formulated to simultaneously check all the assumptions.

Hence, while specification tests are useful diagnostic tests in particular instances, they will never take the place of careful theoretical specifications and assumptions. Indeed, scholars should be particularly careful in drawing conclusions from these tests. Probably the key point to remember is that no test ever enables a researcher to validate the entire model. Unfortunately, this incorrect generalization is often made in tests for omitted variables, which may be calculated in certain instances (see Sections 6.3 and 10.3). In no case can these tests verify other parts of the model and in all cases in which some other part of the model is in doubt these tests are likely to yield fallacious results even about the presence of omitted variables.[18]

## 2.7    Concluding remarks

In this chapter, I have outlined the concepts of probability as a model of uncertainty, and likelihood as a model of inference. The distinctions between likelihood, traditional and inverse probability, and different interpretations of probability are subtle but critical to the analyses that follow. Although likelihood as a relative measure of uncertainty is fundamentally different from traditional probability, it is firmly built on twin foundations of probability theory and statistical modeling. Thus, in Chapter 3, I provide a brief overview of the probability model and relevant features of probability and distribution

---

[18] See Sims (1988) for an excellent discussion and comparison of specification tests, sensitivity testing, and forecast performance in model building.

theory that follow from it. Chapter 4 details the method of likelihood, using a series of simple linear regression models as a running example. Finally, in Chapters 5 to 8, likelihood is applied to a variety of more sophisticated statistical models.

# CHAPTER 3

# The probability model of uncertainty

What we commonly call "probability" is really a formal model of uncertainty with only three axioms. These axioms are neither true nor false; they are assumed. By applying the rules of logic to these axioms, all of probability theory and distribution theory emerges. In what follows, I state these three axioms and provide a sense of a portion of the rich theory that developed from them. My general purpose is not to provide a complete treatment of any of these subsidiary topics, as that would require a library of additional volumes. Instead, I concentrate on a review of the fundamental rules and ideas of primary use in statistical modeling and likelihood inference.

My notation is slightly nontraditional from the perspective of probability theory. However, it closely follows the notation introduced in Chapter 1, emphasizing the important role of the probability model in specifying the complete statistical model. Since I assume most readers have seen some probability theory before, this chapter builds on the basics by demonstrating that it is not necessary to fit one's data to an existing, and perhaps inappropriate, stochastic model. Instead, we can state first principles at the level of political science theory and derive a stochastic model deductively. For the same reasons, the organization below does not follow the traditional approach in increasing order of complexity (discrete, continuous, compound, multivariate, etc.). Instead, this chapter is structured to emphasize how one builds distributions and stochastic models of political phenomena, grouping primarily by the similarity of substantive problems and data. Aside from that presented in this chapter, considerably more probability theory is described and derived in the course of the specific methods developed in Part II.

## 3.1    The probability model

The set of all possible outcomes of an experiment is the *sample space, $\mathscr{S}$*. The elements of this set are mutually exclusive and exhaustive outcomes of the experiment. Sample spaces may be *discrete and finite,* such as the outcome of presidential elections, $\mathscr{S}$ = {Democratic, Republican, Other}. They may be *discrete, but countably infinite,* such as the number of Israeli raids into Southern Lebanon a year, $\mathscr{S}$ = {0,1, . . . }. Sample spaces may also be *continuous,* where listing events becomes impossible; for example, the duration of a parliamentary coalition is a continuous variable.

A *random variable* is a *function* that assigns a real number to every possible random output from a particular experiment, that is, to every element in the sample space. For example, the random variable for presidential elections might assign 1.0 to the event "Democrat wins," 2.0 to "Republican wins," and 3.0 to "other party wins." The word "random" in random variable refers to the stochastic variation in the outputs across experiments for each observation. "Variable" is used to emphasize that in actual runs of the experiment, the observed values of this process vary over observations, even for a single experiment. By contrast, since the parameter $\mu_i$ varies over observations but is constant in repeated experiments, it is called a *nonrandom variable*.[1]

Let $Y_i$ be the random variable for observation $i$ ($i = 1, \ldots, n$). In this chapter, only stochastic models of this single observation will be considered. Subsequent chapters will tie together all $n$ observations into a single model by adding the systematic component. Many of the stochastic models developed below are defined as aggregates (sums, counts, means, etc.) of processes occurring over time that are observable only at the end of some period. Thus, even though stochastic *processes* occur through time, this entire stochastic model for $Y_i$ still results in only a single observation. The set of all $n$ observations may still vary over time, across space (as in cross-sectional data), or both (as in pooled time series-cross-sectional data).

I use $y_i$ to denote a realization or hypothetical value of the random variable $Y_i$ and $y_{ji}$ to denote a real number. The subscript $i$ still refers to the observation number ($i = 1, \ldots, n$), and $j$ is a symbolic label for one possible outcome of the experiment. Furthermore, a set of outcomes is called an *event* and a particular event is labeled $z_{ki}$. An event of type $k$ may include no outcomes (the null set, $z_{ki} = \{\phi\}$), a single outcome ($z = \{y_{ji}\}$), several outcomes ($z_{ki} = \{y_{1i}, y_{2i}, y_{5i}\}$), a range of outcomes [$z_{ki} \in (2,3)$], or the entire sample space ($z_{ki} = \{\mathcal{S}\}$).

The probability model for a particular experiment assigns a measure of uncertainty to every possible event. The three axioms of the model of probability are defined on the basis of these definitions:

1. For any event $z_{ki}$, $\Pr(z_{ki}) \geq 0$.
2. $\Pr(\mathcal{S}) = 1.0$.
3. If $z_{1i}, \ldots, z_{Ki}$ are $K$ mutually exclusive events, then

$$\Pr(z_{1i} \cup z_{2i} \cup \cdots \cup z_{Ki}) = \Pr(z_{1i}) + \Pr(z_{2i}) + \cdots + \Pr(z_{Ki}).$$

---

[1] Strictly speaking, a random variable is neither random – because the probability model is extrinsic to this function – nor variable – since the function remains constant over observations. However, I adopt the somewhat less formal and more intuitive usage in the text.

Axiom 1 requires that for any event, all numerical values produced by the function Pr($\cdot$) be greater than or equal to zero. If an event is not in the set of possible events $\mathscr{S}$, its probability is zero. Axiom 2 is the obvious requirement that something must happen in every run of the experiment (if you flip a coin, either heads or tails must appear). Since events outside the sample space $\mathscr{S}$ occur with probability zero, the event $\mathscr{S}$ must occur with probability one. Axioms 1 and 2 combine to require that any probability range only between zero and one, $0 \geq \Pr(z_{ki}) \geq 1$, for any event $z_{ki}$. Axiom 3 provides the basic additive rule for calculating the probabilities of mutually exclusive events.

Together, these three axioms define a probability model on the sample space $\mathscr{S}$, as the real valued function, Pr($\cdot$). From these axioms one can derive all the rules of probability theory. Before moving on to complete stochastic models for a single observation, I mention three particularly important results here: First, probabilities of events $z_{i1}$ and $z_{k2}$ that are not necessarily mutually exclusive (i.e., may have one or more outcomes in common) may be calculated as:

$$\Pr(z_{1i} \cup z_{2i}) = \Pr(z_{1i}) + \Pr(z_{2i}) - \Pr(z_{1i} \cap z_{2i}),$$

where "$z_{1i} \cap z_{2i}$" represents the intersections of events $z_{1i}$ and $z_{2i}$. This is derived from Axiom 3, since the overlapping part is subtracted out in the last term. If $z_{1i}$ and $z_{2i}$ are *mutually exclusive,* the last term drops out and this rule reduces to Axiom 3. Second, if two random variables, $Y_{1i}$ and $Y_{2i}$, are *stochastically independent,* the probability law governing one has no influence on the probabilities governing the other. Accordingly, one can calculate their joint probability (of both occurring) from their marginal probabilities (of each occurring separately):

$$\Pr(Y_{1i} = y_{ji}, Y_{2i} = y_{li}) = \Pr(Y_{1i} = y_{ji})\Pr(Y_{2i} = y_{li}).$$

Since this applies for all possible events, it may also be written more conveniently as

$$\Pr(Y_{1i}, Y_{2i}) = \Pr(Y_{1i})\Pr(Y_{2i}). \tag{3.1}$$

For example, if we were to assume that elections to Congress and the Presidency are independent, we could calculate the probability of undivided Democratic government by multiplying the probability that the Democrats win control of the majority of both houses of Congress by the probability that they will win the Presidency.

The final result, on *conditional probability,* was already used in Chapter 1:

$$\Pr(Y_{1i}|Y_{2i}) = \frac{\Pr(Y_{1i}, Y_{2i})}{\Pr(Y_{2i})}. \tag{3.2}$$

By combining this result with Equation (3.1), one can see that independence also implies that $Y_{2i}$ has no influence on the probability of $Y_{1i}$,

$\Pr(Y_{1i}|Y_{2i}) = \Pr(Y_{1i})$, and $Y_{1i}$ has no influence on the probability of $Y_{2i}$, $\Pr(Y_{2i}|Y_{1i}) = \Pr(Y_{2i})$.

## 3.2    Univariate probability distributions

The *probability distribution* of a random variable $Y_i$ is a complete accounting of the probability of $Y_i$ taking on any conceivable value $y_i$. Several different methods exist for representing these probabilities.

For example, the random variable $Y_i$ is assigned 1 for heads and 0 for tails in a coin tossing experiment. To specify a probability distribution in this case, one only needs to write

$$\Pr(Y_i = 1) = \pi,$$
$$\Pr(Y_i = 0) = 1 - \pi,$$
$$\Pr(Y \neq 0,1) = 0.$$

$\pi$ is the parameter of this distribution, where $\pi = 0.5$ when the coin is fair. The range of possible values of a parameter is called the *parameter space* and is usually denoted $\Theta$. In this example, the parameter space for $\pi$ is the range from 0 to 1 inclusive (i.e., $\pi \in \Theta = [0,1]$).

In this simple example, merely listing or graphing the probabilities of each outcome in the sample space is relatively convenient. For most interesting examples, however, the number of possible events is very large or infinite. For example, the random variables representing income (in dollars and cents), public approval of the president (in percentages) and occupation can each produce very large numbers of events with nonzero probability. Further analysis thus requires a more concise means of representation.

A mathematical formula is the solution. As most readers know, the usual method of presenting these formulas is merely as a list. However, although not often discussed in introductory books, each distribution was originally derived from a very specific set of theoretical assumptions. These assumptions may be stated in abstract mathematical form, but they may also be interpreted as political assumptions about the underlying process generating the data. The ultimate mathematical form for most distributions is usually not very intuitive, but the first principles from which they were originally derived represent models of interesting political science situations and are much closer to both data and theory. When a list of these first principles is known, understanding them is critical to the correct application of a particular probability distribution. If at any time in this chapter, the mathematics become too difficult, the reader should pay close attention to the first principles (usually appearing in italics) and final form of each distribution. The intervening steps of the derivation may be considered a black box.

Ultimately, political scientists will benefit from learning considerably more about stochastic modeling. This will enable scholars to develop probability distributions that closely match whatever social science processes they desire to model. Fortunately, enormous numbers of distributions have already been developed by statisticians and others.[2] Although often developed for other purposes, analysts can marshal this wealth of raw material for modeling problems in political science. In so doing, researchers need not get bogged down in understanding precisely how every probability distribution is derived from first principles, but we must completely understand these initial substantive assumptions and be able to apply the final distributions. For each distribution in this chapter, I present the first principles and final distribution form. For some, I also present the full derivation. Chapter 4 demonstrates how to apply these distributions in problems of inference.

### Bernoulli distribution

The simplest distribution represents the situation where a random variable has only two possible events with nonzero probability. A coin flip can be represented easily with the Bernoulli distribution. More generally, this distribution can represent one observation of any dichotomous random variable. Vote choice for Bush or Dukakis, employed or unemployed, and developing or industrialized nations are a few of the many possible examples.

The two first principles required to derive the Bernoulli probability distribution are quite simple: the random variable $Y_i$ must have two *mutually exclusive* outcomes, $y_i = 0$ and $y_i = 1$, that are *exhaustive*. This distribution is usually written so that zero and one are the outcomes, but any other coding of a dichotomous variable could be mapped onto this representation. These are the only first principles required. Mutual exclusivity indicates that $\Pr(Y_i = 1 | Y_i = 0) = 0$. If voters were permitted to vote for both Bush and Dukakis, the Bernoulli distribution would not apply. Being exhaustive indicates that the probability of one event occurring is the complement of the probability of the other happening:

$$\Pr(Y_i = 1) = 1 - \Pr(Y_i = 0).$$

Hence, the Bernoulli distribution is a better approximation to the underlying process generating election outcomes, for example, when no popular third party candidates are in the race. Many binary variables fit these two simple assumptions.

From these first principles, deriving a single probability distribution is straightforward. To begin, define a parameter $\pi$, such that

---

[2] The four volumes written by Johnson and Kotz (1969, 1970a, 1970b, 1972) are the standard references on these matters. Rothschild and Logothetis (1987) is a more affordable paperback. See also Shapiro and Gross (1981).

$$\Pr(Y_i = 1) = \pi$$

A direct consequence of the events being mutually exclusive and exhaustive is that:

$$\Pr(Y_i = 0) = 1 - \pi.$$

The full probability distribution is then a way of putting together these two separate parts into a single equation:

$$Y_i \sim f_{\text{Bern}}(y_i|\pi) = \begin{cases} \pi^{y_i}(1 - \pi)^{1 - y_i} & \text{for } y_i = 0, 1, \\ 0 & \text{otherwise.} \end{cases} \tag{3.3}$$

In combination with an appropriate systematic component, this simple distribution will provide a useful model of dichotomous random variables.

Since this is a discrete probability distribution, $f(y_i|\pi) = \Pr(y_i|\pi)$; the same is obviously not true for continuous distributions. Once a probability distribution is completely specified, any feature of the random variable of interest may be calculated. For example, the mean of $Y_i$ is calculated by taking the expected value:

$$\begin{aligned} E(Y_i) &= \sum_{\text{all } y_i} y_i f(y_i) \\ &= 0 f_i(0) + 1 f_i(1) \\ &= 0 + \pi \\ &= \pi. \end{aligned}$$

Hence, if heads is 1 and tails is 0, then one flip of the coin will yield, on average, the number $\pi$. If a vote for Dukakis is assigned a 1 and Bush a 0, then individual $i$ will have a $\pi$ probability of voting for Dukakis.

*Binomial distribution*

Suppose a series of $N$ Bernoulli random variables exists, but *we only observe the sum* of these variables. A political scientist might still be interested in these unobserved binary random variables, but the only data available are based on this sum. For example, data might exist on the number of elections, out of the last five, in which a survey respondent recalled voting. The survey researcher might not have had the time or money to include separate questions about voting participation in each election. Indeed, this aggregate recall question may be subject to fewer recall problems since positive and negative errors in the individual (unobserved) binary questions would tend to cancel out.

By assuming that the unobserved binary variables (e.g., the five decisions to vote or not) are *independent* and *identically distributed,* one can derive a binomial distribution to model this situation. Thus, we suppose that the same

Table 3.1. *Deriving the binomial distribution*

| $Y_{1i}$ | $Y_{2i}$ | $Y_{3i}$ | $\Sigma_{j=1}^{3} Y_{ji} \equiv Y_i$ | $\Pr(Y_i)$ |
|---|---|---|---|---|
| 0 | 0 | 0 | 0 | $(1-\pi)^3$ |
| 1 | 0 | 0 | 1 | $\pi(1-\pi)^2$ |
| 0 | 1 | 0 | 1 | $\pi(1-\pi)^2$ |
| 0 | 0 | 1 | 1 | $\pi(1-\pi)^2$ |
| 0 | 1 | 1 | 2 | $\pi^2(1-\pi)$ |
| 1 | 0 | 1 | 2 | $\pi^2(1-\pi)$ |
| 1 | 1 | 0 | 2 | $\pi^2(1-\pi)$ |
| 1 | 1 | 1 | 3 | $\pi^3$ |

Bernoulli distribution, with the same parameter $\pi$, describes each of the five constituent elections. A constant $\pi$ implies that the probability of individual $i$ voting is the same for each election. The independence assumption, as interpreted here, means that participation by individual $i$ in one election is unrelated to participation by that individual in other elections, except that $\pi$ is the same in each election.

To get a feel for how the binomial distribution is derived from these first principles, take the case of $N=3$ binary variables. Whereas a Bernoulli variable has two possible outcomes, a binomial with $N=3$ has $2^3=8$. Table 3.1 lists each of these eight outcomes with their associated probabilities, calculated using the three first principles. For example, the first line in the table records the outcome that all three binary random variables $(Y_{1i}, Y_{2i}, Y_{3i})$ were realized as zeros. Since the three variables are independent, their probabilities may be multiplied to derive the probability of the sum taking on the value zero [see Equation (3.1)]. Since they are identically distributed, the same probability in each case $(1-\pi)$ is multiplied. Probabilities for the other rows are calculated similarly.

Suppose one is interested in calculating the probability that the sum of the three variables, $Y_i$, is equal to one. The second, third, and fourth rows of Table 3.1 each have outcomes with a sum equal to one. Since these outcomes are mutually exclusive, they may be added:

$$
\begin{aligned}
\Pr(Y_i=2) \equiv \Pr\left(\sum_{j=1}^{3} Y_{ji}=1\right) \qquad\qquad (3.4)\\
= \Pr(Y_{1i}=1,\ Y_{2i}=0,\ Y_{3i}=0)\\
+ \Pr(Y_{1i}=0,\ Y_{2i}=1,\ Y_{3i}=0)\\
+ \Pr(Y_{1i}=0,\ Y_{2i}=0,\ Y_{3i}=1)\\
= \pi(1-\pi)^2 + \pi(1-\pi)^2 + \pi(1-\pi)^2\\
= 3\pi(1-\pi)^2.
\end{aligned}
$$

If $\pi = 0.5$, as in the case of a fair coin, the probability that only one of three coins would turn up heads is $3\pi(1-\pi)^2 = 3(0.5)(1-0.5)^2 = 0.375$.

In order to derive a single formula, instead of always listing all possible outcomes and associated probabilities, note that the last line in Equation (3.4) has two parts: the number of outcomes (3) and the probability of each of these outcomes $[\pi(1-\pi)^2]$. In this case, the probability of $Y_i$ is calculated by taking the product of these two parts. Indeed, regardless of the number of possible events ($N$), the binomial probability always has these two parts. The first part may be generalized with a little knowledge of combinatorics as $\binom{N}{y_i}$. The second part is simply $\pi^{y_i}(1-\pi)^{N-y_i}$. The result is the familiar binomial distribution:

$$
\begin{aligned}
f(y_i|\pi) &= \begin{cases} \binom{N}{y_i}\pi^{y_i}(1-\pi)^{N-y_i} & \text{for } y_i = 0, 1, \ldots, n, \\ 0 & \text{otherwise} \end{cases} \\[2mm]
&= \begin{cases} \frac{N!}{y_i!(N-y_i)!} \; \pi^{y_i}(1-\pi)^{N-y_i} & \text{for } y_i = 0, 1, \ldots, n, \\ 0 & \text{otherwise,} \end{cases}
\end{aligned}
\tag{3.5}
$$

where $\binom{N}{y_i}$ is shorthand for $\frac{N!}{y_i!(N-y_i)!}$ . If the Bernoulli assumptions of mutually exclusive and exhaustive binary events hold, and the additional assumptions that the $N$ binary random variables are independent and identically distributed also hold, one can use this formula to calculate the probability that the random sum $Y_i$ equals $y_i$, which may be between zero and $N$.

*Extended beta-binomial distribution*

Many situations exist in political science where data on the sums of random binary variables are available, but the binomial assumptions of independence and identical distributions are questionable. The number of members of the U.S. Senate (out of a total of 100) who vote for a particular bill, or the number of school districts in a state banning *The Catcher in the Rye,* are good examples. Although unobserved, one can reasonably hypothesize that the probability $\pi$ of each senator voting for a particular bill is not identical. In addition, school districts, as well as senators, are likely to influence each other rather than be totally independent random variables.

I begin by weakening the binomial assumption that the unobserved binary random variables making up $Y_i$ have constant $\pi$. To derive an alternative distribution, one cannot let $\pi$ vary haphazardly. Instead, we must choose a specific distribution that governs the variation in $\pi$ across these individual binary variables within the single observation, $Y_i$. Although $\pi$ is a fixed parameter in the binomial distribution, it becomes a random variable in this derivation of a new probability distribution. The choice of possible distributions is limited to those where the random variable is bounded as is the parameter space for $\pi$, between zero and one. A variety have been proposed, some leading to intractable expressions, others somewhat less intuitive. The most commonly used distribution for $\pi$ is the *beta* density. Thus, in addition to the assumptions required to derive the binomial distribution, the key first principle required to derive the extended beta-binomial distribution is that $\pi$ *varies according to a beta density*.

The beta distribution has $\pi$ as a random variable and two parameters $\rho$ and $\gamma$ (in my parameterization) and may be written as follows:

$$f_\beta(\pi|\rho,\gamma) = \frac{\Gamma(\rho\gamma^{-1} + (1-\rho)\gamma^{-1})}{\Gamma(\rho\gamma^{-1})\Gamma[(1-\rho)\gamma^{-1}]} \pi^{\rho\gamma^{-1}-1}(1-\pi)^{(1-\rho)\gamma^{-1}-1} \quad (3.6)$$

for $0 < \pi < 1$, and zero otherwise, and where $\Gamma(x)$ is the gamma function:

$$\Gamma(x) = \int_0^\infty z^{x-1}e^{-z}dz. \quad (3.7)$$

One can calculate values of the gamma function for particular values of $x$ either directly from this integral (with $z$ as the integration dummy) or from tables designed for this purpose (see Johnson and Kotz, 1970a: Chapter 17). For integer values of $x$, $\Gamma(x+1) = x! = x(x-1)(x-2)\cdots 1$. Noninteger values of $x$ produce a continuous interpolation.

The beta distribution is relatively flexible, and, depending on different values of $\rho$ and $\gamma$, it can be unimodal, bimodal, or skewed. This distribution is assumed here not because it was derived from some set of first principles about how $\pi$ varies over the individual binary variables, but rather because it is a first principle. The benefit of assuming this distribution is its flexibility in handling a variety of interesting cases. It is also mathematically simple, particularly in combination with the binomial distribution.[3] Substantively, $\rho \equiv E(\pi)$ is the mean of the distribution of $\pi$, and $\gamma$ is an index for how much variation exists in $\pi$ across the binary random variables.

The goal now is to derive the extended beta-binomial probability distribution. The procedure will be to modify the binomial distribution $[f_b(y_i|\pi, N)]$ by letting $\pi$ vary according to a beta distribution $[f_\beta(\pi|\rho,\gamma)]$. This procedure is generally called *compounding* a probability distribution with another distribution. Two steps are required.

First, the joint distribution $(f_j)$ of $Y_i$ and $\pi$ is derived by using the basic equation for conditional probability. Thus, Equation (3.2) may also be presented as this:

---

[3] See Sheps and Menken (1973) on the beta density's mathematical properties and Heckman and Willis (1977: Appendix) for an interesting justification of the application of the beta density to the probability of labor force participation by married women.

$$Pr(AB) = Pr(A|B)Pr(B).$$

Thus, I take the product of the binomial and beta distributions:

$$f_j(y_i, \pi | \rho, \gamma) = f_b(y_i | \pi) f_\beta(\pi | \rho, \gamma), \tag{3.8}$$

where $\gamma$ is just carried through as a conditioning parameter, unaffected by the procedure.[4]

Second, the extended beta-binomial distribution ($f_{ebb}$) is derived by collapsing this joint distribution over $\pi$:

$$f_{ebb}(y_i | \rho, \gamma) = \int_{-\infty}^{\infty} f_j(y_i, \pi | \rho, \gamma) d\pi.$$

Since a distribution was substituted for it, $\pi$ no longer appears on the left hand side of this equation. In the extended beta-binomial distribution $\rho$ is now the mean probability of the unobserved binary variables, as was $\pi$ in the binomial distribution. To make clearer the relationship between the two distributions, I reparameterize the extended beta-binomial by substituting each occurrence of $\rho$ with $\pi$. For $y_i = 0, \ldots, N$, the extended beta-binomial distribution is thus defined as

$$f_{ebb}(y_i | \pi, \gamma) = Pr(Y_i = y_i | \pi, \gamma, N) \tag{3.9}$$
$$= \frac{N!}{y_i!(N - y_i)!} \prod_{j=0}^{y_i - 1} (\pi + \gamma j) \prod_{j=0}^{N - y_i - 1} (1 - \pi + \gamma j) / \prod_{j=0}^{N-1} (1 + \gamma j),$$

where one adopts the convention that $\prod_{i=0}^{y} c_i = 1$ for any $x < 0$.[5] This equation may appear more complicated than the ultimate form of the binomial and other distributions, but it is only algebraically complicated. Conceptually, it is just like any other traditional probability. One sets $N$, and the parameters $\pi$ and $\gamma$, at specific values; then one can easily use arithmetic to determine the probability that $Y_i$ takes on any particular value $y_i$.

In the extended beta-binomial distribution, $\pi$ is an average probability of a binary variable equaling 1.0. In the binomial, $\pi$ is the same for each binary variable and is thus also the same average. However, this distribution has an additional unknown parameter, $\gamma$, which governs the degree to which $\pi$ varies across the unobserved binary variables making up each observation. When $\gamma = 0$, this distribution reduces to the binomial and all the $\pi$s are constant. Larger amounts of variation in $\pi$ lead to larger values of $\gamma$.

---

[4] If $f_\beta$ were reconceptualized as the degree of belief about a constant parameter $\pi$, and $\rho$ and $\gamma$ were fixed to specific numbers representing the prior expectations about $\pi$, then this procedure is equivalent to Bayesian analysis, with $f_\beta$ as the prior and the left hand side of Equation (3.8) as the posterior distribution.

[5] The symbol $\prod_{i=1}^{n}$ means "the product from $i = 1$ to $n$." It is an analog to the summation symbol, $\Sigma_{i=1}^{n}$.

Although this derivation weakened only the binomial assumption of identical distributions of the individual binary variables, one can prove that certain types of *dependence* among the individual binary variables lead to exactly the same extended beta-binomial distribution. Thus, heterogeneity (in $\pi$) and dependence are both modeled in this new distribution by $\gamma$. The different ranges of $\gamma$ have implications for both the underlying binary variables and the aggregate observed count $(Y_i)$.

Thus, when $\gamma = 0$, the binary variables are independent and identically distributed and the extended beta-binomial distribution reduces exactly to the binomial. When $\gamma > 0$, either positive correlation among the binary variables or heterogeneity among the $\pi$s causes *overdispersion* in the aggregate variable $Y_i$. When $Y_i$ is overdispersed, its variance is larger than one would expect under the binomial distribution's assumption of binary variate independence. Finally, $\gamma < 0$ indicates negative correlations among the binary variables and results in *underdispersion*.[6,7]

Since one observes only the total count, and not the individual binary variables, determining which of the possible causes is responsible for observed over- or underdispersion is not possible: dependence among the binary variables and heterogeneity among their expected values have the same observed effect on $Y_i$. Indeed, this is a classic problem of identification. The data contain insufficient information at this aggregated level to distinguish between these two substantively different cases. If one collected data on the individual binary variables, this distinction would be possible. An estimated value of $\gamma$ different from zero should nevertheless alert a researcher to potentially interesting information. On this basis, one could decide whether collecting more disaggregated data is worthwhile.

### Poisson distribution

Another important discrete probability distribution is for a count with no upper bound. The Poisson distribution is theoretically appropriate when the occurrence of one event has no influence on the expected number of subsequent

---

[6] A somewhat more intuitive interpretation of $\gamma$ is that the correlation among the binary variables is a direct function of this parameter: $\delta = \gamma/(1 + \gamma)$. Hence, one could reparameterize the extended beta-binomial model by solving for $\gamma = \delta/(1 - \delta)$ and substituting $\delta/(1 - \delta)$ into the distribution for every occurrence of $\gamma$. Due to the invariance property of ML, estimating $\gamma$ and transforming afterwards, if desired, is as easy.

[7] Because the possible binary variables are always constrained in the extent to which they can be negatively correlated, $\gamma$ is constrained such that

$$\gamma \geq \max[-\pi(N-1)^{-1}, -(1-\pi)(N-1)^{-1}].$$

See Prentice (1986) for details.

events, $\lambda$. With three other first principles, the full Poisson probability distribution may be derived.[8]

Consider the time interval for observation $i$ in which events are occurring. Although the random variable $Y_i$ is a count of the total number of events that have occurred at the end of period $i$, the assumptions required to derive the Poisson distribution are about the generation of events during this unobserved period. As usual, the underlying data generation process is not observed, only its consequences (the total count).

To begin, denote the random variable representing the number of events that have occurred up to time $t$ during observation period $i$ as $Y_{ti}$. Then write the probability of an addition, and of no addition, respectively, to the total count during the interval from $t$ to $t + \Delta t$ as:

$$\Pr(Y_{(t+\Delta t)i} = y_{ti} + 1 | Y_{ti} = y_{ti}) = \lambda\Delta t + o(\Delta t) \tag{3.10}$$

and

$$\Pr(Y_{(t+\Delta t)i} = y_{ti} | Y_{ti} = y_{ti}) = 1 - [\lambda\Delta t + o(\Delta t)], \tag{3.11}$$

where $o(\Delta t)$ is the probability that more than one event occurs during $\Delta t$ and which, when divided by $\Delta t$, tends to zero as $\Delta t$ gets smaller. We can then write the unconditional probability $\Pr(Y_{(t+\Delta t)i} = y_{ti} + 1)$ as the sum of two mutually exclusive situations: (1) $y_{ti}$ events have occurred by time $t$ and one additional event occurs over the next $\Delta t$ interval, and (2) $y_{ti} + 1$ events have occurred at time $t$ and no new events occur from $t$ to $t + \Delta t$:

$$\Pr(Y_{(t+\Delta t)i} = y_{ti} + 1) = \Pr(Y_{ti} = y_{ti})\lambda\Delta t + \Pr(Y_{ti} = y_{ti} + 1)(1 - \lambda\Delta t). \tag{3.12}$$

Although Equations (3.10) and (3.11) are axiomatic, deriving Equation (3.12) from these equations requires two first principles. First, assuming that *two events cannot occur at precisely the same instant,* one can drop the $o(\Delta t)$ terms. In addition, by assuming that *the probability of an event occurring during the period from $t$ to $t + \Delta t$ is independent of any events occurring prior to time $t$,* each of the two terms in Equation (3.12) may be written as the product of their respective marginal probabilities.

From Equation (3.12), observe how $\Pr(Y_{ti} = y_{ti} + 1)$ changes with respect to time as $\Delta t$ gets smaller and smaller:

$$\frac{\partial\Pr(Y_{ti} = y_{ti} + 1)}{\partial t} \equiv \lim_{\Delta t \to 0} \frac{\Pr(Y_{(t+\Delta t)} = y_{ti} + 1) - \Pr(Y_{ti} = y_{ti} + 1)}{\Delta t} \tag{3.13}$$
$$= \begin{cases} \lambda[\Pr(Y_{ti} = y_{ti}) - \Pr(Y_{ti} = y_{ti} + 1)] & \text{for } y_{ti} + 1 > 1, \\ -\lambda\Pr(Y_{ti} = 0) & \text{for } y_{ti} + 1 = 1. \end{cases}$$

---

[8] The following proof relies on insights into the continuous time, discrete space Markov process outlined by Feller (1968: Chapter 17). See also King (1988a).

If we make a third assumption that *zero events have occurred at the start of the period*, $t = 0$, then $\Pr(y_{0i} = 0) = 1$. As such, the probability distribution of the count emerging from this underlying process can begin to be built. First, solve the last part of Equation (3.13) as:

$$\Pr(Y_{ti} = 0) = -\left(\lambda^{-1}\right) \frac{\partial \Pr(Y_{ti} = 0)}{\partial t}$$
$$= e^{-\lambda t},$$

where the last line uses the fact that the exponential function is the only function that is equal to its derivative.[9] Then, substituting into the other part of Equation (3.13) yields the probability of a single event happening between time 0 and $t$:

$$\Pr(Y_{ti} = 1) = \lambda t e^{-\lambda t}.$$

Finally, by successively substituting and solving, one can derive the formula for the probability that $Y_{ti}$ takes on zero, one, and all other nonnegative integers. The general formula for the Poisson distribution may be written as follows:

$$f(y_i | \lambda, t) = \begin{cases} \frac{e^{-\lambda t}(\lambda t)^{y_i}}{y_i!} & \text{for } t > 0, \lambda > 0, \text{ and } y_i = 0, 1, \ldots, \\ 0 & \text{otherwise.} \end{cases} \qquad (3.14)$$

The more usual form of the Poisson distribution emerges from the fourth and final assumption that *all observation periods $(0,t)$ are of the same length*. By convention, we let $t = 1$, for all observations, which yields:

$$f(y_i | \lambda) = \begin{cases} \frac{e^{-\lambda}\lambda^{y_i}}{y_i!} & \text{for } \lambda > 0 \text{ and } y_i = 0, 1, \ldots, \\ 0 & \text{otherwise.} \end{cases} \qquad (3.15)$$

To summarize, three first principles about the dynamics within each observation are required to derive the first form of the Poisson distribution in Equation (3.14): (1) more than one event cannot occur at the same instant; (2) the probability of an event occurring in one time is constant and independent of all previous events; and (3) zero events have occurred at the start of each period. The key substantive assumption here is (2), the other two being more technical requirements. To derive the more usual form of the Poisson distribution in Equation (3.15), one also must assume (4) that the length of each observation period $i$ is identical. An implicit assumption of both distributions is that the rate of event occurrence $\lambda$ remains constant, or at least unresponsive to $y_i$, over the observation period. This rate during the observation is also the expected count in the complete distribution. Indeed, the variance of the

[9] This equation gives a version of the exponential distribution, which is useful for modeling the time between independent events.

random count is also $\lambda$, indicating that the variation around the expected value increases as $\lambda$ grows. This is easy to conceptualize when $\lambda$ is very small: since the count cannot be negative, the variance must also be small. Social science examples include the number of patents a firm is awarded, the number of presidential vetoes a year, and the number of news stories about a candidate per year. In each case, the actual number of events has no effective maximum.

### Negative binomial distribution

Two key substantive assumptions required to derive the Poisson distribution are that events accumulating during observation period $i$ are independent and have a constant (or unresponsive) rate of occurrence, $\lambda$. If either of these first principles does not hold, a different distribution for the total count, $Y_i$, is produced. For example, suppose one were counting publications in a cross-sectional survey of new professors. Assuming the rate of publication $\lambda$ is constant across these individuals is implausible (Allison, 1987). For another example, the number of political kidnappings a year is unlikely to meet the independence assumption because successful attempts are likely to breed other attempts.

To derive a new, more appropriate compound distribution (what is called the negative binomial), I proceed as in the derivation of the extended beta-binomial distribution from the binomial. Thus, the proof proceeds in two steps. First, instead of requiring that $\lambda$ be constant over the observation period as in the Poisson distribution, I must now assume a probability distribution for $\lambda$. The choice is not obvious, but the fact that $\lambda$ is restricted to positive values limits the possibilities some. Using mathematical tractability and substantive flexibility as criteria, the gamma distribution is the usual choice (Greenwood and Yule, 1920). The gamma distribution (in my parameterization) has $E(\lambda) = \phi$ and $v(\lambda) = \phi(\sigma^2 - 1)$. Note that as $\sigma^2 \to 1$, the gamma distribution collapses to a spike over $\phi$, leaving $\lambda$ constant. Hence, to derive the negative binomial distribution, I make all the assumptions of the Poisson distribution with one exception: $\lambda$ *is assumed to vary within an observation according to the gamma distribution*. The gamma density, for $\lambda > 0$, $\phi > 0$, and $\sigma^2 > 0$, is written as:

$$f_\gamma(\lambda | \phi, \sigma^2) = \frac{\lambda^{\phi(\sigma^2 - 1)^{-1} - 1} e^{-\lambda(\sigma^2 - 1)^{-1}}}{\Gamma[\phi(\sigma^2 - 1)^{-1}](\sigma^2 - 1)^{\phi(\sigma^2 - 1)^{-1}}}, \tag{3.16}$$

where $\Gamma(\cdot)$ is the gamma function in Equation (3.7). With this distribution and the Poisson, we can now derive the joint distribution ($f_j$) of $Y_i$ and $\lambda$ again using the basic equation for conditional probability in Equation (3.2):

$$f_j(y_i, \lambda | \phi, \sigma^2) = f_p(y_i | \lambda) f_\gamma(\lambda | \phi, \sigma^2).$$

Second, one can derive the negative binomial distribution ($f_{nb}$) by collapsing this joint distribution over $\lambda$:

$$f_{nb}(y_i | \phi, \sigma^2) = \int_0^\infty f_j(y_i, \lambda | \phi, \sigma^2) d\lambda.$$

The parameter $\phi$ plays the same role of the mean rate of event occurrence as $\lambda$ does in the Poisson distribution. Thus, to maintain comparability, I reparameterize by substituting $\lambda$ for each occurrence of $\phi$:

$$f_{nb}(y_i | \lambda, \sigma^2) = \frac{\Gamma\left(\frac{\lambda}{\sigma^2 - 1} + y_i\right)}{y_i! \Gamma\left(\frac{\lambda}{\sigma^2 - 1}\right)} \left(\frac{\sigma^2 - 1}{\sigma^2}\right)^{y_i} (\sigma^2)^{\frac{-\lambda}{\sigma^2 - 1}}, \tag{3.17}$$

where $\lambda > 0$ and $\sigma^2 > 1$. In a manner analogous to the extended beta-binomial distribution, this distribution was derived by allowing $\lambda$ to vary according to a gamma distribution. However, as Thompson (1954) first showed, the same negative binomial distribution also results from assuming a particular form of contagion among the individual events making up $Y_i$.[10]

In the negative binomial distribution, $\lambda$ is still the expected number of events. The more events within observation $i$ that either have heterogeneous $\lambda$ or are positively correlated, the larger the parameter $\sigma^2$ will be. Although $\sigma^2$ cannot equal one in this distribution, the smaller $\sigma^2$ is, the closer the negative binomial distribution is to the Poisson. In Chapter 5, I use a generalization of the negative binomial and Poisson distributions, called the generalized event count distribution, to derive a more universal statistical model for data of this sort.

The beta and gamma distributions were used in this section only to derive the extended beta-binomial and negative binomial compound distributions, respectively, but they can also be used directly to model certain continuous processes. For example, the gamma distribution can be used to model the time between events as a generalization of the exponential distribution (see Footnote 9) rather than counts of events. Gamma distributions, being non-negative everywhere and skewed, might also be of use to model variation across individuals without a group. The beta distribution might be appropriate for modeling a proportion, since it varies between zero and one.

---

[10] More specifically, Thompson (1954) showed that a limiting form of the contagious Polya-Eggenberger distribution and Neyman's contagious distributions is the negative binomial. See also Neyman (1965).

*Normal distribution*

The most familiar continuous probability distribution is the *Normal* or *Gaussian* distribution:

$$f_N(y_i|\mu, \sigma) = (2\pi\sigma^2)^{-1/2} e^{-(y_i-\mu)^2/2\sigma^2} \tag{3.18}$$
$$\text{for } \sigma > 0, \quad -\infty < \mu < \infty, \quad -\infty < y_i < \infty.$$

The Normal distribution has two parameters, the mean $\mu$ and the variance $\sigma^2$. $\pi$ is the mathematical constant $3.14159\cdots$ and is not a parameter here. Many different axiomatic developments of this distribution have been derived, so a variety of different assumptions can be made in order to apply it appropriately in a substantive example.

The Normal distribution has been applied in the social sciences countless numbers of times. The primary reason for its initial adoption is that its use leads to very simple mathematical and statistical calculations (least squares, linear relationships, etc.). Of course, if computational issues are treated as transparent, as they should now be because of dramatically decreased cost, this justification is no longer adequate. Another reason for using the Normal distribution is the unquestioning application of a version of the *central limit theorem* (the theorem establishing the first principles required to derive Normality): scholars often argue that their disturbance term is the sum of a large number of independent but unobserved factors. If this is the process actually driving the data and a number of other conditions hold, then the Normal distribution is appropriate, but this case must be *explicitly* made. If the process being modeled is the sum of a number of unobserved variables, then researchers ought to speculate what these might be and state exactly how the central limit theorem applies. The specific limit theorems that enable one to derive the Normal distribution from this type of situation are often no more plausible than similar limit theorems that lead to other distributions (Bartels, 1977; Koenker, 1982). The simplest proof of the central limit theorem I am aware of requires only three-quarters of a page, but still relies on concepts beyond of the scope of this book (see Tardiff, 1981; see also Spanos, 1986, for an interesting historical presentation).

When some version of the central limit theorem or other set of first principles leads one to adopt the Normal distribution, the data have certain recognizable characteristics. For example, the distribution is continuous. Hence, *a discrete random variable cannot be directly generated by the Normal distribution*. This is a critical point, since so many researchers have wasted significant amounts of information by assuming a Normal distribution when more specific information exists. Furthermore, the distribution is symmetric about $\mu$. This means that a skewed random variable also could not be generated by the Normal distribution. Finally, a random variable that is Normally distributed has events with nonzero probabilities occurring everywhere on the real number line. This has particular consequences if a variable is bounded (both theoretically and empirically). For example, most measures of income are both bounded below at zero and positively skewed (with fewer people making very large amounts of money).

The idea that the Normal, or indeed any, distribution can be applied to every statistical problem is a distinctly 18th century idea. For back then, statisticians were searching for the "curve of errors" that would apply in all or almost all cases (see Stigler, 1986). Due to the unfortunate application of statistical tests with very low power, many mistakenly believed for some time that the Normal distribution applied to most naturally occurring situations. More modern tests and sophisticated understanding of the processes that drive observed data revealed the fallacy in this assumption. Indeed, with the enormous number of probability distributions that have been developed (Johnson and Kotz, 1969, 1970a, 1970b, 1972), this early notion now seems almost bizarre. Unfortunately, in too many cases, social scientists have yet to get beyond this mode of thinking.[11] "Everyone believes in the [Normal] law of errors, the experimenters because they think it is a mathematical theorem, the mathematicians because they think it is an empirical fact" [Poincaré, c.f. Harvey (1981a: 112)].

### Log-Normal distribution

Normally distributed random variables extend theoretically over the entire number line. One class of continuous processes for which this does not apply involves those that are never negative. Income, population figures, crime statistics, and budget totals are a few examples of positive value random variables.

Many continuous distributions exist that are defined only over the positive number line. The gamma distribution in Equation (3.16) is one example that might be useful in some circumstances. Another distribution, much more closely related to the very popular Normal distribution, is the log-Normal. Suppose $Z_i$ is a Normally distributed random variable, with mean 0 and variance 1, such that

$$Z_i = \frac{\ln Y_i - \mu}{\sigma}. \tag{3.19}$$

Then, $Y_i$ has a log-Normal distribution with mean $\mu$ and variance $\sigma$. Since $Y_i$ is the random variable of interest in this case, and

[11] For example, in a tour de force of econometric analysis, Judge et al. (1985: 201) write, "In practice, normality is assumed most often and we will only consider this case." Cramer (1986: xiii), in a book on maximum likelihood, writes, "the only probability distribution that occurs at all frequently [in this book] is the normal."

$$Y_i = \exp(\sigma Z_i + \mu), \tag{3.20}$$

the distribution should probably be called the exponential (a name already taken), but I will adopt the conventional name.

A general rule exists in stochastic modeling for deriving a distribution of a variable that is a function of another variable with a known distribution. Suppose $X$ is a continuous random variable with distribution $f_x(X)$ and $Y = u(X)$ defines a one-to-one transformation of $X$ onto $Y$. Let the inverse transformation be denoted as $X = u^{-1}(Y)$. For example, $Y = 2X$ and $Y/2 = X$ are the transformation and inverse transformation, respectively. The goal is to determine the distribution of $Y$ from the distribution of $X$ and the function $u(\cdot)$; the rule is as follows:

$$f_Y(y) = f_x\left(u^{-1}(y)\right) \left| \frac{\partial u^{-1}(y)}{\partial y} \right|. \tag{3.21}$$

The last term, the absolute value of the derivative of the inverse function, is called the *Jacobian,* and this procedure for deriving a probability distribution is sometimes called the *Jacobian method.* This procedure also works if the function $u(\cdot)$ is only piecewise invertible, instead of a one-to-one function, like the transformation $Y = X^2$ and inverse transformation $\sqrt{Y} = X$.

In the case of the log-Normal derivation, the transformation $u(\cdot)$ is in Equation (3.20) and the inverse transformation is Equation (3.19). Thus, the log-Normal distribution may be derived as follows. The standard Normal distribution of $Z_i$ is simply the Normal [Equation (3.18)] with $\mu = 0$ and $\sigma = 1$:

$$f_{sn}(z_i) = (2\pi)^{-1/2} e^{-z_i^2/2}.$$

The Jacobian is calculated as:

$$\left| \frac{\partial Z_i}{\partial Y_i} \right| = \left| \frac{1}{\sigma Y_i} \right| = \frac{1}{\sigma Y_i}, \quad Y_i > 0.$$

Then, the full log-Normal distribution is written by combining these two results:

$$f_{ln}(y_i | \mu, \sigma) = f_{sn}\left[ \frac{\ln y_i - \mu}{\sigma} \right] \left| \frac{\partial z_i}{\partial y_i} \right|$$

$$= (y_i \sigma \sqrt{2\pi})^{-1} \exp\left[ \frac{-[\ln(y_i) - \mu]^2}{2\sigma^2} \right].$$

Now $Y_i$ is a positive random variable characterized by the log-Normal distribution. It has mean $E(Y_i) \equiv \exp(\mu + \frac{1}{2}\sigma^2)$, variance $V(Y_i) \equiv e^{\sigma^2}(e^{\sigma^2} - 1)e^{2\mu}$, $E(\ln Y_i) = \mu$, and $V(\ln Y_i) = \sigma^2$.

This distribution was derived from two first principles: (1) $Z_i$ *is a standard Normal variable* and (2) $Y_i$ *is a convenient mathematical function of $Z_i$ in*

*Equation (3.20).* If this function is not motivated completely from substantive arguments in some applications, at least the function is familiar and the resulting distribution more appropriately describes some characteristics of the aggregate level random variables.

### Where derivation from first principles is difficult or indeterminate

The distributions presented above can all be neatly derived from different assumptions about a social system. In general, this sort of derivation from first principles is the best means of choosing a probability distribution for use in the stochastic component of a statistical model. However, in many research situations, such a derivation is very difficult, requires assumptions that are unrealistic simplifications of the true stochastic process, leads to multiple possible distributions, or is just analytically intractable. In these instances, one can choose an existing distribution, or create one, that seems to cover most interesting cases. This procedure is often an adequate compromise, permitting further analysis where otherwise none would be possible.

For example, let $Y_i$ be the proportion of citizens in a legislative district who would cast their ballots for the Democratic candidate in a two-party system. $Y_i$ varies between zero (no Democratic votes) and one (all Democratic votes) *across* legislative districts *within* a state. Since $Y_i$ is an unobserved random variable, one needs a probability distribution, which I call the *mean voter preference distribution,* from which an election in each district is randomly drawn. This distribution must be flexible enough to include cases where it is unimodal, to allow for competitive systems with most districts in the state having proportions near 0.5, bimodal, to allow for uncompetitive party systems with many successful incumbents in both parties, skewed, in the case of bias toward one of the parties, and combinations of these. A histogram of the proportion voting Democratic in each district across an actual state is an empirical version of this distribution, but a model requires an explicit density abstracting the key features of this histogram.

Deriving a distribution by making assumptions about individual voters or their geographical arrangement turns out to narrow the range of possible distributions only negligibly as Quandt (1988) and Gudgin and Taylor (1979) demonstrate. Alternatively, one can choose an existing distribution which is flexible enough to handle most interesting aggregate forms. Unfortunately, none exist in the literature.[12] Thus, as part of a stochastic model and an em-

---

[12] Obvious choices include the Beta distribution or one of those developed for correlation coefficients. Only the Beta distribution allows for bimodality, but it is not flexible enough for present purposes (see Johnson and Kotz, 1970b: Chapter 24).

pirical analysis of legislative redistricting (King, in press-d), I derived a new tractable probability distribution specifically designed to handle most of these forms. This distribution is defined on the interval (0,1); special cases of it are unimodal, bimodal, peaked, uniform, skewed, and various combinations of these features.

This mean voter preference distribution may be defined as follows:

$$f_{mvp}(y_i|\rho,\lambda) = \rho e^{\lambda} \left[ e^{\lambda} + \left( \frac{y_i}{1 - y_i} \right)^{\rho} \right]^{-2} y_i^{-(1-\rho)} (1 - y_i)^{-(1-\rho)}. \qquad (3.22)$$

This distribution has two parameters: $\lambda$, which indexes direction and degree of skewness, and $\rho$, which indexes peakedness (ranging from a single spike to extreme bimodality).

## 3.3 Multivariate probability distributions

A univariate probability distribution provides a model of the stochastic component for a single random observation, $Y_i$. Suppose instead that $Y_i$ were a vector of $N$ random variables. To model this vector, a multivariate distribution must be used.

For example, the multivariate Normal distribution for the $N$ random observations $Y_i$ can be written as a function of an $N \times 1$ vector $\mu$ and $N \times N$ symmetric variance-covariance matrix $\Sigma$:

$$f(y_i|\mu,\Sigma) = (2\pi)^{-N/2} |\Sigma|^{-1/2} \exp \left\{ -\frac{1}{2} (y_i - \mu)' \Sigma^{-1} (y_i - \mu) \right\}. \qquad (3.23)$$

Several features of this distribution are worthy of note. First, if $Y_i$ includes only one random variable, then $N = 1$, $\Sigma = \sigma$, and this multivariate Normal distribution reduces to the univariate Normal distribution in Equation (3.18). Second, suppose $\Sigma$ is a diagonal matrix (i.e., $\Sigma$ has variances on the diagonal and zeros for all the off-diagonal covariances). In this case, it is easy to show that the random variables are independent. Hence, in this special case, the product of univariate Normal distributions $f_n(y_{1i}|\mu_1,\sigma_1^2) f_2(y_{2i}|\mu_2,\sigma_2^2) \cdots f_n(y_{Ni}|\mu_N,\sigma_N^2)$ can be shown to be equal to the multivariate Normal distribution. The proof of this assertion comes from Equation (3.1).

In the general statistical model [Equations (1.3) and (1.4)], an important special case is when $Y_1, \ldots, Y_n$ are independent random variables. By assuming independence, one can derive a multivariate distribution from only the product of univariate distributions. This situation is commonly referred to as the absence of autocorrelation (Chapter 7 demonstrates how to model processes without assuming independence). In the even more special case where every random observation has the same probability distribution, except for a parameter vector, modeling the stochastic component only requires one to specify a single univariate probability distribution.

## 3.4     Concluding remarks

The univariate probability distributions given above represent an extremely small proportion of known distributions. A variety of others are introduced and derived throughout the remainder of this book as needed. Literally thousands of others have been invented. Yet, many interesting data sets still exist for which no adequate probabilistic models have been developed. For many problems, political scientists can afford to be merely consumers of "pure" developments in probability theory and distribution theory. However, since many situations remain for which we cannot rely on statisticians to come to the rescue, political scientists must begin to learn more about probability distributions and, more generally, about stochastic processes. To the extent that political processes differ from natural and physical ones – areas which statisticians seem to pay most attention to – political scientists will be responsible for the development of their own stochastic models.

Probability theory has two roles in scientific inference. First, it is the primary means by which the stochastic components of statistical models are built. Indeed, the systematic component of statistical models uses the probability distribution's parameters to model the systematic portions of statistical relationships. Second, probability theory is the critical tool in likelihood inference. Chapter 4 uses probability for this latter purpose. The remaining chapters tap both uses of probability theory.

# The likelihood model of inference

The concept of likelihood was introduced in Chapter 2. This chapter demonstrates how to use the principle of likelihood in practical problems of statistical inference. Although subsequent chapters apply this general scheme to diverse and sophisticated statistical models, I use the more familiar linear regression model to introduce these methods here. This also permits the inclusion of this popular methodology within the general likelihood framework.

In the first section, I demonstrate the methods of calculating the likelihood function and using it as a summary estimator. In the following section, I calculate likelihood point estimators, most useful for more complicated multiple parameter problems. I then proceed to discuss the properties of these point estimates and methods of assessing their precision. Interval estimators are discussed last.

Throughout this chapter, it pays to remember that the single axiom of likelihood, on which all of the following theory rests, is as follows:

$$L(\tilde{\theta}|y) = k(y)\Pr(y|\tilde{\theta})$$
$$\propto \Pr(y|\tilde{\theta}).$$

That is, likelihood is proportional to the traditional probability, where the constant of proportionality $k(y)$ is an unknown function of the data. Whereas traditional probability is a measure of *absolute* uncertainty, built on the three axioms introduced in Chapter 3, the constant $k(y)$ means that likelihood is only a *relative* measure of uncertainty. However, it is this compromise that makes likelihood most useful as a model of scientific inference. Like the axioms of traditional probability, this likelihood axiom is neither true or false; it is assumed.

## 4.1    Likelihood and summary estimation

Understanding summary estimation is easiest in the context of an example. For these purposes, I use data representing the average annual percent of the American public approving of the president for each year from 1957 to 1984 (see King and Ragsdale, 1988: Chapter 6). The stochastic component can plausibly be considered Normal due to the central limit theorem: each observation is the mean of a large number (1500 to 2500) of independent (approve/

disapprove) survey respondents. In addition, the realized values $y$ never get very close to the theoretical upper (100%) or lower (0%) bounds and do not appear skewed. The Normal distribution is therefore most appropriate. For present pedagogical purposes, however, a single parameter distribution will be clearer. I therefore assume presidential approval follows what I call the *stylized Normal* distribution:

$$Y_i \sim f_{stn}(y_i|\mu_i) = (2\pi)^{-1/2} \exp\left[\frac{-(y_i-\mu_i)^2}{2}\right], \tag{4.1}$$

where $\pi$ is the mathematical constant $3.14159 \cdots$ and $\mu_i \equiv E(Y_i)$ is the only parameter. The stylized Normal distribution happens to be a special case of the Normal distribution with $\sigma^2 = 1$. The stylized Normal distribution is generally used when insufficient information exists in the data to estimate $\sigma^2$ (see Section 5.3 and Chapter 9). Sufficient information does exist to estimate $\sigma^2$ in regression analysis, but for the present, I stick to this special case. Later in this chapter, I consider the more usual regression case with a Normal stochastic component.[1]

Begin with a very simple systematic component, keeping the mean $E(Y)_i \equiv \mu_i$ constant over observations. This is written explicitly as:

$$\mu_i = \beta. \tag{4.2}$$

I also assume the absence of autocorrelation:

$Y_i$ and $Y_j$ are independent for all $i \neq j$.

Like the example in Equation (2.8), this model constrains the expected value of the percent of the public supporting the president to be the same for every year in the sample. The model is not very realistic, since $\mu_i$ probably varies over time, but the single parameter to be estimated is an easy starting point.

The likelihood function for a single observation $i$ is proportional to the

[1] One very unusual feature of the Normal distribution is that the parameters ($\mu$ and $\sigma^2$) are *orthogonal*. Intuitively, this means that as the expected value changes, the entire bell-shaped Normal distribution shifts down the number line without changing shape (or variance). Similarly, when the variance changes the absence of bounds allows the mean to remain constant. Statistically, this allows one to estimate $\mu$ or functions of $\mu$ without reference to $\sigma^2$; relative values of the likelihood remain the same with respect to $\hat{\mu}$ (or $\hat{\beta}$) regardless of what $\sigma$ is. (For almost every other distribution, estimating the effect parameters requires simultaneous estimation of all parameters.) For these reasons, inferences with the stylized Normal distribution about $\mu$ are the same as if we had used the Normal distribution. In practical research situations, however, estimates of $\sigma^2$ provide useful information and are also required to calculate appropriate standard errors; thus, except for the pedagogical purpose of keeping the problem simple, one should generally use the Normal distribution instead of the stylized Normal.

Normal probability distribution in Equation (4.1). Since the model [Equation (4.2)] assumes *independence* of all $Y_i$ and $Y_j$ (for all $i \neq j$), the probability rule in Equation (3.1) may be applied to get a probability distribution for the entire data set by taking the product of the probability distributions for each random observation. Furthermore, since Equation (4.2) assumes that each observation is distributed as the same stylized Normal distribution, writing down the probability distribution for the entire data set is straightforward. The complete stochastic component for the vector of $n$ random variables $Y$ may be expressed as follows:

$$
\begin{aligned}
f_{sn}(y/\mu) &= \prod_{i=1}^{n} f_{sn}(y_i|\mu_i) \\
&= (2\pi)^{-1/2} \exp \left[ \frac{-(y_i - \mu_i)^2}{2} \right] \\
&= (2\pi)^{-1/2} \exp \left[ \frac{-(y_i - \beta)^2}{2} \right].
\end{aligned}
$$

The last line of this equation uses information in the systematic portion of the model by substituting $\beta$ for $\mu_i$. This *reparameterization* expresses the probability distribution directly in terms of the theoretical features of the statistical model. In addition, it reduces the $n$ parameters in $\mu_i$ ($i = 1, \ldots, n$) to the single parameter $\beta$.

Begin by writing down the likelihood function:

$$
\begin{aligned}
L(\tilde{\beta}|y) &= k(y) \prod_{i=1}^{n} f_{stn}(y_i|\tilde{\beta}) \\
&\propto \prod_{i=1}^{n} f_{stn}(y_i|\tilde{\beta}) \\
&= \prod_{i=1}^{n} (2\pi)^{-1/2} \exp \left[ \frac{-(y_i - \beta)^2}{2} \right],
\end{aligned}
\tag{4.3}
$$

where $k(y)$ is the constant of proportionality required in likelihood theory as a way of making the likelihood function a relative measure of uncertainty. This function measures the relative likelihood of a specified hypothetical model $\tilde{\beta}$ producing the data we observed.

As demonstrated in Chapter 2, any monotonic function of the traditional probability can serve as a relative measure of likelihood. Mathematically, the most convenient function is the log-likelihood:

$$
\ln L(\tilde{\beta}|y) = \ln \left\{ k(y) \prod_{i=1}^{n} L_i(\tilde{\beta}|y_i) \right\}
\tag{4.4}
$$

$$= k(y) + \sum_{i=1}^{n} \ln L_i(\tilde{\beta}|y_i)$$

$$= k(y) + \sum_{i=1}^{n} \ln \left\{ (2\pi)^{-1/2} \exp\left[ \frac{-(y_i - \mu_i)^2}{2} \right] \right\}$$

$$= \left[ k(y) - \frac{n}{2} \ln(2\pi) \right] - \frac{1}{2} \sum_{i=1}^{n} (y_i - \tilde{\beta})^2.$$

Since the log of a product is the sum of the logs, a constant multiplied in the likelihood is equivalent to a constant added to the log-likelihood. Hence, the term in brackets in the last line of this equation may be dropped because it is not a function of $\tilde{\beta}$; its value only shifts the entire log-likelihood curve up or down by a constant amount and does not affect relative inferences about $\beta$. The *Fisher-Neyman Factorization Lemma* provides proof that the likelihood function is still a complete summary estimator even after terms not depending on the parameters are dropped. The simplified form of the log-likelihood is then:

$$\ln L(\tilde{\beta}|y) = -\frac{1}{2} \sum_{i=1}^{n} (y_i - \tilde{\beta})^2. \tag{4.5}$$

This is an easy function to use to judge relative likelihoods of different values of $\tilde{\beta}$. One can also see from this equation that its magnitude is driven by the sum of squared residuals, $\sum_{i=1}^{n}(y_i - \tilde{\beta})^2 = \sum_{i=1}^{n} \tilde{e}_i^2$.

To get a feel for what the true model might be, one would now calculate the likelihood for various hypothetical values of $\tilde{\beta}$. Since $\beta$ is interpreted as mean presidential approval, it must range between 0 and 100. I have therefore calculated this function for 1000 values of $\tilde{\beta}$ in this range and have plotted them in Figure 4.1. The likelihood function reaches a maximum value at 54.38 percent approval and declines rapidly on either side of this value. This unimodal, globally concave shape lends more support to using the maximum as a point estimate. Nevertheless, the entire likelihood function in Figure 4.1 is a complete summary estimator, containing all relevant information in the original data. If one were sure that this was the only model to be investigated with these data, the original data could be discarded. Of course, discarding data is never recommended, since many models are typically fit to the same data.

For example, a slight complication of Equation (4.2) is to allow its systematic component to vary as a linear relationship:

$$\mu_i = x_i \beta \tag{4.6}$$
$$= \beta_0 + \beta_1 \text{Inflation}_i,$$

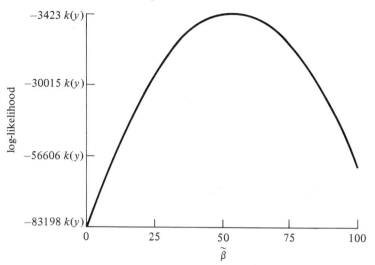

Figure 4.1. Normal, constant.

where $\text{Inflation}_i$ is the percentage increase in the consumer price index and $x_i\beta$ is a matrix expression summarizing a linear functional form with any number of explanatory variables for observation $i$. The substantive hypothesis here is that fewer Americans will approve of the president when inflation rises. That is, $\beta_1$ should be less than zero.

The general likelihood function is a direct generalization of Equation (4.5):

$$\ln L(\tilde{\beta}|y) = -\frac{1}{2} \sum_{i=1}^{n} (y_i - x_i\tilde{\beta})^2 \tag{4.7}$$

or

$$\ln L(\tilde{\beta}_0,\tilde{\beta}_1|y) = -\frac{1}{2} \sum_{i=1}^{n} [y_i - (\tilde{\beta}_0 + \tilde{\beta}_1 \text{Inflation})]^2.$$

The likelihood is still driven by the negative of the sum of squared residuals, but it is now a function of both $\tilde{\beta}_0$ and $\tilde{\beta}_1$. Generally, when more than one parameter is to be estimated, one cannot drop the parameters of less substantive interest (such as $\beta_0$) from the likelihood function.[2] As a result, one can

[2] In this very special case, we could actually take $y$ and Inflation as deviations from their respective means; $\beta_0$ would then drop out. However, since the purpose of this simple example is to portray multiparameter inference problems, and since the latter procedure requires arguments about conditional likelihood, I leave the example as is.

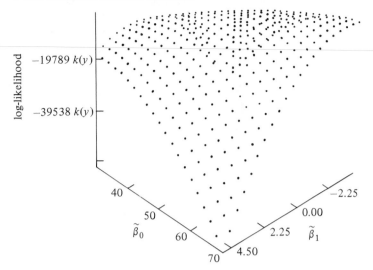

Figure 4.2. Normal, linear.

only assess the relative likelihoods of *pairs* of hypothetical parameter values ($\beta_0$ and $\beta_1$). Thus, instead of the two dimensional graph in Figure 4.1, a three dimensional diagram is now required (see Figure 4.2).

In Figure 4.2, hypothetical values of $\tilde{\beta}_0$ and $\tilde{\beta}_1$ are enumerated along the base. For each pair of parameter values, the height of the *likelihood surface* can be assessed. The single pair of hypothetical values for $\tilde{\beta}_0$ and $\tilde{\beta}_1$ that maximizes the likelihood function is $\tilde{\beta}_0 = 65.38$ and $\tilde{\beta}_1 = -2.30$. From these two values, one can draw the regression line that has the highest likelihood, given the observed data ($y$) and other features of the stated model ($\mathcal{M}^*$). Substantively, these results indicate that a single percentage point increase in inflation leads on average to a 2.3 percentage point drop in public approval of the president. Although somewhat harder to interpret than Figure 4.1, this three dimensional likelihood function is also globally concave and unimodal. The maximum is again a useful summary of available information. Nevertheless, the presentation of the entire log-likelihood surface allows one to assess the likelihood of any other pair of hypothetical values of $\beta_0$ and $\beta_1$. For globally nonconcave likelihood functions, the maximum is not as good a summary and the full likelihood function is more important to retain.

Note that the general form of the likelihood function in linear regression based on a Normal stochastic component requires only substituting the right hand side of Equation (4.6) into the Normal distribution in Equation (3.18) and taking its product over observations:

$$L(\tilde{\mu}, \tilde{\sigma}^2|y) = \prod_{i=1}^{n} f_n(y_i|\tilde{\mu}_i, \tilde{\sigma}^2)$$

$$= \prod_{i=1}^{n} (2\pi\tilde{\sigma}^2)^{-1/2} \exp\left[\frac{-(y_i - \tilde{\mu}_i)^2}{2\tilde{\sigma}^2}\right]$$

$$L(\tilde{\beta}, \tilde{\sigma}^2|y) = \prod_{i=1}^{n} (2\pi\tilde{\sigma}^2)^{-1/2} \exp\left[\frac{-(y_i - x_i\tilde{\beta})^2}{2\tilde{\sigma}^2}\right],$$

where the constant $k(y)$ has been dropped since it is does not vary with $\tilde{\beta}$ or $\tilde{\sigma}^2$. The log-likelihood is then as follows:

$$\ln L(\tilde{\beta}, \tilde{\sigma}^2|y) = \sum_{i=1}^{n} \left\{ -\frac{1}{2} \ln(2\pi\sigma^2) - \frac{1}{2\tilde{\sigma}^2}(y_i - x_i\tilde{\beta})^2 \right\}$$

$$= \sum_{i=1}^{n} \left\{ -\frac{1}{2} \ln(2\pi) - \frac{1}{2} \ln(\tilde{\sigma}^2) - \frac{1}{2\tilde{\sigma}^2}(y_i - x_i\tilde{\beta})^2 \right\} \quad (4.8)$$

where the first term may also be dropped since it is a function of neither $\tilde{\sigma}^2$ nor $\tilde{\beta}$. This function can now be used to evaluate simultaneous hypotheses about $\sigma^2$ and $\beta$.

Although $\beta$ is a vector of effect parameters (regression coefficients), $\sigma^2$ is an ancillary parameter. It gives important information about the dispersion around the population regression line. This is the basic homoscedastic specification where $\sigma^2$ is assumed constant over observations. Alternatively, one might let $\sigma_i^2$ vary over observations as a function of some explanatory variables, just as with $\mu_i$. In this case, the model would have two systematic components, a mean and a variance function (see Davidian and Carroll, 1987). What explanatory variables might be used to explain variation in $\sigma_i^2$? As a mere technical improvement in the specification we might let it vary as a function of the number of people surveyed each year in the presidential approval polls ($S_i$):

$$\sigma_i^2 = \exp(\alpha_0 + \alpha_1 S_i), \quad (4.9)$$

where the $\exp(\cdot)$ function is used because $\sigma^2$ must be positive. $\alpha_1$ in this equation is almost certainly negative, since more survey respondents reduce the variance around the mean. A more interesting use of variance functions is to make it a more central part of the analysis. For some purposes, modeling $\sigma_i^2$ may be more interesting than modeling the expected value. For example, one could address questions such as: why in some years does the public's approval of the president move as a bloc but in other years people have divergent opinions? The following specification allows for the possibility that the variance is a function of the number of survey respondents and foreign policy crises ($C_i = 1$ if a major foreign policy crisis occurs in the year and $C_i = 0$ otherwise):

$$\sigma_i^2 = \exp(\alpha_0 + \alpha_1 S_i + \alpha_2 C_i). \tag{4.10}$$

If $\alpha_2$ is negative, foreign policy crises cause the public to react with a higher degree of unanimity. This specification says nothing about whether average public approval increases or decreases when crises occur; to examine that hypothesis, one would need to put $C_i$ in the systematic component for $\mu_i$. To write down the log-likelihood, one only needs to substitute Equations (4.9) and (4.10) into Equation (4.8).

The list of other explanatory variables that probably belong in the systematic portion of this model is large. Unemployment rates, presidential behavior, international crises, honeymoon effects, among others, all would seem to have an important influence on citizen approval of and agreement about the American president. Indeed, aside from the parameters for these variables, a variety of other parameters might also be included to represent the time series process driving these data. Adding these parameters would require a straightforward complication of Equation (4.6). Indeed, building a likelihood function with any number of parameters is easy mathematically, and, if sufficient data exist, is statistically unproblematic as well. However, evaluating the likelihood function by means of a graph is difficult or impossible with more than two parameters. Conceptualizing four, five, or even $K$-dimensional likelihood hypersurfaces is sometimes conceivable, but substantive interpretation can be extremely difficult or impossible.[3]

## 4.2     Likelihood and point estimation

Because graphical interpretation is difficult or impossible with the typical multiple parameter social science research problem, one must employ more parsimonious estimators. Hence, instead of the likelihood function as a summary estimator, researchers typically use maximum likelihood point estimators in more complicated situations. Interval estimators are easily calculated from these point estimators.

Edwards (1972: 212) and others have criticized the use of maximum likelihood (ML) estimates in place of the full likelihood function due to the loss of information. This criticism is technically correct. ML estimators are not always good summaries of the entire likelihood, such as in the case of a bimodal function with one mode slightly higher than the other. Nevertheless, ML estimators do represent the set of parameter values with a natural and intuitively pleasing interpretation: they have the highest relative likelihood of

---

[3] For attempts to conceptualize in $K$-dimensional space, see Abbott (1952, originally published circa 1884), Banchoff (1987), and Rucker (1984).

having generated the data we observed. In fact, Edwards's criticism of ML is usually directed toward those whose research problems include small numbers of parameters. ML estimation is a reasonable and practical alternative to the problem of conceptualizing in high dimensional space. In research problems with multiple parameters, better alternatives than ML as a point estimator do not yet exist.

In order to find the parameter values at which the likelihood is maximized, one can use either *graphical, analytical,* or *numerical* methods. Since graphical methods are either extremely difficult or fail completely with multiple parameters, one must employ either analytical or numerical methods. I describe these in turn.

### *Analytical methods*

Analytical methods may be used for problems with any number of parameters, but they also fail unless the likelihood function takes a relatively simple form. The advantage of these methods is that the ML estimator may be expressed as an explicit function of the observations. This has obvious computational advantages, but in some cases studying this statistic directly can also yield important intuitive insights.

Analytical methods use calculus to find the maximum of the likelihood function with respect to its parameters. The four step procedure takes advantage of the fact that the slope of the curve at the maximum is flat:

1. Calculate the derivative of the log-likelihood function with respect to the parameter vector, $\bar{\theta}$.
2. Set the derivative equal to zero and substitute every occurrence of $\bar{\theta}$ with $\hat{\theta}$.
3. If possible, solve for $\hat{\theta}$.
4. Take the second derivative of the log-likelihood function. If it is negative, $\hat{\theta}$ is the maximum likelihood estimator. (If $\theta$ is a vector, then the second derivative of the log-likelihood is a matrix and this condition requires that it be negative definite.)

This procedure would yield the identical solution if one used the original likelihood function or any other monotonic function of it. The chief advantage of the *log*-likelihood is that the derivative of a sum is far easier to calculate than the derivative of a product.

As a simple example, I will find an analytical solution to the simple model in Equations (4.1) and (4.2), with the corresponding log-likelihood function in Equation (4.5). [The solution also happens to be the same for the Normal distribution in Equation (4.8).] The four step methodology is straightforward in this case. First, differentiate:

$$\frac{\partial \ln L(\tilde{\beta}|y)}{\partial \tilde{\beta}} = \frac{\partial}{\partial \tilde{\beta}} \left[ -\frac{1}{2} \sum_{i=1}^{n} (y_i - \tilde{\beta})^2 \right]$$

$$= \left( \sum_{i=1}^{n} y_i \right) - n\tilde{\beta}.$$

Then, set the last line in this equation to zero, substitute $\hat{\beta}$ for $\tilde{\beta}$,

$$0 = \left( \sum_{i=1}^{n} y_i \right) - n\hat{\beta},$$

and solve for $\hat{\beta}$:

$$\hat{\beta} = \frac{\sum_{i=1}^{n} y_i}{n}. \qquad (4.11)$$

$\hat{\beta}$ may be recognized as the sample mean of $y$.[4] Finally, since the second derivative $(-n)$ is always negative, we have verified that $\hat{\beta}$ is the ML estimate of $\beta$ in Equations (4.1) and (4.2).

More generally, the maximum likelihood estimator for $\beta$ in Equation (4.6) also has a familiar analytical solution:

$$\hat{\beta} = (X'X)^{-1}X'y, \qquad (4.12)$$

where $\hat{\beta}$ is now a parameter vector. If $X$ is a column of ones, Equation (4.12) reduces to Equation (4.11). This is also the general solution to the linear-Normal regression problem with multiple explanatory variables.

Equation (4.12) is often justified by appealing to the least squares (LS) rule, but this presentation demonstrates that searching for an estimator that minimizes the sum of squared residuals $[\sum_{i=1}^{n}(y_i - x_1\hat{\beta})^2 = \sum_{i=1}^{n} e_i^2]$ is equivalent to finding one that maximizes the negative of the sum of squared residuals [Equation (4.7)]. Whereas Equation (4.12) happens to be the ML estimator from a linear-stylized Normal model and from the more usual linear-Normal model, only the latter has an ancillary parameter, $\sigma^2$. The analytical solution for $\hat{\sigma}^2$ under the Normal distribution is as follows:

$$\hat{\sigma}^2 = \frac{1}{n} \sum_{i=1}^{n} (y_i - x_i\beta)^2.$$

*Remark on least squares:* Before I discuss the numerical methods of point estimation, I pause to comment on these particular analytical results, since

---

[4] This may seem like a substantial degree of work, just to derive the sample mean! However, it does provide a fundamental theoretical background to a result usually justified only on intuitive grounds. In fact, essentially the same ideas used here can be applied to far more sophisticated examples.

LS is in extremely wide use throughout political science. The procedure is usually understood and taught as merely a good way to fit a line to a scatterplot of data points. The results above indicate that *the LS rule may also be justified by appeal to the deeper principle of maximum likelihood under the assumption of a Normally distributed disturbance term.* However, the LS rule is usually applied in political science without this more fundamental justification. Unfortunately, this makes the basis of much empirical analysis purely *descriptive* rather than part of a theory of scientific *inference*.

The likelihood approach leads to the LS rule in the case of Normally distributed disturbances, but that provides no justification for the LS rule as a first principle. LS qua LS is merely a descriptive procedure for drawing a line through a set of points. Drawing this line by minimizing the sum of the squared perpendicular distances between the points and the line seems plausible enough. However, other descriptive rules for drawing lines are at least as plausible. For example, why take squared ($\Sigma_{i=1}^n e_i^2$) rather than absolute ($\Sigma_{i=1}^n |e_i|$) deviations? In addition, most people drawing a line by hand probably informally choose to minimize the perpendicular distance between the points and the regression line (see Mosteller et al., 1981) – the rule behind a statistical procedure called principal components. Others might find horizontal distances to be more intuitive – the rule used in reverse regression.

Unfortunately, reanalyses of the same set of data by these different methods often lead to very different substantive conclusions (see Tukey, 1960). In the absence of a theory of inference which dictates one or another method, we fall back on intuition. However mysterious the initial choice of vertical, squared deviations might have seemed against this backdrop, regression analysis now looks downright ad hoc with LS as a first principle. Without a deeper justification, we are left with the seemingly inescapable conclusions that a large part of empirical political science rests on a rather shaky foundation.[5]

LS is sometimes justified in political science by appeal to the *Gauss-Markov theorem,* which chooses the single estimator that is minimum variance linear unbiased. This theorem is a better justification for LS since it uses inferential rather than merely descriptive criteria. The problem, however, is that the theory of inference this theorem relies on is somewhat arbitrary. For example, why should we insist on unbiased, rather than consistent, estimators? Perhaps the most arbitrary feature of the Gauss-Markov theorem is that it only considers estimators that are *linear* functions of the data.[6] Linearity of the estimator (aside from the functional form) is presumably for alge-

---

[5] Virtually the same argument applies to nonlinear least squares. See Alt (1987) and Gallant (1986) on nonlinear least squares (as well as for a wide variety of interesting statistical models).
[6] Equation (4.12) has $\hat{\beta}$ as a linear function of $y$.

braic or computational efficiency; it certainly is not a reasonable first principle and does not necessarily relate to a plausible theory of statistical inference.

The best reason given for using LS qua LS, or the same LS rule as justified by the Gauss-Markov theorem, is that it usually produces estimators with desirable properties. But LS, or estimators built from a list of ad hoc properties, is still not an integrated theory of inference. Consider four situations likely to arise in practice: (1) In the case of the Normal distribution, ML and LS estimates are identical. By appealing to the philosophy of likelihood, empirical research can be put on a deeper theoretical basis. (2) Suppose the dependent variable is thought to be Normally distributed, but in fact it is not. In this case, the estimator – whether one calls it an ML or LS estimator – still possesses many, but not all, of the desirable properties described in what follows. Whereas specifying some incorrect distributions can lead to damaging results in ML estimation, in this case several of the properties of ML estimators that are to be described may be proved even if the assumption of a Normal distribution is wrong. Again, the likelihood justification is philosophically much deeper.

(3) If we know the distribution of $Y$ and it is not Normal, the alternative ML estimator can have much more desirable properties than the LS estimator. (4) If a researcher is unsure of his or her distributional assumptions, some ML estimators are known to be more robust than others. One of these ML estimators happens to also be the LS estimator, but ML is a much more general, philosophically satisfactory, basis for scientific inference. A growing literature in statistics and particularly econometrics is concerned with estimators where distributional and other assumptions are relaxed. If a complete theory of robust inference is ever successfully developed, it may supplant the likelihood approach. However, although considerable progress has been made in specialized areas, this literature is quite far from this general goal.

The likelihood theory of inference enables one to estimate interesting statistical relationships without criteria such as minimum variance or linear unbiasedness. This theory of inference, along with some regularity conditions, does produce estimators with properties as desirable as or more desirable than "criterion estimators," even judging from their ground rules. In the end, political scientists have no stake in points and lines, and only sometimes have a reason to choose one statistical criterion over another. However, they should be very interested in the underlying processes specified under the likelihood approach. These are, after all, the very subject of political analysis. By providing a formal model of uncertainty and theory of scientific inference, this approach enables one to make reliable inferences about these unobserved political processes directly. Hence, by appealing to the practical properties of estimators, ML outperforms LS. By concentrating on the more fundamental methods of inference, the ultimate justification for LS is either merely descriptive, or inferential but ad hoc. On the other hand, the principle of likelihood provides a much more complete and satisfactory theory of scientific inference.

Perhaps even more important, likelihood permits researchers to analyze problems for which linear regression (and LS) are of little use. This flexibility permits one to adjust or create empirical methods without resorting to the bag of tricks that virtually every standard econometrics text teaches: how to transform variables and "trick" linear regression (and existing regression computer programs) into dealing with the "problems" of autocorrelation, heteroscedasticity, nonlinearity, and others. Unfortunately, these standard procedures may sacrifice information about some of the most interesting political science processes giving rise to one's data. The idea of purging a time series of autocorrelation, and continuing to focus only on regression coefficients of the exogenous variables, is roughly equivalent to book burning. It should not be controversial to argue that the most interesting information in a *time* series is variables that vary and covary over *time!* One should not "control" for this information; one should model it directly and attempt to extract information from it. Indeed, a large variety of very interesting political processes are substantially ignored by the standard linear model.[7]

Clearly, not all political processes should be forced into the same procrustean linear model. Incorporating a broader theory of inference greatly expands the scope of statistical analysis. It enables researchers to model the phenomena of interest *directly,* and to incorporate the features peculiar to the social process hypothesized to be generating one's data. With a more fundamental approach to scientific inference, statistical modeling becomes a much more flexible and creative endeavor. Whether this modeling process leads to a linear-Normal model or not is immaterial.[8]

---

[7] One reason for historical emphasis on least squares is that it leads to very simple computational formulas. The invention of ways to "trick" linear regression programs into doing more sophisticated statistical analyses were, for their time, genuine breakthroughs. At one time this was not only an advantage; it was required if statistical analysis was to be performed at all. Indeed, until very recently, much of the discipline of statistics was devoted solely to achieving maximum computational efficiency. The revolution in computation technology has changed all this. However, by itself, this revolution contributes nothing to statistical theory; but it does *permit* a revolution in the way we think about scientific inference. For the first time in history, computation is within range of being *transparent.* Political scientists can now focus on the theoretical unity of their methods and model their substantive problems directly. For most problems, one no longer need worry about whether a particular approach is computationally feasible.

[8] In fact, dividing up statistical models in this way is like referring to a zoo as a collection of nonelephant animals (paraphrased from Gleick, 1987).

Linear-Normal regression is the leading example of an ML estimator that can be derived analytically. Analytical solutions do exist for many other estimators, but most interesting statistical models in the social sciences require numerical methods.

### Numerical methods

The usual reason for using numerical methods is that although the likelihood function and derivatives of it can be taken and set to zero, solving for the estimator is frequently algebraically impossible. When ML estimators cannot be found analytically one must resort to numerical maximization methods. The solution to iterative numerical maximization procedures cannot be expressed explicitly as a function of the sample observations, so some mathematical intuition may be sacrificed, but no substantive information is lost. These methods also require more computational resources. Of course, with new technologies, this is no longer a serious disadvantage. In fact, with new numerical maximization algorithms, numerical methods are sometimes faster than corresponding analytical (or partially analytical) procedures.

The specific programs require the researcher to write down the likelihood function. Some computer algorithms require analytical derivatives of it as well. The researcher must then either specify *starting values* for each of the parameters or use the program's default values. Numerical computer algorithms then search over the parameter space for values of $\hat{\theta}$ that jointly maximize the likelihood function.

This could be done "by hand," but it would be extremely difficult. Consider a relatively modest problem with fifteen parameters. Now imagine a calculator which, if you typed in a test value for each of the parameters, would compute the likelihood. You have no idea what the fifteen true parameters or fifteen ML estimates are, but, by testing different sets of fifteen, you try to maximize the likelihood. In each turn, you would gradually alter the values. If the likelihood went down, you would try to go in a different direction. If it went up, you would continue adjusting the values in the original direction. The problem is obviously quite difficult, even with this "calculator."

Computers automate this search routine with specific algorithms designed to shorten the time required to find the maximum. The specific algorithms range from *grid searches,* which test values over the entire parameter space, to *gradient methods,* which use the value of the likelihood and the slope of the likelihood surface for each set of the parameter values to choose a new direction in which to move. Many more sophisticated routines also exist. Good algorithms find the correct solution regardless of starting values, although the time required to find the maximum may vary with the given values. In particularly difficult problems, poor starting values can lead iterative procedures to a local rather than global maximum. Other algorithms might never converge. In these difficult cases, running the program several times with different starting values can verify the solution. The computer programs for most standard ML estimators automatically compute good starting values. See Harvey (1981a; Chapter 4), Judge et al. (1985: Appendix B), Press et al. (1986), or Wismer and Chattergy (1978) for a review of numerical estimation methods.

Since neither accuracy nor precision is sacrificed with numerical methods, they are sometimes used even when analytical (or partially analytical) solutions are possible. This avoids having to calculate analytical derivatives, substituting computer time for human efforts and potential errors. As a result, the translation between theory and data is even more transparent.

## 4.3 An alternative representation of the likelihood function

A different representation of the same likelihood function depends on using the *disturbance form* of statistical models. Thus, Equations (1.1) and (1.2) are equivalent. Since $Y$ is closer to theory than the analytical construct $\epsilon$, I use the form of Equation (1.2) exclusively. In addition, many statistical models either have no disturbance form or are very awkward under that representation. However, in those special cases where the systematic component involves the mean, one can write the likelihood function by working with the random variable $\epsilon$. Thus, to derive the disturbance form of the likelihood function, one could state the distribution of $\epsilon$ as a first principle as in Equation (1.1). Instead, I will derive it from what I consider to be the more natural representation in Equation (1.2). The Jacobian method may be used for this derivation, since $\epsilon$ is a function of $Y$ [see Equation (3.21)]:

$$Y_i \sim f_n(y|\mu, \sigma^2),$$

and the transformation $\epsilon = Y - \mu$ implies

$$\epsilon \sim f_n(e|0, \sigma^2)$$

since the Jacobian is 1.0. This is also a special case of the commonly used result that a linear function of a Normally distributed variable is Normally distributed. The likelihood function may then be written as follows:

$$L(\tilde{\mu}, \tilde{\sigma}^2 | y) = \prod_{i=1}^{n} (2\pi\sigma^2)^{-1/2} \exp\left(\frac{-e_i^2}{2\tilde{\sigma}^2}\right),$$

and since the realization of $\epsilon$ is written as $e_i = y - x_i \tilde{\beta}$, this likelihood function may be rewritten as follows:

$$L(\tilde{\mu}, \tilde{\sigma}^2 | y) = \prod_{i=1}^{n} (2\pi\sigma^2)^{-1/2} \exp\left[\frac{-(y - x_i\tilde{\beta})^2}{2\tilde{\sigma}^2}\right],$$

which is the same likelihood function that derives directly from the more natural form of the expression. For most stochastic components, however, the distribution of $\epsilon$ is neither expressed so neatly nor is even in the same family of distributions as $Y$. Thus, in some fields where the Normal distribution is used ubiquitously (as in econometrics), this alternative representation is frequently applied. In fields where other distributions are also common, or where stochastic components involve parameters other than the mean, the representation in Equations (1.3) and (1.4) is much more useful.

## 4.4    Properties of maximum likelihood estimators

From one perspective, the foremost reason to use ML estimation is that the maximum represents an important feature of the likelihood function. The ultimate justification for likelihood, according to this view, depends on its intuitive axioms and associated theory of inference, not on any subsidiary properties.

Others are not quite so convinced. From their perspective, ML is useful primarily as a method of estimation rather than part of a broader theory of inference. For these people, ML is useful *because* of the properties its estimates usually possess. These criteria are also very useful standards to apply when statistical estimators were not derived from within the likelihood theory of statistical inference.[9]

### Regularity conditions

In order to rigorously prove the existence of these properties of ML estimators, one needs to satisfy additional regularity conditions. These conditions are important, but are not easily conceptualized in substantive terms. Indeed, if they were, they would probably be called assumptions! Instead, regularity conditions are technical side conditions required in the course of the proofs.

Many versions of these conditions have been formulated, imposing substantially weaker requirements in general and even more in specialized cases (see Amemiya, 1985; Cramer, 1986; Dhrymes, 1974; Huber, 1981; Norden, 1972, 1973; and Spanos, 1986). I reemphasize here that even ML estimators

---

[9] For example, see Achen's (1979) assessments of normal vote estimates, Brady's (1985) consistency and asymptotic Normality proofs for nonmetric multidimensional scaling methods, Franklin's (in press) consistency proofs for "2SAIV" estimators, and Rivers' (in press) estimators designed to solve the Kramer economic voting problem.

that do not satisfy any form of regularity conditions still produce parameter estimates with the maximum likelihood of having generated the data under the model.

Below are four *sufficient* regularity conditions with which one can derive the properties listed in the remainder of this section. The minimum *necessary* and sufficient conditions to prove the existence of each of these properties are too detailed to present here, and in some cases depend on the special characteristics of individual estimators. In addition, more complicated regularity conditions are required in the case of nonindependent or nonidentically distributed observations. Thus, a model that does not meet these conditions may or may not have the properties listed below; the burden is on the investigator to verify weaker conditions if a claim to some of these properties is desired. These conditions are obviously quite technical and I do *not* expect anyone to understand them in detail on the first reading:

1. The values of $y$ for which $f(y|\theta) > 0$ (i.e., the sample space) do not depend on $\theta$.

2. The probability distribution $f(y|\theta)$ is twice continuously differentiable with respect to $\theta$ for all $\theta \in \Theta$ and $y \in \mathcal{S}$.

3. The *information matrix*,

$$I_n(\theta) \equiv E\left[\left(\frac{\partial \ln f(y|\theta)}{\partial \theta}\right)\left(\frac{\partial \ln f(y|\theta)}{\partial \theta}\right)'\right],$$

is positive definite and finitely bounded.

4.

$$\left|\frac{\partial^j \ln f(y|\theta)}{\partial \theta^j}\right| \le h_j(y), \quad j = 1, 2, 3,$$

where

$$E[h_j(y)] < \infty, \quad j = 1, 2$$

and $E[h_3(y)]$ does not depend on $\theta$.

For ML estimators that meet these (or some weaker form of these) regularity conditions, a list of their finite and asymptotic properties follows.

*Finite sample properties*

*Invariance to reparameterization:* Often researchers prefer to estimate a function of a parameter $u(\theta)$ rather than a parameter $\theta$ itself. The invariance property of ML estimators guarantees that one can estimate either and transform them as needed.[10] For example, in the Normal distribution, one can estimate the standard deviation $\sigma$ and still recover the ML esitmator of $\sigma^2$ by squaring. As another example, King and Browning (1987) posited a model for, among other things, partisan bias in congressional elections. The original form of the partisan bias parameter $\beta$ was between 0 and 1 for Republican bias and between 1 and $\infty$ for bias toward the Democrats. This asymmetric formulation was an unintuitive representation of partisan bias. To make the parameterization symmetric and more interpretable, we transformed $\beta$ by taking the log, making Republican bias negative and Democratic bias positive: for example, $\ln(\beta) = -2$ was now the same amount of Republican bias as $\ln(\beta) = 2$ was Democratic bias. This property of ML enabled us either to estimate $\ln(\beta)$ directly or to estimate $\beta$ and take the log of the estimate. Both estimators have the same desirable properties and yield identical substantive results.[11]

*Invariance to sampling plans:* What is sometimes called the *Likelihood Principle* states that ML estimators depend on the data only through the likelihood function. No other information is relevant for estimation.[12] One implication of the likelihood principle is that ML estimators are the same regardless of the rules for selecting a sample size.

For example, consider how the sample size is typically chosen in political science. For large scale sample surveys, the number of observations depends on the length and cost of each interview. For data collected from archives, the number of observations depends on the patience and wealth of the investigator (or the impatience and poverty of his or her graduate assistants). Suppose the money runs out. Suppose in the midst of a sample survey on presidential approval, the president is assassinated. Suppose the data appear from the ICPSR, and the researcher has no influence on the sample size. Suppose you added new observations to an existing data set. The likelihood principle guarantees that the researcher can use all existing data. The rule used to determine the number of observations is irrelevant to estimation. In addition, the log-likelihoods of independent samples may be added to get a total likelihood for the new combined data set.

---

[10] Due to this property, and the fact that $E[\widehat{u(\theta)}] \neq u[E(\hat{\theta})]$, ML estimators are not generally unbiased. Indeed, if $u(\cdot)$ is a convex function, $u[E(\hat{\theta})] \leq E[u(\hat{\theta}]$ due to Jensen's inequality.

[11] In practice, parameterizations that produce symmetric and unbounded parameter spaces are more likely to be approximately Normal for smaller sample sizes. As detailed subsequently, Normality in ML estimators is guaranteed only at the limit, but the parameterization can influence how quickly the asymptotic approximations apply as $n$ gets larger.

[12] Bayesian statistics violate the likelihood principle.

*Minimum variance unbiasedness: If an unbiased minimum variance estimator exists, then the method of ML estimation chooses it.* In the context of a repeated experiment, an estimator $\hat{\theta}$ is *unbiased* if the average of the estimates produced across experiments equals the parameter one is trying to estimate, $\theta$: $E(\hat{\theta}) = \theta$. This is a relatively popular *property* of estimators, but as a required *criterion* it can be severely flawed. First, unbiased estimators often do not exist. For example, the sample mean, $\bar{y} = \Sigma_{i=1}^{n} y_i/n$, is an unbiased estimator of $\mu$, but no unbiased estimator exists for $1/\mu$. (Due to the invariance property, the ML estimator of $1/\mu$ is $1/\bar{y}$.) Second, unbiasedness can lead to very strange estimators that violate one's intuition (see the examples in DeGroot, 1986: 415–17). Finally, many unbiased estimators of the same parameter often exist. For example, the sample mean, $\Sigma_{i=1}^{n} y_i/n$, and the sample mean of the first $n - 1$ observations, $\Sigma_{i=1}^{n-1} y_i/(n - 1)$, are both unbiased estimators of $\mu$. Hence, unbiasedness is sometimes a desirable property, but one would not always want to require an estimator to be unbiased.

In the context of a repeated experiment, the variance of an unbiased estimator is the degree of variation in these hypothetical numerical estimates around the true parameter value. A minimum variance unbiased (MVU) estimator is the single unbiased estimator with the smallest variance.[13] Put differently, $V(\hat{\theta})$ is minimized with respect to $\hat{\theta}$ subject to $E(\hat{\theta}) = \theta$. In addition, when a MVU estimator exists its variance is called the *Cramer-Rao lower bound*. This property is summarized as follows:

$$E(\hat{\theta}) = \theta,$$

$$V(\hat{\theta}) = CRLB(\theta).$$

The MVU property is quite desirable. It concentrates as much of the sampling distribution as possible around the true parameter value. In addition, when an estimator with this property exists, it is unique. For example, the sample mean (calculated from all the observations) is the single MVU estimator of $\mu$. However, MVU estimators often do not exist. Hence, like unbiasedness, MVU is sometimes a desirable property for estimators but not a generally applicable criterion for selecting them.

*Asymptotic properties*

To establish the asymptotic properties of the ML estimator, think of $\{\hat{\theta}_n\}$ as a sequence of estimators calculated in the same way from larger and larger sample sizes, $n$. Whereas the finite properties evaluate $\hat{\theta}_n$ for fixed $n$, the

[13] Note that this is a more desirable property than that ensured by the Gauss-Markov theorem, since the estimator need not be a linear function of the data.

asymptotic properties evaluate it as $n \to \infty$. Note that for each sample size, $\hat{\theta}_n$ has a distribution across hypothetical experiments (hypothetically performed under identical conditions) called the *sampling distribution*.[14] The asymptotic properties all focus on this sampling distribution.

*Consistency:* An estimator $\hat{\theta}_n$ is consistent when its sampling distribution collapses to a spike over the true parameter value $\theta$ as $n \to \infty$. Consistency, then, is an important property essentially indicating that with an infinite amount of data the estimator will yield the correct answer.

There are several technical variants of consistency, but most estimators are consistent with respect to either all or none. I therefore discuss only one type here: consistency based on the mathematical concept of "almost sure convergence." This form of consistency is expressed as follows:

$$\lim_{n \to \infty} \Pr\left(\max_{m > n} |\hat{\theta}_m - \theta| < \epsilon\right) = 1.$$

The term $|\hat{\theta}_m - \theta|$ indicates how far the estimated value is from the true parameter. The term $[\max_{m > n} |\hat{\theta}_m - \theta|]$ refers to the maximum difference between the estimate and the parameter among all estimates in the series, based on sample sizes greater than $n$. $\Pr(\cdot)$ in this equation then gives the probability that this maximum difference is less than a very small number $\epsilon$. Finally, the limit enables us to evaluate the probability for very large values of $n$.

One way the regularity conditions can be violated so as to produce inconsistent estimators is when the number of parameters increases as fast as or faster than the sample size $n$. The reason this results in inconsistency is that more information is not being brought to bear on the problem as $n$ increases; thus, the variance of the sampling distribution will not decrease. For example, the ML estimators $y_i$ of the parameters $\beta_i$ in Equation (2.11) are inconsistent because the number of parameters is $n$. One should generally prefer to use more than one observation to form an estimator, but this inconsistency does *not* require one to drop $y_i$ as an estimator. If Equation (2.11) is truly the model one wants to estimate, then it is difficult to conceive of a better estimator. The proper ground on which to object to Equation (2.11) is not the estimator that would result; it is the model. A simpler model is much more likely to be useful – for inferential and theoretical purposes.

Consistency is often considered an important and sometimes essential property of estimators. Fortunately, *"it is hard to construct examples in which the*

[14] Imagine running a single experiment that generates $n$ observations a very large number of times. For each run of the experiment (under the same conditions), calculate $\hat{\theta}_n$ from the $n$ observations. Finally, plot the histogram of values of $\hat{\theta}_n$. This histogram would approximate the theoretical sampling distribution of $\hat{\theta}_n$. If one could run this experiment an infinite number of times and plot the histogram on that basis, no approximation would be needed.

*maximum likelihood estimator* (*assuming the likelihood function is correctly specified*) *is not consistent and another estimator is''* (Amemiya, 1985: 120; see also Bahadur, 1958). One can find examples of both consistent, biased estimators (e.g., the ML estimator of $\sigma^2$), and inconsistent, unbiased estimators [e.g., $E(y_1) = \mu$, but $y_1 \overset{p}{\nrightarrow} \mu$].

*Asymptotic Normality:* As $n \to \infty$, the sampling distribution of $\hat{\theta}_n$ collapses to a spike, due to the consistency property, but what is the shape of this distribution for very large $n$? One way to study this question is to standardize $\hat{\theta}_n$ by subtracting out the mean $\theta$ and dividing by the standard deviation $V(\theta)^{1/2}$ of the limiting distribution:

$$
Z_n = \frac{\hat{\theta}_n - \theta}{V(\theta)^{1/2}/\sqrt{n}}
$$
$$
= \frac{\sqrt{n}(\hat{\theta}_n - \theta)}{V(\theta)^{1/2}}.
$$

This standardization is usually called a *z*-score, and its advantage is that it does not permit the distribution to collapse to a spike as $n \to \infty$. Except for the scale factors, $Z_n$ and $\hat{\theta}_n$ will have the same shape and distribution for any finite $n$. The only problem with studying $Z_n$ is that the variance in the denominator is unknown. Thus, we instead study the quantity $\sqrt{n}(\hat{\theta}_n - \theta)$ and seek to determine its distribution and variance.

The theoretical result is this:

$$
\sqrt{n}(\hat{\theta}_n - \theta) \overset{a}{\sim} f_n(z|0, V(\theta)), \tag{4.13}
$$

where $\overset{a}{\sim}$ means "is distributed asymptotically as." Since this quantity has the same distribution as $\hat{\theta}_n$, except for a scale factor, we conclude that $\hat{\theta}_n$ is asymptotically Normally distributed. Because its distribution collapses to a spike, writing $\hat{\theta}_n \overset{a}{\sim} f_n(t|\theta, V(\theta)/\sqrt{n})$ is technically *incorrect*, although it is written this way sometimes for heuristic purposes.

The application of the central limit theorem that results in asymptotic Normality is true regardless of the distribution assumed in the stochastic component for $Y$ and of any other feature of the statistical model, given the regularity conditions. (Similarly, this result in no way justifies assuming a Normal distribution as part of the stochastic component.) The advantage of asymptotic Normality is that it permits hypothesis testing and the calculation of confidence intervals, as I demonstrate in the next section.[15] The key regularity

---

[15] Any known sampling distribution would be of the same use as the Normal distribution is here for hypothesis testing and confidence intervals. However, the central limit theorem guarantees that most estimators with known asymptotic distributions will be functions of the Normal distribution.

condition required for this property is that the likelihood function be differentiable. In certain circumstances, demonstrating asymptotic Normality without this condition is also possible.

*Asymptotic efficiency:* For large *n,* the standardized distribution of $\hat{\theta}_n$ in Equation (4.13) has a variance equal to the Cramer-Rao lower bound. Thus, let

$$I(\theta) = \lim_{n \to \infty} \left[ \frac{1}{n} I_n(\theta) \right].$$

In this equation, $I_n(\theta)$ is the information matrix calculated from a sample size of *n,* just as in the third regularity condition, above:

$$I_n(\theta) \equiv E\left[ \left( \frac{\partial \ln f(y|\theta)}{\partial \theta} \right) \left( \frac{\partial \ln f(y|\theta)}{\partial \theta} \right)' \right].$$

$I(\theta)$ is then the limiting value of the information matrix as the sample size *n* gets very large. In addition, the asymptotic variance is calculated as the inverse of the information matrix and is thus equal to the Cramer-Rao lower bound:

$$V(\theta) = [I(\theta)]^{-1} = CRLB(\theta).$$

In other words, compared to any other consistent and uniformly asymptotically Normal estimator, the ML estimator has a smaller asymptotic variance. Hence, more of the ML estimates that could result across hypothetical experiments are concentrated around the true parameter value than is the case for any other estimator in this class.

No other general method of estimation produces all of these attractive properties as automatically. No other method is as fundamentally intuitive. The leading alternative is to derive an estimator by requiring it to meet a specific list of criteria such as with the Gauss-Markov theorem. Of course, arguing that these estimators meet these criteria better than ML estimators is tautological. More important, the list of criteria selected are usually ad hoc rather than based on some deeper theory of inference. If particular criteria are especially important in specific research projects, these alternative methods of deriving estimators are readily available.[16]

### 4.5    Problems to avoid with maximum likelihood estimators

In this section, I describe two examples of problematic maximum likelihood estimators. In all cases, no problem exists with the theory of likelihood or its

---

[16] Statisticians have attempted to derive the likelihood approach in reverse by beginning with these and other properties as the criteria, but a generally accepted solution remains to be found (see Berger and Wolpert, 1984).

application to inference in these problems. However, the compromise of using the maxima as point estimators in extensions to multiple parameter problems causes problems that should be avoided.

*Infinite parameter problems:* A common problem in statistics occurs when models include parameters that increase in number as the number of observations increases. In most cases, these infinite parameter problems are not very reasonable models. After all, a model is supposed to be an approximation, and thus simplification, of reality. If a model includes an infinite number of unknowns, then the model is just not a very good simplification. (Similarly, a map would be virtually useless as a model of some geographic area if it had an infinite number of details included.)

The example I use here is a modified version of that originally formulated by Neyman and Scott (1948). Imagine that we observed two realizations from each of $n$ Normal populations with separate means, $\mu_i$, and a common variance, $\sigma^2$:

$$Y_{ji} \sim f_n(y_{ji}|\mu_i, \sigma^2)$$

for $i = 1, \ldots, n$ independent observations and $j = 1, 2$ independent realizations from population $i$. Now suppose that the goal is to estimate $\sigma^2$. For example, suppose one had the final predictions from the Gallup and Harris Polls for the outcome of each of $n$ presidential elections. The goal might be to see how much variation existed within each prediction (i.e., the value of $\sigma^2$). Since the predicted election outcomes vary, $\mu_i$ would vary over the observations. However, if both polling organizations use the same techniques, one might reasonably assume that the variance in predictions would be constant.

Since the number of $\mu$ parameters increase as $n$ increases, this model does not meet the regularity conditions for consistency. In fact, the ML estimate of $\hat{\sigma}^2$ converges asymptotically to $\tfrac{1}{2}\sigma^2$, which is very far off the mark. One might object to any model with an infinite number of parameters, but the forecasting example and others reasonably lead us to a situation where $\sigma^2$ was of primary interest and $\mu_i$ $(i = 1, \ldots, n)$ are ancillary.

Fortunately, this problem has an easy solution. We could just use $2\hat{\sigma}^2$ as the estimator, but this has no justification under the likelihood theory of statistical inference. A better justification is a manipulation of the original model by taking the differences between $Y_{1i}$ and $Y_{2i}$, so the ancillary parameters drop out. Thus, let $Z_i = Y_{1i} - Y_{2i}$. Since $Y_{1i}$ and $Y_{2i}$ are independent normal variables, $Z_i$ is also normally distributed with mean

$$
\begin{aligned}
E(Z_i) &= E(Y_{1i}) - E(Y_{2i}) \\
&= \mu_i - \mu_i \\
&= 0
\end{aligned}
$$

and variance

$$V(Z_i) = V(Y_{1i}) - V(Y_{2i}) = 2\sigma^2.$$

So, we can use the following model:

$$Z_i \sim f_n(z_i|0,2\sigma^2)$$

for $i = 1, \ldots, n$. Note that $\mu_i$ does not appear in this distribution. Furthermore, since the number of parameters in this model does not increase in this model as $n$ increases, the ML estimator for $\sigma^2$ meets all regularity conditions and is therefore consistent.

*Unbounded likelihood functions:* Finding the maximum of the likelihood function requires that we find the *finite* maximum. Regularity conditions are violated if, for some values of the parameters, the likelihood function is infinite. This problem occurs most frequently with mixture distributions. For example, consider the Normal mixture:

$$Y_i \sim f_{nm}(y_i|\mu_1,\mu_2,\sigma_1^2,\sigma_2^2,\lambda)$$
$$= \lambda f_n(y_i|\mu_1,\sigma_1^2) + (1-\lambda)f_n(y_i|\mu_2,\sigma_2^2),$$

where $0 \leq \lambda \leq 1$ is the mixing parameter. This model might be appropriate in survey research where some voters are more sophisticated than others (as indexed by $\lambda$) and more sophisticated voters base their votes on different explanatory variables than others (see Bartels, 1988).

In this model, if $\sigma_1^2$ (or $\sigma_2^2$) approaches zero, the height of the first normal hump tends toward infinity. Of course, for most interesting examples, $\sigma_1^2$ and $\sigma_2^2$ are both known to be greater than zero. So, in this case, there is a finite maximum and a series of infinite maxima. Numerical maximization procedures can run into trouble if they wander into the infinite regions, and either the model or the maximization procedures must be modified to prevent this.

Two solutions can be applied. The first is to assume that $\sigma_1^2 = \sigma_2^2$; this solves the problem completely, but it may be more restrictive than is desired. In the political sophistication example mentioned above, one might expect the variance in the opinions of sophisticated voters to be less than that for the unsophisticated voters (but it is certainly above zero). Thus, a second solution to the problem of unbounded likelihood functions is to use the Bayesian theory of inference and put a diffuse prior on the variance parameters (see King and Gelman, 1988).

## 4.6    Precision of maximum likelihood estimators

Once a ML estimate is calculated, whether by analytical or numerical means, a researcher will usually want to know how good an estimate it is. How much information does a particular estimate possess about the underlying parameter? How good a summary of the entire likelihood function is this one point? Across an infinite number of identical experiments, do the estimates vary narrowly or widely around the true parameter value?

Since likelihood is a relative concept, one cannot determine the absolute probability that this estimate equals the unknown parameter. However, one can use information from features of the likelihood function other than the maximum to assess the relative degree of support the estimator gives to a different hypothesis of interest. Hence, *the comparison of hypotheses about the same data is the preferred means of studying the precision of ML estimates.*

Procedures of this sort compare two models, one a more general form of the other. I call these the *unrestricted model* and the *restricted model*. For example, the model in Equation (4.2) may be considered a restricted model and Equation (4.6) the unrestricted model. Equation (4.2) is a restricted version since the parameter $\beta_1$ is fixed at zero. In general, the parameters in the unrestricted model but omitted from the restricted model are the objective of testing. For this purpose, the hypothesis that these *test parameters* are all zero – where the restricted model is the correct one – is called the *null hypothesis* and is symbolized as $H_0$. The *alternative hypothesis* is that these test parameters are not zero – the situation where the unrestricted model is correct.[17]

The three most common hypothesis tests are all calculated directly from the likelihood function. *Wald's test* corresponds to using standard errors of the coefficients and may be calculated by estimating only the unrestricted model. The *likelihood ratio test* requires the estimation of both models and the comparison of their likelihoods; it is a generalization from using likelihood ratios for interpretation, described in Chapter 2. Finally, *Rao's score test* (also called the *Lagrange Multiplier test*) may be calculated by estimating only the null hypothesis.[18] In this section, I briefly describe the use of Wald and likelihood ratio tests, since these are most often useful. A complete discussion and comparison of all three may be found in Engle (1984).

Throughout the remainder of this section, distinguishing between *classical hypothesis tests* and *interpretative uses of hypothesis tests and other measures of precision* is critical. Classical hypothesis tests provide explicit measures of the uncertainty one should have about alternative hypothetical state-

---

[17] The names "null" and "alternative" hypotheses are assigned for convenience only. In addition, this procedure can be made more general by testing the null hypothesis that the parameter vector $\beta$ is equal to a particular set of hypothetical values $\bar{\beta}$ rather than zero. One could then either generalize the notation in the text or reparameterize the problem so that $\bar{\beta}$ is a vector of zeros.

[18] In most cases, only large sample justifications for these tests exist, and in large samples the three are equivalent. Their performances in small samples have not been completely established, but their relative advantages are known to vary by application. In linear models, Wald $\geq$ LR $\geq$ Rao holds in small samples.

ments. Although sometimes incorrectly interpreted as inverse probability statements, we shall see below that these are really traditional probability statements. Hence, I will argue that the interpretive understanding of these tests is much more practically useful.

### Likelihood ratio test

Let $L^*$ be the maximum of the unrestricted likelihood under the alternative hypothesis [e.g., Equation (4.2)], and let $L_R^*$ denote the maximum restricted likelihood under the null [e.g., Equation (4.6)]. Thus, $L^* \geq L_R^*$ or, equivalently, $L_R^*/L^* \leq 1$. The likelihood ratio is exactly 1.0 when the restriction has no effect at all. In general, though, adding more parameters, or unrestricting the range of existing ones, can only increase the likelihood. In Figure 4.1, for example, any restriction on the range of $\beta$ that does not include the maximum would make the ML estimate lower.

In Chapter 2, the likelihood ratio was useful in interpreting relative values of the likelihood. The more important question here is whether an observed likelihood ratio is due to systematic differences between the two models or merely to the consequences of sampling error. In the context of a repeated experiment, a result from distribution theory enables one to make this judgment. I first define the likelihood ratio test statistic as a function of the ratio of the two likelihoods:

$$
\begin{aligned}
\mathcal{R} &= -2\ln\left(\frac{L_R^*}{L^*}\right) \\
&= 2(\ln L^* - \ln L_R^*) \\
&\sim f_{\chi^2}(r|m),
\end{aligned}
$$

where $m$ is the number of test parameters and $r$ is a realized or hypothetical value of $\mathcal{R}$. This equation displays a particular function of the likelihood ratio that is distributed in the context of a repeated experiment as a chi-square variable with $m$ degrees of freedom in large samples. This result derives from the asymptotic Normality property of ML estimators.[19] Since $\ln L^*$ is always greater than or equal to $\ln L_R^*$, $\mathcal{R}$ is either zero or a positive number. Without considering random error, if the unrestricted model were no better than the restricted model, $\mathcal{R}$ would be exactly zero. However, random error alone might cause $\mathcal{R}$ to be larger than zero.

Hence, the relevant question is how much greater than zero does $\mathcal{R}$ have to be in order to convince one that it is due to systematic differences between

---

[19] The sum of squares of $K$ independent standard Normal variables is a chi-square variable with $K$ degrees of freedom.

the two models? Intuitively, under the assumption that the null hypothesis is true (i.e., the restrictions are valid), $\mathcal{R}$ has an expected value of $m$. Thus, $m$ is the amount by which one should expect $\mathcal{R}$ to vary from zero solely due to random error. If the observed value of the test statistic $\mathcal{R}$ is near its expected value, then one should conclude that no perceptible systematic rather than random differences exist between the two models. If the observed value of $\mathcal{R}$ is much larger than $m$, the observed estimates of the two models are more likely to be due to systematic rather than random differences; one would therefore be more likely to adopt the unrestricted model.

One can also quantify these probabilities under the rubric of classical hypothesis testing by looking up the observed value of $\mathcal{R}$ in a chi-square table with $m$ degrees of freedom. For example, the log-likelihood under the restricted model in Equation (4.2) is $-81.27$; the unrestricted log-likelihood in Equation (4.6) is larger, $-72.86$.[20] The null hypothesis ($H_0$) is that the additional parameter in the unrestricted model is zero: $\beta_1 = 0$. Hence, the observed value of $\mathcal{R}$ with $m = 1$ degree of freedom is

$$\hat{\mathcal{R}} = 2(\ln L^* - \ln L_R^*)$$
$$= 2(-72.86 - -81.27)$$
$$= 16.8.$$

Since $\mathcal{R} = 16.8$ is substantially larger than the expected value of $\mathcal{R}$ [$E(\mathcal{R}) = 1$], I conclude that the restriction is unwarranted and opt for the model in Equation (4.6).[21]

In addition, one can more formally test this hypothesis by looking up the probability of getting a value of $\hat{\mathcal{R}} = 16.8$, given the null hypothesis, in a chi-square table. With one degree of freedom, this probability is extremely small:

$$\Pr[\mathcal{R} \geq 16.8 | H_0, m = 1] = \int_{16.8}^{\infty} f_{\chi^2}(\mathcal{R} | H_0, m = 1) \, d\mathcal{R} \qquad (4.14)$$
$$= 0.000041.$$

[20] These values are from the full log-likelihood as functions of both $\sigma$ and $\beta$. The values on the vertical axis of Figure 4.1 correspond only to the sum of squared residuals, from which this particular ML estimator for $\beta$ may also be calculated.

[21] The only statistical procedures for which computer programs do not routinely report log-likelihoods directly are those for linear regression. In this case, the log-likelihood can be obtained by calculating

$$\ln L(\theta | y) = -n \ln\left(\frac{\sqrt{n-k}}{\sqrt{n}} \breve{\sigma}\right),$$

where $\breve{\sigma}$, the unbiased estimate of the standard error of the regression, is usually reported. This expression is derived by substituting the ML estimator for $\hat{\sigma}^2$ in the full likelihood [Equation (4.3)], taking logs, and simplifying. When multiplied by $\sqrt{n-k}/\sqrt{n}$, $\breve{\sigma}$ becomes $\hat{\sigma}$.

I am therefore again led to the conclusion that the restrictions are invalid. However, we should not interpret this exact number as being precise enough so that we can know all six decimal places confidently. For empirical research, it would be sufficient (and advisable) to conclude just that this number is "small."[22]

*Remark on classical hypothesis testing:* Note that Equation (4.14) is neither a likelihood nor an inverse probability. It is the traditional probability understood in the context of a repeated experiment: We suppose that the null hypothesis is true and imagine an infinite number of samples randomly drawn and test statistics $\mathcal{R}$ computed. The distribution of values of $\mathcal{R}$ form a chi-square ($f_{\chi^2}$) sampling distribution. With this distribution, one can calculate the probability of getting an observed result as far or farther from the result as expected, given that the null hypothesis is true. Since, in this case, this probability is very small, one probably would conclude that the null hypothesis is false. However, one *could* conclude instead that the null hypothesis is correct (i.e., $\beta_1 = 0$), but we would then also have to believe that these data $y$ were one of the 41 cases in 1,000,000 that deviated from expectations under the null hypothesis purely due to random error.

Unfortunately, many still misinterpret classical hypothesis tests as providing inverse probability statements (see Oakes, 1986: 79). The probability that the observed case was one of the 41 unusual ones or one of the 999,959 more typical ones *cannot* be calculated since it is an inverse rather than traditional probability. Since classical hypothesis tests are based on a notion of traditional probability, one *can* make statements of absolute uncertainty but only those like Equation (4.14). This probability may be of some use, but it is not the measure of uncertainty in which political scientists are typically interested: these tests still do not permit one to assess the probability that the null hypothesis is true, given the data.

Of what use, then, is classical hypothesis testing? Interpreted correctly, these tests are of only limited use. Even with these tests, we are still completely ignorant about whether an estimate is one of the usual or unusual ones (one of the 41 or of the 999,959, for example). However, interpreting the precision of the ML estimators is still critical. Understanding how much information is behind a point estimate, and how good a summary of the entire likelihood func ion the maximum provides, is as important. Classical hypothesis tests do not permit one to judge the probability of a hypothesis being true,

---

[22] In the most formal of classical hypothesis testing procedures, one would set a probability level *before* the analysis (like 0.05). If the observed probability is smaller than this, then the decision-rule requires one to accept the alternative hypothesis; otherwise the null is accepted.

given the data, but they do provide a framework by which one can get a feel for the precision and value of individual ML estimates.

### Direct measures of precision

As long as one can estimate both the restricted and unrestricted models, the likelihood ratio can be used to examine complicated hypotheses, even with large numbers of test parameters. However, in some cases, one either has no specific alternative hypothesis or has many potential alternatives. In these cases, the likelihood ratio test is not of much use. Fortunately, procedures do exist for these cases. In this subsection, I concentrate on direct measures of the value of a ML estimate. These measures indicate, among other things, how well the estimate summarizes the entire likelihood function. In the next subsection, I use these measures to derive Wald's test statistic. The advantage of this test statistic is that only the unrestricted model need be estimated; from that model, one can perform tests against any number of alternatives.

Since likelihood is a relative concept, the maximum must be evaluated only in comparison with other values. Whereas the likelihood ratio test compares likelihoods at the maximum and at one other specific value (corresponding to a restricted model), one can use the degree of the likelihood function's *curvature* to implicitly compare the maximum to all other values. To understand this idea, imagine two different unidimensional likelihood functions: for one, the likelihood function is highly curved (like Figure 2.4); for the other, the function is relatively flat. Since, for *any* restricted hypothesis, a curved function would yield higher likelihood ratios than a flat function, the ML estimate contains more information when the likelihood is curved. Hence, *a measure of the likelihood function's curvature is also a measure of the precision of the ML estimate.*

What is a reasonable measure of the likelihood function's curvature? To answer this question generally, I first provide an answer in the simple case of the log-likelihood function for linear regression models in Equation (4.8). I then generalize this solution for all types of log-likelihoods. After dropping terms that do not depend on $\beta$, note that this equation may be written as a quadratic equation in $\tilde{\beta}$:[23]

$$\ln L(\tilde{\beta}|y) = -\frac{1}{2\tilde{\sigma}^2} \sum_{i=1}^{n} (y_i - \tilde{\beta})^2 \qquad (4.15)$$

$$= \left(\frac{-\Sigma_{i=1}^{n} y_i^2}{2\tilde{\sigma}^2}\right) + \left(\frac{\Sigma_{i=1}^{n} y_i}{\tilde{\sigma}^2}\right) \tilde{\beta} + \left(\frac{-n}{2\tilde{\sigma}^2}\right) \tilde{\beta}^2,$$

---

[23] A quadratic equation is a representation of a line with one bend in it (a polynomial). $E(Y) = \beta_0 + \beta_1 X + \beta_2 X^2$ is probably familiar to most readers.

where the terms in parentheses in the second line can be considered constant quadratic coefficients of the $\bar{\beta}$s. Since the coefficient of the squared term ($-n/2\bar{\sigma}^2$) is negative, the parabola drawn from this equation must be concave downward, and Figure 4.2 demonstrates that this is indeed the case. The more negative the coefficient is (the larger $n/\bar{\sigma}^2$ is), the more curved will be the parabola. Indeed, two features of the result in this simple case are quite intuitive: The more observations (the larger $n$), the more curved the log-likelihood; hence, the maximum contains more information, is more precise, and is a better summary of the entire log-likelihood. In addition, the ML estimate is more precise when the variance of the disturbance term ($\sigma^2$) is smaller.

Hence, whenever the log-likelihood takes the form of a quadratic equation, a measure of the function's curvature is the coefficient of the squared term. This is a very useful result here, but it is not directly useful when the log-likelihood takes on other geometric forms. In this more general situation, one could separately analyze the mathematical form of each likelihood function, but this would require more background in analytical geometry than is usual and more focus on the algebraic details than should be the case in substantive research.

As an alternative to either intensive mathematical inquiry or conceptualizing graphs of multidimensional hypersurfaces, one can use the simple parabolic form in Figure 4.1 as an *approximation* to any log-likelihood. The specific means by which an arbitrary function may be approximated by a quadratic function is called a "second order Taylor series expansion of the log-likelihood with respect to $\bar{\theta}$ around the maximum $\hat{\theta}$." Through a particular combination of derivatives, the Taylor series method produces the best quadratic approximation to the log-likelihood:

$$\ln L(\bar{\theta}|y) \approx \ln L(\hat{\theta}|y) + \ln L'(\hat{\theta}|y)(\bar{\theta} - \hat{\theta}) + \frac{\ln L''(\hat{\theta}|y)}{2}(\bar{\theta} - \hat{\theta})^2, \quad (4.16)$$

where the primes denote differentiation of the log-likelihood with respect to $\hat{\theta}$. Since this equation applies generally, it is written as a function of $\bar{\theta}$; in this specific example, $\bar{\theta} \equiv \bar{\beta}$. In the special case where the original log-likelihood is quadratic, this quadratic approximation is exact; thus, when applied to the log-likelihood in Equation (4.15), the Taylor series operation in Equation (4.16) exactly reproduces Equation (4.15). Whereas the coefficient of the squared term in Equation (4.15) is $-n/2\bar{\sigma}^2$, the coefficient in the more general case is half the second derivative of the log-likelihood with respect to $\bar{\theta}$, evaluated at $\hat{\theta}$, $\ln L''(\hat{\theta}|y)/2$.

For the general situation where the log-likelihood may or may not be quadratic, the *information* in the data is defined in terms of this second derivative:

$$I(\hat{\theta}|y) = -E \left[ \frac{\partial^2 \ln L(\bar{\theta}|y)}{\partial \bar{\theta} \partial \bar{\theta}'} \right]_{\bar{\theta}=\hat{\theta}}, \tag{4.17}$$

where the constant 1/2 is dropped for convenience. If $\theta$ is a single parameter, then the larger $I(\hat{\theta}|y)$ is, the more curved is the log-likelihood and, therefore, the more information exists in the data and the more precise $\hat{\theta}$ is. If $\theta$ is a vector of $K$ parameters, then $I(\hat{\theta}|y)$ is a $K \times K$ matrix with diagonal elements containing the information of each corresponding element of $\hat{\theta}$. Because of the expected value operator, $E$, Equation (4.17) must be estimated. Several estimators exist. but the most intuitive is:

$$I(\hat{\theta}|y) = - \left[ \frac{\partial^2 \ln L(\bar{\theta}|y)}{\partial \bar{\theta} \partial \bar{\theta}'} \right]_{\bar{\theta}=\hat{\theta}}. \tag{4.18}$$

The core intuition behind this measure is that when the information is larger, the log-likelihood is more curved; hence, the ML estimate is a better summary of the entire likelihood function, and one should be proportionately more confident of the point estimates in $\hat{\theta}$ relative to *any* more restricted hypothesis. Specifically, Equation (4.18) is an *estimator* of a *quadratic approximation* to the curvature of the log-likelihood and thus a measure of information in the ML estimate. Although information is a very useful measure alone, one can improve on intuition by conceptualizing it in the context of a repeated experiment and then formalizing it as a test statistic.

First, the asymptotic Normality property of ML estimators guarantees that, in the context of a repeated experiment, $\hat{\theta}$ has a Normal distribution as the sample size grows. Remarkably, the information in the ML estimator in one set of data is closely related to the asymptotic variance of this Normal distribution across an infinite number of hypothetically identical experiments:

$$V(\hat{\theta}) \approx \lim_{n \to \infty} [I(\hat{\theta}|y)/n]^{-1} \tag{4.19}$$

$$= \lim_{n \to \infty} \frac{1}{n} E \left[ \frac{-\partial^2 \ln L(\bar{\theta}|y)}{\partial \bar{\theta} \partial \bar{\theta}'} \right]_{\bar{\theta}=\hat{\theta}}^{-1}.$$

If the log-likelihood is of quadratic form, Equation (4.19) is exact rather than an approximation. Due to the asymptotic efficiency property of ML estimators, $V(\hat{\theta})$ is smaller than the variance of any other consistent uniformly Normal estimator. In a sample of data, one can estimate $V(\hat{\theta})$ on the basis of the estimated information:

$$\widehat{V(\hat{\theta})} \approx \left[ \widehat{I(\hat{\theta}|y)} \right]^{-1} \tag{4.20}$$

$$= -\frac{1}{n} \left[ \frac{\partial^2 \ln L(\bar{\theta}|y)}{\partial \bar{\theta} \partial \bar{\theta}'} \right]_{\bar{\theta}=\hat{\theta}}^{-1}.$$

In general, $\widehat{V(\hat{\theta})}$ is a $K \times K$ matrix. The diagonal elements of this matrix are estimates of the variances of $K$ parameter estimates. The square roots of these variances are the standard errors of the elements of $\hat{\theta}$.[24]

For the simple case of linear regression [Equations (4.2) and (4.6)], $V(\hat{\beta})$ has a relatively simple form. In the general case with an arbitrary number of explanatory variables,

$$\widehat{V(\hat{\beta})} = \hat{\sigma}^2 (X'X)^{-1},\tag{4.21}$$

where the ML estimator of $\sigma^2$ is

$$\hat{\sigma}^2 = \frac{\sum_{i=1}^{n}(y_i - x_i\hat{\beta})^2}{n}.$$

In the simplest regression model [Equation (4.2)] $(X'X)^{-1}$ is just $1/n$.

Since the variance and information are functions of one another, reporting both is repetitive. The most common procedure is to report the corresponding standard error along with each element of $\hat{\theta}$.[25]

### Wald's test

Since Wald's test is a generalized version of the $t$-test from regression analysis, it is often just called a "$t$-test." From the measures of precision presented above alone, one can formally calculate this $t$-test as:

$$\mathcal{W} = \frac{\hat{\beta}_j - \tilde{\beta}}{\hat{\sigma}_j}\tag{4.22}$$
$$\sim f_N(w|\mu = 0, \sigma^2 = 1),$$

where $\hat{\beta}_j$ is the $j$th element of $\hat{\beta}$, $\hat{\sigma}_j$ is the standard error of $\hat{\beta}_j$, the square root of the $j$th diagonal element of $\widehat{V(\hat{\beta})}$, $w$ is a particular value of $\mathcal{W}$, and $\tilde{\beta}$ is a particular hypothesized value of $\beta$. $\mathcal{W}$ is an asymptotic standard Normal random variable under the assumption that $\tilde{\beta} = \beta$.[26] The formal Wald test is $\mathcal{W}^2$. It and

---

[24] In linear models, one should not confuse what is called the standard error of the

regression, $\hat{\sigma}^2$, and the standard error of the parameter estimates, $\sqrt{\widehat{V(\hat{\theta}_j)}}$.

[25] To the uninitiated, the elements in the information matrix are probably more intuitive, but standard errors are so commonly reported that it pays to go this extra step. It would also be more meaningful to call the standard errors the "curvatures," but this name is already taken for an unrelated statistic (Efron, 1975).

[26] In some cases, distributional results can be obtained for finite samples. In linear regression, for example, $\mathcal{W}$ is distributed as a $t$ distribution with $n - k$ degrees of freedom. The difference between the $t$ and standard Normal distributions is relatively minor, with the $t$ assigning slightly larger probabilities to events farther from zero. As the degrees of freedom become large, the $t$ becomes a standard Normal.

the likelihood ratio statistics are directly comparable since the distribution of $\mathcal{W}^2$ is the same as a likelihood ratio test statistic ($\mathcal{R}$) with one degree of freedom:

$$\mathcal{W}^2 \sim \chi^2(1).$$

However, $\mathcal{W}^2 \neq \mathcal{R}$, except in very large samples.[27]

As an example, consider again the linear model in Equation (4.6). By applying this model to presidential approval as a linear function of the inflation rate, I previously calculated ML point estimates as $\hat{\beta}_0 = 65.37$ and $\hat{\beta}_1 = -2.30$ and now use the same data to calculate the variance of $\hat{\beta}$, and then a specific test statistic. Applying the general rule in Equation (4.20) for calculating the estimated variance, or the specific rule in the case of linear models in Equation (4.21), to the model and data in Equation (4.6) yields the following result:

$$V(\hat{\beta}) = \begin{pmatrix} 8.23 & -1.18 \\ -1.18 & 0.25 \end{pmatrix}.$$

Hence, the variance of $\hat{\beta}_1$ is 0.25, and the standard error is $\sqrt{0.25} = 0.50$. To test the hypothesis that $\beta_1 = 0$, one calculates the Wald test statistic as follows:

$$\mathcal{W} = \frac{\hat{\beta}_1 - \tilde{\beta}_1}{\hat{\sigma}_1}$$
$$= \frac{-2.30 - 0}{0.50}$$
$$= -4.60.$$

Under the hypothesis that $\beta_1 = 0$, the expected value of $\mathcal{W}$ is zero. The observed value $\hat{\mathcal{W}}$ in this case is more than four and a half standard deviations from its expected value. Under the assumptions of classical hypothesis testing, the probability of getting a value of the Wald test statistic as unusual as or more unusual than $-4.60$, given the null hypothesis ($H_0$) that $\beta_1 = 0$ is true, is written as follows:

$$\Pr[(\mathcal{W} < -4.6) \cup (\mathcal{W} > 4.6)|H_0] = \Pr(\mathcal{W} < -4.6|H_0) \qquad (4.23)$$
$$+ \Pr(\mathcal{W} > 4.6|H_0)$$
$$= 2 \int_{4.6}^{\infty} f_N(w|\mu = 0, \sigma^2 = 1)dw$$
$$= 0.000004.$$

If the chi-square distribution with one degree of freedom were used, this same numerical value of the probability results:

---

[27] Finite sample size results are also available for the linear regression model, where an $F$ distribution may be used. The $F$ distribution is asymptotically related to the chi-square distribution.

$$\Pr(\mathcal{W}^2 > 4.6^2|H_0) = \Pr(\mathcal{W}^2 > 21.16|H_0) \qquad (4.24)$$
$$= \int_{21.6}^{\infty} f_{\chi^2}(w^2|m=1)dw^2$$
$$= 0.000004.$$

One can avoid calculating the integrals in Equations (4.23) and (4.24) by using the widely available chi-square and standard Normal distribution tables. But regardless of how one calculates it, the probability of getting this result, given the data and the null hypothesis, is exceedingly small. I am therefore again led to the conclusion that the null hypothesis is false.

Note that this traditional probability calculated using the Wald hypothesis test [0.000004 from Equation (4.23) or (4.24)] is different from the traditional probability calculated using the likelihood ratio test [0.000041 from Equation (4.14)]. Both are estimates of the unobserved probability of the results given the data and null hypotheses. The tests are asymptotically equivalent, but in this necessarily finite sample, there is an observable difference, although, from a substantive perspective, the probabilities are virtually identical.

Just as with the likelihood ratio, one cannot make an inverse probability statement with Wald's test statistic. Saying anything about the *probability* that the null hypothesis is true is still not possible.

### 4.7    Likelihood and interval estimation

For a given unknown parameter $\theta$, the stated goal of interval estimation is to provide estimators for the lower and upper bounds, $\hat{\theta}_L$ and $\hat{\theta}_U$, such that

$$\Pr(\hat{\theta}_L \leq \theta \leq \hat{\theta}_U) = \pi, \qquad (4.25)$$

where $\pi$ is a "confidence level" fixed in advance of the analysis. The procedures for estimating $\hat{\theta}_L$ and $\hat{\theta}_U$ are closely related to procedures for hypothesis testing, and I shall not detail them here. The meanings of the "probability" and "confidence level" in Equation (4.25) are of most importance.

A way of conceptualizing interval estimation in the framework of a model of uncertainty is to write the interval estimator as $(\hat{\theta}_L, \hat{\theta}_U)$. Note, however, that this estimator, like all others, is a particular function of the data: $h(y) \equiv (\hat{\theta}_L, \hat{\theta}_U)$. The level at which $\pi$ is set influences the particular function of the data (it governs, for example, how far apart $\hat{\theta}_L$ and $\hat{\theta}_U$ may be). Given this notation, I rewrite Equation (4.25) as a traditional probability:

$$\Pr[h(y) \equiv (\hat{\theta}_L, \hat{\theta}_U)|\theta] = \pi.$$

A confidence level is then the probability of a function of the data, given the parameters.

Unfortunately, after the data analysis, Equation (4.25) is often *incorrectly* interpreted as the inverse probability of $\theta$ being in the indicated interval. The inverse probability interpretation of Equation (4.25) is written as

$$\Pr[\theta|h(y) \equiv (\hat{\theta}_L, \hat{\theta}_U)] = \pi$$

and is unfortunately interpreted as if $\hat{\theta}_L$ and $\hat{\theta}_U$ were known before the data analysis and $\pi$ was unknown! Since Equation (4.25) was derived by fixing $\pi$ in advance of the analysis, it could not be a measure of uncertainty and cannot be an inverse probability. In referring to $\pi$ as a confidence level, rather than a probability, the problem with this interpretation has been avoided on technical grounds. However, in order for the confidence level interpretation to make sense, its model must be developed explicitly. However, no such explicit model exists.

Just like measures of uncertainty in hypothesis testing, the probability statement associated with an interval estimate is but a traditional probability – stating the probability of the data, and functions of the data $\hat{\theta}_L$ and $\hat{\theta}_U$, given the model and its parameters, $\theta$. The statement is not an inverse probability and does not, and cannot, directly address the questions of interest to political scientists.

However, one need not abandon the use of interval estimators. Instead, one can use interval estimates in place of point estimates as convenient summaries of the entire likelihood function. One only need be careful of the interpretation of it as a measure of uncertainty in the context of inference. Given this, interval estimators combine features of point estimation with assessments of the likelihood's curvature at the maximum: the more curved the likelihood, the smaller the confidence interval (for a fixed confidence level). Indeed, given the ML estimate and the variance matrix, one can calculate an interval estimate, so the two are very closely related. In some instances, confidence intervals might provide a slightly more intuitive way to summarize the likelihood function than point and curvature estimates.

## 4.8    Concluding remarks

This chapter has presented the operational and conceptual details of the likelihood model of statistical inference. The method of likelihood provides a summary estimator of unchallenged superiority, although it falls short of the goals of inverse probability; measuring absolute uncertainty seems an inherently unattainable goal in scientific inference. Instead, likelihood provides a means of measuring the relative uncertainty of alternative hypothetical inferences. Likelihood as a summary estimator can be used *in theory* for any empirical political science problem capable of formalization. However, it is of little use in most *practical* problems with multiple parameters.

In political science research, multiple parameter models are far more common. The practical solution in these cases is to use point and interval estimates as summaries of the likelihood function. The parameter values that maximize the relative likelihood are commonly used. Point estimators also happen to have a variety of desirable properties. Once fully understood as permitting only traditional rather than inverse probability, classical hypothesis tests are of less use in most research situations. However, likelihood ratios and estimates of the curvature of the likelihood function provide evaluations of the ML point estimator and of how well it summarizes the entire likelihood. Interval estimators provide a different means of summarizing the entire likelihood.

In sum, the likelihood approach provides a general model of statistical inference. It derives summary, interval, and point estimators from deep principles of scientific inference rather than as descriptive methods that satisfy arbitrary lists of desirable properties.

# PART II

# Methods

# CHAPTER 5

# Discrete regression models

In the previous four chapters, I outlined a model of the basic theoretical unity of statistical inference: Traditional probability serves as an absolute measure of uncertainty; likelihood is the key to scientific inference. With these concepts, one can go a long way toward understanding and even extending most existing methods. However, in all of this, I have only directly considered very simple statistical models. This helped to focus attention on the deeper concepts of scientific inference without having to worry about the details of less familiar statistical models. Accordingly, the remainder of this book analyzes a wide variety of models, all of which are special cases, or straightforward generalizations, of the generic statistical model in Equations (1.3) and (1.4). One can estimate each with the theory of inference described in Part I.

In the present chapter, I discuss a variety of statistical models for a particular class of discrete dependent variables. Since only continuous variables can be Normally distributed, none of the models discussed in this chapter have stochastic components with Normal distributions. Many of the data generation processes in this chapter are based, in different ways, on *binary outcomes*. In the simplest case, the dependent variable is itself dichotomous. The observation is Democrat/Republican, pass/fail, or employed/unemployed. In other cases, one does not observe the binary outcome, but only specific groups of outcomes. The observation here is the number of binary variables that occur in a particular way; for example, the number of passes on ten exams. In these cases, the underlying binary variables that go into making up each observation may be independent, as with the binomial distribution, or correlated. In still other cases, the number of unobserved binary variables that goes into each observation is essentially infinite; one observes only a count, as, for example, with the number of news stories per year on the budget deficit. These event counts may also be correlated or uncorrelated.

Discrete regression models enable one to study this important class of processes. Although logit models for binary variables are relatively common, the other models discussed below appear in the scholarly literature far less frequently than the corresponding data generation processes appear in political science data. A few of the models presented appear here for the first time. Note that Section 5.2 should be read even if one prefers to skip this chapter.

## 5.1     Binary variables

Dichotomous outcomes are perhaps the simplest of all variables. Indeed, due to the absence of ancillary parameters, models of binary variables are in some ways even simpler than linear regression models, although perhaps not as familiar.

When confronted with a binary dependent variable, researchers often conceptualize the problem as one of explaining variations in $Y_i$, or a list of observed zeros and ones $(y_i)$, across observations. Since the ultimate goal is to determine the underlying process that drives observed data, this is appropriate. However, the problem is much clearer if one considers the stochastic and systematic components of the problem separately.

Consider first a single binary random variable, $Y_i$. Since only $Y_i = 0$ and $Y_i = 1$ have nonzero probabilities of occurring, the Bernoulli distribution provides a convenient model of the stochastic component [See Equation (3.3)]. Hence, let $Y_i$ be distributed as a Bernoulli random variable

$$Y_i \sim f_{\text{bern}}(y_i | \pi_i),$$

and assume that

$Y_i$ and $Y_j$ are independent random variables for all $i \neq j$.

For $y_i = 0,1$, the probability of $Y_i = y_i$ may therefore be calculated as follows:

$$f_{\text{bern}}(y_i | \pi_i) \equiv \Pr(Y_i = y_i | \pi_i) = \pi_i^{y_i}(1 - \pi_i)^{1 - y_i.} \tag{5.1}$$

The Bernoulli distribution has a single unknown parameter that happens to be the expected value of $Y_i$, as well as the probability that $Y_i$ takes on the value 1 across repeated experiments:

$$E(Y_i) = \Pr(Y_i = 1 | \pi_i) = \pi_i.$$

Hence, the $i$th random observation $Y_i$ takes on the value one (e.g., vote yes) with probability $\pi_i$ and zero (e.g., vote no) with probability $1 - \pi_i$. This is an adequate model of the stochastic component of this statistical model. The distinction between the stochastic component's variation across repeated hypothetical experiments and the systematic component's variation across observations is critical. For a single observation, the expected value is fixed; $Y_i$ varies stochastically around that expected value. The systematic component is a model of variation in the $n$ expected values across observations. Thus, the goal of specifying a systematic component for binary variable problems is to model the variation of $\pi_i$ (not $Y_i$ or $y_i$.) *across observations* $(i = 1, \ldots , n)$. Since $y_i$ varies across experiments, we are less interested in this variation than in $\pi_i$, which is constant across experiments. In addition, since the parameter $\pi_i$ happens to be a probability, ranging between zero and one, the expected value may never be realized exactly in any single run of the experiment. Indeed, one would not know anyway, since $E(Y_i) \equiv \pi_i$ is never observed.

I now let $E(Y_i) = \pi_i$ vary over $i$ as a function of a set of explanatory variables $x_i$. The key problem in specifying a systematic component is to choose the appropriate functional form. In general, we set

$$\pi_i = g(x_i, \beta)$$

and choose the functional form $g$ on the basis of the substance of the research problem. This choice is probably never obvious, since many possibilities always exist. But narrowing down the list of options is usually not difficult.

Since $\pi_i$ varies between zero and one, any value of $x_i$ put into the functional form $g(x_i, \beta)$ should yield a value between zero and one. If one were to restrict the values of $x_i$, or if $\pi_i$ were known not to approach its extremes, a linear form might be feasible. For large or small enough values of $x_i$, a linear model would yield probabilities greater than one or less than zero. In addition, $\pi_i$ is not generally known but probably varies close to extremes for at least *some* observations. Hence, the linear model might be a reasonable approximation in some cases, but, as a general model for binary variables, it is unacceptable. Although the linear model might be the most familiar, it is not the most obvious and should not be an automatic choice. In this case, $\pi_i$ is bounded from above and below. Hence, as $x_i$ increases, $\pi_i$ should increase too, but, as $\pi_i$ approaches its upper bound (near one), the rate at which it increases must slow.

For example, more years of education should generally increase the probability that an individual is employed. $\pi_i$ (the probability of employment) is probably higher for someone with a college than a high school degree. In addition, $\pi_i$ should continue to rise for each additional year of education but not at as steep a rate. Consider two people, alike in all respects except that one has two years of education after high school and the other has three. The person with more education should have a slightly higher $\pi_i$. Now consider two other people, alike in all other respects except that one had ten years of post-high school education and the other had eleven. In principle, $\pi_i$ should be very slightly higher for the person with more education. However, the advantage in the probability of employment for one additional year of education is not likely to be as great for this second pair of individuals. A similar story holds when $\pi_i$ becomes small: as $\pi_i$ approaches its lower bound (near zero), the rate at which it decreases in response to a change in $x_i$ must also decrease.

This reasoning excludes a linear form for $g$, as well as a variety of others, but many possibilities still remain. One can narrow down the possibilities somewhat further by requiring the curve to be symmetric with respect to its bounds. For example, I could as easily assign ''1'' to ''vote yes'' and ''0''

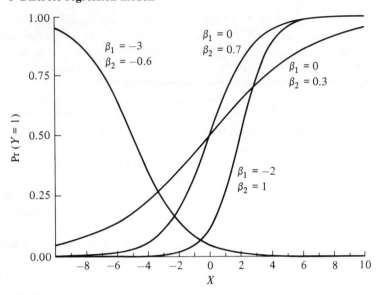

Figure 5.1. Logit curves.

to "vote no" as the reverse. The symmetry requirement is that if one switched the assignment of numbers to events, the substance of the model should remain unchanged. For an asymmetric substantive hypothesis, one of these alternatives could be used (as is done in Section 9.5); however for a large variety of models, symmetry is more appropriate (Aldrich and Nelson, 1984).

A number of functional forms still meet these requirements (see Cox, 1970: 25–9). Among these, *logit* and *probit* are most commonly used. Since the two curves produce essentially identical inferences in practical social science problems, I opt for the mathematically simpler logit functional form for the systematic component of this model (the probit model appears in Section 5.3):

$$\pi_i = \frac{1}{1 + \exp(-x_i\beta)}.$$  (5.2)

For a single explanatory variable, Figure 5.1 plots typical graphs of $1/[1 + \exp(\beta_1 + \beta_2 x_i)]$ for several different parameter values. From this figure, one can see that positive values of the slope $\beta_2$ are upwardly sloping and negative values are downwardly sloping. The intercept $\beta_1$ shifts the curve vertically. In addition, the curve becomes steeper when $\pi_i$ gets closer to 0.5.

One can include multiple explanatory variables by letting $x_i\beta$ be a matrix expression so that

$$x_i\beta = \beta_1 x_{i1} + \beta_2 x_{i2} + \cdots + \beta_K x_{iK},$$  (5.3)

where $x_{i1}$ is typically a column of ones, making $\beta_1$ an analogue to the intercept in linear regression. In this case, the two dimensional curve in Figure 5.1 becomes a surface for two explanatory variables and a $(K+1)$-dimensional hypersurface for $K$ explanatory variables. Just as graphing the full likelihood becomes infeasible with multiple dimensions, alternative means of interpretation become necessary here as well. I leave the specific methods by which one interprets this form and its parameters to the next section, where I also provide general procedures for interpreting parameters of any functional form.

For now, consider how one would estimate the parameter vector $\beta$. With the likelihood approach, the procedure is quite simple. First, derive the full model for the stochastic component by combining Equation (5.1) with the assumption of independence of $Y_i$ and $Y_j$ for all $i \neq j$:

$$\Pr(Y|\pi) = \prod_{i=1}^{n} \pi_i^{y_i}(1 - \pi_i)^{1-y_i}.$$

Then, by substituting the right hand side of Equation (5.2) for $\pi_i$ in this equation (i.e., by reparameterizing), I write the stochastic component as a function of $\beta$, the parameter of interest:

$$\Pr(y|\beta) = \prod_{i=1}^{n} \left(\frac{1}{1+\exp(-x_i\beta)}\right)^{y_i} \left(1 - \frac{1}{1+\exp(-x_i\beta)}\right)^{1-y_i} \quad (5.4)$$

$$= \prod_{i=1}^{n} [1+\exp(-x_i\beta)]^{-y_i}[1+\exp(x_i\beta)]^{-(1-y_i)}.$$

Finally, since the likelihood function $L(\beta|y)$ is proportional to Equation (5.4), the log-likelihood may be written simply by taking logs:

$$\ln L(\tilde{\beta}|y) = \sum_{i=1}^{n} \{-y_i \ln [1+\exp(-x_i\tilde{\beta})] - (1-y_i) \ln [1+\exp(x_i\tilde{\beta})]\}. \quad (5.5)$$

One can use this log-likelihood as a summary estimator for $\beta$ directly, but the usual problems of interpretation occur when $\beta$ contains many elements. Hence, I use the ML estimator for $\beta$, along with the variance matrix, as a practical compromise. This log-likelihood is differentiable, and the derivative can be set equal to zero, but solving for $\hat{\beta}$ is impossible with analytical methods. Thus, a numerical method of maximization must be applied, and many have been implemented for this problem. Measures of the precision of this ML estimator may also be derived through numerical means. In the next section, I discuss an example of logistic regression analysis in the context of the general procedures for interpreting functional forms (see also Merelman and King, 1986).

## 5.2    Interpreting functional forms

The general problem to be considered in this section is the substantive interpretation of the effect of parameters $\beta$ in different functional forms $g$ in the
equation $\theta = g(X, \beta)$. The single most important point of this section is that *if
$\beta$ has no substantive interpretation for a particular model, then that model
should not be estimated.* I say this so emphatically because of the inordinate
number of journal articles that report logit and other coefficients only to eventually describe them as "unintuitive" or even "meaningless." The authors
of these articles then usually resort to classical hypothesis testing, only to
misinterpret these tests as measures of inverse, rather than traditional, probabilities! If $\beta$ has no meaning, why would one want to estimate it? Without
meaning in the original model, the entire motivation for deriving stochastic
and systematic components, forming the likelihood, and finding the ML estimates is lost.

Of course, in most cases, $\beta$ does have a meaningful interpretation. I consider four general procedures by which to interpret it: *graphical methods,
fitted values, first differences,* and *derivatives.* Graphical methods are generally the easiest to conceptualize, but hardest to implement in the multiple
parameter problems typically encountered in political science. Calculating fitted values and first differences is generally not difficult and are quite intuitive,
but it is not as automatic as either graphical methods or derivatives. Derivatives are probably the easiest to calculate and most automatic, but interpretation requires more care. Other methods do exist and are introduced later (see
Section 5.3, for example).

I illustrate each of these methods with a specific application of logistic
regression. The substantive question to be addressed is: Are major national
addresses by U.S. presidents random events, or are they predictable consequences of measurable variables? The dependent variable is binary, representing the presence ($Y_i = 1$) or absence ($Y_i = 0$) of a discretionary presidential
address for each month, from the Truman through the Carter presidencies.
Those months with obligatory speeches, such as inaugural and State of the
Union addresses, were omitted from the data set. Lyn Ragsdale (1984) was
the first to systematically address this question, and, except for a few modifications, the data used here are the same.[1] The explanatory variables include
(1) the monthly change in the proportion of the public that approve of the way

---

[1] Ragsdale included extra observations for months with more than one discretionary
speech. Since the rule for including these extra observations is obviously correlated
with the dependent variable, this procedure creates an unnecessary selection bias
(see Chapter 9). To avoid this nonrandom selection problem, I omit these extra
observations. Since presidents gave multiple discretionary speeches for only a few
months, omitting these observations changed the coefficients but did not markedly
alter the substantive results.

the president is handling his job, the number of (2) positive and (3) negative presidential events (usually zero or one), the percent (4) unemployment and (5) inflation, and (6) the change in the number of military personnel on active duty.[2]

I first use these data to form the log-likelihood in Equation (5.5). Then, with numerical methods, I find the values of the parameters $(\beta_0, \ldots, \beta_6)$ such that the log-likelihood is maximized. These ML estimates are

$$\hat{\beta} = \begin{pmatrix} \hat{\beta}_0 \\ \hat{\beta}_1 \\ \hat{\beta}_2 \\ \hat{\beta}_3 \\ \hat{\beta}_4 \\ \hat{\beta}_5 \\ \hat{\beta}_6 \end{pmatrix} = \begin{pmatrix} 1.515 \\ 0.188 \\ 2.317 \\ 2.796 \\ -0.709 \\ -0.013 \\ -0.341 \end{pmatrix}$$

I also calculated the estimated variance matrix of the ML estimator across repeated hypothetical experiments with numerical methods:[3]

$$\widehat{V(\hat{\beta})} =$$

$$\begin{pmatrix}
0.55099 & 0.00240 & 0.07159 & 0.09263 & -0.11478 & -0.00044 & -0.03282 \\
0.00240 & 0.00138 & 0.00230 & 0.00541 & -0.00123 & -0.00004 & -0.00023 \\
0.07159 & 0.00230 & 0.15792 & 0.06891 & -0.02624 & -0.00030 & -0.01234 \\
0.09263 & 0.00541 & 0.06891 & 0.28204 & -0.02916 & 0.00020 & -0.01325 \\
-0.11478 & -0.00123 & -0.02624 & -0.02916 & 0.02671 & 0.00025 & 0.00782 \\
-0.00044 & -0.00004 & -0.00030 & 0.00020 & 0.00025 & 0.00003 & 0.00001 \\
-0.03282 & -0.00023 & -0.01234 & -0.01325 & 0.00782 & 0.00001 & 0.01847
\end{pmatrix}.$$

$$(5.6)$$

One can interpret the diagonal elements of this matrix directly as *variances,* which one would generally want to be small. They are also a function of the *information* in the ML estimates, the degree of *curvature* of the log-likelihood function at the maximum, and the *precision* with which the ML estimate is measured. The off-diagonal elements of this matrix are measures of the co-variances of the estimates across hypothetical samples.

ML estimates and variances of all types are generally presented in research reports in the format of Table 5.1, where the "standard error" is the square root of the respective diagonal element of the variance matrix in Equation (5.6). Sometimes a *"t* statistic," the ratio of the parameter estimate to the

---

[2] Presidential events are defined "as relatively long-lived, prominent happenings that are national or international in scope, have either negative or positive consequences for the president, and specifically involve some form of presidential action." See Ragsdale (1984) for operational definitions of these variables.

[3] Five decimal places are provided only to show that variances and covariances in the sixth column and row are nonzero.

Table 5.1. *Logistic regression of presidential speechmaking*

| Explanatory variable $(x_j)$ | Parameter estimate $(\hat{\beta}_j)$ | Standard error $\sqrt{\widehat{V(\hat{\beta}_j)}}$ | $t$ statistic $(\hat{W})$ |
|---|---|---|---|
| Constant | 1.515 | 0.742 | 2.042 |
| $\Delta$ Approval | 0.188 | 0.037 | 5.045 |
| Positive | 2.317 | 0.397 | 5.832 |
| Negative | 2.796 | 0.531 | 5.266 |
| Unemployment | −0.709 | 0.163 | −4.340 |
| Inflation | −0.013 | 0.005 | −2.527 |
| Military | −0.341 | 0.136 | −2.513 |

*Note:* Log-likelihood = − 132.016. Number of observations = 318.

standard error, is also reported. In most cases, this is really Wald's test statistic with $\tilde{\beta}=0$. Thus, in all ML models the statistic is distributed Normally in large samples; for linear regression and some other cases one can appeal to the $t$ distribution in small samples. Sometimes, "p-values" are also reported. These are classical probabilities under the null hypothesis that $\tilde{\beta}=0$.

*Graphical methods*

Graphing the functional form for different parameter values is probably the most obvious means of interpreting $g(X,\beta)$. For example, Figure 5.1 graphs different hypothetical values of $\beta_0$ and $\beta_1$ from the logistic functional form. Contemplating this figure and others provides considerable insight into this form.

One can also use graphical methods with two explanatory variables by using a three dimensional graph. However, just as with a multidimensional log-likelihood, three dimensional graphs can be somewhat difficult to interpret.[4]

To demonstrate this, I will use the empirical example in Table 5.1 rather than another hypothetical example. Since this example has six explanatory variables, a seven dimensional graph would be required to fully display these results. As an alternative, I will analyze only the effect of unemployment on the probability of giving a speech. To do this, one must incorporate the other variables in the relationship in some way. A particularly useful way is to hold

---

[4] The basic reason for this interpretive problem is that the three dimensional image must be projected onto a two dimensional page, as in Figure 4.2. Because only one perspective can be viewed, some detail is necessarily lost.

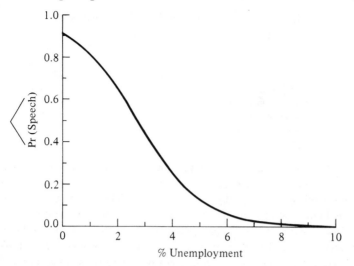

Figure 5.2. Presidential speeches.

the other variables constant at their means, thus reducing the dimensions to only two. Thus, Figure 5.2 plots $\hat{\pi}$ by unemployment. $\hat{\pi}$ is defined as:[5]

$$\hat{\pi} = \frac{1}{1 + \exp[-\overline{X}\hat{\beta}^- - U(-0.709)]} ,$$

where $\overline{X}$ is a vector of means for all the explanatory variables except unemployment and $\hat{\beta}^-$ are the corresponding parameter estimates in Table 5.1.[6] $-0.709$ is the parameter estimate for the effect of unemployment. A different value of $\hat{\pi}$ is calculated for any hypothetical value of unemployment, $U$. Figure 5.2 plots values of $\hat{\pi} \equiv \widehat{\text{Pr(Speech)}}$ for a range of values of $U$ from 0 to 12.

Since the coefficient of unemployment is negative, the relationship in Figure 5.2 is downward sloping: more unemployment leads presidents to give

[5] The usual notation here for what is generally called "fitted" or "predicted" values is either $\hat{y}$ or $\hat{Y}$. The former is unacceptable because $y$ is observed and need not be estimated. The latter is undesirable because $Y$ is a random variable rather than its expected value.

[6] The means in $\overline{X}$ include 1, for the constant term, $-0.044$, the mean change in approval, $0.167$, mean negative events, $0.063$, mean positive events, $-24.003$, mean inflation, and $0.222$, mean change in the number of military personnel on active duty. $\overline{X}\hat{\beta}^-$ is then $1.515(1) + 0.188(-0.044) + 2.317(0.167) + 2.796(0.063) - 0.013(-24.003) - 0.341(0.222) = 2.323$.

Table 5.2. *Estimated probability of presidential speech making*

|  | ΔApproval = −5 | ΔApproval = 5 |
|---|---|---|
| % Unemployment = 4 | 0.188 | 0.603 |
| % Unemployment = 5 | 0.102 | 0.428 |
| % Unemployment = 6 | 0.053 | 0.269 |

fewer major addresses. As unemployment gets much higher, the probability of the president giving a speech continues to drop but at a slower rate since the probability can never drop to below zero. The ceiling effect for this particular logit relationship does not really come into play here since it occurs only for negative levels of unemployment. Note that since this relationship is not very close to linear, particularly near the mean level of unemployment (5.203), a linear relationship would not be a very satisfactory approximation in this case.

Graphical methods such as this can have valuable interpretive power. Unfortunately, using these methods to interpret equations with many explanatory variables can quickly become unwieldy. One of the following three options therefore provides alternative methods of interpretation in these instances.

*Fitted values*

A $K$-dimensional hypersurface is difficult to interpret because of the difficulty of representing it in the three dimensional space people inhabit and the two dimensional space of the published page. However, it is also difficult because so many possible combinations of the $K$ parameters need to be plotted.[7]

One solution to this problem is to evaluate the functional form for only some combinations of the explanatory variables. One selects values of the explanatory variables and calculates the fitted value $\hat{\pi}$ by using knowledges of the substantive research problem. For example, one can get a good feel for the underlying curves from Table 5.1 by evaluating only a few points. Table 5.2 presents $\hat{\pi}$ for six substantively interesting values holding the other four variables constant at their means. These fitted values lead one to conclusions

---

[7] Think of how much more ''space'' is required to represent a three rather than two dimensional graph. If the explanatory variables could only take on a finite number of values, one could calculate the number of possible combinations of explanatory variables by multiplying. The total number of points to be plotted therefore increases geometrically with the number of variables. If one could find a place on a two dimensional page to put these additional points, graphical methods could be extended to these situations.

similar to those ascertained directly from Figure 5.2 for the effect of unemployment, but they also show that an increase in approval leads to a dramatic increase in the probability of a speech. In addition, the absolute effect of unemployment is larger in months with increases, rather than decreases, in public approval.

*First differences*

A slight modification of the method of using fitted values to interpret functional forms is the use of first differences. These statistics are estimates of how much $\theta$ would change given a particular change in a single explanatory variable, while statistically holding constant the other variables in the equation. To derive the formula for first differences, let $X_j$ be the $j$th of the $K$ explanatory variables and let $X_*$ be a vector of the remaining $K-1$ explanatory variables. The effect of variable $X_j$ on $\theta$ is the focus of interpretation.

By definition, the systematic component may now be redefined as $\theta \equiv g(X, \beta) = g(X_j, X_*, \beta)$. Hence, the estimated first difference statistic $\hat{\mathcal{D}}$ may be calculated as

$$\hat{\mathcal{D}} = g(X_j^{(b)}, X_*, \hat{\beta}) - g(X_j^{(a)}, X_*, \hat{\beta}),$$

where $X_j^{(a)}$ and $X_j^{(b)}$ are different hypothetical values of $X_j$. The estimated effect on $\mu$ of an increase in $X_j$ from $X_j^{(a)}$ to $X_j^{(b)}$, after one holds constant all the variables in $X_*$, is $\hat{\mathcal{D}}$.

For a linear model, the first difference takes on a very simple form:

$$\begin{aligned}\hat{\mathcal{D}}_{\text{linear}} &= (X_j^{(b)} \beta_1 + X_* \beta_*) - (X_j^{(a)} \beta_1 + X_* \beta_*)\\ &= X_j^{(b)} \beta_1 - X_j^{(a)} \beta_1\\ &= (X_j^{(b)} - X_j^{(a)}) \beta_1.\end{aligned}$$

Indeed, the effect of a one unit change [i.e., $(X_j^{(b)} - X_j^{(a)}) = 1$] in a variable $X_j$ on $\hat{\mu}$ is exactly equal to its corresponding regression coefficient $\beta_1$. Note that this same effect holds regardless of whether $X_j$ is increasing from 4 to 5 or from 445 to 446. This explains the precise reason for the interpretation of the ML estimate for the effect of inflation on presidential approval [see Equation (4.6)]: A one percentage point increase in inflation led to an average 2.3 percentage point drop in presidential approval, holding constant any other variables in the equation (of which there happened to be none).

For the logistic model, the first difference is as easy to interpret, but it does take a more complicated form:

$$\begin{aligned}\hat{\mathcal{D}}_{\text{logit}} &= [1 + \exp(-X_j^{(b)} \beta_j - X_* \beta_*)]^{-1}\\ &\quad - [1 + \exp(-X_j^{(a)} \beta_j - X_* \beta_*)]^{-1}.\end{aligned}$$

Although this equation cannot be simplified any further, calculating values of $\hat{\mathcal{D}}$ is straightforward. $\hat{\beta}_j$ and $\hat{\beta}_*$ are known from the ML estimation procedure.

Table 5.3. *First difference effects of presidential speechmaking*

| Variable | Estimate | Change in $X$ (from, to) | First difference |
|---|---|---|---|
| Constant | 1.515 | | |
| ΔApproval | 0.188 | $(-2,2)$ | 0.121 |
| Positive | 2.317 | $(0,1)$ | 0.488 |
| Negative | 2.796 | $(0,1)$ | 0.601 |
| Unemployment | $-0.709$ | $(4,6)$ | $-0.246$ |
| Inflation | $-0.013$ | $(-30, -20)$ | 0.021 |
| Military | $-0.341$ | $(-1, -2)$ | $-0.114$ |

Values of $X_*$ are to be held constant as $X_j$ changes. The value at which they are held constant in the linear case is irrelevant, since they drop out of the equation for $\hat{\mathcal{D}}$, but the values do matter in the general case of nonlinear equations. Probably the most obvious value to use is the most typical, the sample mean of each variable. Once this is done, everything in $\hat{\mathcal{D}}$ is constant except $X_j^{(b)}$ and $X_j^{(a)}$, which ultimately must be chosen on the basis of the substantive problem at hand. To get a good feel for the change in $\hat{\pi}$ that occurs on the basis of changes in $X_j$ in this logit equation, one should evaluate $\hat{\mathcal{D}}$ at several relevant points. As in all nonlinear equations, a single unit change in $X_j$ will have a different effect on the expected value of $Y$ depending on the points at which the curve is evaluated.

One way to present first differences is in a format like Table 5.3. The first column of numbers in this table repeats the coefficients from Table 5.1 for convenience. The second column gives the hypothetical values of the explanatory variables that were used to calculate the first differences in the third column. For example, when the number of positive events increases from zero to one, the probability of a speech being given in a month increases by 0.488, with the other variables held constant at their means. Since first differences are evaluated only at some points, the original logit coefficients should always be presented along with them.

### Derivative methods

A modification of the method of first differences is to measure the effect of a very small change in $X_j$ on $\hat{\theta}$. Thus, we define the instantaneous effect of $X_j$ on $\hat{\theta}$ as the deriviative of $\hat{\theta}$ with respect to $X_j$:

$$\frac{\partial \hat{\theta}}{\partial X_j} = \lim_{X_j^{(b)} \to X_j^{(a)}} \left[ \frac{g(X_j^{(b)}, X_*, \hat{\beta}) - g(X_j^{(a)}, X_*, \hat{\beta})}{X_j^{(b)} - X_j^{(a)}} \right]$$

$$= \frac{\partial g(X_j, X_*, \hat{\beta})}{\partial X_j}.$$

In the linear model,

$$\frac{\partial \hat{\mu}}{\partial X_j} = \hat{\beta}_j.$$

So, in this special case, the instantaneous effect is equal to the first difference statistic with $X_j^{(b)} - X_j^{(a)} = 1$. Indeed, only in the linear case does this hold. For *every* other functional form, these two measures differ. For the linear model, appealing to the first difference interpretation is probably more intuitive.

In the logit model, the instantaneous effect is calculated in the same manner:

$$\frac{\partial \hat{\pi}}{\partial X_j} = \frac{\partial}{\partial X_j} [1 + \exp(-X_j\hat{\beta}_j - X_*\hat{\beta}_*)]^{-1}$$
$$= \hat{\beta}_j \hat{\pi}(1 - \hat{\pi}).$$

This demonstrates that the instantaneous effect of $X_j$ on $\hat{\pi}$ depends on two factors: $\hat{\beta}_j$, the coefficient of $X_j$, and $\hat{\pi}(1 - \hat{\pi})$. $\hat{\beta}_j$ determines the sign and general size of the effect, whereas $\hat{\pi}(1 - \hat{\pi})$ controls where on the curve the effect is greatest. Since this latter term is always largest when $\hat{\pi} = 0.5$, the effect of $X_j$ on $\hat{\pi}$ is greatest at that point (i.e., Figure 5.1 is steepest at the middle). Closer to the floor ($\hat{\pi} = 0$) or ceiling ($\hat{\pi} = 1$), this term becomes gradually smaller (and the curves in Figure 5.1 become flatter).

The instantaneous effect is usually very easy to calculate. For example, $0.5(1 - 0.5)\hat{\beta}_j; \equiv \hat{\beta}_j/4$ is always the maximum instantaneous effect of $X_j$ in the logit form. One need not do any graphing or calculate any fitted values; only the coefficient need be presented. Although closely related, this method is even easier than the first differences procedure. For these reasons, using the derivative method is best for a quick first look at empirical results. For some cases, it is even the most substantively interesting. However, for most political science problems, first differences is considerably more intuitive.

Consider again my running example. An estimate of a typical fitted value $\hat{\pi}$ is just the sample mean of the binary variable $y$, in this case 0.274.[8] Thus, for the typical month, one should interpret $\hat{\beta}_j$ after multiplying by $\hat{\pi}(1 - \hat{\pi}) = 0.274(1 - 0.274) = 0.199$. For example, the instantaneous effect of a negative event is $2.796(0.199) = 0.556$. One should *not* say that one additional negative event leads to a 0.556 increase in the probability of a president giving a speech in a month. If this were true, sufficient negative events would lead to a probability greater than 1.0, a substantively meaningless and contradictory statement. Instead, one must interpret this only as the slope at the point $\hat{\pi} = 0.274$. For other values of $\hat{\pi}$, the slope is different.

---

[8] One could calculate $\sum_{i=1}^{n} \hat{\pi}_i/n$, but this is equal to $\sum_{i=1}^{n} y_i/n$ in the logit model with an intercept. The two are similar for other models but not always equal. In probit, for example, the two are not equal.

One might extend this interpretation by calculating this instantaneous effect for other values of $\hat{\pi}$, and thus for $\hat{\beta}_j\hat{\pi}(1-\hat{\pi})$. This provides a tool with which one can make a speedy interpretation of a given functional form. However, a more detailed, substantively intuitive, procedure is probably graphing when possible or first differences in other cases.

## 5.3    Alternative justifications for binary variable models

This section briefly describes two alternative methods of deriving the systematic component for dependent variables with binary outcomes. Section 5.1 derives the functional form from either an implicit assumption that the observed discrete variables are naturally discrete or the conviction that thinking about it directly is most natural. Both of the alternative justifications discussed here begin with the assumption that discrete variables are grouped realizations of unobserved continuous variables.

### Threshold models

Threshold models assume that $Y_i^*$ is a continuous unobserved variable distributed in some specified way:

$$Y_i^* \sim f(y_i^* | \mu_i).$$

Since $Y_i^*$ is continuous and unbounded, a linear relationship may be a reasonable assumption for the systematic component:

$$\mu_i = x_i\beta.$$

Then an observed realization $y_i$ is assumed to be related to $y_i^*$ by the following grouping mechanism:

$$y_i = \begin{cases} 1 & \text{if } y_i^* > \tau, \\ 0 & \text{if } y_i^* \leq \tau, \end{cases}$$

where $\tau$ is the threshold parameter. For example, suppose $y_i$ represents life or death and $Y_i^*$ is health; then $\tau$ is the threshold at which death occurs. For another example, $y_i$ might refer to vote or not vote. The $Y_i^*$ would represent the continuous unobserved propensity to vote, and $\tau$ would represent the threshold at which a nonvoter turns into a voter. One might think of $\tau$ as an additional unknown parameter to be estimated, but I set it to zero ($\tau = 0$), as is the usual practice to ensure identification, since the scale of the unobserved variable $Y_i^*$ is generally arbitrary. The functional form is then derived directly from the distribution and grouping mechanism specified above.

$$\Pr(Y_i = 1) = \Pr(Y_i^* \le 0)$$
$$= \int_{-\infty}^{0} f(y_i^* | \mu_i) dy_i^*$$
$$= F(0|\mu_i),$$

where $F(0|\mu_i)$ is the continuous distribution evaluated at zero, corresponding to the probability density function, $f(y^*|\mu)$. For example, suppose $Y_i^*$ follows a *standardized logistic* distribution:

$$Y_i^* \sim f_{sl}(y_i^*|\mu_i) = \frac{\exp[(y_i^* - \mu_i)]}{\{1 + \exp[(y_i^* - \mu_i)]\}^2}.$$

The standardized logistic distribution is very similar to the stylized Normal distribution, with a mean and no variance parameter.

In this case, $\Pr(Y_i = 1)$ follows the logit functional form:

$$\Pr(Y_i = 1) = \Pr(Y_i^* \le 0)$$
$$= \int_{-\infty}^{0} f_{sl}(y_i^*|\mu_i) dy_i^*$$
$$= [1 + \exp(-\mu_i)]^{-1}$$
$$= [1 + \exp(-x_i\beta)]^{-1}.$$

Note that by definition this equation is also the cumulative standardized logistic distribution. In fact, the functional form for the binary regression problem must always be a cumulative distribution; both are nondecreasing functions that give only values between zero and one.

The standardized logistic distribution happens to be a special case of the *logistic* distribution (see Johnson and Kotz, 1970b: 6), with the variance $\sigma^2$ set to $\pi^2/3$. The full logistic distribution is as follows:

$$Y_i^* \sim f_l(y_i^*|\mu_i, \sigma^2) = \frac{-\pi \exp[-\pi(y_i^* - \mu_i)/(\sigma\sqrt{3})]}{\sigma\sqrt{3}\{1 + \exp[-\pi(y_i^* - \mu_i)/\sigma\sqrt{3})]\}^2},$$

where one must be careful to recognize that $\pi$ in this equation is the mathematical constant $3.14159\ldots$, not the parameter I use in this section for the probability that $Y_i^*$ takes on the value of $1.0$. The special case of this distribution (with $\sigma^2 = \pi^2/3$) is generally used because one cannot estimate both $\sigma^2$ and $\beta$ with only the observed dichotomous realization $y$.

Given this, one might reasonably ask why the variance is fixed at $\sigma^2 = \pi^2/3$. The reason for this is purely mathematical aesthetics: At this value, the logistic distribution takes on the relatively simple form of the standardized logistic. However, for substantive purposes, a variance of $\pi^2/3$ is not particularly interesting, and the algebraic form of most probability densities is neither particularly relevant nor in any way beautiful to a political scientist. As an alternative, therefore, one might set $\sigma^2$ to the variance one would expect an unobserved variable to have. In other cases, it probably makes sense to set it to 1.0; this way, the coefficients can be interpreted as the linear effect of $x_i$ on $\mu_i$, where the random variable $Y_i^*$ is in standard deviation units. Of course, since logit analysis (with $\sigma^2 = \pi^2/3$) is very widely used, this change would probably be more confusing than it is worth.

Indeed, this latter idea happens to be the situation for probit analysis. Thus, if one makes the assumption that $f(y_i^* | \mu_i)$ is a stylized Normal distribution [a Normal distribution with mean $\mu$ and variance $\sigma^2 = 1$; Equation (4.1)], the functional form becomes a *probit:*

$$
\begin{aligned}
\Pr(Y_i = 1) &= \Pr(Y_i^* \leq 0) && (5.7)\\
&= \int_{-\infty}^{0} f_{stn}(y_i^* | \mu_i) dy_i^* \\
&= \int_{-\infty}^{0} (2\pi)^{-1/2} e^{-(y_i - \mu_i)^2/2} dy_i^* \\
&= F_{stn}(0 | \mu_i) \\
&= F_{sn}(\mu_i).
\end{aligned}
$$

This probit form is also the cumulative stylized Normal probability distribution evaluated at zero, which is the same as the standardized Normal distribution evaluated at $\mu_i$. Unlike the logit curve, the integral in this equation cannot be expressed in closed form. However, it can be evaluated easily with numerical methods. Recall that the stylized Normal distribution is just the Normal with $\sigma^2 = 1$; this restriction is used here because, just as in the logistic case, insufficient information exists about $Y^*$ to estimate its variance as well as its mean.

The full logistic and Normal distributions are extremely similar, as are the logit and probit functional forms. Justifications do exist in the literature for choosing one over the other, but in political science data these are theoretical differences with no practical import. Because of the differing variances of the standardized logistic and stylized Normal distributions ($\pi^2/3$ and 1.0, respectively), $\beta$ has different interpretations across the two models. To see this, one can use one of the methods of Section 5.2. However, if one conceptualizes this as a linear regression problem with a standardized, but unobserved, dependent variable, a more direct comparison can be made. If the stylized form of both distributions were used (i.e., with variance 1.0 or with any other common variance, for that matter), the coefficients would be on approximately the same scale. Alternatively, one can use the traditional forms of both and divide the logit coefficients by the logit standard deviation, $\pi/\sqrt{3} \approx 1.8$, to make the logit and probit coefficients on approximately the same scale.[9]

---

[9] Amemiya (1981) shows that 1.6 produces a slightly better approximation. To go from the probit to the logit scale, the coefficients should be multiplied by 1.6.

Table 5.4. *Comparing logit and probit models of presidential speech making*

| Variable | Logit | Logit/1.8 | Probit | Probit s.e. |
|---|---|---|---|---|
| Constant | 1.515 | 0.842 | 0.878 | 0.432 |
| ΔApproval | 0.188 | 0.104 | 0.109 | 0.021 |
| Positive | 2.317 | 1.287 | 1.369 | 0.228 |
| Negative | 2.796 | 1.554 | 1.644 | 0.300 |
| Unemployment | −0.709 | −0.394 | −0.417 | 0.093 |
| Inflation | −0.013 | −0.007 | −0.008 | 0.003 |
| Military | −0.341 | −0.190 | −0.198 | 0.078 |

*Note:* Logit log-likelihood = −132.016. Probit log-likelihood = −131.182. Number of observations = 318.

As an example of the probit model, I reanalyzed the presidential speeches data. The parameter estimates and standard errors appear in the last two columns of Table 5.4. For example, one additional positive presidential event increases $Y^*$ by 1.369 standard deviations; since 95% of the variation in the unobserved Normally distributed variable $Y^*$ is between $\mu - 2$ and $\mu + 2$, this is a fairly substantial effect.[10] Interpreting parameters in terms of an unobserved variable, like this, is thus an additional method of parameter interpretation beyond those in Section 5.2.

In addition, the second column includes the logit coefficients divided by 1.8. Because of this calculation, the middle two columns of coefficients are very similar. Also, because of the small difference between the two log-likelihoods, the two models fit the data essentially the same. Indeed, I have never seen an example with political science data where the difference between these two log-likelihoods is very large.

One also could specify some other distribution for $Y_i^*$ and, in turn, derive a new functional form. Presumably, if one believes that the unobserved variable $Y_i^*$ really exists, one should also have some idea of how it is distributed.

*Utility maximization models*

Another approach to justifying the functional form in binary regression models derives from a version of economic theory. This basic idea is most plausible when individual $i$ is considering a choice between two options, $Y_i = 1$ and $Y_i = 0$. From each option, the individual derives a level of utility, $U_{i1}$ and $U_{i0}$, respectively. One begins the specification by assuming that these utilities are random; that is, an individual will not know the exact level of utility he or

[10] The 95% figure comes from integrating the stylized Normal distribution between these bounds.

she will derive from a choice, but will know the probability distribution from which the utility is to be drawn. Thus, a researcher might assume that

$$U_{0i} \sim f(u_{0i}|\mu_{0i}),$$    (5.8)

$$U_{1i} \sim f(u_{1i}|\mu_{1i}),$$

where $\mu_{0i}$ and $\mu_{1i}$ are expected utilities and linear functions of vectors of explanatory variables. A postulate of rational economic behavior has individuals choosing the option with the higher expected utility. In other words, the probability of choosing option 1 may be written as follows:

$$\Pr(Y_i = 1) = \Pr(U_{1i} > U_{0i}) = \Pr(U_{0i} - U_{1i} < 0).$$

The functional form is derived by completing this calculation. Once we know the distribution for $(U_{0i} - U_{1i})$, the procedure is essentially the same as for the threshold model. The distribution of $(U_{0i} - U_{1i})$ is formed from the two distributions in Equation (5.8). If $U_{0i}$ and $U_{1i}$ follow a Weibull distribution (see Johnson and Kotz, 1970a: 250; Judge et al., 1985: 770), the distribution of the difference is logistic, and the resulting probability follows a logit functional form. On the other hand, if the two initial distributions are Normal, the difference is also Normal, and the functional form is a probit. Of course, the choice of the Weibull or Normal is based more on grounds of tractability (the distribution being closed or in closed-form under subtraction) than on substantive criteria. One could base these judgments more on political science theory, but building a plausible story is not always easy this far from the data.

*First principles of first principles*

The threshold justification for the logit and probit functional forms pushes the first principles back one step before the level presented in Section 5.1. The utility maximization justification goes back even another step. In principle, one could go back many more steps. The critical question, then, is when to stop.

For example, if a well informed voter in 1988 is choosing between George Bush and Michael Dukakis for president, then a utility maximization story is plausible: An individual might actually assign utilities to each option and then make a choice by maximizing his or her expected utility (Brady and Ansolabehere, 1988). But how are each of these individual utilities distributed? A reasonable choice of distribution could be made on the basis of a detailed knowledge of the types and qualities of Democratic and Republican presidents in general, an understanding of how voters perceive them, and how these two candidates are likely to handle the job. Selecting these two distributions would be difficult. The two distributions need not even be the same: Bush was vice-president at the time and thus the variance in expectations about how he would be as president in the future was reasonably low. On the other hand, Dukakis was neither president nor had ever held any federal office; exactly how he would perform in office was very unclear, campaign statements notwithstanding. Modeling this situation with Normal distributions that have different variances yields the same inferences as if the variances were equal. On the other hand, in a situation like this, we might consider using two different distributions.

However, consider the situation of whether or not a citizen is employed. Some of the observed state of employment may be an active choice of the individual, but much of it depends on the state of the economy or other factors. Thus, the idea of maximizing utility does not apply. In these cases, using a utility maximization scheme to derive a functional form goes artificially back beyond the substance of the research problem. Although one can technically derive a functional form from the initial distributions in these cases, an applied researcher would likely be more comfortable translating one's detailed political knowledge into a formal mathematical theory at a higher level of aggregation – either with the threshold model or at the level of the functional form itself. Thus, these alternative justifications can provide quite powerful methods in order to bring one considerably closer to the data and substantive theory, but an inappropriate use of them merely puts extraneous mathematical overhead between a scholar and his or her model. In the end, a researcher should choose a justification at a level closest to his or her substantive research problem. The availability of these three levels of first principle makes it much easier to do this in binary variable problems.

## 5.4 Ordered categorical variables

This section addresses the case of ordered polychotomous dependent variables. An example of ordinal variables is the very common seven point Likert scales, with categories from strongly agree to strongly disagree. These scales are typically analyzed by making the assumption that each of the six intervals is of equal length. The "solution" then is to merely number these from 1 to 7 and run a linear regression. Of course, if the equal interval assumption is incorrect, this procedure can give biased results (see Achen, 1988, for a deeper justification for this procedure based on a threshold model).

Instead of making these relatively strong equal interval assumptions, we can use a straightforward generalization of the binary threshold model. This procedure enables one to include a set of additional parameters representing the unobserved thresholds between the categories. The likelihood function can then be maximized with respect to the effect and threshold parameters simultaneously. The procedure, popularized by McKelvey and Zavoina (1975; see also Maddala, 1983: 46–9) is as follows.

Define a continuous stylized Normally distributed unobserved dependent variable, $Y^*$:

$$Y_i^* \sim f_{stn}(y_i^* | \mu_i)$$

with systematic component

$$\mu_i = x_i\beta. \tag{5.9}$$

Note that the realization $y_i^*$ is also unobserved and that choosing the stylized Normal distribution, rather than the Normal, does not change the substantive results. It is required to anchor the scale of $Y_i^*$ for identification purposes, just as in the binary threshold model (Section 5.3). Since the variance of $Y_i^*$ is 1.0, it may be interpreted in standard deviation units; for example, an increase of two points would be very large, covering about half the area. If this continuous unobserved dependent variable had more meaning in a particular case, $\sigma^2$ could be chosen on more substantive grounds.

Now define threshold parameters $\tau_j$, $j = 1, \ldots, m$, such that $\tau_1 = -\infty$, $\tau_m = \infty$, and

$$\tau_1 < \tau_2 < \ldots < \tau_m.$$

These parameters ($m-2$ of which are unknown) group $Y_i^*$ into $m$ categories. Although the realization $y_i^*$ is unobserved, we do observe which of the $m$ categories it belongs to. That is, $y_i^*$ belongs to category $j$ if

$$\tau_{j-1} < y_i^* \leq \tau_j, \qquad (j = 2, \ldots, m).$$

The observed realization is then defined for later convenience as a set of $m$ dichotomous variables as follows:

$$y_{ji} = \begin{cases} 1 & \text{if } \tau_{j-1} < y_i^* \leq \tau_j, \\ 0 & \text{otherwise} \end{cases}$$

for $j = 2, \ldots, m$ categories and $i = 1, \ldots, n$ observations. Thus, one and only one of these $m$ dichotomous variables equals 1 for each observation $i$.

The likelihood function may then be derived because the distribution of the continuous unobserved variable enables one to calculate the probability that $y_i^*$ will fall into category $j$:

$$\begin{aligned} \Pr(Y_{ji} = 1) &= \Pr(\tau_{j-1} < Y_i^* < \tau_j) \\ &= \int_{\tau_{j-1}}^{\tau_j} f_{stn}(y_i^* | \mu_i) dy_i^* \\ &= F_n(\tau_j | \mu_i, 1) - F_n(\tau_{j-1} | \mu_i, 1) \\ &= F_n(\tau_j | x_i\beta, 1) - F_n(\tau_{j-1} | x_i\beta, 1), \end{aligned}$$

where $F_n$ is the cumulative Normal distribution with variance 1, and the last line substitutes the right hand side of the systematic component in Equation (5.9) for $\mu_i$. The likelihood function for a single observation $i$ is the last line of this equation, but only for the correct category $j$. In other words, if $y_i^*$ fell into the first category, the likelihood should be proportional to the probability of only this event occurring. As a result, one could not just take the product of $\Pr(Y_{ji} = 1)$ over all $m$ categories and then over all $n$ observations. Instead, we use the dichotomous variables $y_{ji}$ to fit together a single equation expressing these ideas:

$$L(\tilde{\tau}, \tilde{\beta}|y) = \prod_{i=1}^{n} \left\{ \prod_{j=1}^{m} \left[ F_n(\tilde{\tau}_j | x_i \tilde{\beta}, 1) - F_n(\tilde{\tau}_{j-1} | x_i \tilde{\beta}, 1) \right]^{y_{ji}} \right\},$$

where $\tau$ is a vector of only threshold parameters that still need to be estimated $(\tau_2, \ldots, \tau_{m-1})$. Note that the term in braces is a single term equal to $\Pr(\tau_{j-1} < Y_i^* < \tau_j)$ for the category that $y_i^*$ falls into (i.e., for which $y_{ji} = 1$). The log-likelihood is then:

$$\ln L(\tilde{\tau}, \tilde{\beta}|y) = \sum_{i=1}^{n} \sum_{j=1}^{m} y_{ji} \ln \left[ F_n(\tilde{\tau}_j | x_i \tilde{\beta}, 1) - F_n(\tilde{\tau}_{j-1} | x_i \tilde{\beta}, 1) \right].$$

This function is then easily maximized to yield simultaneous estimates of the effect parameters $\beta$ and the $m-2$ threshold parameters $\tau$ that have the maximum relative likelihood of having generating the data.

## 5.5 Grouped uncorrelated binary variables

Suppose that instead of observing the realization of each binary random variable, as in Section 5.1, one only observed the realization of groups of independent binary variables. In this case, *each* observation $Y_i$ ($i = 1, \ldots, n$) represents the joint outcome of a *group* of $N$ individual binary variables. $Y_i$ therefore has nonzero probabilities only for the values $0, \ldots, N$. Furthermore, due to the critical assumption that the binary variables making up $Y_i$ are independent and identically Bernoulli distributed random variables, enough information exists to prove that $Y_i$ is distributed as a binomial random variable [see Equation (3.5)].

To build a statistical model of this sort of data generation process, I start with the single random observation, $Y_i$, and assume that it is distributed binomially,

$$Y_i \sim f_b(y_i | \pi_i),$$

and that $Y_i$ and $Y_j$ are independent (for all $i \neq j$). The stochastic component is then written as the product of the individual probability distributions:

$$\Pr(Y|\pi) = \prod_{i=1}^{n} f_b(y_i|\pi_i) \tag{5.10}$$

$$= \prod_{i=1}^{n} \frac{N!}{y_i!(N-y_i)!} \pi_i^{y_i}(1-\pi_i)^{N-y_i}.$$

Since $Y_i$ is binomially distributed,

$$E(Y_i) \equiv \mu_i = N\pi_i.$$

Since the $N$ individual binary variables that went into making up $Y_i$ each have expected value $\pi_i$, this result should not be surprising. We can think of modeling either the expected value $\mu_i$ directly, or $\pi_i$, but the model is essentially the same in either case. My preference is to opt for modeling $\pi_i$, since it focuses on the underlying processes that gave rise to this observed count. Modeling parameters, rather than expected values, is also a more general procedure.

Although $\pi$ includes unknown parameters, $N$ is usually known.[11] Thus, $N$ is considered known in the likelihood function. The preliminary log-likelihood then follows directly from Equation (5.10):

$$\ln L(\tilde{\pi}|y, n) = \sum_{i=1}^{n} \ln f_b(y_i|\tilde{\pi}_i, N)$$

$$= \sum_{i=1}^{n} \left\{ \ln\left(\frac{N!}{y_i!(N-y_i)!}\right) + y_i \ln(\tilde{\pi}_i) + (N-y_i)\ln(1-\tilde{\pi}) \right\}.$$

Since the first term in parentheses on the right hand side in the second line of this equation is constant for all values of $\tilde{\pi}$, it makes no contribution to *relative* values of the log-likelihood. I therefore drop it and represent the preliminary log-likelihood as

$$\ln L(\tilde{\pi}|y, N) = \sum_{i=1}^{n} \{ y_i \ln(\tilde{\pi}_i) + (N-y_i)\ln(1-\tilde{\pi}_i) \}. \tag{5.11}$$

The systematic component of a grouped independent binary variable is very similar to the model for binary variables discussed in the Section 5.1. The reason is that the same parameter $\pi_i$ is being modeled and is thus still bounded between zero and one. Indeed, although the data differ, the underlying process being modeled is virtually the same as in the binary logit case. Hence, we can apply the logit functional form of Equation (5.2). Though this logit form is still a function of $\pi_i$, it is no longer equal to the expected value,

$$\pi_i = [1 + \exp(-x_i\beta)]^{-1}, \tag{5.12}$$

although an obvious relationship does exist: $E(Y_i)/N = \pi_i$. I therefore reparameterize by substituting the logit functional form in Equation (5.2) into the log-likelihood in Equation (5.11).

$$\ln L(\tilde{\beta}|y, n) = \sum_{i=1}^{n} \left\{ y_i \ln\left[1 + \exp(-x_i\tilde{\beta})\right]^{-1} \right.$$

---

[11] $N$ could easily be estimated from the data as well, but this is generally unnecessary.

$$+ (N - y_i) \ln \left[ 1 - [1 + \exp(-x_i\tilde{\beta})]^{-1} \right] \Big\}$$
$$= \sum_{i=1}^{n} \left\{ -y_i \ln \left[ 1 + \exp(-x_i\tilde{\beta}) \right] - (N - y_i) \ln \left[ 1 + \exp(x_i\tilde{\beta}) \right] \right\}.$$

Note how similar this log-likelihood is to that for ungrouped binary outcomes in Equation (5.5). In fact, for one independent binary variable ($N = 1$), this equation reduces exactly to Equation (5.5). This log-likelihood is easily maximized with numerical methods, and parameter interpretation is the same as in the binary logit model. Indeed, the beauty of this model is that one can estimate features of the unobserved binary variables while observing only the aggregate count.

## 5.6 Grouped correlated binary variables

The stochastic model introduced in the previous section is quite useful in many circumstances when modeling groups of binary variables. In other situations, the assumptions of the binomial distribution may be too restrictive. For example, each binomially distributed observation is built on a series of $N$ *independent* and *identically distributed* binary variables. In many cases, these twin critical assumptions are implausible.

For example, suppose one had data on the number of members of the Senate Judiciary Committee voting for presidential nominees to the Supreme Court. In these data, each senator's vote is a binary variable. However, the *observed* random variable is a count of "ayes" ranging from 0 to $N$ senators for each observation $i$ (the committee size, $N$, is usually about 15). The binomial distribution assumes that each senator makes up his or her mind independently. However, due to cue-taking and other typical patterns of influence on the committee, assuming independence is quite unrealistic. Furthermore, assuming that each member of the committee has the same underlying probability $\pi$ of voting for the nominee ignores the typically fundamental divisions among senators along partisan, regional, and ideological lines.

For situations such as these, researchers need a different stochastic model. Although designed for other purposes, a variety of appropriate probability distributions have been derived and could be combined with the statistical models discussed here (see Haseman and Kupper, 1979). More recently, Prentice (1986) derived an even more general distribution. This *extended beta-binomial* distribution allows for both dependence among the unobserved random binary variables, and heterogeneity in $\pi$ across these variables.[12] Hence, I assume that

$$Y_i \sim f_{ebb}(y_i | \pi_i, \gamma),$$

---

[12] Prentice's extended beta-binomial distribution is a conceptual rather than algebraic extension of the beta-binomial distribution. See Heckman and Willis (1977).

where the complete extended beta-binomial distribution is defined in Equation (3.9).

Although individual senators may not vote independently, committee decisions on different nominees are still assumed independent. Put differently, $Y_i$ and $Y_j$ are independent for all $i \neq j$. As a result, the full stochastic component is just the product, from $i = 1$ to $n$, of the component for each observation in Equation (3.9). Thus, by then substituting the logistic form in Equation (5.12) for each occurrence of $\pi_i$, I write the full stochastic component of this statistical model as follows:

$$
\begin{aligned}
\Pr(Y = y \mid \beta, \gamma, N) = \prod_{i=1}^{n} & \left( \frac{N!}{y_i!(N - y_i)!} \right) \\
& \times \prod_{j=0}^{y_i - 1} \left\{ [1 + \exp(-x_i\beta)]^{-1} + \gamma j \right\} \\
& \times \prod_{j=0}^{N - y_i - 1} \left\{ [1 + \exp(x_i\beta)]^{-1} + \gamma j \right\} \Big/ \prod_{j=0}^{N-1} (1 + \gamma j).
\end{aligned}
$$

The complete likelihood of the parameters $\tilde{\beta}$ and $\tilde{\gamma}$ given the data is then proportional to this equation. The log-likelihood is then:

$$
\begin{aligned}
\ln L(\tilde{\beta}, \tilde{\gamma} \mid y) = \sum_{i=1}^{n} \Bigg\{ & \ln\left( \frac{N!}{y_i!(N - y_i)!} \right) \\
& + \sum_{j=0}^{y_i - 1} \ln \left\{ [1 + \exp(-x_i\tilde{\beta})]^{-1} + \gamma j \right\} \\
& + \sum_{j=0}^{N - y_i - 1} \ln \left\{ [1 + \exp(x_i\tilde{\beta})]^{-1} + \tilde{\gamma} j \right\} - \sum_{j=0}^{N-1} \ln(1 + \tilde{\gamma} j) \Bigg\}.
\end{aligned}
$$

Since the first term is a function of neither $\tilde{\beta}$ nor $\tilde{\gamma}$, it again has no influence on relative values of the likelihood. I therefore rewrite this equation as

$$
\begin{aligned}
\ln L(\tilde{\beta}, \tilde{\gamma} \mid y) = \sum_{i=1}^{n} \Bigg\{ & \sum_{j=0}^{y_i - 1} \ln \left\{ [1 + \exp(-x_i\tilde{\beta})]^{-1} + \gamma j \right\} \\
& + \sum_{j=0}^{N - y_i - 1} \ln \left\{ [1 + \exp(x_i\tilde{\beta})]^{-1} + \tilde{\gamma} j \right\} - \sum_{j=0}^{N-1} \ln(1 + \tilde{\gamma} j) \Bigg\}
\end{aligned}
\tag{5.13}
$$

This equation appears more complicated than others I have considered, but it is really only *algebraically* complicated. *Conceptually,* the only difference is that this log-likelihood is a function of the effect parameters $\beta$ and an ancillary parameter $\gamma$. For ML estimation, only a conceptual distinction exists between these two types of parameters. In practice, one maximizes $\ln L(\tilde{\beta}, \tilde{\gamma} \mid y)$ with respect to both $\tilde{\beta}$ and $\tilde{\gamma}$, as if $\tilde{\gamma}$ were another element of the $\beta$ vector. The origin of the right hand side of Equation (5.13) is critical – allowing several types of relationships among the elementary binary variables that are aggregated into $Y_i$ – but the algebraic details can be considered as a black box, producing values of the relative likelihood of a hypothesized model.

How should one choose between the binomial and the extended beta-binomial models? The answer lies in the tradeoff between restrictive and non-restrictive models discussed in Section 2.5. The binomial model has one fewer parameter, so the effect parameters $\beta$ may be estimated more precisely. In addition, estimates from using a binomial distribution have the desirable property of consistency, even if the true distribution is the extended beta-binomial. However, these estimates are sometimes substantially inefficient, and the standard errors are biased.[13] For the complete ML result, this binomial model is inevitably more restrictive, requiring an assumption of independence among the unobserved binary variables. If independence were implausible, the extended beta-binomial model would be preferable. Unfortunately, since the same data must now be used to estimate an ancillary parameter too, the precision with which the effect parameters are estimated is accordingly less.[14]

An alternative, more data analytic, approach is to estimate both models and assess the estimated value of $\gamma$, the likelihood ratio, and differences in the parameter estimates. If the two sets of estimates provide substantively different results, the extended beta-binomial model is to be preferred. Or, one could just estimate the extended beta-binomial model and examine $\hat{\gamma}$ and the corresponding curvature of the likelihood function. If $\hat{\gamma}$ is near zero, dropping back to the more restrictive binomial model may be worthwhile.

If the data already provide an insufficient degree of precision, then the choice is difficult. If sufficient data exist, then the extended beta-binomial model is probably safer. However, more than just safety comes from applying this model. The ancillary parameter $\gamma$ may, in some cases, provide critical substantive information in understanding what drives one's observed data.

## 5.7    Counts of uncorrelated events

Another type of discrete random variable is an *event count*. Examples of event counts include the number of cooperative and conflictual international incidents (Azar and Sloan, 1975), the number of triplets born in Norway in each

---

[13] Except that the estimator is inefficient, one could use the binomial model for parameter estimates and then attempt to take into account the over- or underdispersion in estimating the standard errors. This is essentially the strategy of McCullagh and Nelder (1983). They provide a method of calculating a separate estimate of the dispersion parameter from the residuals of the first stage analysis. One could also use White's (1980) heteroscedasticity-consistent standard errors. This two stage strategy is probably best when the data include many observations and efficiency is not as much of a worry. See also Allison (1987).

[14] In the extremely unusual situation where one knows the correlation among the elementary binary variables, $\gamma$ could be fixed and the effect parameters $\beta$ could be estimated with the same precision as in the binomial model.

half-decade (El-Sayyad, 1973), the annual number of presidential appointments to the Supreme Court (King, 1987a), the number of coups d'etat in black African states (Johnson, Slater, and McGowan, 1984), and the number of medical consultations for each survey respondent (Cameron and Trivedi, 1986). For each of these examples, the upper limit on the number of observed events is theoretically infinite.

One can think of event counts formally in one of two ways. In one, they represent the outcome of an infinitely large group of binary variables, where an "event" is the probability of a designated outcome from each binary variable. However, identifying the list of separate random variables is problematic even in theory; we can count the number of coups d'etat in a year, but even conceiving of a list of potential random coup/no coup situations is improbable.

Alternatively, imagine a social system that produces events randomly during some fixed period. At the end of the period, only the total count of these events is observed. The data include $n$ such periods, with an observed count, $y_1, \ldots, y_n$, at the end of each. Although it remains unobserved the underlying process that drives each observed count may be of considerable substantive importance. Indeed, by making only two critical assumptions about this process (and two additional minor assumptions detailed in Chapter 3), one can derive a formal probability distribution. First, I assume that during each observation period $i$, the *rate* of event occurrence $\lambda_i$ remains constant. In other words, the occurrence or nonoccurrence of events during the observation period has no influence on $\lambda_i$. For example, if a single coup d'etat encouraged coups in neighboring states, this assumption would not hold. Second, I assume that the probability of two events occurring at precisely the same instant is very close to zero. This second assumption is more of a technical than substantive requirement.

An event count is the aggregation of this underlying process. Event counts that result from processes meeting these two assumptions are distributed according to the *Poisson distribution*. For a single observation, the Poisson distribution appears in Equation (3.15). For all $n$ observations, the stochastic component may be written as the product of these individual distributions:

$$\Pr(Y|\lambda) = \prod_{i=1}^{n} \frac{e^{-\lambda_i}\lambda_i^{y_i}}{y_i!}. \tag{5.14}$$

To derive the systemic component, first note that the rate of event occurrence during the observation period, $\lambda_i$, is also the expected count at the end of the period, $E(Y_i) = \lambda_i$ (as was demonstrated in Chapter 3). Since $Y_i$ is always positive, so as $\lambda_i$. Whereas $\pi_i$ in the logistic functional form is bounded from below (0) and above (1), $\lambda_i$ is bounded only from below (0). Thus a

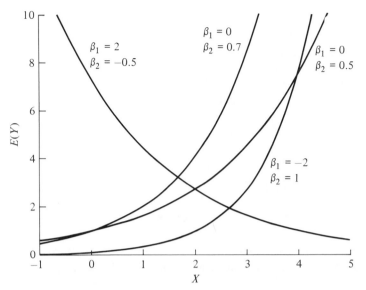

Figure 5.3. Exponential curves.

logit function is inappropriate here. Indeed, a linear form is also inappropriate, since it would not constrain the expected number of events $\lambda_i$ to be positive. I therefore limit $g(\cdot, \cdot)$ to the class of positive valued functions. To narrow this class to a uniquely appropriate function, I reason backward from what the instantaneous effect of $X_j$ on $\lambda_i$, $(\partial\lambda_i/\partial X_j)$, should be. I have already established that this effect should not be $\beta_j$, since that would imply a linear function and would leave open the possibility of the expected number of events being less than zero. Instead, I propose that the simplest and most reasonable effect is $\beta_j\lambda_i$, so that a fixed change in $X_j$ would have a greater effect on the expected value if the expected value were larger. In other words, this specification indicates that the "effort" (in terms of a change in $X_j$) that it would take to move $Y_i$ from 0 to 1 should be proportionally greater than the effort required to move $Y_i$ from (say) 20 to 21. If $\beta_j\lambda_i$ is the appropriate effect, then the functional form is

$$E(Y_i) \equiv \lambda_i = \exp(x_i\beta),\tag{5.15}$$

using the fact that the exponential is the only function that is its own derivative. Although other functions exist that would restrict the expected value to be positive, few *also* have plausible effects. By simultaneously applying both of these criteria, I am led to this particular function. Exponentiation is also most commonly used with the Poisson distribution.

Figure 5.3 portrays several examples of how this curve gets steeper as

$\lambda_i \equiv E(Y_i)$ gets larger. It also makes apparent how the zero bound on the predicted number of events "bends" the curve up from the bottom. Indeed, this form is both intuitively and mathematically the bottom half of the logit curve with no upper limit.

To derive the full log-likelihood, I substitute the functional form in Equation (5.15) into the probability distribution in Equation (5.14) and take logs:

$$\ln L(\tilde{\beta}|y) = \sum_{i=1}^{n} \{(x_i\tilde{\beta})y_i - \exp(x_i\tilde{\beta}) - \ln y_i!\}.$$

Since the last term is not a function of $\tilde{\beta}$, it has no effect on relative values of the likelihood and may be dropped:

$$\ln L(\tilde{\beta}|y) = \sum_{i=1}^{n} \{(x_i\tilde{\beta})y_i - \exp(x_i\tilde{\beta})\}. \tag{5.16}$$

This globally concave log-likelihood may be maximized easily with numerical methods. An empirical example appears in the Section 5.9.[15]

## 5.8    Counts of uncorrelated events with unequal observation intervals

Consider now a situation where the number of possible events $N$ was not infinite, but nevertheless the expected value $\lambda_i$ came nowhere near this upper bound. For example, the expected number of members of the House of Representatives who switch political parties each year is generally very small. If a maximum of one switch per member is counted in any year, the upper limit $N_i$ is the number of members of the House – a quantity that has varied considerably over the last two centuries. Since the upper bound is approximated with only extremely small probability, the stochastic component remains based on the Poisson distribution. In addition, the lack of an effective upper bound means that the functional form need not change to a logit (see King, 1988a; King and Benjamin, 1985).

Nevertheless, $N_i$ is a variable that might generally influence the level of the expected value, $\lambda_i$. In order to divide out this value, one might want to change the functional form in Equation (5.15) to this:

$$\frac{E(Y_i)}{N_i} = \exp(x_i\beta). \tag{5.17}$$

Or, equivalently, one could write Equation 5.17 as

[15] In King (1988a), I provide a more detailed analysis of this estimator. I also demonstrate the substantial biases in linear regression and other common procedures with data such as these.

$$E(Y_i) = \exp(x_i\beta + \ln N_i). \tag{5.18}$$

This latter expression implies that the log of $N_i$ be included as an explanatory probability, with its coefficient constrained to 1.0.[16] For later reference, note that the log-likelihood for this alternative model is as follows:

$$\ln L(\tilde{\beta}|y) = \sum_{i=1}^{n} \{-\tilde{\lambda}_i + y_i \ln \tilde{\lambda}_i - \ln y_i!\} \tag{5.19}$$

$$= \sum_{i=1}^{n} \{-e^{x_i\tilde{\beta} + \ln N_i} + y_i(x_i\tilde{\beta} + \ln N) - \ln y_i!\}$$

$$= \sum_{i=1}^{n} \{y_i(x_i\tilde{\beta}) - N_i e^{x_i\tilde{\beta}}\},$$

where, in the last line, $\ln(y_i!)$ is dropped because it does not vary with $\tilde{\beta}$.

This procedure has been suggested before (Maddala, 1983: 53), but we can now develop a more fundamental justification for it by conceptualizing this problem in a slightly different manner. Instead of thinking of limiting the theoretical value of the maximum count, one can think of allowing the time interval in which events are accumulated and counted to vary. For example, suppose we counted the number of wars in which each nation of the world has been involved. A good stochastic model of this variation would need to take into account how long each nation was in existence. Although a variable maximum count and variable time interval are substantively different social processes, there is no reason to model them any differently.

Nevertheless, consider how one might derive a direct stochastic model for the process generating these data. The answer can be found in Chapter 3, where, during the derivation of the Poisson distribution, the penultimate result included a variable $t$, the length of time in the interval [Equation (3.14)]. At the conclusion of the proof, $t$ was set to one for the final form of the distribution [Equation (3.15)], but this step is not required if information on $t$ exists. In fact, if we add a subscript $i$, allowing $t_i$ to vary over observations, the full stochastic model can easily be written:

$$f_{pt}(y|\lambda, t) = \prod_{i=1}^{n} \frac{e^{-\lambda_i t_i}(\lambda_i t_i)^{y_i}}{y_i!}.$$

One can assign to $t_i$ the number of years since independence for country $i$ in the example above. The log-likelihood is derived by taking the logarithms of this equation and substituting $\exp(x_i\beta)$ for each occurrence of $\lambda_i$:

---

[16] As a somewhat more general control, one would include an additional parameter and estimate it like the other elements of $\beta$ (see Maddala, 1983: 53).

$$\ln L(\tilde{\beta}|y) = \sum_{i=1}^{n} \{ -\tilde{\lambda}_i t_i + y_i \ln(\tilde{\lambda}_i t_i) - \ln(y_i!) \} \tag{5.20}$$

$$= \sum_{i=1}^{n} \{ -e^{x_i\tilde{\beta}} t_i + y_i \ln(e^{x_i\tilde{\beta}} t_i) - \ln(y_i!) \}$$

$$= \sum_{i=1}^{n} \{ y_i(x_i\tilde{\beta}) - t_i e^{x_i\tilde{\beta}} \},$$

where, in the last line, $\ln(y_i!)$ is dropped because it does not vary with $\tilde{\beta}$.

The surprise in Equation (5.20) is its equivalence to the last line in Equation (5.19), with $t_i = N_i$. This stochastic modeling effort provides a more fundamental justification for the procedure of explicitly controlling for the maximum count, $N_i$. It also demonstrates the formal equivalence of variable maximum counts and variable time intervals. Finally, and perhaps most importantly, this example reemphasizes the idea that the stochastic component is as least as important as the systematic component; this feature of the underlying process generating observed data in this example can be modeled with either, resulting in exactly the same empirical result.[17]

### 5.9    Counts of correlated events

Just as grouped binary variables may deviate from independence, so too can event counts. Indeed, assuming that the social system produces events independently may not be appropriate for many interesting research situations. For example, consider a count of the number of news stories about a candidate. Many of the stories that go into this count are probably generated from the earlier stories of competing news organizations. A situation such as this results in overdispersion, just as it did for grouped binary variables.

One way to think about a deviation from independence among the individual events is to observe its effect on the variance of the event count. In general, let the variance of $Y_i$, given $X$, be written as

$$V(Y_i) = \lambda_i \sigma^2 \tag{5.21}$$

for $\lambda_i > 0$ and $\sigma^2 > 0$. $\lambda_i$ is the expected value of $Y_i$ and $\sigma^2$ is an ancillary parameter. The key feature of the Poisson distribution is that independence among events implies that $\sigma^2 = 1$ (which makes the variance of $Y_i$ equal to the expected value of $Y_i$). When events are correlated, or when the rate of event occurrence $\lambda$ is heterogeneous, overdispersion in $Y_i$ implies that $\sigma^2 > 1$. Con-

---

[17] Other modifications can also be made such as this one. For example, a modified Poisson distribution permits one to model situations where measurement error exists only between zero and one count (as is often the case in international event count data, for example). See Haight (1967) for other possibilities.

versely, negatively correlated events result in underdispersion, the situation when $\sigma^2 < 1$.

Whereas the Poisson distribution models independence among the individual events, one can model underdispersion with the *continuous parameter binomial* and overdispersion with the *negative binomial* probability distributions (see Chapter 3 and King, in press-a). Instead of presenting models based on these individual distributions, I use a more general solution. A theoretical result by Katz (1965) has established a certain relationship among these distributions, and, in King (in press-a), I use this result to derive a new single probability distribution that encompasses overdispersion, underdispersion, and independence. Although algebraically more complicated than other distributions discussed here, what I call the *generalized event count* distribution has only one ancillary parameter and is as conceptually simple as the extended beta-binomial distribution for grouped binary variables. Since I derived it elsewhere, I omit the derivation here.

Accordingly, I assume that $Y_i$ is distributed as a generalized event count random variable:

$$Y_i \sim f_{gec}(y_i | \lambda_i, \sigma^2),$$

where the full probability distribution is written as follows:

$$\Pr(Y_i = y_i | \lambda_i, \sigma^2) \equiv f_{gec}(y_i | \lambda_i, \sigma^2)$$

$$= \begin{cases} \Pr(y_i = 0 | \lambda_i, \sigma^2) \, \Pi_{j=1}^{y_i} \left[ \frac{\lambda_i + (\sigma^2 - 1)(j-1)}{j\sigma^2} \right] & \text{for } y_i = 1, 2, 3, \ldots, \\ e^{-\lambda_i} & \text{for } y_i = 0 \text{ and } \sigma^2 = 1, \\ (\sigma^2)^{-\lambda_i/(\sigma^2 - 1)} & \text{for } y_i = 0 \text{ and } \sigma^2 > 1, \\ (\sigma^2)^{-\lambda_i/(\sigma^2 - 1)}/D_i & \text{for } y_i = 0 \text{ and } 0 < \sigma^2 < 1, \\ 0 & \text{otherwise}, \end{cases}$$

$$(5.22)$$

where $D_i$ is the sum of a binomial distribution from $m = 1$ to $[-\lambda_i/(\sigma^2 - 1)] + 1$, and if $\sigma^2 < 1$ the probability of $Y_i$ being greater than $[-\lambda_i/(\sigma^2 - 1)] + 1$ is zero. Since the values of $y_i$ for which $f(y_i) > 0$ depend on the parameters, the first regularity condition in Section 4.4 does not hold. As a result, one cannot automatically assume that all the desirable properties of ML point estimates apply. This estimator would still provide the maximum likelihood estimates, but consistency and other properties are not guaranteed without further analysis. However, one can still prove consistency even given these nonstandard conditions.

To calculate probabilities from this distribution for $Y_i = 0$, one only needs to use the appropriate line from among the last four in Equation (5.22) depending on the value of $\sigma^2$. To calculate the probability for any larger value of $Y_i$, the probability that $Y_i$ is zero, $\Pr(Y_i = 0 | \lambda, \sigma^2)$, must be multiplied by the second term on the first line.[18]

This procedure for calculating probabilities should be viewed as merely a technical complication. This is still a traditional probability, where the probability of $Y_i$ taking on any value $y_i$ may be calculated, given values of the two parameters $\lambda$ and $\sigma^2$. The key intuition behind this distribution is that the variance of $Y_i$ is given in the general form in Equation (5.21). When events are independent, $\sigma^2 = 1$ and Equation (5.22) reduces exactly to the Poisson distribution [Equation (3.15)]. When events are correlated or expected values heterogeneous, $Y_i$, is overdispersed, $\sigma^2 > 1$, and Equation (5.2) reduces to the negative binomial distribution [Equation (3.17)]. Finally, when events are negatively correlated, $Y_i$ is underdispersed, $\sigma^2 < 1$, and Equation (5.21) reduces to the continuous parameter binomial (not shown; see King, in press a).

Since the expected value of $Y_i$ is still $\lambda_i$, the same functional form in Equation (5.15) is still appropriate. The log-likelihood is then the log of the product (from $i = 1$ to $n$) of Equation (5.21). Dropping terms that do not depend on $\beta$ or $\sigma^2$, this may be written as follows:

$$\ln L(\beta, \sigma^2 | y) = \sum_{i=1}^{n} \left\{ C_i - y_i \ln(\sigma^2) + \sum_{j=1}^{y_i} \ln \left[ \exp(x_i \beta) + (\sigma^2 - 1)(j - 1) \right] \right\},$$

where

$$C_i = \begin{cases} -\exp(x_i \beta) & \text{for } \sigma^2 = 1, \\ -\exp(x_i \beta)\ln(\sigma^2)(\sigma^2 - 1)^{-1} & \text{for } \sigma^2 > 1, \\ -\exp(x_i \beta)\ln(\sigma^2)(\sigma^2 - 1)^{-1} - \ln(D_i) & \text{for } 0 < \sigma^2 < 1. \end{cases}$$

With numerical methods, this equation may be maximized with respect to $\beta$ and $\sigma^2$ just like any other log-likelihood.

How should one proceed when the degree of over- or underdispersion is unknown? The problem is analogous to the one in choosing between the binomial and extended beta-binomial. The Poisson distribution produces consistent estimates, even if the generalized event count distribution is correct; however the estimates will be inefficient and the standard errors biased. On the other hand, the generalized event count distribution is less restrictive but puts more demands on existing data, requiring the estimation of an additional parameter. In practice, the choice ought to be made as much as possible on the basis of theory. Failing that, one could estimate both models and examine

---

[18] Since

$$\lim_{\sigma^2 \to 1} (\sigma^2)^{-\lambda_i/(\sigma^2 - 1)} = e^{-\lambda_i}$$

the distribution is continuous in both $\sigma^2$ and $\lambda$.

the differences, or just estimate the generalized event count model and test the hypothesis that $\sigma^2 = 1$. See Lee (1986) for other specification tests for Poisson regression models.[19]

As an example, consider the number of U.S. presidential vetoes that Congress challenges each year. Some of these challenges successfully overturn presidential vetoes; others do not. However, each challenge is a significant event in American national politics and executive–legislative relations. Only 16.56 occur on average each year. The original data are reported in King and Ragsdale (1988).[20] I include three explanatory variables: Election year (coded one for presidential election years and zero otherwise), Congress (coded as the percent of both houses of Congress who are members of the president's party), and Approval (the average annual percent of the public approving of the president). Theory suggests that fewer congressional challenges should occur during election years, when the president has many members of his party in Congress, and when public approval of the president is relatively high. Since the number of vetoes per year provides a theoretical maximum on annual veto challenges, I also include the natural log of the number of vetoes.

The key question for present purposes is the underlying process that generates the annual number of congressional challenges. If one were to collect data on individual challenges, this process could be modeled in the systematic component of the statistical model, but in the available data this process remains unobserved. Nevertheless, one can still theorize and test hypotheses about it. The basic Poisson model is appropriate if the generation of one challenge has no influence on subsequent challenges. Since challenges are major events in U.S. politics, independence is probably not a reasonable assumption. Indeed, since each congressional challenge involves a substantial amount of political organization and lobbying efforts among both the president's friends and enemies, individual challenges are likely to be spread out. Thus, a negative contagion seems probable: one challenge reduces the prob-

[19] In Footnote 13, I discuss an alternative to choosing between the binomial and extended beta-binomial distributions when many observations are available. McCullagh and Nelder (1983: 131–3) suggest that the same approach can be taken with event count data and provide a means of estimating the dispersion parameter from the Poisson residuals. They also suggest that this dispersion parameter may be used to correct an initial estimate of the Poisson standard errors. However, in King (in press-a), I demonstrate for small samples that, although this separate estimate of $\sigma^2$ is consistent and only modestly inefficient, the correct Poisson standard errors still substantially underestimate the true standard errors.

[20] A congressional challenge is defined as any veto for which at least one house of Congress held a formal roll call vote attempting to overturn the veto. A roll call vote is usually held if the issue has some reasonable chance of passing, although many challenges are not successful (see King and Ragsdale, 1988).

Table 5.5. *Models of congressional veto challenges*

| Variable | Poisson estimate | S.e. | GEC estimate | S.e. | Poisson s.e. ÷ GEC s.e. |
|---|---|---|---|---|---|
| Constant | 0.516 | 1.888 | 0.838 | 0.211 | 8.95 |
| ln(Vetoes) | 0.888 | 0.351 | 0.847 | 0.034 | 10.23 |
| Election year | −0.050 | 0.577 | −0.077 | 0.083 | 6.95 |
| Congress | −0.009 | 0.026 | −0.011 | 0.004 | 5.50 |
| Approval | −0.005 | 0.022 | −0.007 | 0.003 | 8.67 |
| $\sigma^2$ | | | 0.121 | 0.043 | |

*Note:* Poisson log-likelihood = 605.11. GEC log-likelihood = 621.35.

ability of another challenge during the next interval of time. The statistical description of this substantive political process is underdispersion, $\sigma^2 < 1$.

To demonstrate the effects of too narrowly specifying the statistical model, Table 5.5 presents both the Poisson and generalized event count (GEC) estimators. The estimated effect parameters for both models are quite similar. I use the GEC model for the following interpretation. Additional vetoes permit more challenges. Using the derivative interpretation of these effects, presidential election years have about $0.077 \times 16.56 = 1.27$ fewer challenges than other years. For each ten percent increase in members of the president's party, Congress challenges about $0.11 \times 16.56 = 1.82$ fewer presidential vetoes. And for each additional ten percent of the public who approve of the way the president is handling the job, $0.07 \times 16.56 = 1.16$ fewer vetoes are challenged.

Although generally in accord with what one might expect from theory, the Poisson model indicates that these effects are quite imprecise. The Wald statistic (estimate/s.e.) indicates very high traditional probabilities that these data were drawn from a population where all the coefficients are really zero. Except for ln(Vetoes), these probabilities are all above 0.72. These results would cause most traditional investigators to conclude that challenges are some kind of random process, to drop these variables and add different ones, or to just give up the project entirely.

However, a more interesting stochastic model of the process generating congressional challenges to presidential vetoes yields very different substantive conclusions. Since $\sigma^2$ is precisely estimated to be substantially less than one, the underdispersion hypothesis is clearly confirmed. Either a Wald test of the $\sigma^2$ estimate or a likelihood ratio test for the difference between the two models confirms the substantial improvement to be gained by moving to the more realistic GEC model. In addition, although the coefficients are similar to those obtained from the Poisson model, their standard errors are strikingly smaller. A comparison of the standard errors in the last column of Table 5.5 indicates that by allowing the model to be underdispersed, the resulting standard errors are between 5.5 and 10.23 times smaller than under the Poisson model.

Whereas an analysis with only the Poisson model would have led most researchers to draw conclusions about the absence of empirical effects, the generalized event count model was able to extract significantly more information from the same data. Some of the improved information came from more precise estimates of the effect parameters. But additional information about the underlying process generating congressional challenges to presidential vetoes was also made available with this method. As this example demonstrates, these points are not merely technical qualifications; they permit one to extract considerably more information from existing data and to more creatively and appropriately model interesting processes.

## 5.10  Concluding remarks

By directly estimating the models discussed in this chapter, one can also appeal to some results on robust statistics. For example, estimators of the Poisson and binomial parameters are consistent even if the true distribution is not the one specified, but is within what is called the linear exponential family of distributions. However, under these conditions, standard errors will still be biased and the estimates inefficient.

A different category of robust results proffers new nonML estimators, with weaker regularity conditions and more general distributional assumptions (see McCullagh and Nelder, 1983). For example, Gourieroux, Monfort, and Trognon (1984) have developed a three stage robust estimator for event count data. What they call a "quasi-generalized pseudo-maximum likelihood" (QGPML) estimator permits one to avoid certain distributional assumptions and retain consistency as well as certain other desirable properties.[21] However, the technique necessarily puts more demands on the data – estimating what is assumed in more standard ML estimators. Put in the notation of Section 2.5, QGPML moves some elements from $\mathcal{M}^*$ to $\theta$; as usual, the model is more realistic, but only at some cost in the precision with which $\theta$ is estimated. Hence, for a given set of data, the variance of the QGPML estimator is necessarily larger than that of the standard ML estimator.

Many other discrete regression models exist and many others could be sug-

---

[21] The procedure requires first the consistent estimation of $\beta$, usually from the Poisson model. Then one must calculate a consistent estimate of $\sigma^2$, usually from the Poisson residuals. Finally, one substitutes these estimates into parts of a distribution in the linear exponential family, like the negative binomial, and maximizes with respect to the remaining $\beta$ parameters.

gested. Those presented here include an important class of models, representing a set of interesting political science processes. For a variety of other interesting and related discrete and limited dependent variable regression models, see Maddala (1983) and Manski and McFadden (1982), as well as the next chapter. One potential difficulty in future research is the specification of mathematically intractable, but substantively plausible, stochastic models. For example, suppose in the analysis of overdispersed event counts one wanted to let the Poisson parameter $\lambda$ vary according to a log-Normal, instead of gamma, distribution. The resulting distribution cannot be written in closed form due to an intractable integration, but the likelihood function can still be evaluated, and parameters estimated, with numerical methods. For a discussion of this and other similar models, see Schoenberg (1985).

# CHAPTER 6

# Models for tabular data

A special type of discrete regression model is particularly useful when the dependent and explanatory variables all happen to be categorical. In this case, the data may be cross-classified, presented, and analyzed in familiar tabular form. An example appears in Table 6.1.

Although countless contingency tables have been presented and analyzed in the social science literature, few represent the original or natural form of the data. Hence, since the object of the analysis is usually to model the process by which the social system generates the observed data, a table is probably the wrong initial representation. It may be a useful method of presentation, particularly as a different kind of descriptive statistic, but in many cases the data were not generated as a table.

Nevertheless, models of tabular data are justifiable in at least four special instances. First, a few types of data do appear more natural in this form, such as occupational mobility tables (see Hout, 1983). Second, other data appear first or only in this form, such as when published in journal articles and books. If the original data are not accessible, only methods based on tabular data make further analysis possible. This tendency of authors to report tabular data, and of journal editors to permit their publication, is in contrast to almost every other form of political science data. Since many authors neither provide sufficient information so that another researcher could collect exactly the same data nor archive their data for use by others, more use of formal models of tabular data can increase at least the possibility of replication in the social sciences – a desirable goal that has been achieved far too infrequently (Ceci and Walker, 1983; Dewald, Thursby, and Anderson, 1986). By maintaining the distinction between the way the data are presented and the underlying data generation process, valuable information can still be extracted from tabular data.[1]

---

[1] When I teach this material, I usually have each student find a contingency table in some political science journal. They are then instructed to reanalyze the table with the methods of this chapter, attempting to extract more information from the data than the author of the original article. Since the dominant method of contingency table analysis is still only percentage calculation, usually more than half the students learn more from the reanalysis than from merely reading the text of the original article. When the students' brief papers are complete, I assign Dewald, Thursby,

Table 6.1. *Frequencies of grades by intelligence, effort, and social class*

| Social class | Effort | Intelligence | High grades | Low grades |
|---|---|---|---|---|
| Middle | High | High | 60 | 20 |
| Middle | High | Low | 40 | 24 |
| Middle | Low | High | 40 | 24 |
| Middle | Low | Low | 24 | 12 |
| Lower | High | High | 40 | 16 |
| Lower | High | Low | 6 | 32 |
| Lower | Low | High | 18 | 38 |
| Lower | Low | Low | 2 | 54 |

Third, a few data sets are so large that even present day computational facilities fall short. The leading example is individual level census data. Fortunately, asymptotically equivalent statistical analyses can be performed on the much more parsimonious tabular form. As long as we concentrate on the underlying process, rather than the table itself, models for tabular data can be a valuable and convenient alternative to reconstructing the original data.

Finally, if all variables are categorical, and a few other key assumptions hold, the tabular form is a complete summary of the original data. Since in these cases, the original data may be completely reconstructed from a table, no information is lost. Of course, if some of the explanatory variables were originally continuous (such as income) but were collapsed into categories (such as poor and nonpoor), the table would be an incomplete, and potentially biased, representation of the original data (see Bishop, Fienberg, and Holland, 1975: 47). This is a very important point, since it implies that one should almost never collapse continuous variables merely to use these methods. Instead, one should apply the corresponding individual level methods of the other chapters in Part II of this book. Other cases when the table is not a sufficient form are discussed below.

In this chapter, I analyze four common models of tabular data: *logit, log-proportion, linear-proportion,* and *log-frequency.* These models are often presented and interpreted in ways that do not emphasize their common features, but, as I demonstrate below, they are all special cases of the framework presented in Equations (1.3) and (1.4), and all closely resemble the models in Chapter 5.[2]

and Anderson (1986), or another work on replication, give each student's paper to a different student, and have them replicate each other's replication. In this second round, usually about a third of the class finds something that either the author of the original article, or the first student, missed.

[2] Parts of the following presentation can be incorporated into the *generalized linear model* framework summarized in McCullagh and Nelder (1983) and conveniently implemented in the GLIM computer program.

## 6.1    Notation

I develop these four models for tabular data with reference to the specific example in Table 6.1. The primary advantage of these data is that they have been analyzed in print many times before (e.g., Blalock, 1972: 306; Kritzer, 1978a: 192). The question addressed by the analysis of the table should be familiar to any academic: Is the influence of intelligence on grades still evident after controlling for social class and effort? This is a relatively simple example that illustrates all the main issues with this type of model. It does only include dichotomous dependent variables. However, although the model can be generalized to multicategory dependent variables, this complication is unnecessary for the present purpose of understanding how models of tabular data may be built in the first place.

I begin with several definitions and redefinitions of the general framework of Equations (1.3) and (1.4): instead of letting $Y_i$ represent the individual level random observations, I let $Y_{1i}$ represent a count of items in category 1 of the contingency table for row $i (i = 1, \ldots, n)$. In Table 6.1, the observed figures $y_{1i}$ $(i = 1, \ldots, 8)$ refer to the number of students who received high grades in each cross-classified category. The $k$ explanatory variables $X$ also have $n$ rows, but are now composed exclusively of categorical variables. I also define $Y_{2i}$ as a vector of random counts and $y_{2i}$ as a vector of observed counts, corresponding to category 2 (low grades). Furthermore, let $N_i = y_{1i} + y_{2i}$ be the number of events recorded in each row and $N = \Sigma_{i=1}^{n} N_i$ be the total number of events in the entire table. Whether or not $N_i$ is assumed known prior to the experiment is a key factor in distinguishing among the four models of this chapter.

I denote the expected counts for high and low grades, respectively, as:

$$E(Y_{1i}) = \mu_{1i}$$

and

$$E(Y_{2i}) = \mu_{2i}$$

for the $i$th observation. Each of the four special cases of models for tabular data have different systematic and stochastic components. The following three preliminary assumptions are usually made. First, the number of cells in the contingency table must be fixed, and observations that are collected can fall in one, and only one, of the mutually exclusive categories. This assumption is probably violated with regularity in practical situations, since researchers tend to collapse large tables into smaller ones when cell values become particularly sparse. When this is done, the number of cells $(2n)$ is actually a function of the total number of events in the table, $\Sigma_{i=1}^{n} N_i = N$. Although special tests designed specifically for tabular data are misspecified if this assumption is violated (see Section 6.3), the general statistical models and tests of Part I all apply. The reason for this is that the asymptotic properties of ML estimators hold for tabular models by allowing either $n$ to remain constant as $N$ goes to infinity, or $N$ to remain constant as $n$ goes to infinity.

Second, $Y_{1i}$ and $Y_{1j}$, and $Y_{2i}$ and $Y_{2j}$ (for all $i \neq j$) are assumed independent. Since contingency tables do not usually represent time series data, this requirement is virtually always met in practice. In fact, when the tables do have a time component, such as in panel studies, it is usually explicitly modeled, so this assumption is unlikely to be violated in any event.

Finally, I assume that the mean rate of event occurrence for each cell, $\mu_{1i}$ and $\mu_{2i}$, remains constant, and independent of the number of events $y_{1i}$ and $y_{2i}$ observed during data collection. For the data in Table 6.1, this implies that the expected number of events in each cell remains the same during the administration of the class survey. For many surveys and other types of data, this is not a problem. However, suppose that half of the students were surveyed at the start of the school year (when effort would be high) and half later in the year (when effort may have trailed off and grades may have dropped). In this case, the assumption would have been violated. Alternatively, suppose that students were tested and graded sequentially. Since a good grade from one student might foster competition and increased effort from the next, assuming that $\mu_{1i}$ and $\mu_{2i}$ are constant would be implausible. In the case of tabular data, part of this assumption may be conceptualized as avoiding omitted variable bias. One can assure that $\mu_{1i}$ and $\mu_{2i}$ are constant by explicitly including enough explanatory variables so that expected counts are kept constant within individual cells. If the random occurrence of some events leads to other events within an observation, then including additional variables will be of no help. I discuss alternative models below for processes that do not fit this assumption.

For each of the four models discussed below, I show the model as it exists in the sociological literature and then translate it into an algebraically equivalent form that, for present purposes, is more directly interpretable. I also use the regression, rather than the equivalent analysis of variance, parameterization. This translation and reparameterization are partially a matter of taste, but they also help reveal the unity of these models and their close relationship to the discrete regression models of individual level data in Chapter 5.

## 6.2    The log-odds (logit) model

In the log-odds model, the contingency table is conceptualized by row. Each of the $n$ rows contains information on the outcome of the $N_i$ binary random variables, where $N_i$ *is assumed to be known in advance of the experiment.* One example where $N_i$ is known a priori is where a controlled experiment is conducted and the $N_i$ individual level binary experiments are fixed ahead of

time. In the present example, suppose the data were generated by first selecting 80 students from the middle class who put in high amounts of effort and
were highly intelligent, 64 students from middle class homes, who had also
put in high amounts of effort, but had only low levels of intelligence, and so
forth for all eight rows in Table 6.1. Only after selecting students in this way
are the students sent to school and grades recorded. If the data were really
generated in this manner, the log-odds model would be most appropriate.
They were not in this example, but I nevertheless apply this model by thinking
of the stochastic component as conditional on $N_i$. Each of these unobserved
binary variables has the same expected value $\pi_i$. For example, in the first row
of Table 6.1, the one random draw from each of the $60 + 20 = 80$ random
observations yielded sixty students with high grades and twenty with low
grades. (Another run of the same experiment would yield a different alloca-
tion of the 80 random observations.) The expected grade for each of these 80
students is $\pi_1$, an unobserved number between zero (for low grades) and one
(for high grades).[3]

The log-odds model takes advantage of the assumption that the $N_i$ events
in each row of the table are *independent* and *identically distributed* random
binary variables. Hence, from the Bernoulli distribution for each binary variable, one can derive a binomial distribution for the number of events in category 1, $Y_{1i}$.[4] A model for the entire vector is then:

$$\Pr(Y = y_{1i} | \pi) = \prod_{i=1}^{n} \frac{N_i!}{y_{1i}!(N_i - y_{1i})!} \, \pi_i^{y_{1i}} (1 - \pi_i)^{N_i - y_{1i}},$$

where $\pi_i = \mu_{1i}/N_i$.

The original form of the systematic component of the log-odds model in
the sociological literature is written as this:

$$\ln\left(\frac{\mu_{1i}}{\mu_{2i}}\right) = x_i \beta, \tag{6.1}$$

where $x_i$ is row $i$ in a matrix $X$ that includes a constant term and a set of
dummy variables corresponding to the categories of explanatory variables in
Table 6.1. Although this form seems natural to some researchers, particularly
in sociology where it was originally proposed (see Goodman, 1968, 1972,
1975), a particular translation of it is more comparable to the models discussed in Chapter 5.[5]

---

[3] A reasonable guess for the value of $\pi_i$ is $60/80 = 0.75$, but this is only a sample
proportion rather than unobserved probability. Indeed, better estimates of $\pi_i$ may be
derived by developing a model of the entire table, as described in the text.
[4] See page 44 for a proof.
[5] The reason Equation (6.1) seems like a natural form will become apparent in Section
6.7.

Since the expected value of a ratio is not equal to the ratio of the two expected values,

$$E\left(\frac{Y_1}{Y_2}\right) \neq \frac{E(Y_1)}{E(Y_2)} \equiv \frac{\mu_1}{\mu_2}$$

and thus Equation (6.1) is *not* $E(Y_1/Y_2) = \exp(X\beta)$.

The correct procedure is to solve for $\mu_{i1}$ in Equation (6.1). Of use in this solution is that $N_i$ is known in advance, and thus the two expected values are related:

$$\begin{aligned} E(Y_{1i}) + E(Y_{2i}) &\equiv \mu_{1i} + \mu_{2i} \\ &= N_i. \end{aligned}$$

Thus, since $\mu_{2i} = N_i - \mu_{1i}$, the systematic model need only be a function of one unknown, $\mu_{1i}$. In addition, since the stochastic component is essentially identical, the systematic component of this tabular statistical model ought to be very similar to that for the individual level grouped binary variable model. This can be shown by exponentiating both sides of Equation (6.1) and solving for $\mu_{1i}$:

$$\begin{aligned} E(Y_{1i}) \equiv \mu_{1i} &= \mu_{2i}\exp(x_i\beta) \\ &= (N_i - \mu_{1i})\exp(x_i\beta) \\ &= N_i\exp(x_i\beta) - \mu_{1i}\exp(x_i\beta), \end{aligned} \tag{6.2}$$

which implies that

$$\begin{aligned} \mu_{1i} + \mu_{1i}\exp(x_i\beta) &= N_i\exp(x_i\beta) \\ \mu_{1i}[1 + \exp(x_i\beta)] &= N_i\exp(x_i\beta), \end{aligned}$$

and, finally, dividing both sides by the bracketed term on the left leaves

$$\begin{aligned} \mu_{1i} = N_i\, &\frac{\exp(x_i\beta)}{1 + \exp(x_i\beta)} \\ &= N_i[1 + \exp(-x_i\beta)]^{-1} \end{aligned}$$

or

$$\begin{aligned} \pi_i &\equiv \frac{\mu_{1i}}{N_i} \\ &= \left[1 + e^{-x_i\beta}\right]^{-1}. \end{aligned}$$

This equation is almost identical to the individual level model for grouped binary variables in Equation (5.12). Indeed, the only difference is that the number of unobserved binary variables $N_i$ now varies over "observations."

The complete log-likelihood is then the same as the individual level binomial model in Equation (5.11), except that $N_i$ is substituted for $N$, and the summation is over the $n$ rows in the table rather than the individual level observations (the number of which in this case is $\Sigma_{i=1}^{n} N_i$).

$$\ln L(\tilde{\beta}|y, N) = \sum_{i=1}^{n} \{-y_i \ln[1 + \exp(-x_i\tilde{\beta})] - (N_i - y_i)\ln[1 + \exp(x_i\tilde{\beta})]\}. \tag{6.3}$$

One can use numerical methods to maximize this log-likelihood, just as one would for individual level problems. If one unpacked the table into individual level data, one could estimate the binary regression model in Equation (5.1). In finite samples, the individual level analysis and this tabular analysis will not produce identical results. However, in my experience, the two models usually yield similar conclusions. Indeed, if all assumptions hold, the tabular level analysis is asymptotically equivalent to the corresponding individual level binary regression model. The key point is that *whether one uses the tabular or individual level forms for the data and analysis, these are models of the same underlying process.*

I illustrate this model by analyzing the data in Table 6.1. The dependent variable is the dichotomous measure of grades in school. For independent variables, I code class as low (0) and middle (1), effort as high (1) or low (0), and intelligence as high (1) or low (0). Since analyses of tabular data have an unusual setup, I present the relevant data matrices here:

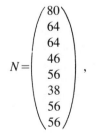

$$y_1 = \begin{pmatrix} 60 \\ 40 \\ 40 \\ 24 \\ 40 \\ 6 \\ 18 \\ 2 \end{pmatrix}, \tag{6.4}$$

$$N = \begin{pmatrix} 80 \\ 64 \\ 64 \\ 46 \\ 56 \\ 38 \\ 56 \\ 56 \end{pmatrix}, \tag{6.5}$$

$$X = \begin{pmatrix} 1 & 1 & 1 & 1 \\ 1 & 1 & 1 & 0 \\ 1 & 1 & 0 & 1 \\ 1 & 1 & 0 & 0 \\ 1 & 0 & 1 & 1 \\ 1 & 0 & 1 & 0 \\ 1 & 0 & 0 & 1 \\ 1 & 0 & 0 & 0 \end{pmatrix} \tag{6.6}$$

where the columns of the $X$ data matrix refer to (from left to right) a constant term, social class, effort, and intelligence.

One could code the explanatory variables in other ways, but the substantive results would be identical. The results for this model appear in the first three columns of numbers in Table 6.2. I also fit another model with each of these explanatory variables plus an interaction between class and intelligence. The reasoning behind including this interaction can be seen by writing down a more structural version of the model:

$$\pi_i = [1 + \exp(-x_i\beta)]^{-1},$$

where

$$x_i\beta = \beta_1 + \beta_2\text{Class} + \beta_3\text{Effort} + \beta_{4i}\text{Intelligence}$$

and

$$\beta_{4i} = \gamma_1 + \gamma_2\text{Class}.$$

This model assumes that the effect ($\beta_{4i}$) of Intelligence on the probability of getting high grades ($\pi_i$) depends on social class. The "interaction" term appears by substituting one equation into the other for purposes of estimation:

$$x_i\beta = \beta_1 + \beta_2\text{Class} + \beta_3\text{Effort} + (\gamma_1 + \gamma_2\text{Class})\text{Intelligence}$$
$$= \beta_1 + \beta_2\text{Class} + \beta_3\text{Effort} + \gamma_1\text{Intelligence} + \gamma_2(\text{Class} \times \text{Intelligence}).$$

Operationally, $\gamma_2$ is estimated by taking the product of the second and fourth columns of $X$ and adding this product as an additional column. The point estimates and standard errors for this model also appear in Table 6.2.

Since each of the explanatory variables is dichotomous, a first difference interpretation is simple to present.[6] For each of the variables, I set $X^{(a)} = 0$ and $X^{(b)} = 1$ and calculate the first difference while holding the other variables constant at $0.5$.[7] I limit my interpretation to the original purpose of the analy-

---

[6] One might also calculate fitted values for each cell in the table, but that is less parsimonious.

[7] The mean would also have been a good choice at which to hold the other variables constant.

Table 6.2. *A log-odds model of grades*

| Variable | Estimate | $\hat{\mathcal{D}}$ | S.e. | Estimate | S.e. |
|---|---|---|---|---|---|
| Constant | −1.84 | | 0.13 | −2.76 | 0.54 |
| Class | 1.47 | 0.35 | 0.14 | 2.85 | 0.55 |
| Effort | 0.85 | 0.21 | 0.22 | 0.80 | 0.18 |
| Intelligence | 1.12 | 0.27 | 0.20 | 2.44 | 0.55 |
| Class × intel. | | | | −2.11 | 0.72 |

*Note:* Log-likelihood model 1: −262.03. Log-likelihood model 2: −252.03.

sis: assessing the influence of intelligence on grades. The result in the table indicates that when class and effort are held constant at 0.5, the difference in the probability of receiving high grades between someone of high intelligence and another person of low intelligence is a substantial 0.27 (on a scale from 0 to 1 probability). Put differently, imagine a student with an average social class background and degree of motivation, but with low intelligence. Another student, alike in all respects except that he or she is highly intelligent, would have a 0.27 point higher probability of receiving a high grade.

A derivative interpretation of these coefficients is quite similar to this first difference interpretation, since $\beta\pi(1 - \pi)$ calculated for $\pi = 0.5$ (that is, $\beta/4$) happens to be very close to the first difference for each coefficient. Since dividing by four is simpler than calculating the first difference for this method, a researcher might use a derivative interpretation during the analysis. The first differences could then be calculated for the final version of the estimates so as to make interpretation easier for the reader.

Model 2 of Table 6.2 includes an interaction term between class and intelligence. To interpret this model I also calculate the first difference for the effect of intelligence, but I do so twice: once for high social class and once for middle social class. The first difference for intelligence is then:

$$\hat{\mathcal{D}} = \begin{cases} 0.433 & \text{if class} = 0, \\ 0.073 & \text{if class} = 1. \end{cases}$$

Thus, the difference in grades between high and low intelligence students of middle social class is very small (0.07). However, for lower class students, intelligence can make an enormous difference by increasing the probability of receiving a high grade by 0.43. Substantively, intelligence is of more consequence for lower class students. Perhaps this is because of a bias toward these students or due to prior training.

Although the stochastic component of this statistical model is binomial, the underlying process generating these data is really Bernoulli. Only by summarizing the data in tabular form does the explicit model become binomial.

In order to get from a Bernoulli process to a binomial distribution, one relies on the key assumptions that the individual unobserved binary variables are *independent* and *identically distributed*. With these assumptions, and also assuming that no variables were collapsed in forming the table, one could reconstruct the original data set without any loss of information. For the data in Table 6.1, the first eighty observations would have identical values of the explanatory variables (middle class, high effort, and high intelligence). The dependent variable would take on the value one for the first sixty of these observations and zero for the remaining twenty. In this manner, the entire individual level data set may be rebuilt. Once this is done, the asymptotically equivalent individual level binary regression model in Section 5.1 may be applied. Of course, since the data are presumably already in tabular form, the model presented in this section is more convenient.

Suppose that the individual binary variables in each row of the table were actually dependent or did not have constant expected values $\pi_i$. In this case, one could *not* reliably reconstruct the individual level data from the tabular form. One needs more information than exists in the table. In Table 6.1, for example, one could correct for heterogeneity in $\pi_i$ among the binary variables represented in the first row of the table. However, in order to do this, one would need to further classify the first 80 individual binary variables according to new explanatory variables, or new categories of existing variables. For example, suppose the teacher encourages male students more than female students. In this case, boys from middle class families who expend high degrees of effort and have high intelligence probably have higher values of $\pi_1$ (the probability of having high grades) than girls who fall into the same category. If the original data were available, one could test this hypothesis with either an individual level binary model, or by creating another table with an additional classification by gender.

What happens when the original data are not available, but these assumptions still do not hold? In this case, $\pi_i$ may be treated as an average of the expected values of the binary variables in each row of the table. The systematic component is therefore still plausible. However, if either the independence or identical distribution assumptions are violated, the binomial distribution no longer provides an adequate stochastic model of the process generating these data. Indeed, the situation of having data in the tabular form, without also possessing the original data, is directly analogous to having individual level grouped binary variables without details of the separate binary variables in each group (see Sections 5.5 and 5.6). Since, in both cases, only the total count (out of either $N$ or $N_i$) is available, assumptions must be made about the process generating these individual level binary variables in order to proceed with statistical analyses. If the assumptions of independence and identical distributions hold, the binomial distribution suffices. If the individual binary variables are dependent, heterogeneous, or both, then the extended beta-binomial distribution (with its additional ancillary parameter) could be substituted for the binomial. The log-likelihood in this case would therefore be directly analogous to that in Equation (5.13). Since considerably fewer "observations" (cells) exist in analyses of tabular rather than individual level data, the additional ancillary parameter is relatively more costly in terms of the tradeoff between restrictive and nonrestrictive models of Section 2.5.

## 6.3    A specification test

Wald, likelihood ratio, and other methods of assessing the precision of one's ML estimates may be applied in models of contingency tables just as with individual level data. However, the special nature of tabular data permits one to also conduct a *specification test*. Specification tests help the data analyst judge the adequacy of the model assumed. In this section, I describe this very widely used statistical test and then explain why I believe it should be used much less frequently and in vastly different ways than is now common practice. The argument here extends that of Section 2.6. Essentially the same test that I describe here for the log-odds model also applies to the other three models of contingency tables to be described in what follows.

This test is based on a likelihood ratio comparison of two alternative hypotheses: (1) the current model is correct and (2) some relevant variables are left out of the current model. The test parameters thus represent the influence of all possible omitted variables on the dependent variable. If any of these test parameters are nonzero, one should include the corresponding variable and reestimate the model. The specification test for models of tabular data permits one to conduct a joint test of the null hypothesis that all the test parameters – that is, all possible omitted variables – are zero. If this null hypothesis cannot be rejected, then the current model is assumed adequate.

Since the likelihood ratio is based on the likelihoods for two very specific models, it may seem strange that this test could even be formulated. Calculating the log-likelihood for the current model is easy, but how can one calculate the log-likelihood for the second model with every other variable in the world? In most cases, this is obviously impossible. However, in models of tabular data, one can rely on the assumption that the number of cells in the table $(2n)$ is fixed in order to limit the number of other possible explanatory variables.

For example, the eight observations (rows) of Table 6.1 limit the number of parameters to be estimated in the log-odds model to eight. The three obvious variables in the table are class (C), effort (E), and intelligence (I). In Table 6.2, I used an interaction between class and intelligence (CI). A model with all eight parameters includes a constant term and coefficients for the variables C, E, I, CI, CE, EI, and CEI. A model with the same number of parameters as observations is called a *saturated model* and always fits the data perfectly. That is, the fitted values will exactly reproduce the data. Since no other variation in the fitted values remains to be accounted for, including additional variables will only be repetitive; attempting to do so would yield a model that is inestimable because many possible parameter values lead to the same data. If the current model includes only C, E, and I, the test parameters would include the coefficients of CI, CE, EI, and CEI. It is thus straightforward to calculate $\hat{\mathcal{R}}$ as minus twice the difference in the log-likelihoods from the current and saturated models.

A special feature of this likelihood ratio test is that it may be written as a direct function of the observed ($y_{ij}$) and predicted ($\hat{\mu}_{ij}$) cell frequencies:

$$\hat{\mathcal{R}} \equiv -2\ln\left(\frac{L_R^*}{L^*}\right)$$

$$= 2\sum_{i=1}^{n}\sum_{j=1}^{2} y_{ij}\ln\left(\frac{y_{ij}}{\hat{\mu}_{ij}}\right),$$

where, using the notation from Chapter 4, $L_R^*$ is the log-likelihood from the restricted model and $L^*$ is the log-likelihood from the unrestricted model. $\hat{\mu}_{ij}$ is calculated from the current, rather than the saturated, model.[8] For this reason, this procedure is often conceptualized as a test of whether the "model is one whose expected cell frequencies . . . significantly differ from the observed data" (Knoke and Burke, 1980: 31).

Computer programs for models of tabular data routinely report this statistic, and data analysts frequently use it as a measure of the adequacy of their models.[9] If $\hat{\mathcal{R}}$ is much larger than its degrees of freedom ($m$), the analyst concludes that important variables have been omitted. Since the table is considered fixed, the only recourse is to keep including additional interactions until $\hat{\mathcal{R}}$ shrinks sufficiently.

As attractive as the concept of an omnibus specification test is, however, four critical reasons cause me to be very wary of their interpretation and to generally discourage their use. First, the test relies heavily on the assumption that the number of cells in the table ($2n$) is fixed. In practice, the number of cells in the table almost always depends on the number of events $N$. When very few items appear in a few cells, the cells are generally collapsed into one. The reason is that the analyst is willing to give up some additional information to get more precise estimates of the means in the remaining cells. This procedure is perfectly reasonable, as a general form of this fundamental choice

[8] $\hat{\mu}_{ij}$ calculated from the saturated model is exactly equal to $y_{ij}$.
[9] $\hat{\mathcal{R}}$ is similar but not identical to the Pearson chi-square statistic used to test for independence in simple contingency tables (see Blalock, 1979: 281).

underlies virtually all statistical analyses (see Section 2.5). However, it also invalidates this test. Technically, the reason is that the likelihood ratio is no longer distributed as a chi-square variable. Substantively, if the number of cells can increase, so can the number of variables; in addition to class effort, and intelligence, one might further break down the counts in the table by gender, race, and the quality of instruction. Unfortunately, since $\mathcal{R}$ only tests against the alternative hypothesis of all possible interactions among class, effort, and intelligence, it might give one the false impression that the current model is the correct one. In fact, it might be that class, effort, and intelligence are substantively irrelevant to explaining variation in grades, but, along with a few interactions, they might still account for most of the variation in the table. In the end, no hypothesis test can tell a researcher whether the table was appropriately set up to begin with.

Second, if the total count of cell frequencies $N$ is very large, both absolutely and in relation to the number of cells in the table, this specification test will almost always lead one to conclude that the saturated model is the correct one. An unquestioning use of this test with large $N$, therefore, will generally lead to a more complicated model than is desired. With large cell frequencies, the additional parameters might be interesting, but the researcher should be the one to decide whether the abundance of information is used to estimate additional parameters or improve the estimation of existing ones.

Third, even if the table is considered fixed and the number of cells do not increase with the sample size, the test parameters are not necessarily the omitted interactions among the original variables. For example, suppose the current model includes class, effort, and intelligence, and the test indicates an omitted variable. In this case, a substantive understanding of the research problem might suggest that middle class, low effort students are fundamentally different from all other student types. A researcher might then code a variable as one for students in this special category and zero for all others. Using standard interactions, as is usually recommended in the literature, this sort of effect could be ascertained, but neither directly nor without extraneous parameters. In fact, even if this specification test indicates that the model fits the data, another model with an equivalent number of parameters could fit the data just as well; only a close substantive understanding of the research problem will enable one to choose which model is appropriate. In general, this specification test is not designed to choose the theoretically appropriate form of one's variables.

Finally, under no circumstances should this or any specification test be interpreted as confirmation that the given model is the correct one. The test is conditional on the functional form and stochastic components being correct (and part of $\mathcal{M}^*$, in the notation of Section 2.5). If the functional form is incorrect, but every relevant variable is included, a specification test can nevertheless indicate that there are omitted variables. An unquestioning application of this test would therefore lead a researcher to include superfluous interactions or other variables or parameters.

For example, the test is also conditional on the stochastic component being the correct one. Suppose the binomial distribution is used, but contagion is present among the unobserved binary variables making up the count in each table cell. Suppose further that a specification test indicates that something was omitted. The usual procedure is for the researcher to include additional variables or interactions and reestimate the model. Unfortunately, this usual procedure may lead to a completely fallacious model: the included variables might be the only correct ones, and the omitted parameter instead of some other variable. This test would then cause one to include the irrelevant variables and to leave the incorrect stochastic component unchanged. Since this specification test is heavily used, and alternative distributional assumptions that take into account contagion and heterogeneity are very rarely used or tested for, a fair number of published analyses are probably significantly misspecified. (I have more to say about this latter point in Section 6.6.)

Although very widely used, this specification test is in fact only very rarely appropriate. It cannot be used to prove the veracity of one's model. Its only use is as a check on the current model compared to a very specific alternative. But this is no different from any likelihood ratio test. In general, one is rarely sure of any part of a statistical model. For this reason, researchers usually estimate many models for each data set. Although procedures are being developed to help researchers decide which model is more appropriate (Leamer, 1978), the automatic and atheoretical use of this or any specification test should be avoided.

## 6.4     The log-proportion model

Although the log-odds model may seem like the only plausible form, other conceptualizations of tabular data lead to reasonable statistical models. For example, the log-proportion model also conceptualizes the table in rows, but the focus is no longer on the *binary variables* in each row. Instead, this model is focused more directly on the *events* occurring in the first column (high grades in Table 6.1). The number of possible events $N_i$, again assumed to be known in advance, can constrain the number of events in column 1.

To derive a distribution, I assume that the individual events that make up $Y_{1i}$ occur with a constant rate $\mu_{1i}$. In addition, if I also assume that the occurrence of each event has no influence on $\mu_{1i}$, then the total count of events $Y_{1i}$ is generated according to a Poisson distribution. The functional form should therefore be similar to that for the individual level event count models. The only qualification is that the number of possible events $N_i$ does influence $\mu_{1i}$ in some way.

Two approaches to deriving a stochastic component for this model are possible here, and both lead to the identical model (see the last part of Section 5.7). One way to model the problem is in the systematic component so that $N_i$ influences $\mu_{1i}$ in a very specific manner. This can be seen in the original form of the log-proportion model, as presented in the sociological literature,

$$\ln \left(\frac{\mu_{1i}}{N_i}\right) = x_i\beta,$$

but this is easily translated into a more interpretable form as a modification of the standard exponential relationship:

$$E(Y_i) \equiv \mu_i \equiv \pi_i N_i = \exp(x_i\beta + \ln N_i).$$

This leads to an intuitive interpretation of this model, since it can be understood as an effort to explain the number of people in the high grade category as an exponential function of a set of explanatory variables, while literally controlling for the "marginals," the number of people in the high *and* low categories, $N_i$.

This functional form implies that the slope of the curve is steeper as the expected value of $Y_{1i}$ gets larger. This can be interpreted to mean, for example, that the number of people in the high grade-high intelligence category is likely to be larger than the number in the high grade-low intelligence category. However, this relationship is likely to be even stronger when considering a case when the expected number of high grade students is already very high. On the other hand, when the expected count $\mu_{1i}$ approaches the floor (zero) the expected difference between the two categories is likely to be even smaller.

Note that this is a somewhat different approach from that taken in the log-odds model. Choosing between the two should be based in practice on an understanding of the process which gave rise to the observed table. The two models represent different ways of dealing with the same general problems and in many cases should yield similar, although not identical, substantive conclusions.

An alternative approach is to appeal to the direct stochastic model of this process at the end of Section 5.7. In this way the systematic component would not include the $\ln N_i$ term but would otherwise remain unchanged. Instead, the stochastic component would be modified. In any event, the log-likelihood would be identical in either case. The log-likelihood may be written as follows:

$$\ln L(\tilde{\beta}|y) = \sum_{i=1}^{n} \{y_{1i}(x_i\tilde{\beta} + \ln N_i) - \exp(x_i\tilde{\beta} + \ln N_i)\}$$

$$= \sum_{i=1}^{n} \{y_{1i}(x_i\tilde{\beta}) - N_i\exp(x_i\tilde{\beta})\},$$

Table 6.3. *A log-proportion model of grades*

| Variable | Estimate | $\hat{\mathcal{D}}$ | S.e. | Estimate | S.e. |
|---|---|---|---|---|---|
| Constant | −1.62 | | 0.09 | −2.60 | 0.78 |
| Class | 0.68 | 0.29 | 0.08 | 1.94 | 1.37 |
| Effort | 0.36 | 0.16 | 0.17 | 0.32 | 0.29 |
| Intelligence | 0.49 | 0.21 | 0.17 | 1.78 | 0.79 |
| Class × intel. | | | | −1.67 | 1.40 |

*Note:* Log-likelihood model 1: −360.78. Log-likelihood model 2: −350.20.

where, in the second line, terms not depending on $\tilde{\beta}$ are dropped. Indeed, this is essentially the same as the log-likelihoods in Equations (5.19) and (5.20) for individual level event counts with variable maximum counts and time intervals, respectively.

I illustrate the log-proportion model by reanalyzing Table 6.1. As with the log-odds estimation, I estimate two models, one with class, effort, and intelligence, and the other with these three variables plus an interaction term allowing the effect of intelligence to vary by social class. The data matrixes remain the same as in Equations (6.4), (6.5), and (6.6) and the results appear in Table 6.3.

The parameter estimates in this table are not comparable to those in Table 6.2, since the two sets are estimates of different underlying parameters from nonequivalent models. As set up, this is an analysis of the expected value of the number of students receiving high grades, $\mu_{1i}$. By defining $\pi_i \equiv \mu_{1i}/N_i$, one could equivalently interpret these results as modeling the probability of receiving high grades. Even given this translation, however, the two models are still fundamentally different representations of the underlying process driving these data. Most times, a researcher would only estimate one of these models, the choice between the two being made on substantive grounds. For present purposes, however, a comparison is useful.

Any of the four methods of interpreting parameters in arbitrary functional forms are useful for comparing these estimates with the ones from the log-odds model (see Section 5.2). Since all the explanatory variables are dichotomous, first differences are again relatively convenient; the second column of Table 6.3 presents these statistics. Note that the effects are similar, but slightly smaller, than the corresponding first differences from the log-odds model in Table 6.2. Whereas the difference between high and low intelligence students in the probability of receiving high grades is about 0.27 points for the log-odds model, it is a slightly smaller 0.21 points here. Indeed, all the first differences are smaller for the log-proportion than the log-odds model, but this result does not necessarily generalize to other examples.

Model 2 is also similar here. The first difference for intelligence is now:

$$\hat{\mathscr{D}} = \begin{cases} 0.431 & \text{if class} = 0, \\ 0.069 & \text{if class} = 1, \end{cases}$$

which is virtually identical to the log-odds model. The substantive result is again that intelligence has a considerably larger effect on grades received for lower than for middle class students.

Just as with the log-odds model, the assumptions with which the stochastic component was derived may not hold in the log-proportion model. In particular, suppose that $E(Y_{1i}) \equiv \mu_{1i}$ were not constant for every event in a category or suppose that the rate of event occurrence on a category $\mu_{1i}$ was influenced by the number of events accumulating in that category. If the individual level data were available, one could remedy the first problem, and perhaps even the second, by including sufficient variables and categories so that the expected count in each cell was constant.

However, when tabular data are available the original individual level data often are not. In these situations, alternative assumptions about the process generating the data may lead to over- or underdispersion in the count variable $Y_{1i}$. The process generating these data can be better modeled as a generalized event count distribution than as a Poisson distribution. The derivation of this likelihood is directly analogous to that for the individual level data in Section 5.9.

## 6.5     The linear-proportion model

The linear-proportion (linear categorical regression) model is probably the simplest to calculate. However, it is probably also the least plausible and most statistically inefficient of the four models of tabular data.

In order to explain each of these points, I begin with one version of the model:

$$Y_{1i} \sim f_N(y_i | \mu_i, \sigma_i^2), \tag{6.7}$$

where

$$\frac{\mu_{1i}}{N_i} = \pi_i = x_i \beta$$

and

$$\sigma_i^2 = \pi_i(1 - \pi_i)/N_i. \tag{6.8}$$

This model does posit a systematic component over observations for both the mean $\mu_i$ and variance $\sigma_i^2$. However, only the mean is of direct interest; the variance is still considered an ancillary parameter. The computationally attractive feature of this model is that ML estimator is very simple. Although the solution still must be numerical, an iterative weighted least squares algorithm has been shown to be very fast.[10] In addition, Wald (1943) has shown that the first iteration of this algorithm, a straightforward weighted least squares estimator (with $\pi_i$ estimated by $y_{1i}/N_i$), has many, but not all, of the desirable properties of ML estimation. This alternative estimator was popularized in biostatistics by Grizzle, Starmer, and Koch (1969), and promoted in political science by Kritzer (1978a, 1978b). It is particularly attractive if only linear regression programs (and relatively slow computers) are available. Although the weighted least squares estimator can be used for other models in this chapter, it is primarily associated with the linear-proportion model. Indeed, the similarity of it to regression analysis has enabled Kritzer (1978a, 1978b) to successfully convince political scientists familiar only with linear regression of the merits of explicit models of contingency tables. This has taken some researchers far beyond the usual percentage calculations.

As attractive as this model may be to those schooled only in linear regression analysis, it is unattractive on several theoretical and practical grounds. First, the model is not realistic. The dependent variable is a proportion, ranging between zero and one, but the model is still linear. Hence, the estimator can lead to meaningless values of $\hat{\pi}$ – fitted values greater than one or less than zero. Kritzer (1978a: 280) has defended the model by writing "In practice, one very seldom obtains out of range probability estimates . . . , *particularly if the model being used is correctly specified,* and if the number of cases upon which the proportions are based is fairly large." Indeed, if $\pi_i$ is always between about 0.25 and 0.75, fitted values from this model tend to be very similar to those from the log-odds model. If one or more elements of $\pi_i$ are outside of that range, the linear-proportion model runs into trouble. In these cases, whether or not the model yields predicted values that are outside the $[0,1]$ interval, the relationship near the bounds will be misrepresented, resulting in biased estimates and fitted values.

But even if the data contain no extreme values of $\pi_i$, the stochastic component remains unrealistic. A Normal distribution does not generate values between zero and one only. Although $y_i/N_i$ can take on any value between zero and one, $y_i$ is discrete. If $N_i$ is considered known, or if we model $y_{1i}$ and $y_{2i}$ without reference to $N_i$ (as in the log-frequency model which follows), considerably more information exists than one takes advantage of by merely assuming that we are modeling a continuous variable. By taking this information into account, considerably more precise estimates may be obtained.

These points may be illustrated by reanalyzing the data in Table 6.1 with

[10] The computer program GLIM implements this algorithm.

Table 6.4. *A linear-proportion model of grades*

|  | Model 1 | | Model 2 | |
| --- | --- | --- | --- | --- |
| Variable | Estimate | S.e. | Estimate | S.e. |
| Constant | 0.20 | 0.16 | 0.02 | 0.15 |
| Class | 0.35 | 0.14 | 0.58 | 0.16 |
| Effort | 0.11 | 0.13 | 0.14 | 0.10 |
| Intelligence | 0.18 | 0.13 | 0.42 | 0.16 |
| Class × intel. | | | −0.40 | 0.21 |

*Note:* Log-likelihood model 1: 28.82. Log-likelihood model 2: 30.46.

the linear-proportion model.[11] The same data matrices in Equations (6.4), (6.5), and (6.6) are used in this model to derive model 1 in Table 6.4. An interaction term between class and intelligence is again included in model 2, and it too is presented in Table 6.4.

In this model, the first differences, derivatives, and parameter estimates are all identical. For comparability between models, the estimates for model 1 may be compared to the first differences presented with the previous two models. Thus, a high intelligence student will have an 0.18 higher probability of receiving high grades than a low intelligence student, controlling for the effects of social class and effort. This is a slightly smaller estimate than the 0.21 for the log-proportion model and a much smaller estimate than 0.27 for the log-odds model. If the values of class and effort were held constant at different values in the log-odds and log-proportion models, these first differences might be closer.

Model 2, which includes the interaction term between class and intelligence, also appears in Table 6.4. The first difference for intelligence is as follows:

$$\hat{\mathcal{D}} = \begin{cases} 0.431 & \text{if class} = 0, \\ 0.069 & \text{if class} = 1, \end{cases}$$

which is again similar, but not identical, to that for the other models.

All of these results indicate the very substantial imprecision with which these parameters were estimated. From a theoretical perspective, the Normal distribution with a linear stochastic component cannot be generating these data. If, for some reason, a researcher really wanted to retain a linear systematic component, more precise estimates could be made by using a more realistic stochastic component. Poisson or binomial distributions would be far better than a Normal density, even with a linear systematic component. Since

[11] Weighted least squares was used as an estimator.

the information exists that the underlying variables are discrete, it should be exploited.

In fact, the linear-proportion model is internally inconsistent, since the weights in Equation (6.8) are derived by assuming that the dependent variable is distributed as a binomial [that is, $\pi(1 - \pi)/N$ is the variance of a binomial]. But this implied assumption conflicts with the explicit assumption that $Y_i$ is distributed Normally in Equation (6.7).[12] The inconsistency is partially reconciled because the binomial distribution approaches the Normal with large sample sizes.

Of course, if a researcher were willing to include this sort of stochastic information, then he or she might as well improve on the systematic component too.

### 6.6    The log-frequency (log-linear) model

The log-frequency model is set up in a very different manner from the other three but is nevertheless very closely related. Most important, the distinction between independent and dependent variables is blurred. The left hand side variable still represents the data in the table, but the variable grades is now on the right hand side. In addition, the row totals ($N_i$) are not assumed known in advance. The meaning of these peculiarities will become apparent as I develop the model.

The log-frequency model is defined by first stacking the relevant vectors. Let

$$\mu_i = \begin{pmatrix} \mu_{1i} \\ \mu_{2i} \end{pmatrix},$$

$$y_i = \begin{pmatrix} y_{1i} \\ y_{2i} \end{pmatrix},$$

$$Y_i = \begin{pmatrix} Y_{1i} \\ Y_{2i} \end{pmatrix}.$$

The dimensions of all matrices, including $X$, increase to $2n$. Then the model is defined with a Poisson stochastic component as follows:

$$Y_i \sim f_p(y_i|\mu_i),$$

[12] Furthermore, if the data are over- or underdispersed, these weights will be incorrect.

where

$$\mu_i = \exp(x_i\beta).$$

In the sociological literature, this model is generally called the log-linear model because this last equation can be rewritten as:

$$\ln \mu_i = x_i\beta.$$

As defined, this is roughly equivalent to the Poisson regression model of Section 5.7. The difference is that $y_i$ now only includes the frequencies, with all meaningful variables defined on the right hand side. This is quite unusual, since in most cases researchers are more interested in explaining some real variable than in explaining the raw frequencies. The log-likelihood function should now be familiar, since it is essentially the same as for individual level event counts:

$$\ln L(\tilde{\beta}|y) = \sum_{i=1}^{2n} \{ y_i(x_i\tilde{\beta}) - e^{x_i\beta} \}. \tag{6.9}$$

To get a better feel for this model and to explain the information it can extract from the data, I move directly to an analysis of the example in Table 6.1. First, define the data matrix as follows:

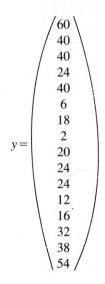

$$y = \begin{pmatrix} 60 \\ 40 \\ 40 \\ 24 \\ 40 \\ 6 \\ 18 \\ 2 \\ 20 \\ 24 \\ 24 \\ 12 \\ 16 \\ 32 \\ 38 \\ 54 \end{pmatrix}$$

The $X$ matrix then includes a constant term and one variable each for grades, social class, effort, and intelligence, respectively:

$$X = \begin{pmatrix} 1 & 1 & 1 & 1 & 1 \\ 1 & 1 & 1 & 1 & 0 \\ 1 & 1 & 1 & 0 & 1 \\ 1 & 1 & 1 & 0 & 0 \\ 1 & 1 & 0 & 1 & 1 \\ 1 & 1 & 0 & 1 & 0 \\ 1 & 1 & 0 & 0 & 1 \\ 1 & 1 & 0 & 0 & 0 \\ 1 & 0 & 1 & 1 & 1 \\ 1 & 0 & 1 & 1 & 0 \\ 1 & 0 & 1 & 0 & 1 \\ 1 & 0 & 1 & 0 & 0 \\ 1 & 0 & 0 & 1 & 1 \\ 1 & 0 & 0 & 1 & 0 \\ 1 & 0 & 0 & 0 & 1 \\ 1 & 0 & 0 & 0 & 0 \end{pmatrix}$$

Table 6.5 presents results from one very simple model, useful primarily for understanding the log-frequency model.

The variables in this model explain only the "marginals" in the table. For example, the coefficient on intelligence is an estimate of the relative number of high and low intelligence students. This is not the influence of intelligence on grades and as such is probably of relatively minor scholarly interest. Nevertheless, consider an interpretation of the parameter estimate for intelligence, 0.28. Holding grades, social class, and effort constant at 0.5, the average number of high intelligence students is $\hat{\mu} = 31.98$ and for low intelligence students it is $\hat{\mu} = 24.17$.[13] The first difference then indicates that $31.98 - 24.17 = 7.81$ more high than low intelligence students are in the sample. Of course, this information is only of minor interest.

Although a little awkward, one can use the log-frequency model to evaluate the influence of some variables on others. I explain how to do this in the next section by demonstrating the equivalence of a special case of this log-frequency model and the log-odds model.

First, however, I present a different example, where explaining the frequencies of a table directly is of more intrinsic interest. Table 6.6 presents a typical occupational mobility table. This table has also been analyzed many times before (see Duncan, 1979; Glass, 1954; or Miller, 1960).

The rows represent the father's occupation and the columns the son's. Occupation codes are classified in rough order of prestige as follows:

[13] These fitted values were calculated according to the procedures in Section 5.2, but using $\hat{\mu}_i = \exp(x_i\hat{\beta})$.

Table 6.5. *A log frequency model of grades*

| Variable | Estimate | S.e. |
|----------|----------|------|
| Constant | 3.02 | 0.03 |
| Grades | 0.04 | 0.04 |
| Class | 0.17 | 0.04 |
| Effort | 0.12 | 0.04 |
| Intelligence | 0.28 | 0.04 |

*Note:* Log-likelihood: 1058.25.

Table 6.6. *British occupational mobility table*

|      | I  | II | III | IV  | Va | Vb  | VI  | VII |
|------|-----|-----|-----|-----|-----|-----|-----|-----|
| I    | 50 | 19 | 26 | 8  | 7  | 11 | 6  | 2  |
| II   | 16 | 40 | 34 | 18 | 11 | 20 | 8  | 3  |
| III  | 12 | 35 | 65 | 66 | 35 | 88 | 23 | 21 |
| IV   | 11 | 20 | 58 | 110 | 40 | 183 | 64 | 32 |
| Va   | 2  | 8  | 12 | 23 | 25 | 46 | 28 | 12 |
| Vb   | 12 | 28 | 102 | 162 | 90 | 554 | 230 | 177 |
| VI   | 0  | 6  | 19 | 40 | 21 | 158 | 143 | 71 |
| VII  | 0  | 3  | 14 | 32 | 15 | 126 | 91 | 106 |

 I.    Professional and high administrative;
 II.   Managerial and executive;
 III.  Inspectional, supervisory, and other nonmanual (high grade);
 IV.   Inspectional, supervisory, and other nonmanual (lower grade);
 Va.   Routine grades of nonmanual;
 Vb.   Skilled manual;
 VI.   Semiskilled manual;
 VII.  Unskilled manual.

Many features of this table may be of scholarly interest, but two are of most immediate concern. First, with what rate do sons inherit their father's occupation? Second, are children upwardly or downwardly mobile? Both of these questions can be answered most naturally by directly modeling the frequencies in this table. The "dependent variable" includes the sixty-four numbers in Table 6.6. The $X$ matrix includes a constant term and two explanatory variables. The first variable (Inherit) takes on the value 1 for cases where sons have the same occupation as their father (i.e., for frequencies that fall on the diagonal) and 0 otherwise. The second variable (Mobility) takes on the value

Table 6.7. *Mobility table analysis*

| Variable | Estimate | $\hat{\mathcal{D}}$ | S.E. | $\hat{\mathcal{W}}$ | $\Pr(\hat{\mathcal{W}} \geq w | \bar{\beta} = 0)$ |
|----------|----------|------|------|------|------|
| Constant | 3.829 | | 0.0033 | | |
| Inherit | 1.232 | 119.73 | 0.0046 | 266.96 | 0.0000 |
| Mobility | 0.144 | 13.18 | 0.0052 | 27.46 | 0.0000 |

*Note:* Log-likelihood = 10925.46.

1 for upwardly mobile sons (frequencies above the diagonal) and 0 otherwise. To estimate this model, I merely maximize the log-likelihood in Equation (6.9). For later reference, I also present the Wald statistics (under the null hypothesis that $\bar{\beta} = 0$) and their approximate associated traditional probabilities.[14] The results appear in Table 6.7.

Since both coefficients are positive, the results are in the expected direction: Sons do tend to inherit their father's occupation. The first difference indicates that, controlling for mobility, about 119.73 more sons inherit their father's occupation than do not. Since the average number of father-son pairs per cell is 54.66, this is quite a sizable effect. The Mobility coefficient indicates that about 13.18 more sons are upwardly than downwardly mobile. This is a more modest effect, but the standard errors indicate that both coefficients are extremely precise.

This presentation should give the reader a flavor for the type of data most suited to the log-frequency model. This model provides an important conceptual and methodological advantage over individual level analyses of this type of data. One can think of other types of tables that might be similarly analyzed, but occupational mobility tables provide the leading examples.

Considerable further analysis of this table could also be conducted. For example, do these effects hold up when the general tendency for the middle class to grow is controlled? One could also test some very specific hypotheses, such as whether the rate of upward occupational mobility is quicker for more prestigious occupations or whether movement occurs more frequently between skilled and semiskilled than between managerial and professional categories.

As with the other three models, if the assumptions made to derive the stochastic component are implausible, another model should be used. In particular, if the events making up each cell of a contingency table are either dependent or do not have constant rates of occurrence, then the Poisson assumption does not hold. As far as I can tell, an alternative stochastic component that takes this into account has never been specified and estimated in the sociolog-

---

[14] The true probabilities are extremely small but are greater than zero.

Table 6.8. *Occupational mobility table: reanalysis*

| Variable | Estimate | $\hat{\mathcal{D}}$ | S.e. | $\hat{\mathcal{W}}$ | $\Pr(\hat{\mathcal{W}} \geq w \mid \hat{\beta} = 0)$ |
|----------|----------|------|------|------|------|
| Constant | 3.918 | | 0.204 | | |
| Inherit | 1.014 | 96.97 | 0.332 | 3.057 | 0.0033 |
| Mobility | 0.186 | 17.07 | 0.274 | 0.679 | 0.4995 |
| $\hat{\sigma}^2$ | 61.51 | | 12.305 | 4.998 | 0.0000 |

*Note:* Log-likelihood = 12683.89.

ical or political science literatures (but see Kleinman, 1973; McCullagh and Nelder, 1983: Chapter 6; and Williams, 1982, in the statistics literature). Unfortunately, ignoring this problem can have very serious consequences. Although either over- or underdispersion can result from violating these two assumptions, overdispersion tends to be empirically much more likely. Just as with individual level event counts, a Poisson model estimated in the presence of overdispersion can result in standard errors that are much too small. Indeed, the frequently analyzed data in Table 6.6 are probably overdispersed.

To illustrate this problem, consider a reanalysis of Table 6.6. The only change I will make is to alter the stochastic component by allowing overdispersion. This is essentially the model in Section 5.9 for counts of dependent events, using the generalized even count distribution Equation (5.22). The results, appearing in Table 6.8, include estimates for all the parameters of the original model, plus the dispersion parameter, $\sigma^2$.

Several factors indicate that this model is a substantial improvement over that in Table 6.7. First, the log-likelihood has grown substantially. Second, under the assumption of the Poisson distribution, $\sigma^2$ in this model ought to be only 1, but it is instead strikingly large (61.51) with a relatively small standard error. Judging from any or all of these factors, these data are severely overdispersed. Since the data set comes from a sample survey of isolated pairs of individuals, dependence among the different father-son pairs is unlikely. Much more likely is that the rate of event occurrence is not constant within each cell. Since a valid categorization and ranking of occupational prestige categories is probably far more complex than the eight in Table 6.6, heterogeneity is probably what is causing the observed overdispersion. What were the consequences of ignoring the heterogeneity of event occurrence in this example? Although the parameter estimates are relatively stable from Tables 6.7 and 6.8, the standard errors in the Poisson model are between fifty and seventy times smaller than they should be! If judged by conventional significance levels, Mobility changes from highly, to not at all, significant.

Researchers limited to the Poisson model are likely to believe their estimates to be much more precise (and have much higher levels of "statistical significance") than is justified. In sociology, a very large number of important articles may have data that do not support their substantive arguments anywhere near as strongly as the standard errors they present indicate. Since these researchers tend to carefully check the fit of their model to the data, some of these problems may be avoided in practice. The occupational mobility table I present above, for example, is very likely missing several key explanatory variables. If they were included, the standard errors would probably be much more realistic.[15] Fortunately, these articles almost always present their original data, so reanalysis is relatively straightforward.[16]

### 6.7    The log-odds model as a special case of the log-frequency model

In this section, I demonstrate that the log-odds model is a special case of the log-frequency model. As a concrete example, consider again the grades and intelligence example in Table 6.1. The derivation that follows starts with the log-likelihood for the log-frequency model, makes the additional assumption that $N_i$ is known in advance, and derives the log-likelihood for the log-odds model.

In the notation of the log-odds model, there are $2n = 16$ cells in this table. The stochastic component may then be written simply as follows:

$$\Pr(Y = y|\mu) = \prod_{i=1}^{2n} \frac{e^{-\mu_i} \mu_i^{y_i}}{y_i!} \propto L(\tilde{\mu}|y),$$

where $\mu_i = e^{x_i\beta}$. The log-likelihood is then

$$\ln L(\tilde{\mu}|y) = \sum_{i=1}^{2n} \{y_i \ln \tilde{\mu}_i - \tilde{\mu}_i\} \qquad (6.10)$$

$$= \sum_{i=1}^{n} \{y_{1i} \ln \tilde{\mu}_{1i} - \tilde{\mu}_{1i}\} - \sum_{i=n+1}^{2n} \{y_{2i} \ln \tilde{\mu}_{2i} - \tilde{\mu}_{2i}\}.$$

---

[15] If one includes additional (even superfluous) explanatory variables, $\hat{\sigma}^2$ will usually be smaller, regardless of the size of $\sigma^2$. Even if $\sigma^2$ is very large, enough explanatory variables can make its estimate look small; on the other hand, if $\sigma^2 = 1$, leaving out relevant explanatory variables can lead to larger values of $\hat{\sigma}^2$ (see Prentice, 1986). Tests of over- and underdispersion are thus predicated on the inclusion of the correct list of explanatory variables. In the end, deciding on most aspects of a statistical model is a theoretical rather than empirical decision.

[16] Mobility tables, and other data in similar forms, might also be analyzed by asymmetric cluster analysis (Hubert, 1973, 1974) or network analysis (Knoke and Kuklinski, 1982). Since these alternatives do not yet have firm statistical bases (Ling, 1973), they must still be regarded as more descriptive than inferential procedures.

No assumption is generally made in the log-frequency model about $N_i$, but in order to derive the more restrictive log-odds model, I assume it is known in advance. Thus, although it is always true that $y_{1i} + y_{2i} = N_i$, we now know that $\mu_{1i} + \mu_{2i} = N_i$. Thus, in Equation (6.10), I replace each occurrence of $y_{2i}$ with $N_i - y_{1i}$, and each occurrence of $\tilde{\mu}_{2i}$ with $N_i - \tilde{\mu}_{1i}$:

$$\ln L(\tilde{\mu}|y) = \sum_{i=1}^{n} \{y_{1i}\ln\tilde{\mu}_{1i} - \tilde{\mu}_{1i}\} \tag{6.11}$$

$$+ \sum_{i=1}^{n} \{(N_i - y_{1i})\ln(N_i - \tilde{\mu}_{1i}) - (N_i - \tilde{\mu}_{1i})\}$$

$$= \sum_{i=1}^{n} \{y_{1i}\ln\tilde{\mu}_{1i} + (N_i - y_{1i})\ln(N_i - \tilde{\mu}_{1i})\},$$

where, in the second line, terms independent of $\tilde{\mu}_{1i}$ are dropped. To go further than Equation (6.11), we need to write down the model for $\mu_{1i}$. Since $\mu_i = \exp(x_i\beta)$, the ratio of the two parts of $\mu_i$ is also equal to the ratio of the two elements in $\exp(x_i\beta)$:

$$\frac{\mu_{1i}}{\mu_{2i}} = \frac{\exp(x_{1i}\beta_1)}{\exp(x_{2i}\beta_2)}.$$

Furthermore, since this is equivalent to the original form of the log-odds model,

$$\ln\left(\frac{\mu_{1i}}{\mu_{2i}}\right) = x_{1i}\beta_1 - x_{2i}\beta_2,$$

one can solve for $\mu_{1i}$ just as in Section 6.2, Equation (6.2). Thus, the result is that the exponential form for $\mu_i = \exp(x_i\beta)$ translates into a log-odds (logit) form for $\mu_{1i}$:

$$\mu_{1i} = N_i[1 + e^{-(x_{1i}\beta_1 - x_{2i}\beta_2)}]^{-1}. \tag{6.12}$$

By itself, this is a very interesting intermediary result. Simply by assuming that $N_i$ is an upper bound to the frequency of events in cell $i$ of the contingency table, and is known in advance, this shows that an exponential relationship logically *implies* a logistic one. This result also implicitly confirms the intuition behind the models given for individual level binary variables in Sections 5.5 and 5.6 and their logical connections with the models for individual level event counts in Sections 5.7 and 5.9.

I continue now by substituting the result in Equation (6.12) into the log-likelihood of Equation (6.11) to get:

$$\ln L(\tilde{\beta}|y) = \sum_{i=1}^{n} \left\{ y_{1i}\ln N_i\left(1 + e^{-(x_{1i}\tilde{\beta}_1 - x_{2i}\tilde{\beta}_2)}\right)^{-1} \right.$$

$$\left. + (N_i - y_i)\ln\left[N_i - N_i\left(1 + e^{-(x_{1i}\tilde{\beta}_1 - x_{2i}\tilde{\beta}_2)}\right)^{-1}\right]\right\}$$

$$= \sum_{i=1}^{n} \left\{ -y_{1i}\ln\left(1 + e^{-(x_{1i}\tilde{\beta}_1 - x_{2i}\tilde{\beta}_2)}\right) \right.$$
$$\left. - \left(N_i - y_{1i}\right)\ln\left(1 + e^{(x_{1i}\tilde{\beta}_1 - x_{2i}\tilde{\beta}_2)}\right) \right\}.$$

The only difference between this equation and that for the log-likelihood for the log-odd model [Equation (6.3)] is the notation in the term $(x_{1i}\tilde{\beta}_1 - x_{2i}\tilde{\beta}_2)$. Since this is just another form of a linear relationship, one could write it simply as, say, $X\tilde{\beta}$, which would make this model identical to that for the log-odds model. However, slightly more intuition can be gained into this problem by giving further attention to this term. In general, it can be rewritten as follows:

$$x_{1i}\beta_1 - x_{2i}\beta_2 = [\beta_{11} + D_i\beta_{21} + X_i\beta] - [\beta_{12} + D_i\beta_{22} + X_i\beta]$$
$$= \gamma + X_i(\beta_1 + \beta_2),$$

where, in the first line, $\beta_{11}$ and $\beta_{12}$ are the two constant terms and $D$ is the variable designated as "dependent." Since $D$ takes on the value 1 for category one and 0 for category two, $\beta_{22}$ may be dropped in the second line. Also, in the second line, $\gamma$ is just a reexpression of $\gamma = (\beta_{11} - \beta_{12} + \beta_{21})$. Except for $D_i$, $X_{1i}$ and $X_{2i}$ are equivalent. This feature is also used in the second line of this equation. Thus, we have proved that *one can begin with the log-frequency model, add the key assumption that the row marginals $N_i$ are known in advance, and get the log-odds model.*

This information would enable one to use the log-frequency model (and existing log-frequency computer programs) to estimate the log-odds model. However, if one is interested in analyzing the influence of one variable on another, estimating the log-odds model directly is certainly much easier.

## 6.8    Concluding remarks

The models in this chapter represent an extremely small percentage of existing methods for contingency tables analysis. More generally, at least three separate scholarly literatures on models for tabular data exist. The distinctions between these literatures are primarily due to varying numerical algorithms that put different constraints on the possible models to be estimated, as well as diverse substantive concerns. The most general algorithm is a direct ML estimation or an equivalent (but faster) iterative weighted least squares procedure appearing primarily in the British statistics literature (see McCullagh and Nelder, 1983, for a review). This literature is closest to the presentation in this chapter. The only difference is that statisticians tend to use the analysis of variance, instead of regression, parameterization.

The second literature on contingency tables is in sociology, identified most closely with Leo Goodman (e.g., 1978). These models are presented in a very different form from the models in the British statistics literature, but I have demonstrated in this chapter that the two are algebraically equivalent. For mostly historical reasons, sociological models of tabular data are usually estimated with an "iterative proportional fitting" algorithm (see Fineberg, 1970a, 1970b, 1980). This algorithm produces the same ML estimates as the iterative weighted least squares algorithm, with one important exception: it can only estimate "hierarchical models." A model is hierarchical if, for every interaction included, each of the variables making up the interaction is also included separately. All of the models fit in this chapter are hierarchical; they could therefore be fit with either algorithm. However, sometimes nonhierarchical models are more reasonable. For example, the nonhierarchical model in Equation (2.10) is probably more natural than its hierarchical version. Although this algorithm was designed to fit the log-frequency model, the log-odds model may be estimated as a special case by using the proof in Section 6.7.

The final literature on cross-tabulations is primarily focused in biostatistics (Grizzle, Starmer, and Koch, 1969; see also Kritzer, 1978b, in political science). This literature uses the (noniterative) weighted least squares algorithm. Although this algorithm permits a relatively flexible systematic component, it has a single stochastic component, centering on the consequences of the Normal distribution. Weighted least squares does not produce an ML estimator, except in one very special case; it is therefore not as statistically efficient. However, it is relatively robust to misspecification, can easily be estimated with existing regression computer programs, and can estimate many models other than the linear-proportion.

The most commonly used models of cross-classified categorical variables are the four presented in this chapter, but many other models do exist and others could easily be developed. In doing so, and in using these, researchers ought to concentrate on the process that produces the observed contingency table. If it is the researcher that created the table, rather than it being generated naturally, the methods of Chapter 5 are probably preferable, although a table may still be a very useful and intuitive descriptive statistic. When the original data are unavailable, particularly in replications of analyses from published tables, models for tabular data are quite useful. More generally, this chapter has demonstrated how to apply the likelihood theory of inference in Part I to this very different form of quantitative data.

# CHAPTER 7

# Time series models

The statistical models presented thus far may all be described according to a special case of the general framework in Equations (1.3) and (1.4). More specifically, I have always made the following three assumptions:

1. $Y_i \sim f(y_i|\theta_i,\alpha)$.
2. $\theta_i = g(x_i,\beta)$.
3. $Y_i$ and $Y_j$ are independent for all $i \neq j$.

The key difference between models that fit this framework and time series models is assumption 3. For example, in a cross-sectional study of presidential popularity, individual $i$'s approval of the current president is likely to be unrelated to individual $(i+1)$'s approval. In fact, the order of the observations in a sample survey is usually irrelevant. Assuming that an observation at one time is independent of the next period's observation is often implausible. For example, the set of monthly presidential approval polls of the entire nation represents a time series. Even conditional on the past level of mean approval, an unusually high level of public support for the president in one month is likely to remain high for at least the next month. Monthly unemployment statistics, also collected through sample surveys, and annual trade figures are two other examples where successive observations are likely to be dependent.

Data with time series *properties* need not have been collected over time in a series. For example, an extensive survey of a neighborhood at one point in time might result in observations that are serially correlated if neighbors influence one another. The correlations among observations would then be over space rather than over time, but successive observations would still be correlated. A considerable part of politics is fundamentally geographic. Unfortunately, much of our data is collected in surveys that almost completely ignore relationships among neighborhoods, districts, states, and individuals. On the other hand, aggregate electoral data sources do preserve some of these spatial relationships; developing and applying models with spatial relationships should be an important topic for future research in political science. For another example, suppose one wanted to do a survey of a rare group, such as lesbian mothers. Because so few of these people exist, a random sample of the U.S. population would be very costly and grossly inefficient. An alternative might be to use "snowball sampling." The basic procedure is to find one lesbian mother, interview her, and ask her for the names of other people in a similar situation (TenHouten, Stern, and TenHouten, 1979). Since, by definition, each mother knows the next person in the sample, successive observations are likely to be correlated.

What happens if one estimates a model based on assumption 3, but some random observations are actually dependent? From a technical perspective, the parameter estimates would be inefficient and the standard errors biased. For many models the parameter estimates would also be inconsistent. Dependence also means that each observation adds something less than one additional piece of information; in effect, standard errors are biased because they are based on the apparent, rather than effective, sample size.[1] One could "correct" for these "violations," as many econometrics texts teach, but this would obliterate some of the most interesting information in *time* series data. A central goal of this analysis should be to model the underlying process by which the random observations vary and covary over time. In a sense, the task of time series analysis is to model how history repeats itself or how it influences future events.

In order to understand how to alter assumption 3, consider first its specific role in the models introduced in previous chapters. The primary purpose of this assumption is as a very specific model of the process producing the observed data. Under this assumption, the stochastic process for each observation is a function of a set of unknown parameters, $\theta$ and $\alpha$. In addition, $\theta$ is usually allowed to vary over the random observations. Conditional on these parameters, large values of one observation do not necessarily lead to large (or small) values of the next observation.

In previous chapters, I used the independence assumption, along with assumption 1 about the stochastic process for a single observation, as first principles with which to derive the full stochastic component [Equation (1.3) in the general case]. The derivation is quite simple:

$$f(y\,|\,\theta,\alpha) = \prod_{i=1}^{n} f_i(y_i|\theta_i,\alpha), \qquad (7.1)$$

where $f_i$ is specified in assumption 1 and the product may be taken because of assumption 3. The resulting multivariate distribution (of the vector $y$ on the left hand side) is proportional to the likelihood function which is then used for inference purposes.

One could easily avoid assumption 3 (and assumption 1 as well) by directly specifying the multivariate distribution for the entire data vector, $f(y|\theta,\alpha)$.

---

[1] In the extreme case of perfect autocorrelation, the first observation would contain all the information in the data set. In this case, even if one collected an infinite number of additional observations, no more information would be added.

Independence or any form of dependence could then be incorporated directly into this multivariate distribution. However, theorizing about multivariate distributions is generally "harder" than for univariate distributions. I use quotation marks because, although we tend to be more comfortable theorizing about univariate distributions and independence, the two sides of Equation (7.1) are still equal. The additional degree of comfort exists with respect to the right hand side because its two assumptions are simpler and closer to the substantive process we are trying to model than the single, more complicated, assumption on the left hand side.

Thus, choosing fundamental first principles is probably a better approach in modeling time series or any other processes than directly assuming a multivariate distribution for the entire set of random observations. Since assumption 3 no longer holds, we need a different set of first principles and a different method of deriving a multivariate distribution from them. The solution is provided by a version of the basic rule for conditional probabilities in Equation (3.2). To illustrate the use of this equation, consider a simple problem with only two observations. Whether or not they are independent, the bivariate distribution of $Y_1$ and $Y_2$ can be written as follows:

$$f(y_i, y_2|\theta,\alpha) \equiv f(y|\theta,\alpha)$$
$$= f(y_1|\theta_1,\alpha)f(y_2|y_1,\theta_2,\alpha).$$

If $Y_1$ and $Y_2$ are independent, $f(y_2|y_1,\theta_2,\alpha) = f(y_2|\theta_2,\alpha)$, and this equation reduces to Equation (7.1). The first principles in this case are assumptions about the distribution of $Y_1$ and the conditional distribution of $Y_2|Y_1$. No assumption of independence is required. Of course, we will also need to specify the functional form that indicates precisely how the parameters of $Y_2$ depend on $Y_1$, just as for previous analyses we had to specify how they depended on the exogenous variables, $X$.

This result may be expressed in a more general form for $n$ observations as follows:

$$f(y|\theta,\alpha) = f(y_1|\theta_1,\alpha)f(y_2|y_1,\theta_2,\alpha)f(y_3|y_1,y_2,\theta_2,\alpha) \cdots$$
$$= f(y_1|\theta_1,\alpha) \prod_{i=2}^{n} f(y_i|y_1, \ldots, y_{i-1},\theta_i,\alpha).$$

However, for many problems, this form is excessively general. In time series data, $Y_i$ often depends on $Y_{i-1}$, perhaps on $Y_{i-2}$, and maybe even on a few prior random observations. However, whether the observations were taken each second, minute, month, or year, only in unusual situations would $Y_i$ depend on $Y_{i-k}$ for very large $k$, especially after the earlier lags were taken into account. Thus, one simplifying alternative is to assume in general that

$Y_i$ and $Y_{i-k}$ are conditionally independent for $k > t$.

This is a property of *Markov processes*. Markov processes basically assume that, conditional on the present, the future of a process is independent of the past (see, for example, Spanos, 1986: 148–9). For example, in many cases an assumption that today is influenced only by yesterday (and not the day before or previous days) is adequate. That is, $t = 1$, which in turn gives:

$$f(y|\theta,\alpha) = f(y_1|\theta_1,\alpha) \prod_{i=2}^{n} f_i(y_i|y_{i-1},\theta_2,\alpha). \tag{7.2}$$

For a setup such as this, one needs to make assumptions about the distribution of the first observation $Y_1$, the conditional distribution of $Y_i|Y_{i-1}$, and the value of $t$. These first principles thus enable one to derive the full stochastic component and, in turn, the complete likelihood function.

Conditional distributions are far easier to hypothesize about than a full $n$-dimensional multivariate distribution. One issue that must be addressed is the role of $y_{i-1}$ in the conditional distribution, $f(y_i|y_{i-1},\theta_i,\alpha)$. The easiest interpretation of this lagged dependent variable is as an additional explanatory variable. For example, one simple model of the way $Y_2$ depends on $Y_1$, and a vector of explanatory variables, is the following equation:

$$\mu_i = x_i\beta + y_{i-1}\phi. \tag{7.3}$$

When the realization of the previous observation, $y_{i-1}$, increases by one unit in this linear model, the expected value of $Y_i$ ($\mu_i$) increases by $\phi$.

To make the situation even clearer, one could even change the notation so as to include $y_{i-1}$ as an extra column of the $X$ matrix. The only difficulty with this interpretation is that until now $X$ has included only *known features* of the social system – that is, they were exogenous. At time $i$, $y_{i-1}$ is known for certain, so we might interpret it as merely an additional known feature. Although this works well on one level, $y_{i-1}$ is not really a feature of the social system; it is only a realized value of the random variable $Y_{i-1}$. If essentially the same experiment were run again, a different value of $y_{i-1}$ would result. What are the consequences of including explanatory variables that are realizations of stochastic processes rather than known features of the social system? I take a brief aside in the next section to answer this essential question. Following that section, I return to specifying and analyzing a variety of complete time series models more sophisticated than the systematic component in Equation (7.3).

## 7.1 Stochastic explanatory variables

Suppose instead of $X$ being a vector of known features of the social system, it represents a single realization from an unknown multivariate probability distribution. These realizations could be lagged values of the dependent variable or just stochastic explanatory variables. In this section, I demonstrate that this situation of stochastic explanatory variables results in the same likelihood function and parametric inferences as if $X$ had been exogenous.

Begin with the usual model

$$Y \sim f(y|\theta,\alpha),$$

$$\theta = g(X,\beta)$$

and, for clarity, substitute the second equation into the first:

$$Y \sim f(y|g(X,\beta),\alpha) = f(y|X,\beta,g,\alpha). \tag{7.4}$$

Suppose now that $X$ is not fixed and known in advance, but instead is a random variable distributed in some unknown manner:[2]

$$X \sim f_?(X).$$

The only assumption I make about this distribution is that its parameters, if there are any, are not functions of $\theta$ or $\alpha$.[3] Indeed, this assumption is equivalent to assuming that $X$ is *weakly exogenous* with respect to $Y$ (see Hendry and Richard, 1983).[4]

The full stochastic component must always reflect all randomness in the model. Thus, $X$ should not be taken as given in Equation (7.4). Instead, one must derive a stochastic component as a function of both $y$ and $X$. To do this, I use a procedure similar to that used in Chapter 3 to derive the extended beta-binomial distribution [see Equation (3.8) and the discussion that follows]. Thus a joint distribution of $y$ and $X$ may be derived by taking the product of the conditional and marginal distributions:

$$f_j(y,X|\theta,\alpha) = f(y|X,\beta,g\alpha)f_?(X).$$

The log-likelihood is then written as follows:

$$\ln L(\tilde{\beta},\tilde{\alpha}|y,X,g) = \ln f_j(y,X|\tilde{\beta},g,\tilde{\alpha})$$
$$= \ln f(y|X,\tilde{\beta},g,\tilde{\alpha}) + \ln f_?(X).$$

---

[2] For the dependent variable, I have used $Y$ for the random variable and $y$ as the realization. Since this section demonstrates that treating $X$ as either stochastic or exogenous is inconsequential, I avoid introducing new notation by using $X$ to take on both meanings, depending on the context.

[3] A more traditional way to make this point is by saying that $X$ is independent of the disturbance term, $\epsilon \equiv Y - \mu$ (see Hanushek and Jackson, 1977). Thus, the existence of shared parameters driving the two processes (of $Y$ and $X$) and a correlation between $X$ and $\epsilon$ are different ways of expressing the same point. I prefer the former because it involves only variables close to political science theory rather than the analytical construct $\epsilon$. In addition, the disturbance form of the relationship is only conceivable in those special cases where the systematic component involves the mean.

[4] One must also assume that parameters of $f_?$ have no relation to $\theta$ and $\alpha$.

Note that since the last term does not depend on either $\tilde{\beta}$ or $\tilde{\alpha}$, it merely shifts the function up and down, not affecting inferences based appropriately on relative values of the log-likelihood. Therefore, regardless of which multivariate function $f_?$ represents, it may be safely dropped during estimation:

$$\ln L(\tilde{\beta},\tilde{\alpha}|y,X,g) = \ln f_j(y|\tilde{\beta},g,\tilde{\alpha}).$$

Fortunately, this result is identical to the log-likelihood that results if $X$ is assumed to be a known feature of the social system. Thus, from here on, I do not distinguish between explanatory variables that are known features and those that are realizations of stochastic processes. Note also that this result is consistent with, and indeed a result of, the likelihood principle – the concept that the only information used to make inferences is that of the data.


## 7.2    The influence of history

Equation (7.3) represents one process by which history influences later events. It states that $\mu_i$ is a simple linear function of a vector of explanatory variables $x_i$ and a single lag of the observed dependent variable $y_{i-1}$. This simple model is quite powerful for many substantive research problems, but it is not the only way that past events can influence the present. In general, the goal is to formulate a systematic model of some parametric feature of the stochastic component, $\theta_i$, as it varies over time as a function of past and present events. For this section, however, I stick to systematic components that attempt to account for variation in the expected value $\mu_i$ over time.

In the time series literature, the expected value $\mu_i$ is almost always assumed to be a linear function of a vector of explanatory variables with a Normal stochastic component. Part of the reason for this, as will shortly become obvious, is that the range of "reasonable" specifications increases vastly when data have time series properties. Of course, by itself, this provides little justification for choosing a linear-Normal model or any other. Perhaps the best justification is that applications of this model have been quite successful in forecasting: "The linearity is a convenient mathematical fiction only. Experience suggests that a model of [this form] will fit a wide range of data" (Hannan, 1970: 9). Partial theoretical justification for linear systematic components can be found in the *Wold decomposition theorem* (Wold, 1954). Wold demonstrated that any stationary time series process $Y_i$ could be decomposed into two independent processes, $Y_i = S_i + U_i$ where $S_i$ is a systematic component and $U_i$ is a stochastic component with a known time series process (moving average of infinite order). This theorem does not prove that linear time series models are always or even usually best, but it does suggest that they may be a good approximation in a wide variety of cases. Even after all this reasoning and argument, little theoretical justification exists for choosing a linear-Normal model without further reflection. Nevertheless, I use it in this section to introduce the variety of ways the influence of the past on the present can be modeled. Perhaps because linear models have been so successful, the theory of nonlinear, non-Normal time series models is still in its infancy. Writing down these new models is relatively easy, but ascertaining their theoretical consequences is somewhat more difficult (see Ashley, Patterson, and Hinich, 1985; Granger, and Newbold, 1986: 303–12; Harvey, 1986b; Hinich and Patterson, 1985; Priestley, 1980).

To specify the complete stochastic component in the time series context, one must use a derivation like that in Equation (7.2). Three initial assumptions are therefore key: (1) the distribution of the first observation, (2) the conditional distribution of the remaining random observations, and (3) the length of the dependency among the observations. For all the models in this section, I assume that the distribution for the first observation and the conditional distributions are Normal.[5] Finally, I assume that only one lag is relevant; two observations farther apart than one period are assumed independent, conditional on the previous observation. These assumptions may be written as follows:

1. $Y_1 \sim f_N(y_1|\mu_1,\sigma^2)$.
2. $Y_i|Y_{i-1} \sim f_N(y_i|\mu_i,\sigma^2)$.
3. $\mu_i = g(x_i,\beta,Y_{i-1},\phi)$.
4. $Y_i$ and $Y_{i-t}$ are independent for all $t > 1$.

In this section I assume further that $g$ in assumption (3) is linear. Some feature of $Y_{i-1}$, and not the random variable itself, is to be part of this assumption. Since $\sigma^2$ is written without a subscript, it is constant over observations – the assumption of homoscedasticity – although this could be generalized to include a variance function as in Equation (4.10). For time series research that is relevant to this specification, see Engle (1982) and Granger, Robins, and Engle (1985) on AutoRegressive Conditional Heteroscedastic (ARCH) models. From this, the general form of the stochastic component may be written as follows:

$$f_N(y|\mu,\sigma^2) = f_N(y_1|\mu_1,\sigma^2) \prod_{i=2}^{n} f_N(y_i|\mu_i,\sigma^2)$$
$$= (2\pi\sigma^2)^{-1/2} e^{-(y_1-\mu_1)^2/2\sigma^2} \prod_{i=2}^{n} (2\pi\sigma^2)^{-1/2} e^{-(y_i-\mu_i)^2/2\sigma^2}.$$

---

[5] The Normal density is the only example of a distribution where the conditional distributions take the same form as the marginal distributions. With non-Normal stochastic components, therefore, one must introduce new forms for the conditional distributions.

Dropping terms that do not depend on $\tilde{\sigma}^2$ and $\tilde{\beta}$, the log-likelihood can then be written in preliminary form as:

$$\ln L(\tilde{\mu}_i, \tilde{\sigma}^2 | y) = -\frac{1}{2}\left[\ln(\tilde{\sigma}^2) + \frac{(y_1 - \tilde{\mu}_1)^2}{\tilde{\sigma}^2}\right] - \frac{1}{2}\sum_{i=2}^{n}\left[\ln(\tilde{\sigma}^2) + \frac{(y_i - \tilde{\mu}_i)^2}{\tilde{\sigma}^2}\right].$$

(7.5)

The terms in brackets in this equation cannot be combined, with summation going from 1 to $n$, because $\mu_i$ is a function of past values of $y_i$, and $y_0$ is unknown. This form does make it clear that this log-likelihood is a function of the sum of squared residuals in a manner similar to that in Chapter 2.6 for standard cross-sectional regression models.

I now move to various forms of systematic components for data with time series properties. Below is a list of four possible influences on $\mu_i = E(Y_i)$. The first was considered in previous chapters. The others are all functions of the lagged dependent variable, $Y_{i-1}$:

1.  exogenous variables, $x_i$;
2.  past expectations, $\mu_{i-1} \equiv E(Y_{i-1})$;
3.  past realizations, $y_{i-1}$;
4.  past shocks, $\xi_{i-1} \equiv y_{i-1} - \mu_{i-1}$.

Previous lags of any of these variables can also be relevant. Although most substantive applications involve only some of these variables, the most general form of a relationship with a single lag can still be written as follows:

$$\mu_i = g(x_i, \mu_{i-1}, y_{i-1}, \xi_{i-1}).$$

For presentation, I simplify this general relationship and use only a linear form as I consider each of these in turn.

*Exogenous variables*

The exogenous variables $(x_i)$ at time $i$ can influence $\mu_i$ in time series or cross-sectional data in roughly the same manner. As an example, consider a time series of monthly presidential approval ratings. Exogenous influences might include economic variables and international conflict. Thus, we might write:

$$\mu_i = x_i\beta.$$

Estimating this equation is straightforward. Since no time series component is included, $x_i\beta$ may be directly substituted for $\mu_i$ in the Normal density to form the likelihood. Exogenous variables are included in most time series models. In some, lags of exogenous variables are included as well. For example, public approval toward presidents is likely to depend on current economic concerns, but a deep recession six months ago is unlikely to be entirely forgotten. Hence, one can write:

$$\mu_i = x_i\beta_1 + x_{i-1}\beta_2. \tag{7.6}$$

Estimation here would also not be a problem, since the right hand side of this equation could easily be incorporated in the log-likelihood in Equation (7.5). The only unusual feature is that $x_{1-1} \equiv x_0$ is generally unknown. The first observation is a persistent problem in most models of times series. However, with large sample sizes, it usually has little consequence. The easiest procedure is then to drop this first observation, although more efficient methods have been developed (see Harvey, 1981a). Because exogenous variables are almost always present, I include them as I introduce the remaining ways the past may influence the present.

### Past expectations

Since the true level of presidential approval seems to change only gradually over time, high past expectations ($\mu_{i-1}$) of presidential approval are likely to lead to high current levels of expected approval. $\mu_{i-1}$ represents one feature of the systematic portion of the random variable $Y_{i-1}$. Other systematic features of $Y_{i-1}$ might also influence $\mu_i$, but the leading example is very often the mean at time $i-1$. Thus, one might hypothesize the following:

$$\mu_i = x_i\beta + \mu_{i-1}\phi, \tag{7.7}$$

where $\phi$ and $\beta$ are effect parameters. This is the first systematic component we have considered with an unobserved nonrandom variable on the right hand side of the equation for the systematic component. When past mean approval increases by one percentage point, $\mu_i$ would be expected to increase by $\phi$. Note that $\mu_{i-1}$ is very different from $y_{i-1}$. The former is the expected value of the random variable $Y_{i-1}$ measured without error; the latter is merely one realization from the random variable. As such, $y_{i-1}$ is a function of the mean plus random error. In data with a fair amount of random error, significant theoretical and empirical differences can be found between the two specifications. With presidential popularity, each observation comes from a separate sample survey and necessarily contains sampling error. Since Americans' attitudes toward presidents tend to be quite stable, current approval is likely to depend more on past mean approval than on sampling error in any individual poll.

Writing down the likelihood function for this model is somewhat more complicated than for previous models. The reason is that if the right hand side of Equation (7.7) is substituted into the log-likelihood function in Equation (7.5), $\mu_{i-1}$ is still in the equation. If $\mu_{i-1}$ were known, this would cause no difficulties. Thus, further reparameterization is necessary so that the only unknown parameters are $\beta$ and $\phi$. The simplest means of thinking about this problem is to reformulate the systematic component by *recursive reparameterization*. Note that Equation (7.7) implies that

$$\mu_{i-1} = x_{i-1}\beta + \mu_{i-2}\phi, \tag{7.8}$$

which is only Equation (7.7) shifted back one observation. Now repeatedly substitute the right hand side of Equation (7.8) for $\mu_{i-1}$ in Equation (7.7):

$$\begin{aligned}
\mu_i &= x_i\beta + \mu_{i-1}\phi \tag{7.9}\\
&= x_i\beta + (x_{i-1}\beta + \mu_{i-2}\phi)\phi\\
&= x_i\beta + x_{i-1}\beta\phi + \mu_{i-2}\phi^2\\
&= x_i\beta + x_{i-1}\beta\phi + (x_{i-2}\beta + \mu_{i-3}\phi)\phi^2\\
&= x_i\beta + x_{i-1}\beta\phi + x_{i-2}\beta\phi^2 + \mu_{i-3}\phi^3\\
&= \mu_1\phi^{i-1} + \sum_{j=0}^{i-2} x_{i-j}\beta\phi^j\\
&= \sum_{j=0}^{\infty} x_{i-j}\beta\phi^j.
\end{aligned}$$

Several features of this result are worthy of comment. First, in the final step, all of previous history is included as previous lags. Since data collection only begins at time $i = 1$, some assumption must be made about the effects of prior unobserved lags. This *truncation assumption* is a problem that reoccurs in most time series models. No wholly satisfactory solution exists, so compromises must be made. In general, the practical solution is to assume that $y_1$ is fixed across experiments and equal to $\mu_1$. Thus, one substitutes the right hand side of the penultimate line in Equation (7.9), with $y_1 = \mu_1$, into the log-likelihood in Equation (7.5). It may then be easily maximized with respect to $\hat{\beta}$ and $\hat{\phi}$. Alternatively, one could use the penultimate line of Equation (7.9) to estimate $\mu_1$ as an additional ancillary parameter. This is less restrictive and more realistic than assuming $y_1 = \mu_1$, but it does put additional burdens on one's data by requiring that an additional parameter be estimated. Assuming $y_1 = \mu_1$ is the most common truncation assumption, but it is not necessarily the best in every instance; with a fair amount of data, estimating $\mu_1$ can result in substantial improvements.

The calculations in Equation (7.9) may be considered merely a technique for writing the likelihood without $\mu_i$ appearing directly. If they are, then $\beta$ and $\phi$ may be interpreted as in Equation (7.7): they are effect parameters representing the influence of $x_i$ and $\mu_{i-1}$, respectively. However, the reformulation in Equation (7.9) leads to a very different interpretation. This point can be made a little clearer by writing out the last line of that equation:

$$\mu_i = x_i\beta + x_{i-1}(\beta\phi) + x_{i-2}(\beta\phi^2) + x_{i-3}(\beta\phi^3) + x_{i-4}(\beta\phi^4) + \cdots. \tag{7.10}$$

In this formulation, the current mean $\mu_i$ is written as a function of all past values of the explanatory variables. If $\phi$ is between $-1$ and $1$, exogenous variables with longer lags have proportionately smaller effects on the current $\mu_i$. If $\phi$ is outside the $[-1,1]$ interval, the longer lags have larger effects;

indeed, for very long lags, the effect "explodes," eventually going to positive or negative infinity. Since the latter is implausible for most political science applications, we will generally assume that $\phi \in (-1,1)$. This restriction is a special case of a standard assumption in time series, that of *stationarity*.[6]

Note that Equation (7.7) and Equation (7.10) are substantively very different but still algebraically equivalent. In the former, $\phi$ is interpreted as the effect of $\mu_{i-1}$ on $\mu_i$. In the latter, $\phi$ may be interpreted as a constraint on the structure of the lagged effects of the exogenous variables. As written, the coefficients on past values of the exogenous variables decline geometrically as the length of the lag increases. Because of this interesting interpretation, Equation (7.10) is often the original form of the specification and is called the *geometric distributed lag* (or Koyck distributed lag) model (Harvey, 1981a: 222–6; Koyck, 1954). The closer $\phi$ is to $-1$ or 1 [given $\phi \in (-1,1)$] the longer a change in an exogenous variable will have an effect on $\mu_i$. For most values of $\phi$ the effects of lagged values of $x$ become very small, very quickly. For example, a plausible specification for presidential approval might have the mean current approval as a geometrically distributed lag of all states of the economy over the incumbent president's term. Recent months would be weighted more heavily, and events even many months ago would have some very small residual effects.

A generalization of the geometric distributed lag may be written in preliminary form as follows:

$$\mu_i = x_i \gamma_0 + x_{i-1} \gamma_1 + x_{i-2} \gamma_2 + \cdots + x_1 \gamma_{i-1}.$$

This is only preliminary because this model is far too unrestrictive. Some additional structure must be put on all of the $\gamma$ parameters. The geometric distributed lag structure is only one special case where all the $\gamma$ coefficients are replaced by only two parameters by using the following equation to reparameterize:

$$\gamma_j = \beta \phi^j.$$

Equation (7.6) is another, even more restrictive form. Still another is due to Almon (1965) who proposed approximating the $\gamma$ coefficients with a polynomial having many fewer coefficients. For example,

$$\gamma_j = \beta_0 + j\beta_1 + j^2\beta_2 + j^3\beta_3.$$

---

[6] In more sophisticated models, stationarity is a critical assumption requiring considerably more attention than I have given it here. In general, it is the assumption that the only factor governing the relationship between two observations is the distance that separates them in time. Thus, the models in this chapter hold regardless of what $i$ is. See Granger and Newbold (1986) for a more complete treatment. Note that although stationarity is a technical requirement, it stems from fundamental substantive assumptions about the process giving rise to one's time series data.

Lütkepohl (1981) proposed an exponentially distributed lag structure, and Tsurumi (1971) introduced the idea of estimating the model by letting the parameters follow a gamma distribution. Dhrymes (1971), Griliches (1967), Jorgenson (1966), Judge et al. (1985: Chapters 9–10), and Trivedi (1984) introduce a variety of other interesting possibilities.[7]

*Past realizations*

From another perspective, the relevant influence on the current mean might be $y_{i-1}$, the actual realization of the random variable $Y_{i-1}$. Suppose one is interested in explaining public support for a presidential candidate during the primary season. Support for candidates tends to be quite volatile. In addition, since citizens prefer to vote for the winner, actual poll results influence voter preferences. Thus, the random error from one poll (perhaps even funded by one of the candidates) would have as much predictive power as the true proportion of the population supporting each candidate. If this is the case, then using past expectations [Equation (7.8)] would be inappropriate. However, the past realization could easily be included in the equation:

$$\mu_i = x_i\beta + y_{i-1}\phi. \tag{7.11}$$

Since everything on the right side of this equation is either to be estimated directly or is known, the estimation of this model requires no recursive reparameterization. One only needs to insert the right hand side of this equation into the log-likelihood in Equation (7.5) and then maximize it with respect to $\tilde{\beta}$ and $\tilde{\phi}$.

The time series component of this model is generally referred to as an AR($p$) model, an *autoregressive process* with $p$ lags. Equation (7.11) is then AR(1). See Box and Jenkins (1976).

*Past shocks*

A past shock is defined as the difference between the realization and the mean of the random variable $Y_{i-1}$:[8]

$$\xi_{i-1} \equiv y_{i-1} - \mu_{i-1}. \tag{7.12}$$

---

[7] A key distinction usually made in this literature is between finite and infinite numbers of distributed lags. This distinction is important, but primarily for technical reasons: convergence of infinite sums is often easier to represent than for finite sums. Although an infinite distributed lag does allow for the (implausible) possibility that some event an infinite number of periods ago would still have an influence, the parameters usually allow for the effect to die out to essentially zero after only a few periods.

[8] One could think of $\xi_i$ as an unobserved realization of the disturbance, $\epsilon \equiv Y_i - \mu_i$.

In explaining a time series such as stock market prices, measured systematic variables like the inflation rate are surely important. However, with a phenomenon as sensitive as market pricing, random unobserved shocks are also likely to have powerful effects. We might therefore write

$$\mu_i = x_i \beta + \xi_{i-1} \phi \tag{7.13}$$

to represent the situation where a random shock has an effect for a single period.

To estimate this model, one cannot directly substitute the right hand side of Equation (7.13) into the likelihood in Equation (7.5). The problem here is similar to the problem with past expectations – a right hand side variable is unobserved. Fortunately, with recursive reparameterization, Equation (7.13) can be redefined as a function of $\beta$ and $\phi$ only. First, substitute Equation (7.12) into Equation (7.13), and then successively substitute previous lags of Equation (7.13) into itself:

$$
\begin{aligned}
\mu_i &= x_i \beta + \xi_{i-1} \phi \\
&= x_i \beta + (y_{i-1} - \mu_{i-1}) \phi \\
&= x_i \beta + y_{i-1} \phi - \mu_{i-1} \phi \\
&= x_i \beta + y_{i-1} \phi - (x_{i-1} \beta + y_{i-2} \phi - \mu_{i-2} \phi) \phi \\
&= x_i \beta + y_{i-1} \phi - x_{i-1} \beta \phi - y_{i-2} \phi^2 + \mu_{i-2} \phi^2 \\
&= x_i \beta - (y_1 - \mu_1)(-\phi)^i - \sum_{j=1}^{i-1} (y_{i-j} - x_{i-j} \beta)(-\phi)^j \\
&= x_i \beta - \sum_{j=1}^{\infty} (y_{i-j} - x_{i-j} \beta)(-\phi)^j .
\end{aligned}
\tag{7.14}
$$

Since only observations $i = 1, \ldots, n$ are available, the last line of this equation is useful for interpretation but not estimation. Instead, the penultimate line is generally used in one of two ways. First, one may substitute this entire expression for $\mu_i$ in the log-likelihood in Equation (7.5); the log-likelihood is then maximized with respect to $\tilde{\beta}$, $\tilde{\sigma}^2$, and $\tilde{\mu}_1$. Second, one might choose to assume that $y_1$ is fixed across experiments and known to be equal to $\mu_1$. Note that this assumption is relatively strong, since it implies that $\xi_1 = \xi_0 = \xi_{-1} = \cdots = 0$. If this assumption is made, the second term in the penultimate line is equal to zero and thus drops out; the rest of the equation is substituted into the log-likelihood in Equation (7.5), which is then maximized with respect to only $\tilde{\beta}$ and $\tilde{\sigma}^2$.

This is a relatively complicated expression for the effects of the exogenous variables and previous realized values of $Y$, but it may still be used to substitute into the log-likelihood in Equation (7.5) for estimation. $\beta$ is an effect parameter for the exogenous variables and $\phi$ is the effect of the random shock

Table 7.1. *Senate roll call participation*

| Variable | Estimate | S.e. |
|----------|----------|------|
| Constant | 90.39 | 0.76 |
| Weekend | −6.08 | 1.21 |
| $\xi_{i-1}$ | 0.58 | 0.07 |
| $\xi_{i-2}$ | 0.41 | 0.08 |
| $\xi_{i-3}$ | 0.26 | 0.08 |
| $\xi_{i-4}$ | 0.13 | 0.07 |

on $\mu_i$. The time series component of this model is generally called a *moving average process* with parameter $q$, or MA ($q$). See Box and Jenkins (1976).

Additional lags of previous random shocks can be used to model the situation where a shock has a longer lasting influence. For example, suppose one were interested in modeling participation rates by U.S. senators on roll call votes (see King, 1986b; Riker, 1959). One could include measured exogenous variables like the day of the week (senators tend to be in their constituency from Friday through Monday), the policy area of the roll call, interparty competition, and interparty cohesion. However, a critical factor is likely to be the occasional roll call votes that are especially important. When an important vote occurs, many senators are likely to rush to Washington to participate. Then, once the senators get to Washington they are likely to stay for the rest of the day or week and continue to vote on roll calls. Thus, a shock (an important roll call) that hits the system is likely to raise participation initially and keep it high for several additional roll calls. This phenomenon could be modeled by deriving an explicit measure of roll call importance; unfortunately, no satisfactory measure exists. Thus, one could estimate a model like the following (see King, 1986b):

$$\mu_i = x_i\beta + \xi_{i-1}\phi_1 + \xi_{i-2}\phi_2 + \xi_{i-3}\phi_3 + \xi_{i-4}\phi_4.$$

Table 7.1 gives empirical estimates of this model using senate roll call votes from the first six months of 1980.[9] The estimates indicate that when an unexpectedly important roll call reaches the senate floor and increases the number of senators participating, about 58% of the additional senators remain to vote on the next roll call, 41% on the next, 26% on the next, and 13% on the fourth. This simple model provides a look into the unobserved process that

---

[9] Exogenous variables that did not substantially influence values of the other coefficients were omitted from the model. Estimations with different numbers of lags produced similar results.

generates observed senatorial participation rates. Even though $\xi_i$ cannot be directly measured, estimates of its impact can be reliably made.

An alternative interpretation of a single lag random shock model comes from the third line of Equation (7.14). This model is equivalent to one with a single lag of both the realization ($y_{i-1}$) and expectation ($\mu_{i-1}$) of the random variable $Y_{i-1}$, with the coefficients of each constrained to be the negative of one another. One can generalize this model slightly by unconstraining the two parameters:

$$\mu_i = x_i\beta + y_{i-1}\phi_1 + \mu_{i-1}\phi_2. \tag{7.15}$$

Is it true that $\phi = -\phi_2$? If it is, then one can use this additional information in the model in Equation (7.13) to get more precise parameter estimates. Otherwise, the slightly less restrictive Equation (7.15) can be used since it only requires one additional parameter. If the answer to this question is unclear, then Equation (7.15) can be estimated and one can test the hypothesis that $\phi_1 = -\phi_2$. It also demonstrates how one can model more complicated processes by which the past influences the present.

### Combinations

Any number or types of combinations of the above methods by which the past can influence the present might provide useful models in particular substantive situations. One can use expectations, realizations, random shocks, previous values of the exogenous variables, or any other combination of factors. In addition, multiple lags of any or all of these might be included in many situations. For example, in forecasting annual social welfare expenditures, incremental budgeting can be modeled by including the past realization. Since members of Congress prefer higher social welfare spending to help them out in election years, a lag at time $i-2$ might also be included. Of course, the quadrennial presidential elections may also lead to spending increases. The result might be a model with lags at times $i-1$, $i-2$, and $i-4$:

$$\mu_i = x_i\beta + y_{i-1}\phi_1 + y_{i-2}\phi_2 + y_{i-4}\phi_4.$$

Since social welfare expenditures probably have few random shocks, one might expect that past realizations, as in this equation, would give similar results to lagged expectations.

### 7.3    Theoretical ambiguities

In the previous section, each model was given at least two algebraic representations. The first might be called the structural or theoretical model. The second is the reduced form, most useful for estimation. However, many of the reduced forms, calculated with recursive reparameterizations, were also interesting structural models in their own right. A theoretical specification might begin with either representation, depending on the substance of the research problem.

With a little reflection, the theoretical ambiguities in time series models become even more apparent. For example, is a given set of data generated by a process in which the current mean depends on current exogenous variables and a single lag of the expected value [as in Equation (7.7)], or is it generated by an infinite geometric distributed lag of the exogenous variables [Equation (7.10)]? The question is unanswerable because the two seemingly different processes are mathematically equivalent. Researchers should therefore be very careful about the cases made for particular time series models; very often, they are not mutually exclusive specifications.

Another example can be found in the third line of Equation (7.14) and its generalization in Equation (7.15). From that calculation, and from the relationship $\xi_i = y_{i-\mu_i}$, one can see that a single lag of an expectation, a realization, *or* a shock may be rewritten solely in terms of the other two with certain constraints on the parameters.

In fact, the ambiguities in time series models run even deeper than those presented in the last section. For example, any two of the three functions of $Y_{i-1}$ – shocks, realizations, and expectations – used in the same model are equivalent to including any of the other two. For example, here is a model for the current mean as a function of a vector of exogenous variables, a shock, and realization at time $i-1$:

$$\mu_i = x_i\beta + \xi_{i-1}\phi_1 + y_{i-1}\phi_2.$$

However, since $\xi_{i-1} = y_{i-1} - \mu_{i-1}$, this equation may be written as follows:

$$\begin{aligned}\mu_i &= x_i\beta + (y_{i-1} - \mu_{i-1})\phi_1 + y_{i-1}\phi_2 \qquad (7.16)\\ &= x_i\beta + y_{i-1}\phi_1 - \mu_{i-1}\phi_1 + y_{i-1}\phi_2\\ &= x_i\beta + y_{i-1}(\phi_1 + \phi_2) + \mu_{i-1}(-\phi_1)\\ &= x_i\beta + y_{i-1}\theta_1 + \mu_{i-1}\theta_2,\end{aligned}$$

where $\theta_1 = \phi_1 + \phi_2$ and $\theta_2 = -\phi_1$. Although no past expectation existed in the original form of this model, the last line in this equation has the current mean as a function of the same vector of exogenous variables, a past realization, and a past expectation. The past shock is no longer explicitly in the model.

One can take this a step further by writing the previous model in a still different form. Since $\xi_{i-1} = y_{i-1} - \mu_{i-1}$, $y_{i-1} = \xi_{i-1} + \mu_{i-1}$. Substituting this into the last line of Equation (7.16) gives:

$$\mu_i = x_i\beta + y_{i-1}\theta_1 + \mu_{i-1}\theta_2$$
$$= x_i\beta + (\xi_{i-1} + \mu_{i-1})\theta_1 + \mu_{i-1}\theta_2$$
$$= x_i\beta + \xi_{i-1}\theta_1 + \mu_{i-1}\theta_1 + \mu_{i-1}\theta_2$$
$$= x_i\beta + \xi_{i-1}\theta_1 + \mu_{i-1}\gamma,$$

where $\gamma = \theta_1 + \theta_2$. We have now come full circle. The specification began with a shock and realization. That was shown to be equivalent to a realization and expectation. Now, this equation shows those two specifications to be equivalent to including a shock and an expectation.

Two final ambiguities in time series models will suffice for this presentation. First, consider a translation of a model with a vector of exogenous variables and a single lag of past realizations:

$$\mu_i = x_i\beta + y_{i-1}\phi \qquad (7.17)$$
$$= x_i\beta + (x_i\beta + y_{i-2}\phi + \xi_{i-1})\phi$$
$$= x_i\beta + x_i\beta\phi + y_{i-2}\phi^2 + \xi_{i-1}\phi$$
$$= x_i\beta + x_i\beta\phi + \xi_{i-1}\phi + (x_{i-2}\beta + y_{i-3}\phi + \xi_{i-2})\phi^2$$
$$= \left(\sum_{j=0}^{i-1} x_{i-j}\beta\phi^j\right) + \xi_{i-1}\phi + \xi_{i-2}\phi^2 + \xi_{i-3}\phi^3 + \cdots.$$

These calculations prove that a single past realization may always be written as a distributed lag of all past shocks. More generally, an autoregressive process of order $p$ may be written as a moving average process of infinite order. In addition, what were current values of the exogenous variables are now an infinite geometrically distributed lag of all exogenous variables.

Second, consider a model with the current mean as a function of a vector of exogenous variables and one lagged random shock.

$$\mu_i = x_i\beta + \xi_{i-1}\phi$$
$$= x_i\beta + (y_{i-1} - \mu_{i-1})\phi$$
$$= x_i\beta + y_{i-1}\phi - (x_{i-1}\beta + y_{i-2}\phi - \mu_{i-2}\phi)\phi$$
$$= x_i\beta + y_{i-1}\phi - x_{i-1}\beta\phi - y_{i-2}\phi^2 + (x_{i-2}\beta + y_{i-3}\phi - \mu_{i-3}\phi)\phi^2$$
$$= \left(\sum_{j=0}^{i-1} x_{i-j}\beta\phi^j\right) + y_{i-1}\phi - y_{i-1}\phi^2 + y_{i-3}\phi^3 - \cdots.$$

This alternative representation enables one to write this MA(1) regression model as a geometric distributed lag of the exogenous variables plus an autoregressive process of infinite order.

What implications do these results have for actual work with time series models? From one perspective, these results are quite troubling because the story about the underlying data generation process that accompanies each model appears unique. Unfortunately, many are not. Concentrating on the mathematical representations of time series models helps to reveal these substantive equivalences.

This situation should not be confused with the problem in discrete regression models where two very different underlying processes – contagion and heterogeneity – led to identical overdispersed aggregate models. In those models, different underlying processes exist; however, statistical methods cannot distinguish between them given only aggregate data. In time series models, no amount of additional data could distinguish between algebraically equivalent models. Thus, the ambiguities here are *theoretical* rather than statistical.

In practice, then, how should political scientists choose a time series model? In time series models, the scholar is given additional latitude in choosing a theoretical representation for a particular model, and it will often pay to use more than one representation for each model estimated. For example, a student of public opinion might argue that the public's approval of the president's performance can be thought of as a function of the previous month's true level of approval. This emphasizes to public opinion experts that presidential approval is quite stable and, for social science purposes, this is quite important information. However, as advice to the chief executive from one of his advisors, this information seems almost useless. All it seems to say is that if the president wants his popularity high this month, he should make sure that it was high last month! Of course, this completely misses the reason the president might be interested in the question. Fortunately, the alternative representation is of considerable use: current approval is a geometrically distributed lag of all previous values of the exogenous variables. If the president can influence any of these variables (improve the economy, meet with the Soviet leader, give more persuasive speeches), then they will positively influence his popularity for all future time at a geometrically decreasing rate. This theoretically different, but mathematically equivalent, alternative gives the president considerably more useful information. Thus, this theoretical ambiguity can be creatively used in different ways to extract meaningful information from time series models. Used incorrectly, or without recognizing the alternative ways to represent one's model, time series models can lead one down the wrong theoretical path; the different formulations are mathematically identical, but some fit much more easily into political science theories than others. The information to be extracted and its interpretation will obviously differ depending on the purpose for which it is to be used.

For technical issues of estimation, the choice between different representations of the same model is completely arbitrary. However, in practice, the choice is often quite important. For example, whether one chooses an AR(1) process or an equivalent MA($q$) process with very large $q$ and parameters appropriately constrained, the same information will be extracted. However, in political science research a single model is almost never estimated. Instead, several models are usually tested and examined to see if the same substantive conclusions hold up across these different specifications (see especially Leamer,

1978). What alternative models should be tested? If one begins with an AR(1) specification, the next logical alternative would probably be to try an autoregressive specification with additional or no lags. However, if one starts with a high order MA process with parameters constrained as in Equation (7.17), then the next move would probably be to eliminate some of the lags and unconstrain some of the remaining parameters. The problem is that although the two original models are equivalent, the "natural" directions one would move to do sensitivity testing can lead one to models that are completely different from both theoretical and mathematical perspectives. What appear to be benign choices at the start can be quite consequential in practice.

Another consequence of this theoretical ambiguity has been in the field of forecasting (see Box and Jenkins, 1976). Forecasters are often less interested in the process giving rise to one's data than in producing good forecasts of future events. Particularly in the analysis of business trends, and other practical arenas, forecasting is generally the main concern. In the social and behavioral sciences, however, explanation is usually the goal. Forecasters take advantage of the ambiguity of time series models by not worrying about which equivalent mathematical representation is theoretically appropriate. Instead, the dominant procedure has been to arbitrarily choose to represent all time series as a function of past shocks and past realizations. The effect of past expectations is accounted for as part of shocks and realizations, but is never explicitly included in these models. Justification for excluding exogenous variables is usually based on the argument that their past values will get realized in past values of the dependent variable. Thus, for the purpose of relatively quick and efficient forecasts, a univariate time series can be modeled solely as a function of past values of itself. This is not to say that exogenous variables could not improve the forecasts (see Rosenstone, 1983), but in business and other fields the time necessary to collect these additional variables is generally too costly.

The general procedure is to choose an autoregressive, moving average process with $p+q$ parameters, ARMA($p,q$). If the independent variable has to be differenced ($y_i - y_i$) $d$ times to induce stationarity, then the model is called an ARIMA($p,d,q$) process. Powerful techniques have been developed to help identify the values of $p$ and $q$ solely from the data (see Box and Jenkins, 1976; Fuller, 1976; Granger and Newbold, 1986; Nelson, 1973). These techniques are independent of the estimation of the model and are a form of descriptive statistic. With them, forecasters can quickly identify a rough approximation to the structure of the model and easily produce surprisingly good forecasts. Computer programs even exist that will forecast without any specification at all by users (see Newbold and Granger, 1974).

These and other relatively automatic methods of forecasting have their place, but this place is usually outside the scope of most political science, where explanation is central. When imported directly into political science without modification, these techniques are rightfully criticized as being atheoretical. However, this should not cause researchers to consider the entire process of time series modeling as a mere "nuisance" (see Beck, 1986; Hendry and Mizon, 1978). As this chapter has demonstrated, many interesting social science problems are inherently time series processes. Having a set of models with which to study these problems is critical (see also Hendry, Pagan, and Sargan, 1984).

## 7.4 The first differences error correction model

The *first differences* model is quite popular in political science. Instead of the static regression

$$\mu_i = x_i \beta,$$

which explains levels of the expected value of $Y_i$ with levels of the explanatory variables, the first differences model is written as follows:

$$\Delta \mu_i = \Delta x_i \beta, \tag{7.18}$$

where $\Delta$ is the first difference operator such that $\Delta a_i = a_i - a_{i-1}$ for any random (or nonrandom) variable $a$. The static regression ignores any time series component and also makes the implausible assumption that levels of $E(Y_i) \equiv \mu_i$ respond instantly to levels of $x_i$.

Unfortunately, the first differences model also has at least two unattractive features. One is that just as summing tends to cancel out random error, resulting in clearer relationships, differencing can cancel out the systematic component, resulting in additional random error. In the extreme case, imagine two random variables $Y_{1i}$ and $Y_{2i}$, with the same expected value $\mu_i$. Then the difference $Y_{1i} - Y_{2i}$ has expected value zero (for all $i$) whereas the sum has expected value $2\mu_i$. Note that the difference has a systematic component that is constant over the observations and thus does not vary as a function of any explanatory variables. However, the sum varies over the observations in a range even larger than the systematic component for each of the original variables. Thus, as a nearly general rule, models based on differenced series tend to fit less and have higher standard errors and less stable coefficient values. Of course, one does not take differences in order to obliterate the systematic component. Instead, in some cases, differencing can strip the series of a trend that happens to exist in both the explanatory and dependent variables, resulting in spurious relationships in the static regression. In these cases, differencing can therefore help to highlight the interesting portion of the variation in the systematic component. This explains some of the attractiveness of, as well as some of the frustrations political scientists have had with, this model.

However, a more serious problem with the first differences model is that short term changes in $\mu_i$ are assumed to respond only to short term changes in $x_i$. No effect lasts longer than one period. For many research problems in political science, this is a very implausible assumption having quite undesirable implications.

For example, suppose the dependent variable of interest is $\Delta A_i$, where $A_i$ is the proportion of the population in month $i$ that approves of the way the president is handling his job. Thus, under a first differences model, monthly changes in public approval of the president respond only to current changes in inflation and unemployment, for example. An unusually large change in inflation in one particular month will have a correspondingly large influence on approval. If inflation this month were an aberration, the model might correctly predict the *changes* in subsequent months, but this one shock to $\Delta A_i$ would still send the *level* of approval far off in the wrong direction for all future months. Whereas small shocks are not that serious for models with levels as a dependent variable, a random shock can have devastating consequences for a first differences model.

Nathaniel Beck (1987a) recognized this problem with the first differences model of presidential approval and, following Davidson et al. (1978), proposed the *error correcting model* to cope with the situation.[10] Thus, begin by assuming that changes in approval of the president are Normally distributed as with the rest of the models in this chapter. Then let the expected change in approval, $E(\Delta A_i) \equiv \mu_i$, vary as a function of changes in economic variables, a set of dummy variables, and an error correcting term:

$$\mu_i = (\Delta E_i)\beta_1 + x_i\beta_2 + \lambda[A_{i-1} + E_{i-1}\gamma], \tag{7.19}$$

where $E$ is a vector of economic variables, usually inflation and unemployment (and, for convenience, a constant term). $X$ includes a separate "leakage dummy variable" for each new presidency (equaling 1 for the start of each administration and 0 for every other month); these variables prevent the public's approval of one president from leaking into predictions of public approval for the next president. A similar leakage dummy is included for the hostage taking in Iran. In addition, $X$ also includes a dummy variable for Watergate and a variable for the number of Americans killed each month of the Vietnam War (in the ten thousands).

Without the last two terms, this model is the first differences model of

---

[10] The data and models estimated that follow are essentially those in Beck (1987a) with additional observations and a dummy variable for Iran.

Equation (7.18). The $x_i\beta_2$ term is also quite common in models of presidential approval. The novel part of this model is the last term, $\lambda[A_{i-1}+E_{i-1}\gamma]$. This provides an error correcting mechanism to the rest of the model. The term in brackets represents the equilibrium level of popularity at time $i-1$, as represented by a weighted average of the lagged levels of presidential approval and economic conditions. If $\lambda$ is negative, then that fraction of last month's shock is discounted in the current period.

With $\lambda$ multiplied out, this model is then just a straightforward linear regression. Because the error correction component adjusts for shocks that occur only in the current period (i.e., the difference in approval from month $i-1$ to month $i$), I follow Beck (1987a) and also estimate the model with an additional lagged shock.

Since the second model is more complicated, I derive its log-likelihood here. The general form of the log-likelihood is in Equation (7.5). The systematic component is written in preliminary structural form as follows:

$$\mu_i = (\Delta E_i)\beta_1 + x_i\beta_2 + \lambda[A_{i-1}+E_{i-1}\gamma] + \xi_{i-1}\phi. \tag{7.20}$$

Since $\xi_{i-1}$ is not observed, Equation (7.20) cannot be substituted directly into Equation (7.5). Instead, the systematic component must be recursively reparameterized in a fashion similar to Equation (7.14) for past shocks. The final reduced form representation is derived simply by substituting the right hand side of Equation (7.20) for $x_i\beta$ in Equation (7.14):

$$\begin{aligned}
\mu_i &= (\Delta E_i)\beta_1 + x_i\beta_2 + \lambda[A_{i-1}+E_{i-1}\lambda] + \xi_{i-1}\phi \\
&= \{(\Delta E_i)\beta_1 + x_i\beta_2 + \lambda[A_{i-1}+E_{i-1}\lambda]\} \\
&\quad - (y_1-\mu_1)(-\phi)^i - \sum_{j=1}^{i-1}\{y_{i-j}-[(\Delta E_{i-j})\beta_1+x_{i-j}\beta_2 \\
&\quad + \lambda(A_{i-j-1}+E_{i-j-1}\gamma)]\}(-\phi)^j \\
&= \{(\Delta E_i)\beta_1 + x_i\beta_2 + \lambda[A_{i-1}+E_{i-1}\gamma]\} \\
&\quad - \sum_{j=1}^{\infty}\{y_{i-j}-(\Delta E_{i-j})\beta_1+x_{i-j}\beta_2+\lambda[A_{i-j-1}+E_{i-j-1}\gamma]\}(-\phi)^j.
\end{aligned}$$

If we assume that $y_1$ is fixed and equal to $\mu_1$, the second term in the second line of this equation drops out. I tried estimating $\mu_1$ instead of making this assumption, but the substantive results were extremely similar to those presented below; given the large number of observations ($n=411$), this is not surprising. The rest of the second line is substituted into Equation (7.14) to yield the complete log-likelihood. This expression is then maximized with respect to $\tilde{\beta}_1$, $\tilde{\beta}_2$, $\tilde{\lambda}$, $\tilde{\gamma}$, $\tilde{\phi}$, and $\tilde{\sigma}^2$.

Empirical results for both models appear in Table 7.2. The results are similar, with many of the coefficients growing slightly in the second specification. I use this second model for the following interpretation. In the table, $A$

Table 7.2. *Error correction model of presidential approval*

| Variable | Model 1 | | | Model 2 | | |
|---|---|---|---|---|---|---|
| | Estimate | S.e. | $t$ | Estimate | S.e. | $t$ |
| Constant | 12.18 | 2.19 | 5.56 | 9.29 | 2.18 | 4.26 |
| $\Delta U$ | −1.58 | 0.92 | −1.72 | −1.83 | 0.87 | −2.11 |
| $\Delta I$ | −0.11 | 0.07 | −1.50 | −0.07 | 0.08 | −0.87 |
| $A_{i-1}$ | −0.16 | 0.02 | −6.44 | −0.12 | 0.02 | −4.92 |
| $U_{i-1}$ | −0.34 | 0.15 | −2.23 | −0.23 | 0.14 | −1.72 |
| $I_{i-1}$ | −0.31 | 0.07 | −4.53 | −0.26 | 0.06 | −4.21 |
| Vietnam | −3.23 | 0.99 | −3.26 | −2.51 | 0.88 | −2.86 |
| Watergate | −4.07 | 1.28 | −3.18 | −3.24 | 1.12 | −2.89 |
| Iran | −16.20 | 3.97 | −4.08 | −16.01 | 3.88 | −4.12 |
| JFK1 | 12.73 | 3.97 | 3.21 | 13.30 | 3.89 | 3.41 |
| LBJ1 | 20.22 | 3.97 | 5.09 | 20.69 | 3.89 | 5.32 |
| RMN1 | 12.13 | 4.02 | 3.02 | 13.28 | 3.97 | 3.35 |
| GRF1 | 24.60 | 4.05 | 6.08 | 26.57 | 4.01 | 6.62 |
| JEC1 | 18.22 | 3.98 | 4.58 | 19.02 | 3.91 | 4.86 |
| RWR1 | 16.35 | 3.99 | 4.09 | 18.12 | 3.98 | 4.55 |
| $\sigma^2$ | 3.96 | 0.14 | 28.63 | 3.92 | 0.14 | 28.62 |
| $\xi_{i-1}$ | | | | −0.17 | 0.06 | −2.58 |

*Note:* Model 1: log-likelihood = −1145.63. Model 2: log-likelihood = −1142.23.

is public approval of the president, $U$ is unemployment, and $I$ is inflation. Short term changes in both unemployment and inflation cause changes in approval to drop. A single percentage point increase in the change in unemployment decreases the change in approval by nearly two (1.83) percentage points. The coefficient on the lagged shock variable indicates that about seventeen percent of a large random shock that hits the system will be offset in the next period. However, this offsetting effect only lasts a single month. Fortunately, the error correction component is included, where λ is the coefficient of $A_{i-1}$ in Table 7.2. This −0.12 figure indicates that a shock to presidential approval will be adjusted downward toward equilibrium at the rate of about twelve percent each month for the first month and for each subsequent month.

For example, suppose the United States suddenly invaded Nicaragua. The probable effect of this action is a rally-around-the-flag effect of roughly ten additional approval points for the current president. This will be adjusted downward the first period by both the effect of the lagged shock and the error correction, so in the second period it will be about $10(0.12+0.17)=2.9$ points less. Thus, in this next period, approval would still be 7.1 points higher than the equilibrium value. The following period, this value would adjust again, but only as a result of the error correction term; approval would reduce by about $7.1(0.12) = 0.85$ points, still staying about $7.1 - 0.85 = 6.25$ points above the equilibrium value. A year later this rally-around-the-flag incident will still have caused the equilibrium value of approval to be about $10(1 - 0.12 - 0.17)(1 - 0.12)^1 1 = 1.74$ percentage points higher than the equilibrium value.

## 7.5    The "standard" time series regression model

Given the rich variety of models introduced in this chapter for the influence of the past on the present, one would be hard pressed to propose any one model as the standard or default. Unfortunately, the social science literature heavily favors a single model as an alternative to the static linear regression model in the presence of time series data – the linear regression model with AR(1) disturbances. This model is generally written as follows:

$$Y_i = x_i\beta + \omega_i, \tag{7.21}$$
$$\omega_i = \omega_{i-1}\phi + \epsilon_i,$$

where $\epsilon_i$ and $\epsilon_j$ are independent for all $i \neq j$, $\omega_i$ is a random variable combining all the random error in $Y_i$ with all the time series processes. The second equation specifies the time series process that $\omega_i$ follows, where $\epsilon_i$ is a random variable with zero expectation and constant variance.

By segregating time series processes in a separate equation, this presentation emphasizes the similarity of this model with static regression models but, at the same time, gives the influence of the past on the present only subordinate theoretical status (see Beck, 1986). Writing the model in this form stems from the old view of static linear regression as the parent model. Time series "deviations" from, or "violations" of, this model are relegated to the disturbance term, which is then modeled separately.[11] When only linear regression computer programs were available, this strategy was sensible. Indeed, when linear regression is the only statistical model with which one is familiar, it may still be a reasonable choice. However, with better background and computer programs, one can easily estimate more interesting statistical models and give time series processes the same theoretical status as other parts of the model. Thus, the notation of this most commonly used statistical model is quite inadequate.

[11] See almost any econometrics text. Hanushek and Jackson (1977), Johnston (1984), Judge, et al. (1985), Kmenta (1986), and Maddala (1977) are a few of many examples of the "assumption-violation" approach to econometrics.

By substituting the second line of Equation (7.21) into the first line and identifying the systematic component, one can reformulate the model as follows:

$$\mu_i = x_i\beta + \omega_{i-1}\phi. \tag{7.22}$$

One could stop here and interpret $\phi$ as the effect of $\omega_{i-1}$ on $\mu_i$, but what exactly is $\omega_{i-1}$? As the sum total of all time series processes and all random error, $\omega_{i-1}$ remains a relatively uninteresting analytical construct. The best justification for interpreting $\omega_{i-1}$ is probably as the total of all the omitted exogenous variables plus all random error. The time series process is then thought of as having been induced by these omitted variables. My alternative presentation emphasizes that the time series process is an integral part of the systematic component, rather than as a failure of the "more interesting" part of the specification. Thus, to understand this model better, it pays to substitute $\omega_{i-1}$ out of the model, and in its place put the appropriate combination of time series fundamentals: exogenous variables, realizations, expectations, and shocks.

To derive this more interesting interpretation, I substitute the second line of Equation (7.21), lagged one period, into Equation (7.22):[12]

$$
\begin{aligned}
\mu_i &= x_i\beta + \omega_{i-1}\phi & (7.23) \\
&= x_i\beta + (\omega_{i-2}\phi + \xi_{i-1})\phi \\
&= x_i\beta + \xi_{i-1}\phi + \omega_{i-2}\phi^2 \\
&= x_i\beta + \xi_{i-1}\phi + (\omega_{i-3}\phi + \xi_{i-2})\phi^2 \\
&= x_i\beta + \xi_{i-1}\phi + \xi_{i-2}\phi^2 + \omega_{i-3}\phi^3 \\
&= x_i\beta + \xi_{i-1}\phi + \xi_{i-2}\phi^2 + \xi_{i-3}\phi^3 + \cdots.
\end{aligned}
$$

Thus, the standard "AR(1) regression model" may be written as the expected value being a linear function of the exogenous variables and a geometric distributed lag of all previous random shocks. Written in this form, one can see that this is a reasonable and quite interesting model. Of course, no theoretical reason guarantees that it is appropriate for most political science examples. Should all previous lags be included? Why should the lags be geometrically distributed over time, rather than as an exponential, polynomial, or some other form? Why only previous shocks rather than previous expectations, realizations, or exogenous variables? Why should the time series process necessarily be linear? This model could certainly be justified in a large

[12] Realizations of the disturbance term, $\epsilon$, were called shocks and labeled $\xi$ in previous sections. Since, at time $i$, past values of $\epsilon$ are already realized, one lag of $\epsilon_i$ is written as $\xi_{i-1}$. As always, $y$, is a realization of $Y_i$. The reason I use Greek letters for $\epsilon_i \equiv Y_i - \mu_i$ and $\xi_i \equiv y_i - \mu_i$ is that, in this case, the random variable and its realization are both unobserved.

number of situations in political science research, but too many other interesting models exist for this to be the universally designated alternative to the static regression model. Indeed, once scholars begin to think in terms of directly modeling the substantive process that generates one's data, researchers will have no standard model that all analyses of a certain type are forced into. Instead, the particular form of the model will emerge directly from the political content of the research problem.[13,14]

## 7.6    Concluding remarks

This chapter has demonstrated how to model data generating processes with time series properties. Some of the most interesting political data have these properties, so it should not be surprising that these models, by themselves and in combination with those in other chapters of this book, are quite useful in many areas of research.

The algebraic calculations, particularly those requiring recursive reparameterization, do become quite tedious at times and particularly if several lags or combinations of exogenous variables, realizations, expectations, and shocks are included. Although they do sometimes help provide insights into the nature of the model, these calculations can get in the way of one's analysis. The solution is to let the computer do the work. The specific method is to estimate a model in what is called the *state space form* with *Kalman filtering*. The state space form is similar to the form of the model before recursive reparameterization. With a Kalman filter algorithm, the computer then does the recursions numerically. Using this method, one cannot write the likelihood function as a simple equation, but expressing it in this recursive form leads to no loss of statistical information. The only problem is that one gives up the conceptual benefits that are sometimes had by different representations of the same model. However, this difficulty is somewhat offset by the large amount of time Kalman filtering can save in complicated models. See Beck (1987b), Granger and Newbold (1986: 297–303), and Kalman (1960).

The statistical literature on time series, even beyond that which I have made

---

[13] Most regressions performed on time series data report the obligatory Durbin-Watson test statistic. This statistic is essentially a test of whether $\phi = 0$ in this model. Unfortunately, researchers incorrectly use this test to rule out all forms of time series processes. Of course, even if $\phi$ is actually zero, only this particular time series process is ruled out. The infinite number of other processes may still be operating.

[14] The standard truncation assumption, that $y_1$ is fixed across experiments and known to be equal to $\mu_1$ seems relatively innocuous. However, the reformulation of this model in Equation (7.23) suggests a different interpretation. $y_1 = \mu_1$ implies that $\xi_j = 0$ for all $j \le 1$. Thus, terms in the last line of Equation (7.23) prior to observation 2 are dropped from the model. Or, in other words, the model assumes that all random shocks occurring before the observation period are zero (or have no effect).

reference to, is enormous. Other important topics include time-varying parameter regression models (Beck, 1983), representations of causality (Freeman, 1983), spectral or frequency domain analysis (Priestley, 1981), and multivariate ARIMA processes (Hannan, 1970). Pooled time-series–cross-sectional models are briefly discussed in the next chapter.

# CHAPTER 8

# Introduction to multiple equation models

The methods introduced in all previous chapters in Part II require one to specify the distribution of a single random observation, $Y_i$, and how its parameters vary systematically over all observations. Occasionally, more than one equation was used in a single model, but never was more than one output of the social system modeled simultaneously. However, the system does produce multiple observations for many interesting political science research problems. For example, a single observation might include the number of presidential vetoes *and* the number of congressional overrides in a year or the number of hostile acts directed toward the Soviet Union *and* the number directed toward the United States each month. A sample survey might contain a dozen imperfect measures of a citizen's ideological orientation that could jointly be considered one observation. The monthly unemployment and inflation rates are probably jointly generated by the U.S. economy.

For any of these examples, one could use the methods introduced in previous chapters to build a separate model for each individual variable. Indeed, nothing particularly troublesome occurs if this is in fact done. However, by allowing for multiple equation models, one may simultaneously study larger portions of a given social system. This, in turn, allows one to derive more sophisticated, realistic, and interesting models. At the same time, the models can become even less restrictive than the least restrictive single equation model, requiring more of one's finite store of data. If one is willing to make certain additional assumptions, a more restrictive model might result and better estimates of parameters may generally be obtained than with applications run equation by equation. As always, a researcher should carefully consider the tradeoff between unrestrictive, realistic models and restrictive, estimable ones. In multiple equation models, this tradeoff becomes even more apparent.

In this chapter, $i$ still indexes observations, from 1 to $n$, but, at each observation, $Y_i$ is now an $N \times 1$ vector randomly produced by the social system, $Y_i = (Y_{1i}, \ldots, Y_{Ni})'$. The stochastic component of a multiple equation model thus requires a multivariate probability distribution:

$$Y_i \sim f(y_i | \theta_i, \alpha),$$

where $\theta_i$ is an $N \times 1$ vector of parameters at observation $i$, $\theta_i = (\theta_{1i}, \ldots, \theta_{Ni})'$, corresponding to the respective $N$ random observations, $Y_i$, and realized

189

values, $y_i$. $\alpha$ is usually an $N \times N$ matrix of ancillary parameters. The systematic component is then written as a set of $N$ equations for observation $i$:

$$\theta_{1i} = g_1(x_{1i}, \beta_1),$$
$$\theta_{2i} = g_2(x_{2i}, \beta_2),$$
$$\vdots \quad \vdots \quad \vdots$$
$$\theta_{Ni} = g_N(x_{Ni}, \beta_N).$$

Relationships among the various elements of $\theta_i$ are also often specified as part of the systematic component. For example, some of the explanatory variable matrices may include elements of $\theta$ from the other equations. In addition, fewer parameters may be estimated if some of the effect parameters are held constant across equations (e.g., $\beta_1 = \beta_2$).

A multiple equation model is generally chosen when the aspect of the social system one is studying actually produces multiple observations. But when does a multiple equation model yield results different from a set of $N$ separate models? *The results differ in multiple equation models – and in general have more desirable statistical properties – when either the elements of $Y_i$ are (1) stochastically or (2) parametrically dependent;* Gallant (1986: 267–8) calls these two conditions dependence and shared parameters, respectively. These two critical features of a multiple equation model are easiest to understand in the context of a simple proof. For clarity, I use only two equations and suppress the ancillary parameters. This proof shows that if elements of $Y_i$ are stochastically independent and the separate equations are parametrically independent, then an equation-by-equation estimation strategy yields results identical to a multiple equation estimation. If there is no time series component, the full stochastic component is written as usual:

$$f(y|\theta) = \prod_{i=1}^{n} f(y_i|\theta_i).$$

Due to *stochastic independence of $Y_{1i}$ and $Y_{2i}$*, the distribution on the right hand side may be factored according to the probability rule in Equation (3.1):

$$f(y|\theta) = \prod_{i=1}^{n} f(y_i|\theta_i)$$
$$= \prod_{i=1}^{n} f(y_{1i}|\theta_{1i})f(y_{2i}|\theta_{2i}).$$

The log-likelihood is then

$$\ln L(\tilde{\theta}_1, \tilde{\theta}_2 | y) = \sum_{i=1}^{n} \ln f(y_{1i}|\tilde{\theta}_{1i}) + \sum_{i=1}^{n} \ln f(y_{2i}|\tilde{\theta}_{2i}).$$

If, in addition, *the two equations are parametrically independent,* that is, if $\tilde{\theta}_{1i}$ and $\tilde{\theta}_{2i}$ are not deterministic functions of one another, then the second term of this log-likelihood is constant over values of $\tilde{\theta}_{1i}$ (and the first term is constant over $\tilde{\theta}_{2i}$). Thus, if one wanted to make inferences about $\tilde{\theta}_1$, this second term may be dropped leaving the likelihood function identical to that resulting from a single equation model. Thus, with stochastic and parametric independence, the multiple equation and single equation models produce identical inferences.

The particular form of the stochastic and parametric dependence is what distinguishes most of these multiple equation models. The most prominent multiple equation models in the literature include those for factor analysis and unobserved variables, analysis of covariance structures, selection bias, reciprocal causation, and pooled time-series–cross-sectional data. These may include linear and nonlinear systematic components and Normal and other stochastic components. Variables may be discrete, continuous, or mixed, and the data may or may not have time series properties.

I present a few of these in the remainder of this chapter and the two that follow, but throughout I rely on the simplest cases so that the multiple equation framework remains prominent. Thus, I assume the absence of a time series component, although the methods of Chapter 7 can be easily extended to these methods. I describe ''identification'' in the next section, a problem that occurs in models of all types but most frequently with multiple equation models. Succeeding sections present a variety of specific multiple equation models.

## 8.1    Identification

One has almost complete freedom to write down mathematical models of any kind for political science phenomena, but this does not guarantee that these models will be sensible. Whereas many implausible models are never even considered or are easily ruled out, others *seem* plausible enough on the surface to warrant further attention. The criterion that the parameters of a model be ''identified'' is often an important condition of the reasonableness of a statistical model. However, it is not always necessary or even sufficient to guarantee a reasonable model. The problem with identification comes with ML estimation, since unidentified parameters do not have unique ML estimates.

Identification is an issue with models of all types, but, due to their complexity, it is usually much more difficult to recognize in multiple equation models. I describe the problem in this section with three examples of progressively increasing complexity. The first is so simple that no reasonable person would specify such a model. The last example is more difficult to see without further analysis. Important necessary, but not sufficient, criteria for identification are introduced in all three. In the following section on reciprocal causation, I present the first multiple equation model of this chapter and deal explicitly with the problem of identification in multiple equation models.

*Example 1: Flat likelihoods*

Suppose one specified the following model and wanted to make an inference about $\beta$:

$$Y_i \sim f_p(y_i|\lambda_i)$$

$$\lambda_i = 1 + 0\beta.$$

The stochastic component of this model lets $Y_i$ vary according to a Poisson distribution and is quite reasonable. However, the systematic component is another matter. It may obviously be rewritten as $\lambda_i = 1$, but a naive researcher who wants to make inferences about $\beta$ does not immediately make this calculation. Regardless of what further computations are made, values of $\beta$ will have no influence on $\lambda_i$ or on any other part of the model. $\beta$ is not identified. To define the concept of identification more precisely consider the full stochastic component

$$L(\tilde{\lambda}|y) = \prod_{i=1}^{n} \frac{e^{-\lambda}\lambda^{y_i}}{y_i!}$$

and the log-likelihood, with $(1 + 0\beta)$ substituted for $\lambda_i$:

$$\ln L(\tilde{\beta}|y) = \sum_{i=1}^{n} \{-(0\tilde{\beta}+1) - y_i \ln(0\tilde{\beta}+1)\}$$

$$= \sum_{i=1}^{n} -1$$

$$= -n.$$

This result indicates that regardless of the value of $\tilde{\beta}$, the likelihood curve is flat. Thus, the relative likelihood of any value of $\tilde{\beta}$ is indistinguishable from any other.

More generally, *a likelihood function with a flat region or plateau at the maximum has a parameter that is not identified.* A flat likelihood indicates that many ML estimators exist for a single parameter. This particular example is simple because the entire model has only one parameter, and the likelihood function is flat for all values of $\tilde{\beta}$. Thus, the likelihood – and therefore the model – provides no information with which one can make inferences about $\beta$. For other models, the plateau at the maximum may exist for only a small range of values of $\tilde{\beta}$. In these cases, one could use the range of $\tilde{\beta}$ for which the likelihood was maximized to make inferences. Of course, the wider the plateau, the less useful the inferences.[1] The other problem with an unidentified model is that the usual calculations of curvature, information, and standard errors do not directly apply. At any one of the maximum values, the curvature is also flat, indicating no information and an infinite variance in the ML estimate across experiments. Of course, if the plateau region is relatively small, some information does exist; it is just that the usual methods do not apply.

Identification causes no problem for the method of likelihood and the likelihood function as a summary estimator. However, for ML estimation, no generally adequate solution to an unidentified model exists. Thus, particularly in problems with multiple parameters, one merely tries to assure that all parameters are identified. Unfortunately, with multiple parameters and more complex $K$-dimensional likelihoods, even determining whether a plateau exists is often very difficult. Indeed, whereas many necessary conditions for identification can be stated, the full list of sufficient conditions is unknown, making the judgment of identification still more a matter of art than science.

*Example 2: Nonunique reparameterization*

One feature of a problem with identified parameters is that the reparameterization should be unique. For example, suppose one posited a simple linear regression model:

$$Y_i \sim f_N(y_i|\mu_i,\sigma^2), \tag{8.1}$$
$$\mu_i = x_{1i}\beta_1 + x_{2i}\beta_2 + x_{3i}\beta_3.$$

The second equation is the systematic component of this model, but it also represents a reparameterization when the right hand side is substituted for $\mu_i$ in the stochastic component. This particular reparameterization is generally not problematic unless some of the columns of $X$ are perfectly correlated – the problem of multicollinearity. Intuitively, multicollinearity gives the estimation procedure no information with which to ascertain the separate effects of the parameters on the perfectly correlated variables. Multicollinearity is a special case of an unidentified model. For simplicity, consider an even more

---

Averaging the various values in this flat region is *not* a reasonable means of deriving a unique ML estimate. A flat curve indicates that the model plus the data reveal only ignorance about equivalent relative likelihoods of $\tilde{\beta}$. Averaging these implies that one has a uniform prior over these values. However, the latter is a strong Bayesian assumption about which values of $\tilde{\beta}$ one believes are the correct ones; it is hardly an adequate representation of ignorance (see Sections 2.2 to 2.4).

special case of multicollinearity, when $x_{2i} = x_{3i}$.[2] Then the systematic component reduces to the following:

$$\mu_i = x_{1i}\beta_1 + x_{2i}\beta_2 + x_{3i}\beta_3$$
$$= x_{1i}\beta_1 + x_{2i}(\beta_2 + \beta_3).$$

The last line of this equation is a simplified form of the reparameterization required for this problem. Whereas the right hand side may be substituted in for $\mu_i$, this substitution is not unique. So, for example, these parameter values

$$\mu_i = x_{1i}\beta_1 + x_{2i}(5 + 3)$$

yield the same values for $\mu_i$ as these

$$\mu_i = x_{1i}\beta_1 + x_{2i}(3 + 5)$$

or even these

$$\mu_i = x_{1i}\beta_1 + x_{2i}(7 + 1).$$

The same is not true for Equation (8.1) where $x_{2i} \neq x_{3i}$ (and when the variables are not perfectly collinear).[3]

Thus, only unique one-to-one reparameterizations can have identified parameters. Of course, features of the stochastic component, or other parts of the systematic component, can also lead to unidentified parameters, so this is another necessary but not sufficient condition of identification.

*Example 3: Deterministic relationships among the ML estimators*

A final example concerns a single equation "errors-in-variables" or "unobserved variables" problem. The model is as follows:

1.  $Y_i \sim f_N(y_i | \mu_i, \sigma^2)$.
2.  $\mu_i = X_i^* \beta$.
3.  $X_i \sim f_N(x_i | X_i^*, \sigma_x^2)$.

---

[2] Perfect collinearity occurs when two or more variables are linear combinations of one another. Thus, $x_{2i} = \gamma_1 + \gamma_2 x_{3i}$. The example in the text, where $x_{2i} = x_{3i}$, is merely a special case of this with $\gamma_1 = 0$ and $\gamma_2 = 1$.

[3] The problem of nonidentification due to multicollinearity is similar to the problem of having a small number of observations, as both lead to $X'X$ not being invertable in the analytical solution for this ML estimator, $(X'X)^{-1}X'y = \hat{\beta}$. Since more observations is the same as more information, this result is quite intuitive: the more observations, the more curved the likelihood function, and the less problems one will have with identification. In general, adding observations cannot make an unidentified model identified.

4. Conditional on $\mu_i$, the variables $Y_i$, $X_i$, and $X_i^*$ are independent for all $i$.[4]

5. $Y_i$ and $Y_j$ are independent and $X_i$ and $X_j$ are independent, for all $i \neq j$.

The first two equations represent a standard linear-Normal regression problem, except that $X_i^*$ is unobserved. However, we do observe the realization of a stochastic process of which $X_i^*$ is an unknown parameter.[5] Without the third equation, the $X_i^*$ and $\beta$ parameters are obviously not identified since the reparameterization would not be unique: for example, $\mu_i = (3)(4)$ or $\mu_i = (4)(3)$ or $\mu_i = (6)(2)$ give the same value for $\mu_i$.

Are all the parameters identified by including the third equation? This is quite difficult to determine by mere inspection of this five part model. Indeed, examining the likelihood surface directly would also be difficult because of the presence of many parameters (and thus dimensions). I therefore move to an additional method of assessing the identification of the likelihood, the calculation of analytical ML estimators.

Note that the full stochastic component now involves the random variables $Y$ *and* $X$. Since they are independent, the product of the two distributions yields the joint distribution of both:

$$f(y, x | \mu, \sigma^2, \sigma_x^2) = \prod_{i=1}^{n} f_N(y_i | \mu_i, \sigma^2) f_N(x_i | X_i^*, \sigma_x^2),$$

$$f(y, x | \tilde{X}_i^*, \sigma^2, \sigma_x^2) = \prod_{i=1}^{n} f_N(y_i | \mu_i, \sigma^2) f_N(x_i | X_i^*, \sigma_x^2)$$

$$= \prod_{i=1}^{n} (2\pi\tilde{\sigma}^2)^{-1/2} \exp\left[ \frac{-(y_i - \tilde{X}_i^* \tilde{\beta})^2}{2\tilde{\sigma}^2} \right] (2\pi\tilde{\sigma}_x^2)^{-1/2} \exp\left[ \frac{-(x_i - \tilde{X}_i^*)^2}{2\tilde{\sigma}_x^2} \right].$$

Then, taking logs and dropping terms that do not depend on $\tilde{X}_i^*$, $\tilde{\beta}$, $\tilde{\sigma}$, or $\tilde{\sigma}_x$, the log-likelihood is as follows:

$$\ln L \equiv \ln L(\tilde{X}_i^*, \tilde{\beta}, \tilde{\sigma}^2, \tilde{\sigma}_x^2 | y)$$

$$= \sum_{i=1}^{n} \left\{ -\ln(\tilde{\sigma}) - \ln(\tilde{\sigma}_x) - \frac{1}{2\tilde{\sigma}^2} (y_i - \tilde{X}_i^* \tilde{\beta})^2 - \frac{1}{2\tilde{\sigma}_x^2} (x_i - \tilde{X}_i^*)^2 \right\}$$

$$= -\frac{n}{2} (\ln \tilde{\sigma}^2 + \ln \tilde{\sigma}_x^2) - \frac{1}{2\tilde{\sigma}^2} \sum_{i=1}^{n} (y_i - \tilde{X}_i^* \tilde{\beta})^2 - \frac{1}{2\tilde{\sigma}_x^2} \sum_{i=1}^{n} (x_i - \tilde{X}_i^*)^2.$$

We could maximize this likelihood numerically to avoid analytical calculations, but the computer program would never arrive at a proper solution. To

---

[4] In more standard terminology, this is the assumption that $X_i^*$, $X_i$, and $\epsilon_i \equiv Y_i - \mu$ are independent.

[5] Note that the $X^*$ parameters may themselves be either fixed across experiments or the outcome of some other unknown stochastic process. The results of Section 7.1 make this latter difference inconsequential.

see the reason for this, consider the analytical solution. To maximize a likelihood function with one parameter, one derivative needs be taken. Here, the four vectors of parameters require that four derivatives be computed:

$$\frac{\partial \ln L}{\partial \tilde{\beta}} = \frac{1}{\tilde{\sigma}^2} \sum_{i=1}^{n} (y_i - \tilde{X}_i^* \tilde{\beta}) \tilde{X}_i^*,$$

$$\frac{\partial \ln L}{\partial \tilde{\sigma}^2} = -\frac{1}{2\tilde{\sigma}^2} \left[ -n + \frac{1}{\tilde{\sigma}^2} \sum_{i=1}^{n} (y_i - \tilde{X}_i^* \tilde{\beta})^2 \right],$$

$$\frac{\partial \ln L}{\partial \tilde{\sigma}_x^2} = -\frac{1}{2\tilde{\sigma}_x^2} \left[ -n + \frac{1}{\tilde{\sigma}_x^2} \sum_{i=1}^{n} (x_i - \tilde{X}_i^*)^2 \right],$$

$$\frac{\partial \ln L}{\partial \tilde{X}^*} = \frac{1}{\tilde{\sigma}_x^2} \sum_{i=1}^{n} (x_i - \tilde{X}_i^*) + \frac{\beta}{\tilde{\sigma}^2} \sum_{i=1}^{n} (y_i - \tilde{X}_i^* \tilde{\beta}).$$

The next step is to set these four equations to zero, substitute $\tilde{\beta}$, $\tilde{\sigma}^2$, $\tilde{\sigma}_x^2$, and $\tilde{X}^*$ with $\hat{\beta}$, $\hat{\sigma}^2$, $\hat{\sigma}_x^2$, and $\hat{X}^*$, respectively, and simultaneously solve for the ML estimators. This involves substituting the four equations into each other and solving. Carrying out this procedure yields estimators, but also reveals the following key relationship among them:

$$\hat{\beta} = \frac{\hat{\sigma}_x}{\hat{\sigma}}. \tag{8.2}$$

When estimators are deterministic functions of one another, as in this equation, the model is unidentified. The reason is that the multidimensional likelihood surface has a flat ridge at the maximum defined by this equation. Along this ridge, many ML estimators exist for each parameter.

### What to do

Most econometrics texts criticize models with unidentified parameters. For example, Judge et al. (1985: 712) write that the implications of the result in Equation (8.2) are "unreasonable and not true." But, if one really believes the model originally specified, then the result *is* true. It may be undesirable, since the model gives the analyst no information with which to distinguish a range of values of the model's parameters, but it certainly is correct. Indeed, the general likelihood approach works just as well if the parameters are identified as if they are not.

The problem comes with the methods of *maximum* likelihood. If a unique maximum does not exist, then using a single point estimate makes little sense. A noninvertible information matrix and infinitely large standard errors serve to emphasize this point. If, in a particular problem, the plateau were relatively narrow, alternative methods could be used to interpret the information still faithfully represented in the likelihood function.[6] For example, with a unidimensional likelihood function, one might use a range of values and some measure of how steep the drop is off each side of the plateau. Unfortunately, no general procedure has been developed for situations like these, so one could use only relatively ad hoc interpretations (see the end of Section 10.1 for a brief discussion of one such class of method). In addition, whereas for some problems the range of the plateau is relatively narrow, for others it ranges from $-\infty$ to $\infty$. Methods to distinguish even between these two situations would be quite important.

Econometrics texts also teach how to make an unidentified model more restrictive so that more of the parameters will be identified. These are a useful set of tools for understanding the model and its limitations. But these ''methods'' should not be taken literally. One does not assume a particular model and then try to ''identify'' it. Identification is a description, not a process. If one posits a model and finds upon analysis that some of its parameters are not identified, then that by itself does not invalidate the model. On the other hand, it may be an unsatisfactory result for many substantive purposes, causing one to change the model. Indeed, the usual procedure to make more parameters identified is to put further restrictions on the model. For example, if one assumed that $\sigma^2$ or $\sigma_x^2$ were known in Example 3, then $\beta$ would be identified. However, those assumptions change the basic model, probably making it less reasonable, although more restrictive.

Theory enables one to posit arbitrarily complicated statistical models, ones in which even determining whether a model is identified can be very difficult. In general, models are intended to be abstracted, and thus more interpretable, versions of reality. If an analyst cannot assess important features of his or her model, then it is probably not sufficiently abstract. But even when the model is abstract enough so that identification and other features are more obvious, an unidentified model may not be sufficiently restrictive, particularly in large multiple parameter problems. Identification is thus a critical feature of statistical models, one that researchers will often require in many instances.

## 8.2     Reciprocal causation

A popular multiple equation model is one where important features of two or more variables depend on one another. For example, in most models of voting behavior, an individual's voting decision depends on his or her political party

---

[6] See Brady (1985) on the concept of set-valued consistency in the context of models for nonmetric multidimensional scaling. Because of the special nature of the model, the solution turns out to be meaningful even if one locates any value of the parameter in the plateau region.

identification, as well as a variety of other factors. For a long time, political party identification was generally regarded as a stable feature of citizens' psychology, but, from another perspective, party identification might also depend, in part, on changes in voting behavior. Thus, one would conceptualize the social system as producing two random observations, $Y_{1i}$ and $Y_{2i}$, for each $i$.

### A linear model

For any model of this sort of phenomenon, one would need to specify a bivariate stochastic component and a systematic component with two equations. For example, suppose $Y_{1i}$ and $Y_{2i}$ are bivariate Normal:

$$(Y_{1i}, Y_{2i}) \sim f_{bn}(y_{1i}, y_{2i} | \mu_{1i}, \mu_{2i}, \sigma_1, \sigma_2, \sigma_{12}),\tag{8.3}$$

$$\mu_{1i} = x_{1i}\beta_1 + x_{2i}\beta_2 + \mu_{2i}\beta_3,$$

$$\mu_{2i} = x_{1i}\gamma_1 + x_{3i}\gamma_2 + \mu_{1i}\gamma_3.$$

This model has the mean of $Y_{1i}$ (say voting behavior) depending on the mean of $Y_{2i}$ (say party identification) as well as the reverse. In addition, the means of both depend on other factors, including $x_{1i}$ in both equations, and $x_{2i}$ and $x_{3i}$, each in only one. In our running example, $x_{1i}$ probably includes demographic attributes and general ideological orientations of the voters. $x_{2i}$ includes characteristics of the candidates and short term events in the campaign, factors that are likely to explain voting behavior but *not* partisan identification. $x_{3i}$ might include parents' partisan identifications, which probably influence party identification but not one's voting behavior in a particular campaign.[7]

The variances of both dependent variables ($\sigma_1^2$ and $\sigma_2^2$) are assumed constant in this model, although not necessarily equal to each other. Note, in addition, the $\sigma_{12}$, the contemporaneous covariance of $Y_{1i}$ and $Y_{2i}$, is also assumed constant over $i$. If these assumptions are implausible, one could let these parameters vary over observations in a manner analogous to the systematic components for $\mu_{1i}$ and $\mu_{2i}$.[8]

The preliminary stochastic component may be written for both random de-

---

[7] Note that no statistical model really assumes "causation." All this model assumes is that stated above. In general, no causal assumption is required, but political scientists like to attribute causation to the effect parameters. For reviews of attempts to formalize the notion of causality, see Freeman (1983), Geweke (1984), and Holland (1986).

[8] An alternative systematic component would have $y_{1i}$ and $y_{2i}$ on the right hand side of the systematic component equations in place of $\mu_{1i}$ and $\mu_{2i}$, respectively. This is, of course, a different specification and the choice of one over the other should be well grounded in substantive arguments. See Section 7.2 for a discussion of similar questions.

pendent variables by letting $y = (y'_1, y'_2)'$, $y_i = (y_{1i}, y_{2i})'$, $\mu = (\mu'_1, \mu'_2)'$, $\mu_i = (\mu_{1i}, \mu_{2i})'$, and

$$\Sigma = \begin{pmatrix} \sigma_1 & \sigma_{12} \\ \sigma_{12} & \sigma_2 \end{pmatrix}.$$

The result is as follows [see Equation (3.23)]:

$$f(y|\mu, \Sigma) = \prod_{i=1}^{n} f_{mn}(y_i|\mu, \Sigma) \tag{8.4}$$

$$= \prod_{i=1}^{n} (2\pi)^{N/2}|\Sigma|^{-1/2}\exp\left\{ -\frac{1}{2} (y_i - \mu_i)'\Sigma^{-1}(y_i - \mu_i)\right\},$$

where $N = 2$ is the number of equations in this model. In order to proceed, one must first substitute out $\mu_{1i}$ and $\mu_{2i}$ for some function of $\beta_1$, $\beta_2$, $\beta_3$, $\gamma_1$, $\gamma_2$, $\gamma_3$, and the observed data, as specified by the systematic component. However, the right hand sides of the two equations in the systematic component are still functions of $\mu_{1i}$ and $\mu_{2i}$, so some alternative method must be used. Whereas standard models are reparameterized and time series models are recursively parameterized, this model requires *multiple equation reparameterization*. Thus, the right hand side of the second equation is substituted in for $\mu_{1i}$ in the first equation and solved for $\mu_{2i}$:

$$\begin{aligned} \mu_{1i} &= x_{1i}\beta_1 + x_{2i}\beta_2 + \mu_{2i}\beta_3 \\ &= x_{1i}\beta_1 + x_{2i}\beta_2 + (x_{1i}\gamma_1 + x_{3i}\gamma_2 + \mu_{1i}\gamma_3)\beta_3 \\ &= x_{1i}\beta_1 + x_{2i}\beta_2 + x_{1i}\gamma_1\beta_3 + x_{3i}\gamma_2\beta_3 + \mu_{1i}\gamma_3\beta_3 \\ &= \left(\frac{1}{1 - \gamma_3\beta_3}\right)[x_{1i}\beta_1 + (x_{1i}\gamma_1 + x_{3i}\gamma_2)\beta_3 + x_{2i}\beta_2]. \end{aligned} \tag{8.5}$$

In a similar manner, the original first equation of the systematic component is substituted into the second and solved for $\mu_{2i}$:

$$\begin{aligned} \mu_{2i} &= x_{1i}\gamma_1 + x_{3i}\gamma_2 + \mu_{1i}\gamma_3 \\ &= x_{1i}\gamma_1 + x_{3i}\gamma_2 + (x_{1i}\beta_1 + x_{2i}\beta_2 + \mu_{2i}\beta_3)\gamma_3 \\ &= x_{1i}\gamma_1 + x_{3i}\gamma_2 + (x_{1i}\beta_1 + x_{2i}\beta_2)\gamma_3 + \mu_{2i}\beta_3\gamma_3 \\ &= \left(\frac{1}{1 - \beta_3\gamma_3}\right)[x_{1i}\gamma_1 + x_{3i}\gamma_2 + (x_{1i}\beta_1 + x_{2i}\beta_2)\gamma_3]. \end{aligned}$$

Then the right hand sides of the last line of each of these equations may be substituted for $\mu_{1i}$ and $\mu_{2i}$, respectively, in the bivariate Normal stochastic component in Equation (8.4). The result, which is proportional to the likelihood function, can then be maximized by taking logs and then differentiating with respect to all the effect parameters ($\tilde{\beta}_1$, $\tilde{\beta}_2$, $\tilde{\beta}_3$, $\tilde{\gamma}_1$, $\tilde{\gamma}_2$, $\tilde{\gamma}_3$), the two variances ($\tilde{\sigma}_1$ and $\tilde{\sigma}_2$), and the contemporaneous covariance ($\sigma_{12}$). The effect parameters should be interpreted as in the original form of the model, as this particular multiple equation reparameterization does not yield much additional insight into the relationships.[9] For example, when $\mu_{2i}$ increases by one unit, $\mu_{1i}$ increases by $\beta_3$, after controlling for the effects of $X_1$ and $X_2$.

Further analysis reveals that all the parameters of both equations are identified, so long as $X_2$ and $X_3$ differ from each other and are included as specified. A counter example provides some insight into this point. If $X_2$ and $X_3$ were dropped, Equation (8.5) would be written as:

$$\mu_{1i} = \left(\frac{1}{1 - \gamma_3\beta_3}\right)[x_{1i} + x_{1i}\gamma_1\beta_3]$$

$$= x_{1i}\left(\frac{\beta_1 + \gamma_1\beta_3}{1 - \gamma_3\beta_3}\right).$$

This result indicates that different values of the right hand side parameters can lead to the same values for $\mu_{1i}$. For example, the two sets of parameter values $\{\beta_1 = 1, \gamma_1 = 30, \beta_3 = 555, \gamma_3 = -30\}$ and $\{\beta_1 = 1, \gamma_1 = 1, \beta_3 = -999, \gamma_3 = -1\}$ both produce the value $\mu_{1i} = x_i$. Indeed, this answer will result as long as $\beta_1 = 1, \gamma_1 = -\gamma_3$, for any value of $\beta_3$.

Thus, the identification of this model of reciprocal causation leans heavily on the theoretical specification of $X_2$ and $X_3$. If substantive theory provides insufficient guidance to make these specifications, parameter estimates with maximum relative likelihoods are not unique.

In the history of statistics, a large number of estimators have been proposed for this model and its close relatives. Most were proposed due to easier computational efficiency or as incremental improvements over the prior state of the literature. A mutually nonexclusive list includes two stage least squares (also known as 2SLS), three stage least squares (3SLS), generalized least squares (GLS), indirect least squares (ILS), $K$-class estimators, double $K$-class estimators, $K$-matrix-class estimators, limited information maximum likelihood (LIML), instrumental variables estimators (IV), and nonlinear versions of each. None of these methods is as general as maximum likelihood (or what is called in this literature, "full information maximum likelihood," FIML); none derives from as general a theory of inference; and none has as desirable statistical properties.[10] Indeed, Hendry (1976) has demonstrated that each of these estimators is a different numerical approximation to the more general maximum likelihood solution.[11]

---

[9] One point that does become clearer in the reparameterized form of the equations in the systematic component is that $\mu_{1i}$ depends on $x_{2i}$, and $\mu_{2i}$ depends on $x_{1i}$, albeit indirectly, even though these variables do not originally appear to have such effects.

[10] Some do turn out to be relatively more robust than FIML to certain types of misspecification. This is an example, then, where the likelihood approach provides the theoretical unity between this and other apparently diverse models, but where an approximation to it may actually be better.

[11] Hendry's (1976) analysis applies to this model, but it also applies to the more general model in Section 10.4, of which this is a special case.

One final point is worth mentioning before moving on to another multiple equation model. Suppose one posited a model just like the one above, but without reciprocal causation. For example,

$$(Y_{1i}, Y_{2i}) \sim f_{bn}(y_{1i}, y_{2i} | \mu_{1i}, \mu_{2i}, \sigma, \sigma_1, \sigma_2, \sigma_{12}),$$
$$\mu_{1i} = x_{1i}\beta_1 + x_{2i}\beta_2,$$
$$\mu_{2i} = x_{1i}\gamma_1 + x_{3i}\gamma_2.$$

These equations share no parameters, but estimates from this model would not be the same as those from two separate models unless the stochastic component factored into two separate independent Normal distributions. Thus, the contemporaneous covariance, $\sigma_{12}$, would have to be equal to zero. Indeed, viewed this way, one can see that running two parallel regressions separately is equivalent to *restricting* $\sigma_{12} = 0$. Thus, the above model is less restrictive, by allowing $\sigma_{12}$ to vary, but it is also more realistic. Thus, one might take a set of these *seemingly unrelated regressions* and estimate them jointly if a contemporaneous covariance is assumed to be nonzero.

This model could be applied for two (or more) time series collected over different cross-sectional units. An example of this *pooled time-series–cross-sectional* design might be the nationwide percent of Republicans elected to the U.S. House of Representatives as one variable and the percent of Republicans elected to the Senate as another. These two parallel time series of biennial observations would probably be explained by a variety of explanatory variables, but, due to a large number of small unobservable factors, the two variables are likely to be correlated even after the explanatory variables are taken into account. Zellner (1962) first demonstrated that joint estimation of what were once seemingly unrelated regressions could significantly improve estimation.[12] The value of $\hat{\sigma}_{12}$ could also provide additional important substantive information. For other linear and nonlinear models for pooled time-series–cross-sectional designs, see Hausman, Hall, and Griliches (1984), Judge et al. (1985: Chapters 12 and 13), King (in press-b), and Stimpson (1985).

## 8.3    Poisson regression models with unobserved dependent variables

In this final section of this chapter, I develop a new model for multiple dependent event counts with unobserved variables. In order to motivate this rather sophisticated model, I develop it in the context of a somewhat more detailed analysis of a specific empirical question: Does military spending by one superpower deter or provoke the other superpower? The relevant data set is from

---

[12] If the multiple time equations happen to have identical explanatory variables, but $\sigma_{12} \neq 0$, then a linear-Normal model still factors into two separate estimators. With any other stochastic or systematic component, this does not occur.

Table 8.1. *Independent Poisson regressions of U.S.–Soviet conflict*

| Variable | U.S.→Sov. | | | Sov.→U.S. | | |
|---|---|---|---|---|---|---|
| | Est. | Std. err. | $t$-stat | Est. | Std. err. | $t$-stat |
| Constant | 3.888 | 0.030 | | 3.843 | 0.095 | |
| Military$ | −0.003 | 0.001 | −5.050 | −0.002 | 0.002 | −1.042 |
| President | 0.120 | 0.018 | 6.576 | 0.468 | 0.017 | 28.323 |

*Notes:* U.S.→Sov. log-likelihood = −223.72. Sov.→U.S. log-likelihood = −241.80. Mean number of events U.S.→Sov. = 44.53. Mean number of events Sov.→U.S. = 52.64. Observations: 28.

the Conflict and Peace Data Bank (COPDAB; see Azar, 1982). From 1951 to 1978, the number of conflictual actions the United States directed at the Soviet Union, and the number the Soviets directed at the United States, are recorded as annual event counts. The first version of this model was originally proposed in King (in press-c).

I begin by focusing on the underlying continuous process of interest. Thus, let $\theta_{1i}$ be a nonrandom variable representing the degree of conflict originating with the United States and directed at the Soviet Union. Similarly, let $\theta_{2i}$ be the degree of conflict originating with the Soviet Union and directed at the United States.[13] To explain U.S. originated conflict, I include a measure of Soviet military expenditures (in constant 1970 billions of U.S. dollars) and a dummy variable for the party of the U.S. president (coded 1 for Democratic presidents and 0 for Republicans). U.S. military expenditures (also measured in constant 1970 billions of U.S. dollars) and the same president variable are included to explain Soviet originated conflict (military expenditure data are from Ward, 1984: 311).

I begin the empirical estimation with two independent Poisson regression models, allowing $\theta_{1i}$ and $\theta_{2i}$ to be exponential linear functions of military spending of the other superpower and the dummy variable for the party of the U.S. president. Empirical results appear in Table 8.1.

The variable Military$ refers to Soviet domestic military spending in the first equation and U.S. spending in the second. In both models, this coefficient is moderately negative, indicating that military spending by a superpower deters conflict directed at it by the other superpower. In the first equa-

---

[13] Since these are Poisson-based models, $\theta_{1i}$ and $\theta_{2i}$ could be called $\lambda_{1i}$ and $\lambda_{2i}$ to be consistent with previous usage. I introduce this alternative notation here in order to make use of the more consistent usage in the more sophisticated model to be developed below.

tion, explaining the conflict directed from the United States toward the Soviets, for example, a ten billion dollar increase in the Soviet defense budget yields about $0.003 \times 10 \times 44.53 = 1.3$ fewer hostile acts directed at the Soviets per year. The coefficient is smaller in the Soviet→U.S. equation, with a larger standard error. Nevertheless, by running only these two regressions, an analyst might reasonably conclude that deterrence works: the level of conflictual actions directed at a nation appears to drop if that nation increases its defense budget.[14]

Although these results seem intuitive from one perspective, a further analysis yields considerably different insights. The most critical problem in the current setup is defining more precisely what $\theta_{1i}$ and $\theta_{2i}$ should mean. As it is, they represent the overall level of hostility directed from one superpower to the other. However, in theory at least, one can separate out at least two types of conflictual dyadic behavior in each of these nonrandom variables. For example, some of the aggregate level of U.S.→Soviet conflict is surely domestically generated. No matter how good relations were, the United States would probably always object to what it views as Soviet human rights abuses. Similarly, the Soviets are unlikely to stop complaining about effects of U.S.-style capitalism. On the other hand, some of the conflictual behavior between these two nations is merely a response to each others' conflictual actions. For example, the United States claims to have caught a Soviet spy and expels a half dozen members of the Soviet embassy. In response, the Soviets expel a dozen members of the U.S. embassy in Moscow. This tit-for-tat conflictual behavior or specific reciprocity may continue for several more iterations until one side eventually stops.

In international relations theory, reciprocity is of considerable interest. Under certain conditions, reciprocity can lead to cooperation or even a semipermanent "feud" between nations (Axelrod, 1984; Axelrod and Keohane, 1986; Keohane, 1986). Thus, we can define $\lambda_{1i}$ and $\lambda_{2i}$ as the degrees of pure U.S. and Soviet originated conflict, respectively, and a separate variable, $\lambda_{3i}$, for the degree of tit-for-tat conflictual behavior. This specification assumes that superpower responses to each other occur at roughly the same level and intensity; if they did not, one might think about including a separate tit-for-tat variable for each country.

Thus, let $\theta_{1i} \equiv \lambda_{1i} + \lambda_{3i}$ be the total degree of conflict directed from the United States to the Soviet Union. $\lambda_{1i}$ is the domestically originated portion of this conflict. Similarly, let $\theta_{2i} \equiv \lambda_{2i} + \lambda_{3i}$ be the total conflict directed from the Soviet Union at the United States, with $\lambda_{2i}$ as the domestically originated portion. These three variables are each unobserved, nonrandom, and theoret-

---

[14] Note that the two log-likelihoods cannot be compared with each other because they are calculated from different data sets. They are included here for later reference.

ically distinct. The goal is to derive explanatory models for $\lambda_{1i}$, $\lambda_{2i}$, and $\lambda_{3i}$. Just as with the models in Section 5.7, we could easily specify:

$$\lambda_{1i} = \exp(x_i\beta), \tag{8.6}$$

$$\lambda_{2i} = \exp(w_i\gamma), \tag{8.7}$$

$$\lambda_{3i} = \exp(z_i\delta), \tag{8.8}$$

where $x_i$, $w_i$, and $z_i$ are vectors of explanatory variables and $\beta$, $\gamma$, and $\delta$ are effect parameter vectors. However, not only are $\lambda_{1i}$, $\lambda_{2i}$, and $\lambda_{3i}$ unobserved, but we have no obvious empirical measure of the random variables giving rise to any of the three. The COPDAB data set records total conflictual events with an actor and target, but none of the variables distinguish domestically originated from tit-for-tat behavior. With the model I derive below, however, existing data *can* be used to estimate $\beta$, $\gamma$, and $\delta$. This case is quite an interesting example of my approach: Deriving coding rules for distinguishing between the types of international conflict seems difficult, if not impossible. However, existing data combined with this new model are almost sure to reveal more useful information than would an expensive new data collection effort.

I begin by assuming that $Y_{1i}^*$, $Y_{2i}^*$, and $Y_{3i}^*$ are unobserved random Poisson variables representing international conflict of the United States directed toward the Soviet Union and of the Soviet Union directed toward the United States, and tit-for-tat actions directed toward each other, respectively. Thus,

$$Y_{1i}^* \sim f_p(y_{1i}^*|\lambda_{1i}),$$
$$Y_{2i}^* \sim f_p(y_{2i}^*|\lambda_{2i}),$$
$$Y_{3i}^* \sim f_p(y_{3i}^*|\lambda_{3i}),$$

where $E(Y_{ji}^*) = \lambda_{ji}$, for $j = 1,2,3$, and, conditional on these expected values, the three variables are assumed independent. Thus, the expected length of the tit-for-tat behavior, once initiated, may depend on the true levels of U.S.→Soviet and Soviet→U.S. conflict, but the random variation of these three variables around their own expected values is assumed to be independent. If the realizations of these random variables, $y_{ji}^*$ (for $j = 1,2,3$), were each observed, this analysis could proceed just as with the standard Poisson regression model in Section 5.7. Although they are not observed, we do observe realizations of random variables that are two functions of these three variables,

$$Y_{1i} = Y_{1i}^* + Y_{3i}^*,$$
$$Y_{2i} = Y_{2i}^* + Y_{3i}^*,$$

and, because sums of independent Poisson distributed random variables are also Poisson distributed, we can write:

$$Y_{1i} \sim f_p(y_{1i}|\theta_{1i}) = f_p(y_{1i}|\lambda_{1i} + \lambda_{3i}),$$
$$Y_{2i} \sim f_p(y_{1i}|\theta_{2i}) = f_p(y_{2i}|\lambda_{2i} + \lambda_{3i}).$$

Unfortunately, this is still insufficient as an estimable model, however, since the two terms in the expected value in each distribution cause them each to be separately unidentified.

Fortunately, we can modify a result in probability theory due to Holgate (1964: 241; see also Johnson and Kotz, 1969: 297–8; and King, in press-b) to solve this problem. The solution is based on a proof that, given conditions equivalent to those stated above, $Y_{1i}$ and $Y_{2i}$ are distributed as a bivariate Poisson distribution:

$$(Y_{1i}, Y_{2i}) \sim f_{bp}(y_{1i}, y_{2i} | \lambda_{1i}, \lambda_{2i}, \lambda_{3i}) \tag{8.9}$$

$$= \exp(-\lambda_{1i} - \lambda_{2i} - \lambda_{3i}) \sum_{j=0}^{\min(y_{1i}, y_{2i})} \frac{\lambda_{1i}^{(y_{1i}-j)}}{(y_{1i}-j)!} \frac{\lambda_{2i}^{(y_{2i}-j)}}{(y_{2i}-j)!} \frac{\lambda_{3i}^{j}}{j!}.$$

Due to the special properties of this distribution, if no tit-for-tat behavior exists, and thus $\lambda_{3i}$ turns out to be zero for all $i$, then the bivariate Poisson factors into the product of two independent Poisson variates. As such, this distribution is a straightforward generalization of the univariate Poisson, and, since the covariance of $Y_{1i}$ and $Y_{2i}$ is $\lambda_{3i}$, this setup is a generalization of the Seemingly Unrelated Poisson REgression Model Estimator (SUPREME) developed in King (in press-b). Thus, a test for $\lambda_{3i}$ equaling zero is equivalent to a test for whether this model is extracting more information from the data than would two independent Poisson regression models applied to $y_{1i}$ and $y_{2i}$ separately. To the extent that tit-for-tat behavior exists and $\lambda_{3i}$ is different from zero, separate Poisson models produce estimates of $\beta$ and $\gamma$ that are not only statistically inefficient, but are biased and inconsistent as well. And in addition to improvements in the properties of existing estimators, this model also enables one to estimate the explanatory variables' effect on, and the raw extent of, tit-for-tat behavior – answering key substantive questions one could not hope to even address with standard methods.

To estimate $\beta$, $\gamma$, and $\delta$, substitute the right hand sides of Equations (8.6), (8.7), and (8.8) into Equation (8.9), take logs, and sum over the $n$ observations. The result is the log-likelihood function:

$$L(\beta, \gamma, \delta | y_{1i}, y_{2i}) = \sum_{i=1}^{n} \left\{ -\exp(x_i\beta) - \exp(z_i\gamma) - \exp(w_i\delta) \tag{8.10} \right.$$
$$\left. + \ln\left[ \sum_{j=0}^{\min(y_{1i}, y_{2i})} \frac{\exp(x_i\beta)^{(y_{1i}-j)}}{(y_{1i}-j)!} \frac{\exp(z_i\gamma)^{(y_{2i}-j)}}{(y_{2i}-j)!} \frac{\exp(w_i\delta)^{j}}{j!} \right] \right\}.$$

This well-behaved function is then easily optimized to yield the maximum likelihood estimates of the effect parameters $\beta$, $\gamma$, and $\delta$. No identifying restrictions need be put on the three sets of explanatory variables. They may be all identical or may differ, depending on theory.

Consider now a point estimation with the new model developed above.

Table 8.2. *SUPREME2 model of U.S.-Soviet conflict*

| Variable | Estimate | Std. error | $t$-stat |
|---|---|---|---|
| $\hat{\beta}_0$ | 2.673 | 0.119 | |
| SovMilitary\$ | 0.011 | 0.001 | 8.095 |
| President | 0.438 | 0.055 | 7.947 |
| $\hat{\gamma}_0$ | 2.590 | 0.170 | |
| USMilitary\$ | 0.010 | 0.002 | 5.108 |
| President | 0.794 | 0.062 | 12.753 |
| $\hat{\delta}_0$ | 8.598 | 0.745 | 11.534 |
| AvgMilitary\$ | −0.103 | 0.016 | −6.555 |
| President | −0.674 | 0.202 | −3.334 |

*Note:* Log-likelihood $= -397.04$. Observations: 28.

This model now permits the degree of tit-for-tat behavior between the superpowers to be estimated rather than assumed. To estimate this model, I leave the specifications for $\lambda_{1i}$ and $\lambda_{2i}$ as functions of military spending of the other superpower and the party of the U.S. president. These two nonrandom variables are interpreted as international conflict, stripped of any tit-for-tat behavior. In addition, I specify a model for $\lambda_{3i}$, as in Equation (8.8). Although one could develop a long list of explanatory variables, I keep the specification simple by assuming that tit-for-tat behavior is an exponential function of only the average superpower military spending (AvgMilitary\$) and the party of the U.S. president. The empirical results appear in Table 8.2.

The overall improvement in moving from the two Poisson regression models to this joint estimation can be judged by examining the log-likelihoods. Since the two models in Table 8.1 were estimated independently, the log-likelihoods may be summed to arrive at a total log-likelihood, $-223.72 - 241.80 = -465.52$. This number can be compared to the likelihood from Table 8.2 to derive a test statistic. The likelihood ratio test statistic, in this case, is $2(-397.04 + 465.52) = 136.96$. This is a chi-square statistic with two degrees of freedom. Thus, the hypothesis of no difference between the models is comfortably rejected.

The most surprising result is the parameter estimates for military spending. It appears that deterrence does not work as it seemed from the results of the independent Poisson regression models. Instead, U.S. military spending seems to very clearly provoke Soviet hostile action toward the United States. Indeed, Soviet military spending also provokes U.S. conflictual actions at almost exactly the same rate. Whereas the independent Poisson models explained total U.S. and Soviet actions, this model extracts off tit-for-tat behavior as a separate variable. Indeed, this more sophisticated model shows that higher levels of average superpower military spending reduce tit-for-tat behavior, presumably because such superfluous conflictual behavior becomes more dangerous with bigger military budgets. Thus, military spending appears to provoke pure hostile actions but deter superfluous ones.

Since the average value of military spending is 61.44 billion U.S. dollars, the typical value of $\hat{\lambda}_{3i}$ may be calculated as:

$$\hat{\lambda}_{3i} = \exp(\delta_0 + \delta_1 \text{AvgMilitary\$} + \delta_2 \text{President})$$
$$= \exp(8.598 - 0.103 \times 61.44 - 0.674 \times 0.5)$$
$$= 6.9.$$

Thus, of all the conflictual acts occurring between the United States and the Soviet Union, an average of 6.9 of these events a year are merely tit-for-tat actions. This represents 15.5% of the typical yearly U.S.→Soviet acts and 13.1% of the Soviet→U.S. acts. Only with this new model can these three types of behavior be extracted from the two existing data series.

Goldstein and Freeman (1988) show that virtually all previous studies based on annual data are unable to find evidence of reciprocity, and nearly all based on less aggregated data find substantial evidence. The analysis presented here, which used annual data but nevertheless finds clear evidence of reciprocity, dramatically demonstrates how these more powerful models can extract far more information than the commonly used techniques such as linear regression.

The independent Poisson models were biased primarily by the contamination from the tit-for-tat behavior. Once this behavior is separated out analytically, empirical results become much clearer and substantive findings significantly different.

## 8.4 Concluding remarks

This chapter provides a brief introduction to models with multiple equations. The key substantive point is that these methods enable political scientists to deal with situations where part of the social or political system one is studying is producing more than a single output. In these situations, multiple equations enable researchers to build more sophisticated models and address questions not possible with single equation models. Indeed, with access to only single equation models, one might not even think of asking certain important categories of questions. Aside from this additional substantive information, multiple equation models have considerably more desirable statistical properties than equation-by-equation estimations of the same problem, particularly in those situations when parameters are shared among the equations or when some of the outputs are stochastically dependent on one another.

Aside from its immediate benefit, the material introduced here will be of use in developing models with nonrandom selection in Chapter 9 and general classes of multiple equation models in Chapter 10.

# Models with nonrandom selection

Every model introduced so far assumes that all data are randomly generated by the social system and observed by the analyst. These sources of data were generated in a large variety of ways and took on a large number of resulting forms, but every observation appears in the data set. Even in the case of ordinal probit (Section 5.4), where only the ordered categories in which $y_i^*$ fell were known, all data are assumed to be generated and observed randomly.

In this chapter, I show how the same likelihood theory of inference can be used to deal with problems of nonrandom selection. Because some of what we previously called "observations" are now not observed, we refer to rows in the $(Y, X)$ data matrix as "units" (from the phrase "unit of analysis"). A variety of models are derived in this chapter, but an important distinction should be made between two general types of nonrandom selection: *censoring* and *truncation*. In the former, all units are in the data set and all explanatory variables are observed, but some values of the dependent variable are unobserved. The term "censoring" is used because this missing information is sometimes intentionally censored by the government, the survey analyst, or something or someone else. The purpose of this censoring may be to hide the identity of the respondents or, as we shall see below, to actually get more reliable estimates. In *truncation*, units with missing information never even appear in the data set. Thus, whereas censored data have measurements for explanatory and dependent variables, a truncated sample does not even provide information on how many units were truncated from the data set.

The basic intuition about models with nonrandom selection is that *if the rule by which units are censored or truncated is independent of the dependent variable, standard techniques may be used without problem* (see Achen, 1986). Since our explanatory variables are usually assumed fixed or controlled by the investigator, selection rules correlated with $X$ cause no particular problems. However, the models in this chapter become statistically necessary, and also enable one to extract significant new information, if the data selection rule is related to $Y$. These points are formalized and clarified below.

## 9.1    Censoring

Suppose one is interested in modeling data on personal income collected from sample surveys. Getting people to faithfully report their incomes to a survey

208

researcher can be quite difficult. In particular, the very few people with extremely high incomes may not want to even participate in the survey if they are asked to report their earnings. One would quickly lose anonymity with detailed information on such a small group. To get around this problem, one might ask respondents to report their exact income only if it is below $100,000. Everyone making more would merely check the ''$100,000 and over'' category. With this procedure, one gets some information and avoids losing the rest by keeping these people from dropping out of the survey. The resulting measure is continuous from zero up to $100,000. However, information on the individuals in the last category is censored by construction.

A model of censored data can be built by defining $Y_i^*$ as a continuous unobserved variable. Since income is bounded from below by zero, a log-Normal distribution would seem appropriate. However, if the mean is sufficiently far from the bound, the Normal is a reasonable approximation:

$$Y_i^* \sim f_n(y_i^* | \mu_i, \sigma^2),$$

where the systematic component is, for example:

$$\mu_i = x_i \beta.$$

In addition to this basic specification, there is also a deterministic censoring mechanism (a sample selection rule) that governs which units are observed and which remain censored:

$$y_i = \begin{cases} y_i^* & \text{if } y_i^* < c, \\ c & \text{if } y_i^* \geq c. \end{cases} \tag{9.1}$$

Thus, one actually observes the realization of $Y_i^*$ if it is less than the censoring value, $c$ ($100,000, for example). If the realized value is $c$ or greater, one only observes $c$. Since the censoring rule is related to $Y$, alternative methods are called for.

A naive approach would be to merely drop all the censored observations, effectively turning censored data into truncated data. This naive approach is flawed because standard techniques are biased under either censoring or truncation. In addition, discarding useful information is never recommended. One could include the censored units in the analysis, and code them as $c$ or some value larger than $c$ (say $150,000). This approach is also flawed since all these people almost surely do not have identical incomes; and, even if they did, their income levels are still unknown. This approach would also overestimate the certainty with which we know this imputation. Fortunately, one can solve the problem by including all available knowledge in the likelihood function.

Begin by assuming the absence of a time series component: $Y_i^*$ is independent of $Y_j^*$ for all $i \neq j$. Then, the likelihood function can be written as the product of two separate parts, one for $Y_i^*$ observed and one for the censored values. For the former, one merely takes the product over the relevant observations as in a linear-Normal model without censoring:

$$\prod_{y_i^* < c} f_n(y_i|\mu_i, \sigma^2).$$

For the censored observations, all we know is that $Y_i^* \geq c$, so we write the $i$th element as follows:

$$\begin{aligned}
\Pr(Y_i = c) &= \Pr(Y_i^* \geq c) \\
&= \int_c^{\infty} f_n(y_i^*|\mu_i, \sigma^2) dy_i^* \\
&= 1 - \int_{-\infty}^c f_n(y_i^*|\mu_i, \sigma^2) dy_i^* \\
&= 1 - F_n(c|\mu_i, \sigma^2),
\end{aligned}$$

where $F_n(c|\mu_i, \sigma^2)$ is the cumulative Normal distribution function, by definition equal to $\Pr(Y_i^* \leq c)$. Since all units are assumed independent, the censored units are independent of the uncensored ones. Thus, the full stochastic component and likelihood function may be written by taking the product of the two parts:

$$\begin{aligned}
L(\tilde{\mu}_i, \tilde{\sigma}^2|y) &\propto f(y|\tilde{\mu}_i, \tilde{\sigma}^2) \\
&= \left[ \prod_{y_i^* < c} f_n(y_i|\tilde{\mu}_i, \tilde{\sigma}^2) \right] \left[ \prod_{y_i^* \geq c} [1 - F_n(c|\tilde{\mu}_i, \tilde{\sigma}^2)] \right],
\end{aligned}$$

with $\tilde{\mu}_i = x_i\tilde{\beta}$. This likelihood function may then be maximized by numerical methods with respect to $\tilde{\beta}$ and $\tilde{\sigma}^2$. The result is a much more realistic model of the process generating censored data, and $\beta$ may be interpreted as if from a linear-Normal regression with no censoring.

This model is also a variant of the *Tobit model*. The original model was developed by James Tobin (1958) and was named by Goldberger (1964) as shorthand for "Tobin's Probit." McDonald and Moffitt (1980) provide an interesting decomposition of the tobit effects, demonstrating that significant additional information can be extracted from the estimated coefficients.

## 9.2     Stochastic censoring

In the type of censoring considered in the last section, a characteristic of the data gathering mechanism (the survey) obliterates information on some of the units of the dependent variable according to the *deterministic* relationship in Equation (9.1). For some problems of this type, a deterministic rule is not reasonable. For example, suppose one is analyzing the determinants of grades in a college as a function of grades in high school and standardized achievement test (SAT) scores. Data on the explanatory variables exist for all applicants, but one obviously only has data for grades in college for those admitted and attending.

The data gathering mechanism is the admissions committee. Although many factors are taken into account, having a strong *potential* for high grades in college is probably the most important factor. Thus, the bottom of the distribution of the unobserved variable, expected grades in college, is censored. The problem is that the admissions committee is not perfect, so $c$ is not a fixed predicted college grade level. Indeed, some students might be admitted on the basis of extracurricular activities unrelated to academics. Although the method of selection is not deterministically related to $Y$, it is stochastically related (assuming a reasonably good committee). Thus, the standard techniques are not appropriate.

A naive approach to this problem is to drop from the analysis those students not admitted to college. Not only does this discard useful information, but it creates predictable biases: Since those admitted will have relatively uniform high school grades and SAT scores, a regression run with only those admitted will indicate that these variables are poor predictors of performance, whether they really are or not (see Achen, 1986). Indeed, in the situation where the admissions committee does an exceptionally good job (and thus the more highly correlated are the selection rule and $Y$), the standard techniques will indicate that the committee did an especially poor job! The other naive approach is to assign all students not admitted an arbitrary grade. This latter naive approach makes it even clearer that $c$ should not be a constant. Certainly some nonadmitted students would be expected to have done better in college (had they been admitted) than others.

One model of this selection problem may be formed by letting $Y_i$ be the random *outcome* variable (grades in college, for example). $C_i$ is now a random *selection* variable. Begin by assuming that these are two jointly distributed Normal variables:

$$(Y_i, C_i) \sim f_{mn}(y_i, c_i | \mu_{yi}, \mu_{ci}, \sigma_y^2, \sigma_c^2, \sigma_{yc}).$$

The expected values of each of these variables have associated systematic components. Thus,

$$\mu_{yi} = x_{1i}\beta_1 + x_{2i}\beta_2,$$
$$\mu_{ci} = x_{1i}\gamma_1 + x_{3i}\gamma_2.$$

The first equation in the systematic component is for the outcome variable and its effect parameters represent the effects of, for example, high school grades and SAT scores. The second equation is included to model the admissions process. Having variables like $x_{3i}$ in one equation but not the other turns out to be necessary for identification. It might include variables measuring extracurricular activities or whether the applicant's parents were alumni.

Neither of these variables would necessarily affect grades in college; they would therefore be omitted from the first equation.

To the above specifications, we add a data gathering mechanism: $C_i$ is an unobserved random variable and $y_i$ is observed only when $y_i > c_i$.[1]

To simplify matters, let $L_0 \equiv \Pi_{y_i \le c_i} L_{0i}$ be the likelihood function for $y_i$ censored and let $L_1 \equiv \Pi_{y_i > c_i} L_{0i}$ be the corresponding likelihood function for $y_i$ observed. I will now derive each of these separately and then put them together.

The stochastic component for the realization of $Y_i$ observed (where $c_i < y_i$) is then the joint distribution of $y_i$ and $c_i < y_i$. This can be derived by averaging the bivariate Normal distribution over the $c_i$ dimension for $-\infty$ up to $y_i$:

$$L_{1i} = \int_{-\infty}^{y_i} f_{mn}(y_i, c_i | \mu_{y_i}, \mu_{c_i}, \sigma_y^2, \sigma_c^2, \sigma_{yc}) dc.$$

This expression can be simplified considerably by using a version of the standard definition for conditional probability, $\Pr(AB) = \Pr(B)\Pr(A|B)$, to factor the bivariate distribution as follows:

$$
\begin{aligned}
L_{1i} &= \int_{-\infty}^{y_i} f_n(y_i | \mu_{y_i}, \sigma_y^2) f_n(c | \theta_i, \delta^2) dc \\
&= f_n(y_i | \mu_{y_i}, \sigma_y^2) \int_{-\infty}^{y_i} f_n(c | \theta_i, \delta^2) dc \\
&= f_n(y_i | \mu_{y_i}, \sigma_y^2) F_n(y_i | \theta_i, \delta^2) dc,
\end{aligned}
\tag{9.2}
$$

where $F_n$ is the cumulative Normal distribution and $\theta_i$ (a function of $y_i$) and $\delta^2$ are defined, from the definition of the Normal conditional distributions (DeGroot, 1986: 302–3), as

$$\theta_i = \mu_{ci} + \frac{\sigma_{yc}}{\sigma_y^2} (y_i - \mu_{yi}),$$

$$\delta = \sigma_c^2 - \frac{\sigma_{yc}^2}{\sigma_y^2}.$$

Note that the right hand sides of these expressions include the data $y_i$ and all the parameters appearing in the bivariate Normal distribution. In addition, from the definition of the model, $\mu_{yi} = x_{1i}\beta_1 + x_{2i}\beta_2$ and $\mu_{ci} = x_{1i}\gamma_1 + x_{3i}\gamma_2$.

The other part of the likelihood function is from the censored data and thus is based only on the information that $y_i \le c_i$, or equivalently, $(y_i - c_i) \le 0$. To calculate $\Pr[(y_i - c_i) \le 0]$, one first needs to derive the distribution of $(y_i - c_i)$.

---

[1] Note that in the example I used above for censoring, the top of the distribution was deterministically censored. Here, the bottom of the distribution is stochastically censored.

Since linear combinations of bivariate Normally distributed variables are Normally distributed,

$$(y_i - c_i) \sim f_n(y_i - c_i | \mu_{yi} - \mu_{ci}, \sigma_y^2 + \sigma_c^2 - 2\sigma_{yc}).$$

From this, calculations are straightforward:

$$\begin{aligned} L_{1i} &\propto \Pr[(y_i - c_i) \leq 0] \\ &= \int_{-\infty}^{0} f_n(z_i | \mu_{yi} - \mu_{ci}, \sigma_y^2 + \sigma_c^2 - 2\sigma_{yc}) dz_i \\ &= F_n(0 | \mu_{yi} - \mu_{ci}, \sigma_y^2 + \sigma_c^2 - 2\sigma_{yc}), \end{aligned}$$

where $F_n$ is again the cumulative Normal probability distribution.

The resulting likelihood function is the product of these two components multiplied over their respective observations. Thus,

$$\begin{aligned} &L(\tilde{\beta}_1, \tilde{\beta}_2, \tilde{\gamma}_1, \tilde{\gamma}_2, \tilde{\sigma}_y^2, \tilde{\sigma}_c^2, \tilde{\sigma}_{yc} | y) \\ &= \left[ \prod_{y > c} f_n(y_i | \tilde{\mu}_{yi}, \tilde{\sigma}_y^2) F(y_i | \tilde{\theta}_i, \tilde{\delta}^2) \right] \left[ \prod_{y < c} F_n(0 | \tilde{\mu}_{yi} - \tilde{\mu}_{ci}, \tilde{\sigma}_y^2 + \tilde{\sigma}_c^2 - 2\tilde{\sigma}_{yc}) \right]. \end{aligned}$$

This likelihood function can then be easily maximized over all the parameters, $\tilde{\beta}_1$, $\tilde{\beta}_2$, $\tilde{\gamma}_1$, $\tilde{\gamma}_2$, $\tilde{\sigma}_y^2$, $\tilde{\sigma}_c^2$, and $\tilde{\sigma}_{yc}$. Note that this model provides estimates of the effect parameters for both the outcome and selection equations. The main purpose of the analysis is probably the outcome equation, that is, the effect of observable factors on grades in college. Nevertheless, the selection equation also can provide significant additional information. For example, is the admissions committee making decisions based on race or class? These variables could be included in the second equation to test these and related hypotheses.

## 9.3 Stochastic truncation

For problems of both deterministic and stochastic censoring one has observations on the explanatory variables for all individuals, but on the dependent variables for only some units. For example, suppose one were analyzing grades in college but information on applicants not admitted was unavailable or too difficult to collect. A more interesting example involves the Soviet emigrant project (see, for example, Bahry and Silver, 1987). Imagine a model where one was interested in the determinants of political satisfaction in the USSR. Since the Soviet Union prohibits random interviews of its citizens on politically sensitive subjects, the only choice Soviet scholars have had is to interview emigrants. Of course, problems of selection would be expected to be quite severe, as emigrants are much less likely to be satisfied. Since information on explanatory and dependent variables is unavailable for individuals not in the sample, models of censoring and selection are useless.

In cases such as this, a model of stochastic truncation is most appropriate (see Bloom and Killingsworth, 1985). This model may be written by defining the random variable of interest as $Y_i$ and the unobserved random threshold variable as $C_i$. The two are assumed distributed as a bivariate Normal:

$$(Y_i, C_i) \sim f_{mn}(y_i, c_i | \mu_{yi}, \mu_{ci}, \sigma_y^2, \sigma_c^2, \sigma_{yc}), \tag{9.3}$$

where the systematic component of primary interest is

$$\mu_{yi} = x_{1i}\beta_y$$

and a corresponding systematic component for the truncation threshold is written as

$$\mu_{ci} = x_{2i}\beta_c.$$

In addition, $y_i$, $x_{1i}$, and $x_{2i}$ are observed if and only if $c_i > 0$. Since $C_i$ is a random variable, the point of truncation varies over observations and across hypothetical experiments.

The stochastic component of observation $i$ in a model like this would need to be a function of $y_i$, given that $c_i > 0$ and $y_i$ has a univariate distribution: $f(y_i | c_i > 0, \mu_{yi}, \mu_{ci}, \sigma_y^2, \sigma_c^2, \sigma_{yc})$.

The naive approach is to merely take the marginal distribution of $Y_i$ in Equation (9.3), $f(y_i | \mu_{yi}, \sigma_y)$, which yields a standard linear regression of the nontruncated observations. This approach is incorrect because it ignores the fact that we cannot integrate over all of $C_i$ to yield the marginal distribution. In other words, it ignores the relationship between $Y_i$ and $C_i$. Thus, one can calculate the correct univariate distribution and derive a truncated distribution by using the basic rule for conditional probability in Equation (3.2) as follows:

$$
\begin{aligned}
f(y_i | c_i > 0, \mu_{y_i}, \mu_{c_i}, \sigma_y^2, \sigma_c^2, \sigma_{yc}) &= \frac{f(y_i, c_i | \mu_{y_i}, \mu_{c_i}, \sigma_y^2, \sigma_c^2, \sigma_{yc})}{\Pr(C_i > 0)} \\
&= \frac{f_n(y_i | \mu_i, \sigma_y^2)\Pr(C_i > 0 | y_i)}{\Pr(C_i > 0)}
\end{aligned}
\tag{9.4}
$$

All three elements of the right hand side of the second line of this equation can be calculated directly from the bivariate Normal distribution in Equation (9.3). I discuss each in turn. Since all marginal distributions of a multivariate Normal are also Normal, $f(y_i | \mu_{y_i}, \sigma_y)$ is Normal:

$$f_n(y_i | \mu_{y_i}, \sigma_y^2) = \int_{-\infty}^{\infty} f_{mn}(y_i, c_i | \mu_{y_i}, \mu_{c_i}, \sigma_y^2, \sigma_c^2, \sigma_{yc}) dc_i.$$

To calculate $\Pr(C_i > 0 | y_i)$, the conditional distribution of $C_i$ given $y_i$ is required. Since conditional distributions of the multivariate Normal distribution are also Normal, this is also straightforward. This conditional distribution may be written as follows (see DeGroot, 1986: 302–3):

$$f_n(c_i|\delta_i,\phi^2),$$

where

$$\delta_i = \theta_i + \frac{\sigma_{yc}}{\sigma_y^2}\,(y_i - \mu_{y_i})$$

and

$$\phi^2 = \sigma_c^2 - \frac{\sigma_{yc}^2}{\sigma_y^2}.$$

Then the probability needed for Equation (9.4) is calculated as follows:

$$\Pr(C_i > 0|y_i) = \int_0^\infty f_n(c_i|\delta_i,\phi^2)dc_i$$
$$= 1 - F_n(0|\delta_i,\phi^2),$$

where $F_n$ is the cumulative Normal distribution. The denominator of Equation (9.4) is calculated from the marginal distribution of $C_i$ as follows:

$$\Pr(C_i > 0) = \int_0^\infty f_n(c_i|\mu_{c_i},\sigma_c^2)dc_i$$
$$= 1 - F_n(0|\mu_{c_i},\sigma_c^2).$$

Finally, I collect all of these results and, by assuming independence over observations and substituting into Equation (9.4), can write the full likelihood as

$$L(\tilde{\beta}_y,\tilde{\beta}_c,\tilde{\sigma}_y^2,\tilde{\sigma}_c^2,\tilde{\sigma}_{yc}|y)$$
$$= \prod_{i=1}^n f_n(y_i|\tilde{\mu}_{y_i},\tilde{\sigma}_y^2)[1 - F_n(0|\tilde{\delta}_i,\tilde{\phi}^2)]/[1 - F_n(0|\tilde{\theta}_i,\tilde{\sigma}_c^2)],$$

where

$$\tilde{\delta}_i = \tilde{\theta}_i + \frac{\tilde{\sigma}_{yc}}{\tilde{\sigma}_y^2}\,(y_i - \tilde{\mu}_{y_i}),$$

$$\tilde{\phi} = \tilde{\sigma}_c^2 - \frac{\tilde{\sigma}_{yc}^2}{\tilde{\sigma}_y^2},$$

$$\tilde{\mu}_{y_i} = x_{1i}\tilde{\beta}_y,$$

$$\tilde{\mu}_{c_i} = x_{2i}\tilde{\beta}_c.$$

Note that the product is taken over all $n$ observations since, for any individual for which $c_i \leq 0$, no unit appears to the data set. Since nothing at all is known about $C_i$, except its distribution, the parameters of this problem are not all identified. However, without loss of generality, one can set $\sigma_c^2 = 1$. With this constraint, the parameters are identified and only the *scale* for $C_i$ is assumed. With this done, the likelihood function may be maximized with respect to $\tilde{\beta}_y$, $\tilde{\beta}_c$, $\tilde{\sigma}_y^2$, and $\tilde{\sigma}_{yc}$. $\beta_y$ is a vector of effect parameters of primary interest, but some of the other parameters may also be relevant in certain problems. For example, $\beta_c$ are the effect parameters that help determine where the truncation threshold will occur. With a sample of only Soviet emigrants, it is quite remarkable that one can estimate $\beta_c$, which can then be used to study the determinants of the decisions to emigrate; the relatively strong assumptions about the processes generating these data make this sort of inquiry possible. $\sigma_{yc}$ is the relationship between the dependent variable (say, perception of political freedom) and the truncation variable (emigration). This is of obvious substantive interest, but it is of statistical interest as well. That is, if $\sigma_{yc} = 0$, the likelihood above reduces to that for a standard linear-Normal regression model. If it were true that $\sigma_{yc} = 0$, then, one could avoid this procedure and just run a regression with the available data. Of course, in most interesting examples of truncation, this will not occur.

## 9.4    Truncated and variance function event count models

I now consider an application in somewhat more depth so as to motivate a series of new models for truncated event count data. The basic substantive question is:

What explains international cooperation in imposing economic sanctions on a target country? Data available to help answer this, and many other related questions about economic sanctions, have been collected by Lisa Martin (in progress) and Hufbauer and Schott (1983). The data to be used here involve 78 incidents of economic sanctions since the economic blockade of Germany in World War I. An economic sanction is defined as "the deliberate government-inspired withdrawal, or threat of withdrawal, of 'customary' trade or financial relations" (Hufbauer and Schott, 1983: 2).

The observed dependent variable is the number of nations participating in each of 75 instances of economic sanctions – an event count.[2] However, this particular event count has at least two interesting features worthy of further study. I now analyze this model in the way introduced in Chapter 5, and then derive a new model as each of these two special features is defined.

---

[2] I deleted three special cases. Whereas the mean number of senders is 3.4 in the sample of 75, the three omitted sanctions included primarily U.N. sponsored activities where a large proportion of the nations of the world joined the effort.

Consider, first, a simple systematic component for $\lambda_i$, the expected number of nations cooperating:

$$E(Y_i) \equiv \lambda_i = \overline{\exp}(\beta_0 + \beta_1 \text{Stability}_i + \beta_2 \text{Cost}_i), \qquad (9.5)$$

where the variable Stability is a measure of the target country's overall economic health and political stability during the sanctions episode, abstracting from the effects of the sanctions. Stability$_i$ is coded on a scale from 1 (distressed) to 3 (strong and stable). The hypothesis is that more nations will join the sanction if the target country is weak and, thus, the effort is likely to be successful. Cost$_i$ is a measure of the effect of the sanction on the sanctioning (or "sender") country. Hufbauer and Schott's (1983: 84) analysis implies that a more costly sanction will encourage the sender country to obtain cooperation from other nations. Cost is coded from 1 (net gain to sender) to 4 (major loss to sender).

Appealing to the two first principles required to derive the Poisson distribution in this case seems quite unreasonable. Indeed, a key feature of this substantive problem is the contagion among nations. In many cases, the sending nation intentionally tries to get others to join the effort against the target. Hence, the assumption of independence is not only implausible, but it would seem to strip the problem of one of its most interesting features.

Before complicating the model, then, I move from the basic Poisson process to the generalized event count (GEC) distribution [Equation (5.22)]. Since overdispersion (resulting in this case from contagion) is almost certain to be present, $\sigma^2$ will be greater than one. In order to simplify later analysis, I therefore use the negative binomial distribution, a special case of the GEC when $\sigma^2 > 1$ [Equation (3.17)]. Also for later simplification, I reparameterize this distribution so that $\sigma^2 = 1 + \theta$ and $\theta = \exp(\gamma)$. Thus, the expected value is still

$$E(Y_i) \equiv \lambda_i$$

but the variance is now

$$V(Y_i) \equiv (1 + \theta)\lambda_i = (1 + e^\gamma)\lambda_i.$$

The full distribution is then written for a single observation as follows:

$$f_{nb}(y_i | \lambda_i, \theta) = \frac{\Gamma(\lambda_i/\theta + y_i)}{y_i! \Gamma(\lambda_i/\theta)} \, \theta^{y_i} (1 + \theta)^{-(\lambda_i/\theta + y_i)}, \qquad (9.6)$$

where $\theta = \exp(\gamma)$. Note that this reparameterization has no substantive effect on the present analysis, but it will make calculations easier in the models developed later.[3] Larger values of $\gamma$ mean that more overdispersion (and therefore contagion) is present in these data.

---

[3] The other advantage of this parameterization is that all parameters now vary between negative and positive infinity. This is an advantage because the theory and practice of numerical optimization has not yet dealt adequately with bounded parameter spaces.

Table 9.1. *Negative binomial regression of nations sanctioning*

| Variable | Estimate | Std. error | $t$-stat |
|----------|----------|------------|----------|
| Constant | 0.707 | 0.409 | 1.726 |
| Stability | −0.217 | 0.145 | −1.496 |
| Cost | 0.510 | 0.108 | 4.711 |
| $\hat{\gamma}$ | 0.607 | 0.334 | 1.814 |

*Note:* Log-likelihood = 124.769. Observations: 75. Mean number of nations participating = 3.4.

By substituting the right hand side of Equation (9.5) into the probability distribution in Equation (3.17), taking logs, and summing over observations, the log-likelihood may be derived. Maximizing this function gives the maximum likelihood estimates of $\beta_0$, $\beta_1$, $\beta_2$, and $\gamma$. Empirical results appear in Table 9.1.

First note the level of dispersion, $\hat{\gamma}$. If nations chose to participate in economic sanctions independently of one another, the variance of $Y_i$ would equal its mean, $\lambda_i$. In this case, however, the variance is $[1 + \exp(0.607)] = 2.83$ times greater than its mean, indicating moderate contagion in sanctioning decisions (but see the next model).

Both of the explanatory variables appear to have modest effects. The Stability of a target country decreases international participation by about $-0.217\lambda_i$ more nations. Thus, for the typical sanction, with about 3.4 nations participating, an increase on the Stability scale, from a country that is distressed to a strong and stable nation, decreases participation by about $-0.217 \times 2 \times 3.4 = -1.48$ more (or 1.48 fewer) nations, although this effect is not quite significant by conventional standards. For each unit increase in the four point cost-to-sender scale, an additional $3.4 \times 0.510 = 1.73$ more nations are convinced to join in the sanction.

### A truncated negative binomial model

In virtually all substantive problems in political science, one has only a sample of realized values from the process governed by $\lambda_i$. However, in many problems, the sample is either roughly random or is periodic. However, in the present example, realizations of the process are only observed when a major sanction takes place. Thus, these data are likely to have two types of nonrandom selection. The first is that if zero nations cooperate in an economic sanction, the observation never appears in the data set. As a result, the observed data $y_i$ are always greater than zero. A second type of selection bias is that the cases included in the analysis are "somewhat biased toward the 'big case' " (Hufbauer and Schott, 1983: 2). Thus, some cases of economic sanctions with relatively few nations participating did not come to the attention of the coders.

I now construct a model that takes into account the truncation-at-zero problem. This model will not directly address the second type of selection bias, where the truncation threshold is greater than zero and probably stochastic, but this latter problem seems less severe in this substantive example. See Cohen (1960) and especially Grogger and Carson (1988) for studies of truncated count data models.

The present example is an extreme case of nonrandom selection since an international economic sanction is observed and included in the data set only if $y_i > 0$. So the selection rule is deterministically related to the dependent variable. What effect might this truncation have on the empirical results in Table 9.1? An intuitive way to think of the problem is that sample truncation causes the regression line to be artificially bounded (in this case) from below. Thus, the more dramatic the truncation, the flatter one's regression line is estimated to be. Thus, *truncation causes effect parameters to be biased toward zero*. As a result, the estimates in Table 9.1 are probably too small. Estimating these parameters from a model that explicitly takes into account the truncation should yield larger estimates.

A truncated-at-zero count data distribution can be derived from the parent negative binomial distribution using the basic rule for conditional probability in Equation (3.2):

$$
\begin{aligned}
\Pr(Y_i | y_i > 0) &= \frac{\Pr(Y_i)}{\Pr(Y_i > 0)} \\
&= \frac{\Pr(Y_i)}{1 - \Pr(Y_i = 0)},
\end{aligned}
\tag{9.7}
$$

since $\Pr(Y_i)$ is the joint distribution of $Y_i$ and $Y_i | y_i > 0$. $\Pr(Y_i)$ in this case is the standard negative binomial probability distribution in Equation (9.6). Then, the probability of a zero under a negative binomial distribution is derived by substituting $y_i = 0$ into Equation (3.17):

$$f_{nb}(0 | \lambda_i, \theta) = (1 + \theta)^{-\lambda_i / \theta}.$$

Thus, the full truncated-at-zero negative binomial probability distribution may be written by substituting the constituent parts into Equation (9.7):

$$f_{tnb}(y_i | \lambda_i, \theta) = \frac{\Gamma(\lambda_i / \theta + y_i)}{y_i! \Gamma(\lambda_i / \theta)[1 - (1 + \theta)^{-\lambda_i / \theta}]} \, \theta^{y_i} (1 + \theta)^{-(\lambda_i / \theta + y_i)}.
\tag{9.8}$$

Thus, the bracketed term in the denominator is the only difference between this and the untruncated negative binomial. If negative contagion seemed a

Table 9.2. *Truncated negative binomial regression of*
*nations sanctioning*

| Variable | Estimate | Std. error | $t$-stat |
|---|---|---|---|
| Constant | $-0.785$ | 1.623 | $-0.483$ |
| Stability | $-0.869$ | 0.453 | $-1.918$ |
| Cost | 1.265 | 0.619 | 2.045 |
| $\hat{\gamma}$ | 1.531 | 0.428 | 3.578 |

*Note:* Log-likelihood = 155.571. Observations: 75.

reasonable possibility, one could generalize this to a truncated-at-zero GEC distribution. However, since countries such as South Africa, likely to create negative contagion, are not in the habit of imposing economic sanctions on other nations, this generalization seems unnecessary in the present example.

The log-likehood is then derived directly from this distribution:

$$\ln L(\tilde{\lambda}_i, \tilde{\theta}|y) = \sum_{i=1}^{n} \left\{ \ln \Gamma \left( \frac{\tilde{\lambda}_i}{\tilde{\theta}} + y_i \right) - \ln \Gamma \left( \frac{\tilde{\lambda}_i}{\tilde{\theta}} \right) + y_i \ln (\tilde{\theta}) \right.$$
$$\left. - \left( \frac{\tilde{\lambda}_i}{\tilde{\theta}} + y_i \right) \ln (1 + \tilde{\theta}) - \ln \left[ 1 - (1 + \tilde{\theta})^{-\tilde{\lambda}_i/\tilde{\theta}} \right] \right\},$$

with $\lambda_i$ defined as in Equation (9.5) and $\theta = \exp(\gamma)$. The maximum likelihood estimates based on this model appear in Table 9.2.

Note that the log-likelihood has increased significantly, indicating that this model is relatively more likely to have generated the data than the untruncated model estimated in Table 9.1. The key substantive result here is that by explicitly taking into account the truncation, the effect parameters are now estimated to be more than three times as large. Thus, if about 3.4 nations could be expected to participate in an economic sanction on average, a two point increase on the stability scale (from 1 to 3) would now decrease the number of nations participating in the sanction by about $-0.869 \times 2 \times 3.4 = -5.91$ more nations (compared to an estimated effect of $-1.48$ nations from the untruncated negative binomial model). The $t$-statistic has also increased. For each unit increase in the four point cost-to-sender variable, an additional $3.4 \times 1.265 = 4.3$ more nations are convinced to join in the sanction (compared to only 1.73 under the negative binomial). In addition, the truncated model enables one to get a better estimate of contagion among nations in sanction participation: the variance is now $1 + \exp(1.531) = 5.62$ times greater than the mean, reflecting a considerable amount of contagion. The fundamental lesson here is that by explicitly modeling the underlying continuous process, and its relationship to the data, one can get dramatically improved empirical results.

*Truncated negative binomial with variance function*

I now complicate this truncated model further with a more explicit examination of the contagious process by which nations convince other nations to join their economic sanctions. For all the models presented before now, I have assumed that the variance of $Y_i$ was proportional to its mean. Thus, in the present parameterization,

$$V(Y_i) = \lambda_i(1 + \theta).$$

Thus, both the mean and the variance are assumed to vary over the different observations, but the two are closely tied together. In the present substantive example, however, $\theta$ is not a nuisance parameter. It indicates the degree to which participation in economic sanctions is contagious, a fundamental part of the research problem. Thus, whereas theory usually causes us to focus on how the mean $\lambda_i$ varies as a function of a set of explanatory variables, the present substantive example causes us to focus on $\theta$ as well.

The general problem is called *variance function estimation* and, although some work has been done in the area (see Davidian and Carroll, 1987), it has heretofore not been extended to event count models (see also Sections 4.1 and 7.2). I derive this new model by first adding the subscript $i$ to $\theta$ so that it can vary over the observations. $\theta_i$ is then conceptualized as the degree of contagion among nations at time $i$. Like $\lambda_i$, $\theta_i$ is not observed at any point in time, but something like it certainly does exist in theory. We can, however, use the same events data to estimate the influence of specified explanatory variables on $\theta_i$.

Since $\theta_i$ has some of the same formal characteristics as $\lambda_i$, I use the same functional form. Hence,

$$\theta_i = \exp(z_i\gamma), \tag{9.9}$$

where $z_i$ is a vector of $k_1$ explanatory variables and $\gamma$ is now a $k_1 \times 1$ parameter vector. The variables one chooses to comprise $z_i$ can be the same as or different from the ones in the mean function, $x_i$.

The log-likelihood function is derived for this model by substituting Equations (9.9) and (9.5) into the truncated negative binomial probability distribution and taking logs. One could create a simpler version of this model by substituting into the untruncated negative binomial distribution, but the truncated distribution is most appropriate for the present case. Thus,

$$\ln L(\tilde{\beta},\tilde{\gamma}|y) = \sum_{i=1}^{n} \left\{ \ln \Gamma \left[\exp(x_i\tilde{\beta}-z_i\tilde{\gamma}) + y_i\right] - \ln \Gamma \left[\exp(x_i\tilde{\beta}-z_i\tilde{\gamma})\right] \right.$$
$$+ y_i(x_i\tilde{\beta}) - [\exp(x_i\tilde{\beta}-z_i\tilde{\gamma}) + y_i]\ln[1 + \exp(x_i\tilde{\beta})]$$
$$\left. - \ln\left[1 - [1 + \exp(z_i\tilde{\gamma})]^{-[\exp(x_i\tilde{\beta}-z_i\tilde{\gamma})]}\right] \right\}$$

Table 9.3. *Truncated negative binomial regression with variance function of nations sanctioning*

| Variable | Estimate | Std. error | $t$-stat |
|----------|----------|-----------|-------|
| Constant | −0.868 | 1.232 | −0.705 |
| Stability | −0.938 | 0.451 | −2.070 |
| Cost | 1.417 | 0.517 | 2.740 |
| $\hat{\gamma}_0$ | 2.328 | 0.830 | 2.806 |
| US | −1.441 | 0.859 | −1.678 |

*Note:* Log-likelihood = 172.608. Observations: 75.

For present exploratory purposes, I let $z_i$ contain just one variable, US, which is coded as 1 if the United States is the major sender and 0 otherwise. Empirical estimates appear in Table 9.3.

Note first that the log-likelihood for this model is considerably higher than that for the standard negative binomial model and the truncated negative binomial generalization. The advantages of this truncated variance function negative binomial model over the standard models are apparent. First, this more realistic model of the way contagion varies enables one to get better estimates of the $\beta$ parameters; both turn out to be larger here than in the previous negative binomial model and more precisely estimated. Second, this model enables one to extract considerably more information from the same data. For example, the negative coefficient on the US variable says nothing about how many more or fewer nations will participate when the United States is the leading sender, but it does indicate that international cooperation in sanctioning U.S. chosen targets is a less contagious process than when other nations are the leading senders. This effect reflects the fact that the United States tends to make economic sanctioning decisions without receiving prior support from its allies. In these cases, then, decisions to participate by other nations tend to be more isolated.

## 9.5    Hurdle event count models

Hurdle models are used for observations created with random selection rules, but the specific data generating mechanisms make it appropriate to treat the data in distinct parts, as if some of the data were missing. The point is clearest in the context of an example. Do international alliances affect the incidence of war? Deriving statistical models for the analysis of this empirical question is the subject of this section. The data for the analysis come from the classic studies of Singer and Small (1966, 1969, 1972). The dependent variable is the number of nations who entered into a war each year for 1816 through 1965 (excluding data from the World Wars, 1915–19 and 1940–5). The key explanatory variable is the percent of nations in the system involved in formal international alliances. For a sampling of studies on international alliances, see McDonald and Rosecrance (1985), McGowan and Rood (1975), Singer and Small (1968), Siverson and Tannefoss (1984), Wallace (1973) and Walt (1985).

To begin the data analysis, imagine an unobserved nonrandom variable $\lambda_i$, representing the rate at which nations get involved in war at time $i$. $\lambda_i$ is always a positive number, since there is always some small chance of a war breaking out. Thus a larger value of $\lambda_i$ increases the probability of an event, but at no point does it guarantee the occurrence or nonoccurrence of one.

The theoretical question of interest is whether the value of $\lambda_i$ increases or decreases when more nations are involved in international alliances. Of course, $\lambda_i$ is unobservable at any of the infinite number of time points $i$ in the process. However, the list of events and the count of the number of events during each year are available.

Thus, let $Y_i$ denote a random variable representing the number of additional nations that got involved in wars in year $i$. $Y_i$ is assumed to have expectation $E(Y_i) \equiv \lambda_i$. By making the plausible assumptions in this case of conditional independence and homogeneity of the underlying process, we are led to the conclusion that $Y_i$ is a Poisson random variable with mean (and variance) $\lambda_i$. This Poisson assumption is made all the more plausible by all the studies showing a reasonable fit to this distribution.[4]

The systematic component of this model is specified as follows:

$$\lambda_i = \exp(\beta_0 + \beta_1 \text{Alliances}_i).$$

To estimate the parameters $\beta_0$ and $\beta_1$, the right hand side of this equation is substituted into the Poisson distribution in Equation (3.15), logs are taken and summed over all $n$ observations, and the resulting log-likelihood function, in Equation (5.16), is maximized. Estimates of this model appear in Table 9.4.

The focus of attention should be on the coefficient of the "Alliances" variable. To interpret these effects, note that the derivative of $\lambda_i$ with respect to $x_1$ is $\lambda_i \beta_1$. To make the interpretation more concrete, note that the empirical

---

[4] Further analyses indicate that these data are slightly overdispersed, probably as a result of war being somewhat contagious. A reasonable correction, in this particular case only, is to merely double the estimated standard errors. The coefficients presented are consistent, and only marginally inefficient, in the face of modest overdispersion (Gourieroux, Monfort, and Trognon, 1984a, 1984b). One could improve the efficiency of these estimates and get correct standard errors by moving to the negative binomial or GEC distribution. Because of the modest degree of overdispersion, I avoid this complication in this example.

Table 9.4. *Poisson regression of nations in war*

| Variable | Estimate | Std. error | *t*-stat |
|----------|----------|------------|----------|
| Constant | 0.848 | 0.059 | |
| Alliances | 0.007 | 0.001 | 6.454 |

*Note:* Log-likelihood = 49.749. Observations: 139.

range of $y$ is from zero to eighteen nations entering into war, with a mean of 3.029. The percent of nations involved in alliances ranges from zero to eighty. Thus, consider the effect of a fifty percentage point increase in the number of nations involved in alliances in the typical year (that is, with about three nations entering into wars). The effect of this increase in alliances is to lead to $0.007 \times 3.029 \times 50 = 1.06$ more wars.

Since alliances establish peace among their signatories, it is odd that $\beta_1$ is positive. However, alliances are also mutual defense pacts, sometimes formed in order to go to war. Indeed, the standard error on this coefficient is quite small, and the *t*-statistic would surely lead one to conclude that this coefficient is significantly greater than zero. But do alliances really cause wars? If alliances are made in part to ensure a nation's security (Waltz, 1979), this finding is surely questionable.

Further questioning of these results might lead one to respecify the model of the underlying process. One possibility is to imagine that $\lambda_i$ really represents two values, $\lambda_{0i}$ and $\lambda_{+i}$, instead of one. $\lambda_{0i}$ is the rate at which the first additional nation gets involved in a war, or, in other words, the rate at which the international system switches from peace to the first occurrence of war. $\lambda_{+i}$, then, is the rate at which other nations get involved, given that at least one is involved. These processes may very well occur simultaneously. The substantive hypothesis is that the percent of alliances has a small or even negative effect on the probability of any nations being involved in wars. However, once the first nation commits to an international conflict, the existence of additional international alliances will drag new nations into the fray. Vasquez (1987:121), for example, concludes that "alliances not only fail to prevent wars, but make it likely that wars that do occur will expand."

Modeling the onset of war separately from its escalation requires a two part model. Mullahy's (1986) work on hurdle Poisson regression models represents the current state of the art in this area; the discussion in this section draws, in part, on his work. I first define the general form of the hurdle regression model and then derive an estimable model as a special case.

Begin by defining a dummy variable $d_i$ which takes on the value 0 when $y_i = 0$ and 1 otherwise (for $i = 0, \ldots, n$). Then, a Bernoulli distribution may be used to describe the "hurdle" that the system goes through between no nations and some nations getting involved in international wars:

$$f_B(d_i|\pi_i) = \Pr(Y_i = d_i|\pi_i) = \pi_i^{d_i}(1-\pi_i)^{1-d_i} = \begin{cases} 1-\pi_i & \text{for } y_i = 0, \\ \pi_i & \text{for } y_i \geq 1, \end{cases}$$

where $\pi_i$ parameter stands for the probability that $Y_i > 0$ according to a separate stochastic process, $f_0$:

$$\pi_i = \Pr(Y_i = 1) = 1 - f_0(0|\lambda_{0i}).$$

Conditional on at least one nation being involved in a war, the distribution of $Y_i$ is written as a truncated event count distribution. If $f$ represents some event count distribution defined on the nonnegative integers, $f_+$ is a corresponding truncated-at-zero event count distribution for only the positive integers:

$$f_+(y_i|\lambda_{+i}) = \frac{f(y_i|\lambda_i)}{1-f(0|\lambda_i)} \tag{9.10}$$

for $y_i \in \{1,2,\ldots\}$ and zero otherwise.

Note that $f_0$ and $f_+$ define the full stochastic nature of this process. In the standard Poisson regression model, for example, $f_0$ and $f_+$ have the same distribution with the same mean. In hurdle event count models, however, these may differ completely or merely be due to different parameters. Following Mullahy (1986), I restrict attention to the case where these $f_0$ and $f_+$ differ only by letting $\lambda_{0i}$ differ from $\lambda_{+i}$.

To construct the likelihood function, the observations with $y_i = 0$ must be treated differently than observations with $y_i > 0$. The two parts appear in separate brackets in the likelihood function:

$$L(\lambda_{0i}, \lambda_{+i}) = \left[ \prod_{y_i=0} (1-\pi_i) \right] \left[ \prod_{y_i>0} \pi_i f_+(y_i|\lambda_{+i}) \right]$$

$$= \left[ \prod_{y_i=0} f_0(0|\lambda_{0i}) \right] \left[ \prod_{y_i>0} [1 - f_0(0|\lambda_{0i})] f_+(y_i|\lambda_{+i}) \right].$$

This likelihood function specifies $f_0(0|\lambda_{0i})$ for the observations with zeros, the probability of zero nations getting involved in war. For those years where at least one nation took up arms, the probability of a particular number of nations involved in war is equal to $1 - f_0(0|\lambda_{0i})$ multiplied by a truncated event count distribution, with its own parameter.

A special case of this model is the Poisson hurdle regression model. Here we assume that both $f_0$ and $f_+$ are generated by nonidentically distributed Poisson processes (with means $\lambda_{0i}$, respectively). To derive this model, first calculate the probability of zero events under the Poisson distribution [Equation (3.15)]:

$$f_0(0|\lambda_{0i}) = \frac{e^{-\lambda_{0i}}\lambda_{0i}^0}{0!}$$
$$= e^{-\lambda_{0i}}.$$

One then derives the truncated Poisson distribution for the positive integers using the same procedure as for the truncated negative binomial in the last section. The probability that $Y_i = 0$ under the Poisson distribution is:

$$f_0(0|\lambda_{+i}) = e^{-\lambda_{+i}}$$

Then, substituting this result into the formula for constructing truncated distributions in general [Equation (9.10)], produces:

$$f_+(y_i|\lambda_{+i}, y_i > 0) = \frac{\lambda_{+i}^{y_i}}{(e^{\lambda_{+i}} - 1)y_i!}. \tag{9.11}$$

Only $\lambda_{0i}$ and $\lambda_{+i}$ separate the process governing the hurdle crossing from the process governing the number of nations involved in an existing war. These two parameters each vary in some unobserved way over the same time period. In general, we let each vary separately as a function of (possibly different) measured explanatory variables:

$$\lambda_{0i} = \exp(x_{0i}\beta_0),$$
$$\lambda_{+i} = \exp(x_{+i}\beta_+).$$

Reduced to sufficient statistics, the full Poisson hurdle regression model log-likelihood function may then be written as follows:

$$\ln L(\tilde{\beta}_0, \tilde{\beta}_+ | y) = -\sum_{y=0} \exp(x_{0i}\tilde{\beta}_0) + \sum_{y>0} \{\ln[1 - \exp(-\exp(x_{0i}\tilde{\beta}_0))] + y_i(x_{+i}\tilde{\beta}_+) - \ln[\exp(\exp(x_{+i}\tilde{\beta}_+)) - 1]\},$$

which is easily maximized with respect to $\tilde{\beta}_0$ and $\tilde{\beta}_+$. Indeed, since $\tilde{\beta}_0$ and $\tilde{\beta}_+$ appear in separate terms in the log-likelihood function, these terms may be maximized separately. However, in my experience, even simultaneous estimations converge very quickly. Note that if $X_0 = X_+$ and $\tilde{\beta}_0 = \tilde{\beta}_+$,

$$\ln\{1 - \exp[-\exp(x_i\tilde{\beta})]\} - \ln\{\exp[\exp(x_i\tilde{\beta})] - 1\} = -\exp(x_i\tilde{\beta}),$$

and in this special case the Poisson hurdle specification reduces directly to the basic Poisson regression model. Of course, in empirical examples, the effect parameters are not necessarily equal, and the explanatory variables need not be the same.

Another point of interest about this model is the implied parameterization of the probability that the hurdle is crossed:

$$\Pr(Y_i > 0|\lambda_{0i}) = 1 - \exp(-\lambda_{0i}) = 1 - \exp[-\exp(x_{0i}\beta_0)]. \tag{9.12}$$

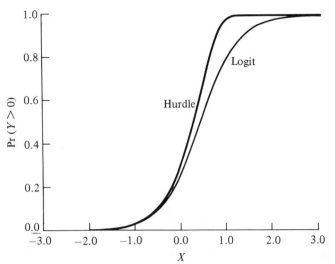

Figure 9.1. The hurdle form.

If one were not deriving a statistical model from basic assumptions made about the deeper underlying process, as done here, but instead were putting together a more data-based model, the first choice would probably be a logit:

$$\Pr(Y_i > 0 | \lambda_{0i}) = [1 - \exp(-x_{0i}\beta_0)]^{-1}. \tag{9.13}$$

Because its justification is derived from first principles much closer to international relations theory, Equation (9.12) should be more satisfying than the ad hoc specification in Equation (9.13). At the same time, however, researchers are probably more familiar with the logistic specification.

A reasonable question, then, is how the two curves differ. Figure 9.1 provides an intuitive answer. There it shows that whereas the logistic curve is symmetric, the one we derived is not. The two curves coincide near the bottom as the lower bound of zero "bends" the line up. However, at the top, the upper bound has an effect much later in our curve than for the logit. However, this asymmetric shape is quite plausible here since, in the hurdle model, the probability of crossing the hurdle might actually get arbitrarily close to 1.0 when the expected number of nations initiating conflict ($\lambda_{+i}$) is high. The existence of the other process, represented by $\lambda_{+i}$, thus serves to release some of the pressure near the top of the curve and creates the small asymmetry.[5]

Of course, without a large number of observations, empirically distinguish-

[5] Equation (9.12) is also closely related to the Gompertz curve (see Zellner and Lee, 1965).

Table 9.5. *Hurdle Poisson regression of nations in war*

| Variable | Estimate | Std. error | $t$-stat |
|----------|----------|------------|----------|
| Constant$_0$ | 0.511 | 0.241 | |
| Alliances | 0.001 | 0.006 | 0.239 |
| Constant$_+$ | 1.010 | 0.068 | |
| Alliances | 0.007 | 0.001 | 5.688 |

*Note:* Log-likelihood = 68.43. Observations: 139.

ing between the fit of these two alternative specifications would be difficult. Nevertheless, having derived this form from deeper principles about the theoretical process being analyzed, discovering such subtle sophistications gives one further confidence in the first principles and the derived model. Having a statistical model this consistent with substantive theory is also satisfying.

Consider again the data on the effects of formal international alliances. Table 9.5 provides estimates of the hurdle Poisson regression model with a constant and the percent of nations involved in alliances in each equation. The key result is the difference between the coefficients of the alliance variable in the two parts of the model. The existence of international alliances has no noticeable effect on the presence of war (see the small coefficient and the near zero $t$-statistic). However, once war has begun (i.e., once the hurdle has been crossed), alliances have essentially the same effect as they were estimated to have in the standard Poisson regression model.

Aside from these important substantive differences between the two models, a likelihood ratio test of the improvement of this model can easily be calculated by taking advantage of the fact that the standard model is nested within this one. With two degrees of freedom, the chi-square statistic is $2(68.43 - 49.74) = 37.36$, so one can reject the hypothesis that no improvement occurred with the hurdle model with considerable confidence.

Further analysis into this substantive problem would require the inclusion of appropriate control variables, as well as testing a number of specifications to check for sensitivity in the empirical results. Although this is obviously not my purpose here, I do present one additional estimation in Table 9.6. This estimation includes a lag of the dependent variable in the first, but not the second, part of the model.

Several features of this alternative specification are worthy of note. First, this model emphasizes that the parameterizations of $\lambda_{0i}$ and $\lambda_{+i}$ need not be the same. Second, the significant positive coefficient for this Nations$_{i-1}$ indicates that when more nations are involved in war this year, the probability that the hurdle will be crossed again next year (i.e., at least one additional

Table 9.6. *Hurdle Poisson regression of nations in war, an alternative specification*

| Variable | Estimate | Std. error | $t$-stat |
|---|---|---|---|
| $\text{Constant}_0$ | 0.141 | 0.290 | |
| Alliances | 0.003 | 0.006 | 0.430 |
| $\text{Nations}_{i-1}$ | 0.143 | 0.031 | 4.587 |
| $\text{Constant}_+$ | 1.010 | 0.068 | |
| Alliances | 0.007 | 0.001 | 5.688 |

*Note:* Log-likelihood = 75.859. Observations: 139.

nation will become involved) increases. The coefficient on alliances does increase somewhat, but it is still only half the size of its standard error, so the substantive interpretation does not change. Third, although I do not provide a full complement of event count models that account for autocorrelation here, this specification is one example of how to model time dependence in $\lambda_{0i}$ and $\lambda_{+i}$. For further analysis, one could include lags in the model for $\lambda_{+i}$ (instead of $y_i$) or include additional lags in either portion of the model. Fourth, note that the two coefficients and standard errors in the model for $\lambda_{+i}$ are identical in Tables 9.5 and 9.6. This is a consequence of $\beta_0$ and $\beta_+$ falling in separate terms in the likelihood function.

Finally, from one perspective, including a lag of the dependent variable makes the model internally inconsistent. The first principles required to derive the Poisson distribution for this model included the assumption that events within each year are independent. However, using the lag of the dependent variable as an explanatory variable implies dependence across years. The inconsistency can be resolved in two ways. In one, we could relax the assumption of independence within observations by using the negative binomial distribution. This would, and does, work fine, but in this empirical case with only modest overdispersion, I find that it has no substantial effect on the results. Alternatively, one could insist that war is not contagious in the short term, but that broad aggregate patterns in the rate of the onset of war are dependent. Just how plausible this latter assertion is depends on the features of one's empirical question and on the length of the observation periods. In fact, the only study that attempts to explicitly model the time series properties in event count models makes this latter assumption (see Holden, 1987).

## 9.6    Concluding remarks

This chapter has derived a variety of models for data with nonrandom selection. The models included censoring and truncation, stochastic and deterministic selection rules, continuous and discrete stochastic components, and linear and nonlinear systematic components. There was even an analysis of randomly selected data for which the insights it provided into models for nonrandom data helped to build a model able to extract significantly more information. The variety of models and methods presented here should make the range of other possibilities more obvious. For example, one could have truncation at the top and bottom or even deterministic censoring at the top and stochastic truncation at the bottom.

Another way to conceptualize some of the models in this chapter is to think of them as standard models, but with missing data. Little and Rubin (1987) develop methods for statistical analysis on incomplete data that are drawn directly from the likelihood theory of inference. See also Rubin (1987) for a method more specifically attuned to sample surveys.

# CHAPTER 10

# General classes of multiple equation models

In a sense, every model introduced so far is really a class of distinct models. Even the linear-Normal regression model includes such diverse special cases as a regression with a single explanatory variable, multiple regression, interaction terms, polynomials, and all the other models that can be squeezed into this framework. In this chapter, I derive several very broad classes of multiple equation models. Each class is so general that no one should even think of estimating it in the completely nonrestricted form in which it is usually presented. Indeed, this general form of these classes of models is not even close to being identified.

What, then, are the advantages of such general classes of models? First, understanding the general form helps one to more quickly see a range of estimable models that happen to be special cases. Such general classes of models also help to unify in a single framework a large set of apparently diverse methods. Classes of models are also popular because computer programming for a single class is more efficient than writing separate programs for each constituent model.

## 10.1 Factor analysis

Factor analysis is an extension of the model for unobserved variables in Section 8.1, Example 3. The factor analysis model differs in two basic ways. It has $N$ dependent variables, instead of one, and neither the explanatory variables nor their realizations are observed (see Goldberger, 1971). Thus, the model may be formally written by first defining $Y_i$ as an $N \times 1$ vector of random observations produced by the social system, $Y_i = (Y_{1i}, \ldots, Y_{Ni})'$. The mean of $Y_i$, $\theta_i$, is also an $N \times 1$ vector, and $\Psi$ is an $N \times N$ covariance matrix. The model is then written by assuming a multivariate distribution for the $N$ elements of $Y_i$. Consider, for example, a multivariate Normal distribution and corresponding systematic component:

$$Y_i \sim f_{mn}(y_i | \theta_i, \Psi), \tag{10.1}$$

$$\theta_i = \beta x_i^* = \beta_1 + \beta_2 X_{2i}^* + \beta_3 X_{3i}^* + \cdots + \beta_k X_{ki}^*,$$

$$X_i^* \sim f_{mn}(x_i^* | 0, \phi),$$

231

where $\phi$ is a $k \times k$ covariance matrix of the $k$ unobserved $X_i^*$ variables. $\beta$ is an $N \times k$ matrix of effect parameters, with $N$ typically much greater than $k$. Each column of $\beta$, $\beta_j$ ($j = 1, \ldots, k$), is an $N \times 1$ vector. Thus, for each of the $N$ observable random variables, $Y_{ji}$, the second line in Equation (10.1) implies a separate equation:

$$
\begin{aligned}
\theta_{1i} &= \beta_{11} + \beta_{12} X_{2i}^* + \cdots + \beta_{1k} X_{ki}^*, \\
\theta_{2i} &= \beta_{21} + \beta_{22} X_{2i}^* + \cdots + \beta_{2k} X_{ki}^*, \\
&\ \vdots\ \ \vdots\ \ \vdots \\
\theta_{Ni} &= \beta_{N1} + \beta_{N2} X_{2i}^* + \cdots + \beta_{Nk} X_{ki}^*.
\end{aligned}
\tag{10.2}
$$

Note that each equation has the same list of $k$ unobserved factors in common, hence the justification for the frequently used name, *common factor analysis*. Nevertheless, this resulting model surely seems odd: It features a set of $N$ seemingly unrelated regressions with no observed explanatory variables! Why would one want to estimate the parameters ($\beta$ and $X^*$) of a model like this? And how could it possibly be done?

Models like these are quite pervasive in psychology and some other areas of the social sciences. The idea is that the key concepts in the social sciences are often unobserved and even unobservable. For example, no one has ever seen ideology, intelligence, utility, community, or economic growth. However, researchers can measure the observable consequences of these unobserved factors. For example, psychologists often ask fifty or a hundred test questions, each of which is only an imperfect measure of intelligence. Political scientists frequently include a dozen or more questions on sample surveys about specific issue positions, in lieu of a more direct measure of political ideology. The purpose of factor analysis is to explore the features of these unobserved variables and how one's observed measures depend upon them. The goal, then, is to estimate the $(N \times k)$ matrix $\beta$. Although the $k$ factors are common to all $N$ equations, the effect parameters are allowed to vary by equation and by factor. Thus, estimates of $\beta$ enable the researcher to see which observable variables depend on which unobservable factors and, in turn, to make inferences about what each of the factors might actually be. Other techniques are available to estimate the unobserved factors ($X^*$) and to use them in more general statistical models, but I leave these to Section 10.4.

In the original form of the model, $\beta$ and $X^*$ are both sets of parameters to be estimated. However, further analysis will reveal that the distributional assumption for the unobserved variables $X^*$ means that they do not appear in the likelihood function, so one need only estimate $\beta$. To demonstrate this, first note that since $X^*$ is a Normal random variable, and $\beta X_i^*$ is a linear combination of $X_i^*$, $\theta_i \equiv \beta X_i^*$ is a Normal random variable as well.[1] Thus,

---

[1] This basic result from distribution theory, that linear combinations of Normally distributed variables are Normally distributed, can be proven by compounding the Nor-

$$\theta_i \sim f_{mn}(t_i|\mu_i, \Phi),\tag{10.3}$$

where $t_i$ is a realization of $\theta_i$, where

$$\begin{aligned}
\mu_i &\equiv E(\theta_i)\\
&= E(\beta X_i^*)\\
&= \beta_1 + \beta_2 E(X_{1i}^*) + \beta_2 E(X_{1i}^*) + \cdots + \beta_k E(X_{ki}^*)\\
&= \beta_1
\end{aligned}$$

because $E(X_{ji}^*) = 0$, for $j = 2, \ldots, k$, and where

$$\Phi \equiv V(\theta) = V(\beta X_i^*) = \beta V(X_i^*)\beta' = \beta\phi\beta'$$

is an $N \times N$ covariance matrix.[2] But if $\theta_i$ is a random variable, then it should not be represented as given in the stochastic component in Equation (10.1). Thus, I compound that distribution with the one for $\theta_i$ in Equation (10.3) in the usual way.

First, form the joint distribution of $(Y_i, \theta_i)$ as:

$$f_j(y_i, t_i|\mu_i, \Phi, \Psi) = f_{mn}(y_i|\theta_i, \Psi)f_{mn}(t_i|\mu_i, \Phi).$$

Since the realization of $\theta_i$, $t_i$, is also not observed, I collapse this joint distribution over $t_i$ as follows:

$$f_{mn}(y_i|\mu_i, \Sigma) = \int_{-\infty}^{\infty} f_j(y_i, t_i|\mu_i, \Phi, \Psi)dt_i,$$

where

$$\mu_i = \beta_1$$

and

$$\Sigma = \Phi + \Psi = \beta\phi\beta' + \Psi.\tag{10.4}$$

Several features of this derivation are worthy of comment before proceeding on to derive the complete likelihood function for this factor analysis model. First, note that the original distribution, $f_{mn}(y_i|\theta_i, \Psi)$, the compounding distribution, $f_{mn}(t_i|\mu_i, \Phi)$, and the final compound distribution, $f_{mn}(y_i|\mu_i, \Sigma)$, are all multivariate Normal (see Johnson and Kotz, 1972: 87–8). Probability distributions with this property are referred to as *closed under compounding*. This

---

mal distribution with another Normal (as is done below in another context). However, texts on distribution theory often prove this with the use of "moment generating functions," a concept outside the scope of this book but quite useful for deriving certain probability distributions. See, for example, Bain and Englehardt (1987: 213). Perhaps an even more surprising characteristic of the Normal distribution is the Cramér-Lévy Theorem: if the sum of two independent variables is Normally distributed, then the separate variables making up the sum must also be Normally distributed.

[2] These two equations use the standard rules for the expectation and variance of linear functions, respectively.

property of the Normal distribution will be useful for other purposes, in succeeding sections. Second, the result that $\mu_i = \beta_1$ (a constant term) may seem odd at first, but it is a direct result of the assumption that the mean of $X_j^*$ is zero in the third line of Equation (10.1). One might question that assumption, but since the only parameters of interest are in $\beta$, adding a constant to $X^*$, such as its true mean, would leave the rest of $\beta$ unchanged, the constant merely being absorbed by $\beta_1$. Thus, since the means of these variables have no effect on the results, I avoid estimating what would be merely a set of additional ancillary parameters. Finally, note that the rest of $\beta$, indeed the part in which we are interested (i.e., $\beta_2, \ldots, \beta_k$), exists in this final distribution only through the $(N \times N)$ variance matrix, $\Sigma$ [see Equation (10.4)]. Since we are generally uninterested in $\beta_1$, the estimation problem primarily involves the parameters in $\Sigma$. Nevertheless, *estimates of the elements of $\beta_2$, $\ldots$, $\beta_k$ are still interpreted as in the second line of Equation (10.1).*

By assuming independence over $i$ for all $Y$ and $X^*$, the full stochastic component is then written as a product of the $n$, $N$-dimensional probability distributions:[3]

$$
\begin{aligned}
f_{mn}(y|\mu,\Sigma) &= \prod_{i=1}^{n} f_{mn}(y_i|\mu_i,\Sigma) \\
&= \prod_{i=1}^{n} (2\pi)^{N/2} |\Sigma|^{-1/2} \exp\left\{ -\frac{1}{2}(y_i - \mu_i)\Sigma^{-1}(y_i - \mu_i)' \right\} \\
&= \prod_{i=1}^{n} (2\pi)^{N/2} |\beta\phi\beta' + \Psi|^{-1/2} \\
&\quad \times \exp\left\{ -\frac{1}{2}(y_i - \beta_1)(\beta\phi\beta' + \Psi)^{-1}(y_i - \beta_1)' \right\}.
\end{aligned}
$$

Then, dropping terms that do not depend on the parameters, the log of the likelihood function is then:

$$
\ln L(\tilde{\beta},\tilde{\phi},\tilde{\Psi}|y) = -\frac{n}{2} \ln|\tilde{\beta}\tilde{\phi}\tilde{\beta}' + \tilde{\Psi}| - \frac{1}{2} \sum_{i=1}^{n} (y_i - \beta_1)(\tilde{\beta}\tilde{\phi}\tilde{\beta}' + \tilde{\Psi})^{-1}(y_i - \tilde{\beta}_1)'.
$$

$$(10.5)$$

Note the parameters that still need to be estimated: $\beta$, which is still of primary interest, $\phi$, a $k \times k$ symmetric matrix of covariances among the unobserved $X^*$ variables, and $\Psi$, and $N \times N$ symmetric matrix of covariances among the observed variables. All of these parameters are assumed constant over $i$, but this assumption could be easily changed. Note that the unobserved $X^*$ parameters are no longer in the likelihood.

Unfortunately, this model is still not identified. To see this, one only needs

---

[3] If $Y$ were time series data, this independence assumption could be changed by applying some of the methods introduced in Chapter 7.

to concentrate on the reparameterization in Equation (10.4) and observe how many different combinations of $\beta$, $\phi$, and $\Psi$ could lead to the same $\Sigma$. The usual approach at this point is to add additional restrictions (see Jöreskog, 1969: 185–6). Indeed, the only reason I present the model in this form is because one can more easily consider a whole class of more specific models. Imposing restrictions on these matrixes leads to a variety of different models as special cases, all of which are identified.

For example, one might assume that the unobserved factors are uncorrelated and have unit variances. In this case, $\phi$ would be set to an identify matrix. In addition, one might assume that all the contemporaneous covariances among the $N$, $Y_i$ variables are zero. The result is the standard *orthogonal factor analysis* model. Allowing some of the $X^*$ variables to be correlated, and adding some additional restrictions on the other matrixes, yields the *oblique factor analysis* model.

A common practice in the psychometric literature is to distinguish between the above, which are generally called *confirmatory factor analysis* methods, and a different procedure, called *exploratory factor analysis*. The latter usually begins with an estimation of an unidentified version of the orthogonal factor model. Then, after one set of nonunique estimates is derived, the analysis proceeds further to systematically consider several other equally good solutions along the likelihood function's plateau. This postanalysis search procedure is called *rotation*. Many methods of rotation have been developed and an enormous literature in psychometrics is concerned with the benefits of these alternative methods. In a sense, the initial unidentified model, plus an appropriate method of rotation, yields a unique identified solution (see Shapiro, 1982). The problem with exploratory factor analysis is that the identifying restrictions are not as obvious, but they are still present. For no particularly good reason, these methods also tend not to present standard errors. As a result, parameter estimates are presented from a model the first principles of which are somewhat hidden and the precision of which is unknown. Armstrong (1967) provides a nice criticism of exploratory factor analysis.

Factor analysis was originally developed as a set of mere algebraic methods of data analysis. They did not emerge as statistical models and thus were not founded on any theory of inference. The statistical foundations of this model have been secured only recently. Harman (1976) gives an extensive review of the large number of analytic factor analysis methods. For other general treatments of this very large literature, see Jöreskog (1969, 1971), Lawley and Maxwell (1971), and Mulaik (1972).

## 10.2    Analyzing covariance structures

In Chapter 6, I demonstrated how one could analyze tabular data, even if the data were not originally generated as a table. The method of analysis was more convenient because a tabular presentation of statistical data is much more parsimonious. It is also quite useful as a sort of descriptive statistic. The analysis was based on the key result that if certain assumptions are fulfilled, a table is a complete summary of the original data.

In this section, I present an analogous statistical procedure for analyzing the factor analysis model, and others to follow. The idea is that data randomly drawn from a multivariate Normal distribution can be summarized without loss of any information as an observed covariance matrix and a list of $N$ sample means. Indeed, since the means are usually unimportant in these analyses (and variables are often taken as deviations from their own sample means), the covariance matrix by itself can be considered a complete summary. Thus, whether one begins with all the individual level data, as in the previous section, or with an $N \times N$ observed covariance matrix calculated from it, the result is an analysis identical to that considered in the previous section.

To demonstrate this equivalent, but more convenient, method of analysis, I first define the $N \times N$ symmetric random covariance matrix, $S$, with elements,

$$S_{mp} = \frac{1}{n} \sum_{i=1}^{n} (Y_{mi} - \bar{Y}_m)(Y_{pi} - \bar{Y}_p), \qquad (10.6)$$

where

$$\bar{Y}_m = \frac{1}{n} \sum_{i=1}^{n} Y_{mi}.$$

Since $Y_i$ are random variables, $S$ is a matrix of random variables. The observed realization of this random matrix is $s$, with elements,

$$s_{mp} = \frac{1}{n} \sum_{i=1}^{n} (y_{mi} - \bar{y}_m)(y_{pi} - \bar{y}_p),$$

where

$$\bar{y}_m = \frac{1}{n} \sum_{i=1}^{n} y_{mi}.$$

On the diagonal of the $s$ matrix are the observed variances of the respective $N$ realized variables. The off-diagonal elements are covariances which can be interpreted easily since the observed *correlation coefficient* is merely a standardized covariance: $s_{mp}/(s_{mm}s_{pp})$. Thus, the covariance matrix is also a very parsimonious and useful descriptive statistic. The idea of *covariance structure analysis* is merely that one can discard the original data ($n$ observations of $N$ variables each) once one has calculated the $s$ matrix and assumed multivariate Normality. (In practice, of course, discarding data is never recommended.)

Note that although a few cases exist where tabular data appear to be the natural form, one could not reasonably suppose that any particular data set was originally generated as a covariance matrix.

The procedure, then, is to derive the distribution of the random matrix $S$ from three of the first principles used in the factor analysis model:

1.  for observation $i$, the $N$ variables $Y_i \equiv (Y_{1i}, \ldots, Y_{Ni})$ are distributed multivariate Normal;
2.  $Y_{pi}$ are independent of the variables $Y_{pj}$ for $p = 1, \ldots, N$ and for all $i \neq j$ (that is, no time series component is included); and
3.  $S$ is calculated as in Equation (10.6).

Wishart (1928) was the first to successfully complete this derivation and the resulting distribution bears his name. I omit this derivation here because it is excessively technical. Johnson and Kotz (1972: 158–62) present a somewhat simpler derivation of the Wishart distribution due to Hsu (1939), but even this is technically quite demanding. Nevertheless, it matters not how difficult the proof is, so long as one understands the first principles and can use the final result.

The resulting Wishart distribution can be written for present purposes as follows:

$$S \sim f_W(s|\Sigma, n) = C|\Sigma|^{-n/2} \exp\left[ -\frac{1}{2}\mathrm{tr}(S\Sigma^{-1}) \right],$$

where $C$ is a complicated function not involving $\Sigma$ (see Johnson and Kotz, 1972: 162; Spanos, 1986: 602–3) and $\mathrm{tr}(\cdot)$ is the trace of a matrix which yields the sum of the diagonal elements of the matrix in its parentheses.

Since $S$ contains all the usable information in $Y$, this probability distribution is proportional to the likelihood function for $\Sigma$. Note that one need not take the product over the $n$ observations, since all the observations are already incorporated in this distribution. The corresponding log-likelihood, dropping terms that do not depend on $\tilde{\Sigma}$, is then:

$$\ln L(\tilde{\Sigma}|s,n) = -\frac{n}{2} \ln|\tilde{\Sigma}| - \frac{1}{2}\mathrm{tr}(S\tilde{\Sigma}^{-1}). \tag{10.7}$$

If one is using this to analyze the factor analysis model, one would reparameterize by substituting $\beta\phi\beta' + \Psi$ for $\Sigma$ in this equation to yield:[4]

$$\ln L(\tilde{\beta},\tilde{\phi},\tilde{\Psi}|s,n) = -\frac{n}{2} \ln|\tilde{\beta}\tilde{\phi}\tilde{\beta}' + \tilde{\Psi}| - \frac{1}{2}\mathrm{tr}[S(\tilde{\beta}\tilde{\phi}\tilde{\beta}' + \tilde{\Psi})^{-1}]. \tag{10.8}$$

---

[4] Different reparameterizations would be used for other models, such as the one to be introduced in the next section.

The key result here is that, after some calculation, the log-likelihood in Equation (10.8) is equivalent to that in Equation (10.5) in the previous section. *Thus, regardless of whether one uses the data in their original form, or one collapses them to a covariance matrix and begins analysis there, identical parametric inferences result.*

## 10.3    A specification test

Section 6.3 describes a specification test for contingency table models. A similar test has been derived for the analysis of covariance structures. In theory, the idea is to compare the current specification to the best possible specification and to conduct a likelihood ratio test for the difference between these two. If this test indicated that the two specifications were significantly different, one would add factors or otherwise unrestrict the current model.

In order to conduct this specification test, the first issue is how to calculate the log-likelihood for the best possible specification. The procedure is essentially the same as in Section 6.3. The maximum number of parameters one could include and still have an identified model is constrained by the number of independent "observations" in the covariance matrix $s$, $N(N-1)/2$. If all these parameters were included, the fitted values would exactly reproduce the observed covariance matrix. Thus, the log-likelihood for the least restrictive but still identified specification possible has the ML estimator of $\Sigma$ equal to $s$.

Thus, the log-likelihood under the current (restricted) model is

$$\ln L_R^* = -\frac{n}{2}\ln|\tilde{\Sigma}| - \frac{1}{2}\mathrm{tr}(S\tilde{\Sigma}^{-1})$$

and the log-likelihood under the completely unrestricted model is

$$\ln L^* = -\frac{n}{2}\ln|s| - \frac{1}{2}\mathrm{tr}(ss^{-1})$$

$$= -\frac{n}{2}\ln|s| - \frac{1}{2}\mathrm{tr}(I)$$

$$= -\frac{n}{2}\ln|s| - \frac{N}{2}.$$

This likelihood ratio specification test may then be written as follows:

$$\mathcal{R} = 2(\ln L^* - \ln L_R^*)$$

$$= 2\left[-\frac{n}{2}\ln|\tilde{\Sigma}| - \frac{1}{2}\mathrm{tr}(S\tilde{\Sigma}^{-1}) + \frac{n}{2}\ln|s| + \frac{N}{2}\right]$$

$$= -n\ln|\tilde{\Sigma}| - \mathrm{tr}(S\tilde{\Sigma}^{-1}) + n\ln|s| + N.$$

As usual, $\mathcal{R}$ is distributed as a chi-square variable with degrees of freedom equal to the number of test parameters. In this case, the degrees of freedom are $[N(N-1)/2] - P$, where $P$ is the number of parameters in the current (restricted) model.

One can easily calculate this specification test. Indeed, most computer programs routinely report it. Unfortunately, the problems with this test are identical to those with the specification test for cross-classified categorical data. I will not repeat all my objections here, in part because they are adequately covered in Section 6.3, but also because the literature on covariance structures tends to be much more sensitive to these issues.[5] For example, Jöreskog (1969: 200–1) writes,

> If a sufficiently large sample were obtained this $\chi^2$ statistic would, no doubt, indicate that any such nontrivial hypothesis is statistically untenable. . . . When to stop fitting additional parameters cannot be decided on a purely statistical basis. This is largely a matter of the experimenter's interpretations of the data based on substantive theoretical and conceptual considerations.

Indeed, a variety of alternative "goodness of fit" criteria have been proposed to "get around" the usual disconcertingly large chi-square statistics. For example, Tucker and Lewis (1973) propose a reliability coefficient and others (e.g., Alwin and Jackson, 1980; Burt, 1973) also recommend using $\mathcal{R}$ divided by its degrees of freedom. Both of these alternatives are reasonable approaches, but one should remember that they are merely descriptive statistics and, as such, can provide only general guidelines rather than rigorous rules deduced from statistical theory or from some more fundamental theory of inference.

## 10.4    A general linear structural equation model

The factor analysis model is very general and quite remarkable. One can estimate the parameters of a set of $N$ regressions without even having observed the explanatory variables. Orthogonal or oblique solutions can be specified. The effect parameters on the common factors for some of the observed dependent variables can easily be constrained to be zero or some other number. Large numbers of equations and unobserved factors may be included.

As general as the factor analysis model is, however, one might consider using the unobserved variables from a factor analytic model for other purposes. For example, consider the models for reciprocal causation in Section 8.2. Suppose that instead of using the observed realization of a variable like partisan identification, one had twenty imperfect measures of a person's partisanship. Then, through some factor analytic scheme, one could use the pure

---

[5] The reason is probably that the sorts of data to which covariance structure analysis is applied usually have large numbers of observations. Analysts of contingency tables are usually not that fortunate.

unobserved factor in the model for reciprocal causation. An approach such as this seems more reasonable and more likely to yield reliable empirical results.

The purpose of this section is to describe such a model. Although the particular *general linear structural model* I consider here is far from the most general model that has been proposed, a large number of popular models are formally special cases of it. Among the special cases are factor analysis models, multiple-indicator–multiple-cause models (MIMIC), multiple group measurement models, simultaneous equations with or without reciprocal causation, some models for panel data, and even a straightforward linear regression model with all variables directly observed.[6]

Because this model begins with the assumption of multivariate Normality and the absence of a time series component, the likelihood function may be derived from the individual level data, as in Section 10.1, or as a method of covariance structure analysis, as in Section 10.2. Although the usual way this model is presented is by skipping directly to the analysis of covariance structures, this can obscure the model and its very sophisticated set of assumptions. Thus, I analyze this model and its estimator here by deriving it from first principles, just as I have for all the other models in this book. The difference here is that the generality of this model makes it much more sophisticated and complicated. At once, it is very restrictive – because it makes strong multivariate assumptions about much larger portions of the output from the social system – and it is very unrestrictive – in that one has great flexibility to specialize this class of general models in a wide variety of ways. Given this, one almost *never* begins with a set of data and concludes that a general linear structural model like this is called for. For almost every possible application, one would use a more specialized version of this model. Indeed, its general form is presented here only to avoid presenting many overlapping models. It is also instructive to see how such large scale models are built. Since many analyses will not precisely meet the general multivariate Normality, independence, or linearity assumptions of this general structural model, one could use a derivation similar to that in this section to develop models with a variety of alternative data generating processes.

I begin by presenting the model in its most general form, deriving the likelihood function, and then demonstrating how one can make restricted versions that encompass a variety of interesting special cases.

### The general model

Equations (10.9) to (10.18), which follow, define the model. These equations fall into three general categories and are presented in the following order:

---

[6] A variety of computer programs has also been written to estimate this model, the most popular of which is called LISREL.

1. the measurement model for the unobserved dependent variables,
2. the structural model, and
3. the measurement model for the unobserved explanatory variables.

The structural model provides the link between the unobserved explanatory and dependent variables.

*1. Dependent variable measurement model:* For each $i(i = 1, \ldots ,n)$, one observes a vector of $N_y$ observations, $y_i = (y_{1i}, \ldots ,y_{N_y1})'$. This $N_y \times 1$ random dependent vector $Y_i = (Y_{1i}, \ldots ,Y_{N_yi})'$ is assumed to be distributed multivariate Normal:

$$Y_i \sim f_{mn}(y_i|\mu_i,\Psi_y),$$ (10.9)

where $\mu_i$ is an $N_y \times 1$ vector of expectations such that

$$\mu_i = \beta_y Y_i^*,$$ (10.10)

and $\Psi_y$ is an $N_y \times N_y$ covariance matrix. $Y_i^*$ is a $k_y \times 1$ vector of unobserved dependent factors. $\beta_y$ is an $N_y \times k_y$ matrix of effect parameters relating the unobserved factors to the resulting observed dependent variables. In addition, the unobserved $Y_i^*$ variables are assumed distributed multivariate Normal:

$$Y_i^* \sim f_{mn}(y_i^*|\mu_i,\Omega).$$ (10.11)

Equations (10.9), (10.10), and (10.11) represent a factor analysis model for what will be the dependent variables in the general model. These equations are generally called the *dependent variable measurement model.*

*2. Structural model:* The parameters of the dependent variable measurement model are now related to the explanatory variables (which will, in turn, have their own measurement model):

$$\Gamma\mu_i = \beta X_i^* \quad \text{or} \quad \mu_i = \Gamma^{-1}\beta X_i^*,$$ (10.12)

$$\Omega = \Gamma^{-1}\phi_y\Gamma^{-1}.$$ (10.13)

In the language of this type of general model, Equation (10.12) is the *structural model.* Without $\Gamma$, Equation (10.12) would be a standard linear component for a set of $N$ regressions. The addition of $\Gamma$ allows for a standard linear model if it is set equal to an identity matrix, but it can also more generally parameterize the special way elements of $\mu_i$ are allowed to influence one another. For example, as I demonstrate below, one set of restrictions on $\Gamma$ would lead to a model for reciprocal causation.

*3. Explanatory variable measurement model:* Also at observation $i$, one observes realization of the $N_x = 1$ random vector $X_i$. This vector of explanatory variables is also assumed to be distributed multivariate Normal:

$$X_i \sim f_{mn}(x|\gamma_i,\Psi_x),$$ (10.14)

where $\Psi_x$ is an $N_x \times N_x$ covariance matrix and

$$\gamma_i = \beta_x X_i^*. \tag{10.15}$$

$X_i^*$ is a $k_x \times 1$ matrix of unobserved common explanatory factors. $\beta_x$ is an $N_x \times k_x$ matrix of effect parameters relating the $k_x$ unobserved factors to the $N_x$ observed explanatory variables. Finally, the unobserved factors are also assumed to be multivariate Normally distributed:

$$X_i^* \sim f_{mn}(x_i^* | 0, \phi_x), \tag{10.16}$$

where $\phi_x$ is a $k_y \times k_y$ covariance matrix.

Two steps remain in the specification of this model. First, the observed dependent and explanatory variables $Z_i \equiv (Y_i', X_i')'$ are distributed multivariate Normal:

$$Z_i \sim f_{mn}(\omega, \Sigma), \tag{10.17}$$

where the definitions of $\omega$ and $\Sigma$ need to be deduced from the previous assumptions. Finally,

$$Y_i \text{ and } Y_j, \text{ and } X_i \text{ and } X_j, \text{ are independent for all } i \neq j, \tag{10.18}$$

which implies that no time series component is included.

### The likelihood function

The stochastic component of all the data at observation $i$ is specified, in very preliminary form, in Equation (10.17). The task now is merely to specify the contents of $\omega$ and $\Sigma$. I do this in three steps: first for $Y_i$, then for $X_i$, and finally for $Z_i \equiv (Y_i', X_i')'$. Each derivation uses the equations above roughly in the order in which they were presented.

Since Equation (10.11) specifies $Y_i^*$ as an unobserved random variable, $\mu_i$ in Equation (10.10) must be a random variable. Thus, $\mu_i$ should not be taken as given in the distribution for the observed dependent variables in Equation (10.9). To remedy this situation, I first derive the distribution of $\mu_i$ and use this to compound the distribution in Equation (10.9). Since $\mu_i$ in Equation (10.10) is a linear combination of Normally distributed variables, it too is a Normal variate:

$$\mu_i \sim f_{mn}[t_i | E(\mu_i), V(\mu_i)], \tag{10.19}$$

where, from the rules for expectations of linear functions and the assumptions in Equations (10.11) and (10.12),

$$E(\mu_i) = E(\beta_y Y_i^*) = \beta_y \mu_i$$

and, using the result for the variance of linear functions and Equations (10.11) and (10.13),

$$V(\mu_i) = V(\beta_y Y_i^*)$$
$$= \beta_y V(Y_i^*)\beta_y'$$
$$= \beta_y \Gamma^{-1} \phi_y \Gamma^{-1} \beta_y'.$$

Then, I use the distribution in Equation (10.19) to compound the original distribution for $Y_i$ in Equation (10.9). One can avoid writing down the joint distribution and integrating by remembering that Normal distributions are closed under compounding (see Section 10.1). The resulting compound distribution has a mean equal to the mean of the compounding distribution and variance equal to the sum of that for the compounding and the original distributions. Thus, the compound distribution for $Y_i$ may be written as follows:

$$Y_i \sim f_{mn}(y_i|\beta_y\mu_i, \beta_y\Gamma^{-1}\phi_y\Gamma^{-1}\beta_y' + \Psi_y). \tag{10.20}$$

However, this is not the final expression for the distribution of $Y_i$ because $X_i^*$ is assumed random [in Equation (10.16)] and, as a result of Equation (10.12), $\mu_i$ must be random as well. Thus, $\beta_y\mu_i$ should not be considered as given in Equation (10.20). $\mu_i$ is a linear combination of Normal variables, so it must be normal:

$$\mu_i \sim f_{mn}[m_i|E(\mu_i), V(\mu_i)],$$

where

$$E(\mu_i) = E(\Gamma^{-1}\beta X_i^*) = \Gamma^{-1}\beta E(X_i^*) = 0$$

and

$$V(\mu_i) = V(\Gamma^{-1}\beta X_i^*) = \Gamma^{-1}\beta\phi_x\beta'\Gamma'^{-1}.$$

Thus, the distribution of $\beta_y\mu_i^*$ is also multivariate Normal:

$$\beta_y\mu_i \sim f_{mn}(d_i|0, \beta_y\Gamma^{-1}\beta\phi_x\beta'\Gamma'^{-1}\beta_y').$$

Finally, this distribution can be used to compound the distribution in Equation (10.20) to yield the complete version of the stochastic component for $Y_i$:

$$Y_i \sim f_{mn}(0, \beta_y\Gamma^{-1}\beta\phi_x\beta'\Gamma'^{-1}\beta_y' + \beta_y\Gamma^{-1}\phi_y\Gamma'^{-1}\beta_y' + \Psi_y). \tag{10.21}$$

I now move to the somewhat simpler task of deriving the stochastic component for $X_i^*$. First note that since $X_i^*$ is random in Equation (10.16), $\gamma_i$ must also be random due to Equation (10.15). The distribution of $\gamma_i$ is easily specified:

$$\gamma_i \sim f_{mn}[g_i|E(\gamma_i), V(\gamma_i)], \tag{10.22}$$

where

$$E(\gamma_i) = \beta_x E(X_i^*) = 0$$

and

$$V(\gamma_i) = V(\beta_x X_i^*) = \beta_x\phi_x\beta_x'.$$

Then, compounding the original distribution in Equation (10.14) with this distribution [Equation (10.22)], we get the final form of the stochastic component for $X_i$:

$$X_i \sim f_{mn}(x_i | 0, \beta_x \phi_x \beta_x' + \Psi_x).$$

Finally, since $C(X_i, Y_i) = \beta_y \Gamma^{-1} \beta \phi_x \beta_x'$ and due to Equation (10.17), the full stochastic component for $Z_i \equiv (X_i', Y_i')'$ may be written as follows:

$$Z_i \sim f_{mn}(z_i | 0, \Sigma),$$

where

$$\Sigma \equiv V(Z_i) = E(Z_i Z_i') \tag{10.23}$$

$$= \begin{pmatrix} V(Y_i) & C(Y_i, X_i) \\ C(X_i, Y_i) & V(X_i) \end{pmatrix}$$

$$= \begin{pmatrix} \beta_y \Gamma^{-1} \beta \phi_x \beta' \Gamma'^{-1} \beta_y' + \beta_y \Gamma^{-1} \phi_y \Gamma'^{-1} \beta_y' + \Psi_y & \beta_y \Gamma^{-1} \beta \phi_x \beta_x' \\ \beta_x \phi_x \beta' \Gamma'^{-1} \beta_y' & \beta_x \phi_x \beta_x' + \Psi_x \end{pmatrix}.$$

The full stochastic component for the most general form of this model may then be written as the product of this distribution over $i$, due to the assumption in Equation (10.18):

$$f_{mn}(z | 0, \Sigma) = \prod_{i=1}^{n} f_{mn}(z_i | 0, \Sigma).$$

The log-likelihood function may then be written in symbolic form as:

$$\ln L(\tilde{\Sigma} | z) \equiv \ln L(\bar{\beta}_y, \bar{\beta}_x, \bar{\Gamma}, \bar{\beta}, \bar{\Psi}_y, \bar{\Psi}_x, \bar{\phi}_y, \bar{\phi}_x | y, x)$$

$$= -\frac{n}{2} \ln |\tilde{\Sigma}| - \frac{1}{2} \sum_{i=1}^{n} (z_i \tilde{\Sigma}^{-1} z_i'),$$

with $\tilde{\Sigma}$ defined as in Equation (10.23). Note that this log-likelihood function may have been derived from the multivariate Normal distribution of all $n$ observations, as was done here, or by appealing directly to the resulting Wishart distribution of the covariance matrix of the dependent and explanatory variables (as in Section 10.2).

### Special cases

Now that the general model and likelihood function have been derived, one can choose from a number of models to specify special cases of this general one. It would be extremely rare for a model to be interesting if left in this completely general and excessively unrestrictive form. Indeed, the purpose of presenting this general class of models is merely convenience. Consider now two special cases of this general model that provide a flavor for the enormous number of special cases one could construct.

First, this general linear structural model becomes a simple linear regression model with no unobserved variables by restricting the matrixes in the following manner. $N_y$ is assumed to be 1, so that $Y_i$ is a scalar. $\Gamma$ is then also equal to 1. By setting $\phi_y$ and $\phi_x$ to matrixes of zeros, $Y_i^*$ and $X_i^*$ become fixed, rather than random, variables. In turn, $\mu_i^*$ becomes merely the mean of $Y_i$. Thus, measurement models for the dependent and explanatory variables drop out and $Y_i^*$ and $X_i^*$ are assumed observed and equal to $Y_i$ and $X_i$, respectively. The resulting stochastic component is the same as for the linear-Normal regression model and the structural model reduces to the linear regression systematic component:

$$Y_i \sim f_{mn}(y_i|\mu_i, \Psi_y),$$

$$\mu_i = \beta x_i,$$

where $\Psi_y$ is a scalar and $\beta$ is a $k_x$ parameter vector. Obviously, it makes little sense to begin with a model as general as this one and then reduce it to a simple regression model in an actual research situation, but it should be comforting to know that this model can be considered a generalization of the very frequently used linear-Normal regression model.

Second, consider a model for reciprocal causation between two unobserved factors. The structural portion of this model is specified by defining the following four matrixes:

$$\Gamma = \begin{pmatrix} 1 & -\Gamma_1 \\ -\Gamma_2 & 1 \end{pmatrix}, \qquad \mu_i^* = \begin{pmatrix} \mu_{1i}^* \\ \mu_{2i}^* \end{pmatrix},$$

$$\beta = \begin{pmatrix} \beta_{11} & \beta_{12} & 0 \\ \beta_{21} & 0 & \beta_{23} \end{pmatrix}, \qquad X_i^* = \begin{pmatrix} X_{1i}^* \\ X_{2i}^* \\ X_{3i}^* \end{pmatrix}.$$

The result of this specification is that the structural portion of the model,

$$\Gamma \mu_i^* = \beta X_i^*,$$

is now written as

$$\begin{pmatrix} 1 & -\Gamma_1 \\ -\Gamma_2 & 1 \end{pmatrix} \begin{pmatrix} \mu_{1i}^* \\ \mu_{2i}^* \end{pmatrix} = \begin{pmatrix} \beta_{11} & \beta_{12} & 0 \\ \beta_{21} & 0 & \beta_{23} \end{pmatrix} \begin{pmatrix} X_{1i}^* \\ X_{2i}^* \\ X_{3i}^* \end{pmatrix},$$

which, in turn, implies

$$\mu_{1i}^* = \Gamma_1 \mu_{2i} + \beta_{11} X_{1i}^* + \beta_{12} X_{2i}^*,$$
$$\mu_{2i}^* = \Gamma_2 \mu_{1i} + \beta_{21} X_{1i}^* + \beta_{23} X_{2i}^*$$

Were the variables in these two equations all observable, this would be equivalent to the systematic portion of the basic linear-Normal model for reciprocal causation in Equation (8.3). Of course, in this formulation, these variables need not be directly observable. Instead, we hypothesize measurement models for both the explanatory and dependent variables and observe only consequences of both $X_i^*$ and $Y_i^*$.

An example of a dependent variable measurement model that would go along with this structural model is specified by assuming that $\Psi_y$ is diagonal (i.e., there are no contemporaneous correlations), $\phi_y$ is an identity matrix (i.e., an orthogonal factor solution), and

$$\mu_i = \begin{pmatrix} \mu_{1i} \\ \mu_{2i} \\ \mu_{3i} \end{pmatrix}, \qquad \beta_y = \begin{pmatrix} \beta_{1y} & 0 \\ \beta_{3y} & \beta_{4y} \\ \beta_{5y} & \beta_{6y} \end{pmatrix}, \qquad Y_i^* = \begin{pmatrix} Y_{1i}^* \\ Y_{2i}^* \end{pmatrix}.$$

Note that the number of observed variables, $N_y$, is always chosen by the analyst, except that it must be larger than the number of unobserved factors, $k_y$. Thus, the systematic component of the dependent variable measurement model, $\mu_i = \beta_y Y_i^*$, can be written as

$$\begin{pmatrix} \mu_{1i} \\ \mu_{2i} \\ \mu_{3i} \end{pmatrix} = \begin{pmatrix} \beta_{1y} & 0 \\ \beta_{3y} & \beta_{4y} \\ \beta_{5y} & \beta_{6y} \end{pmatrix} \begin{pmatrix} Y_{1i}^* \\ Y_{2i}^* \end{pmatrix}$$

and finally reduced to:

$$\mu_{1i} = \beta_{1y} Y_{1i}^*,$$
$$\mu_{2i} = \beta_{3y} Y_{1i}^* + \beta_{4y} Y_{2i}^*,$$
$$\mu_{3i} = \beta_{5y} Y_{1i}^* + \beta_{6y} Y_{2i}^*.$$

Features of the random variable $Y_i^* \equiv (Y_{1i}^*, Y_{2i}^*)'$ from this measurement model are used in the structural model.

The last portion of this model for reciprocal causation is the explanatory variable measurement model. An example of this can be seen by defining $\Psi_x$ as diagonal (i.e., with no contemporaneous correlations) and $\phi_x$ as an identity matrix (i.e., an orthogonal factor solution), both just as in the dependent variable measurement model. Then the three matrixes of the systematic component, $\gamma_i = \beta_x X_i^*$, might be defined as follows:

$$\gamma_i = \begin{pmatrix} \gamma_{1i} \\ \gamma_{2i} \\ \gamma_{3i} \\ \gamma_{4i} \\ \gamma_{5i} \end{pmatrix}, \qquad \beta_x = \begin{pmatrix} \beta_{1x} & \beta_{2x} & \beta_{3x} \\ \beta_{4x} & \beta_{5x} & 0 \\ \beta_{6x} & 0 & \beta_{7x} \\ \beta_{8x} & 0 & 0 \\ 0 & \beta_{9x} & 0 \end{pmatrix},$$

$$X_i^* = \begin{pmatrix} X_{1i}^* \\ X_{2i}^* \\ X_{3i}^* \end{pmatrix}.$$

These matrixes then reduce to the following set of equations:

$$\gamma_{1i} = \beta_{1x}X_{1i}^* + \beta_{2x}X_{2i}^* + \beta_{3x}X_{3i}^*,$$
$$\gamma_{2i} = \beta_{4x}X_{1i}^* + \beta_{5x}X_{2i}^*,$$
$$\gamma_{3i} = \beta_{6x}X_{1i}^* + \beta_{7x}X_{3i}^*,$$
$$\gamma_{4i} = \beta_{8x}X_{1i}^*,$$
$$\gamma_{5i} = \beta_{9x}X_{2i}^*.$$

Just as with the dependent variable measurement model, some elements of the effect parameter matrix were assumed zero. In other words, certain observable variables are taken to be the consequences of some, rather than all, of the unobserved factors. In an even simpler and potentially more powerful model, one might include completely separate sets of observable variables for each of the factors.

*General comments*

An extremely large variety of other interesting models are special cases of this general one [see Jöreskog and Sörbom (1979) for a variety of others]. Possibly because of this richness, even understanding some of the more complicated cases and sophisticated assumptions can be quite difficult – particularly in the context of one's even more specific research design. For example, certain necessary conditions for identification of the parameters of this model have been discovered, but no one has yet been able to specify the sufficient conditions. How reasonable is the assumption that the observable variables are generated by a multivariate Normal distribution? How is it even possible to be confident in the assumption that the unobservable variables are multivariate Normal? Is it reasonable that the three systematic components (one in the structural model and one each in the two measurement models) are all linear in every variable, observed and unobserved?

Unfortunately, even dreaming up an example that permits a satisfactory answer to all these questions is quite difficult. Observed (and unobserved) variables cannot be dichotomous or ordinal scales; the variables cannot be bounded in any way; and all the relationships must be linear. In the end, answers to these and other questions about the reasonableness of this model cannot be stated in the abstract. Instead, one must consider precisely how the observed data one has in hand were actually generated. If a special case of this general linear structural equations model seems like a reasonable approximation, then this formulation, along with the convenient computer programs set up for estimating it, should be used.

How rough an approximation should one allow? From a practical standpoint, the answer to this question is still unknown, as considerable further analysis of the robustness of this model to misspecification is still needed. However, from a more fundamental point of view, one could begin with a theory about the sort of model that would give rise to one's data. Then, by formalizing this theory, a particular statistical model would emerge.

For example, suppose one had some continuous Normally distributed variables, some dichotomous variables, and some ordered categorical variables. Clearly the model presented in this section could not be applied, except as a rough approximation. However, one might assume that some unobserved Normally distributed variables generated the observed categorical variables through some grouping mechanism (such as a generalization of the one suggested in Section 5.3 as an alternative justification for binary variable models). This grouping mechanism could then be appended onto the model in this section to yield an even more general class of models. Indeed, Muthén (1983, 1984) has proposed such a class of models.

Alternatively, one may believe that the unobserved variables are actually discrete, rather than continuous. In this situation, a more straightforward generalization of the models in Chapters 5 to 7 might be called for (see, e.g., the last part of Section 8.2). A variety of these have been proposed, but many others have yet to be invented.

## 10.5    Concluding remarks

Most social systems worthy of analysis output a large variety of interesting variables and data. Political scientists can never completely study all of it. With single equation models, analysts are able to make inferences about only fixed portions of the social system. To expand the scope of analysis, one could repeatedly apply single equation models to the different sources of quantitative data. Indeed, this would probably yield additional interesting information. However, multiple equation models are usually more than the sum of several individual equation models. At the simplest level, the observations from these seemingly unrelated individual equations are frequently correlated. By taking this additional information into account in a joint estimation, significant additional information may be extracted from existing data. At a more theoretical level, one can estimate more sophisticated and interesting models. Multiple equation models permit one to analyze and estimate models of reciprocal causation, unobserved variables, selection bias, and a variety of other plausible structures.

Multiple equation models require more general assumptions, but only because the subject of analysis is broader. As a result, one might consider these more restrictive models. However, the space which one is restricting with one of these models – that is, the area of the social system being studied – is much broader. The combination of these two contradictory forces yields a very broad class of quite flexible models not necessarily more or less restrictive than single equation models. If one is willing to make the broader set of assumptions and simultaneously consider a larger quantity of data, much more realistic models can be constructed with this methodology.

# CHAPTER 11

# Conclusions

The purpose of this book is to unify the apparently disparate methods of political science research and help forge a new subfield of political methodology. The vehicle for this unification is the likelihood theory of statistical inference. In this brief concluding chapter, I touch upon some possible alternative approaches.

The main alternative approach is largely descriptive. Essentially, the idea of this approach is that one begins and ends with the data. Statistical inference to unobserved parameters and models is not really of interest, although still possible. The goal is reducing data rather than estimating parameters. A simple example of this approach is a view of least squares regression, where, based solely on "reasonableness," one minimizes distances between observed and fitted values (see Section 4.2). In a much more general form, this is also called the *minimization of distances in vector spaces,* and the most extensive treatment of this is by Pollack (1979). *Exploratory data analysis* is not entirely based on minimizing distances, but it too is largely descriptive in orientation (see Tukey, 1977).

The chief advantage of most of these descriptive approaches is that they are often quite *computationally* intuitive. The methods of maximum likelihood sometimes produce intuitive estimation formulas, but more often they require the iterative computation of complicated nonlinear expressions. My argument is that as long as an estimator is derived from first principles close to one's substantive problems, the exact computational formulas are not particularly relevant to inference about particular empirical questions. In fact, just as computation should be transparent, algebra should ideally become frictionless as well: it represents merely the intermediary steps between one's theoretical specification and empirical estimates. In the end, political scientists should not sacrifice features of their theoretical models merely to ensure intuitive computational formulas.[1] Description should be an important part of any statistical analysis, but inference must be the ultimate goal.

This statement should be qualified in one sense: sometimes estimation formulas require extraordinary amounts of time for convergence. Since refinement, respecification, and sensitivity analyses should be important parts of any research project, a model this complicated should probably be made somewhat more restrictive. As computers become more powerful this will be less of a concern, but it will probably always remain a consideration.

Another view of quantitative methodology is as a set of *assumptions* associated with a few popular models. When these assumptions are *violated,* one comes up with *corrections*. Once one's statistical procedures are corrected, a researcher can then perform the analysis as if no violation had occurred.

This assumption-violation-correction strategy is primarily a product of a well developed tradition, primarily in econometrics. The reason for the tradition is largely technical: calculations were generally done by hand or on mechanical adding machines.[2] The result was that significant areas of scholarship were appropriately devoted to issues of computation efficiency.[3] For example, discovering how to do partitioned inverses of many small matrixes, instead of an inverse of a single matrix, could literally save a researcher months of work. Even when computers were developed, the available software was geared primarily to simple linear regression models. Given this situation, how would a researcher deal with, for example, time series data? Scholars did not think of modeling this interesting process; they only considered how to "correct for autocorrelation" so that the standard regression model would yield reasonable results. The advantage of this approach is its feasibility; the disadvantage is that it ignores the time series process entirely – probably the most interesting aspect of this sort of data.

Although modern computers virtually eliminate the need for spending inordinate amounts of time ensuring computational efficiency, nearly all modern econometrics texts are still organized in the assumption-violation-correction tradition. Large portions of these books are devoted to "tricking" existing programs into producing what one should want in theory. Aside from the methods of "tricking" models of heteroscedasticity and autocorrelation into standard linear regression programs, some still even include the "definitional" and "computational" formulas for the sample variance and other statistics.[4]

[2] Academics fortunate enough to have assistants often used them as essentially "human computers." Imagine a room filled with graduate students, each doing his or her part in a single multiple regression analysis (see Stigler, 1986: 158).

[3] Indeed, computation has always been an important constraint in quantitative analysis: Some of the first books ever published on mathematics in the seventeenth century spent considerable time demonstrating calculation tricks so that users would not have to waste expensive paper.

[4] In addition, political scientists still too often select a statistical method merely because it is included in SPSS or some other computer package. The result, aside from violating assumptions and discarding significant amounts of information, is that an unquestioning application of standard packages constrains the set of available statistical methods. In turn, the ways one can look at and study the world are severely limited. By focusing on the theory of inference underlying political methodology, instead of the availability of computer programs, one can concentrate on substantive reasons for decisions about research design and analysis. Concentrating on theoretical reasons for methodological decisions was always desirable and, with recent dramatic advances in computer technology, it is now possible.

In the context of a simple model, a realistic political process looks like an unfortunate violation of one's assumptions; with a more sophisticated model, this process can become an integral part of substantive theory. Assumptions, violations, and corrections are also quite distant from the substantive concerns of political science. Instead of this approach, statistical practice should be explicitly grounded in a more fundamental theory of inference. The likelihood framework provides one very widely applicable theory. By so doing, one removes a plethora of not very interesting issues of technical violations and computational efficiency and replaces them with a much more direct means of modeling political relationships.

Section 4.2 touches on "criterion estimators," probably the leading alternative method of deriving estimators for the purpose of statistical inference. Criterion estimators, and the newer robust statistics, have proven quite useful. In some specialized cases, substantive research questions and particular data sets will suggest which criteria to require of one's estimators. In a variety of areas, an estimator derived in this way may be preferable to the ML estimator. However, in most cases these estimators are derived more on the basis of what is feasible in a particular case than on substantive grounds. As an almost universally applicable approach to statistical inference, likelihood is unparalleled.[5]

To summarize: no other theory of scientific inference is as intuitive. None is anywhere near as generally applicable. No other approach produces point estimators with properties as generally desirable – even when judging from the perspective of criterion estimators. None is as easy to modify and extend. Perhaps most importantly, no other theory of inference operates as close to the substance of political science research.

If a political methodology subfield is to ever emerge in full, we must eventually do more than import methods from other disciplines. The data we committed so many resources to require specialized models that will not be developed by anyone but political scientists. The time has come for political scientists to be tool-makers rather than merely tool-users.[6]

If political methodology is to be an important part of political science, it must solve existing problems and generate new ways of looking at the world. In a word, it must be *creative*. Many political science departments want their students to be able to read and criticize the quantitative literature ("read the journals" it is often said) without necessarily being able to contribute to it. This reasoning exhibits two fallacies. The first is that criticizing and contribut-

---

[5] Other approaches exist for unifying only some areas of statistical analysis (e.g., Speed, 1987).

[6] We should also work toward excising courses from our curricula that go by names such as, "Econometrics for Political Scientists." These were useful for some time, but they are now merely insulting.

ing is often a false dichotomy. If you understand a methodology well enough to criticize it, you will often be able to suggest a different or an improved method. Howard Becker (1984: 124) has written that "Intellectual life is a dialogue among people interested in the same topic. You can eavesdrop on the conversation and learn from it but eventually you ought to add something yourself." New methods should obviously not be created in the many situations when suitable ones exist. However, political scientists ought to be able to create methods when necessary. In response to a similar creative process, well-developed (and well-respected) methodological subfields have emerged in every other social science. It is time the same happened in political science.

The second fallacy inherent in this reasoning implies that political science needs methods only for a series of technical fixes – not as fundamental contributions. The problem with this reasoning is that methodology is not plumbing. A methodological contribution affects not only one discovery but potentially a whole range of future studies: for example, the invention of the alphabet is as least as important as all the works of Shakespeare and Schattschneider combined. New methodologies can help extract information from data that were previously unknowable, provide precise models of new ideas, and create fundamentally new ways to understand existing substantive problems.

# References

Abbott, Edwin A. 1952 (originally published circa 1884). *Flatland: A Romance of Many Dimensions*. New York: Dover.

Achen, Christopher H. 1988. "The Polychotomous Linear Probability Model." Presented at the annual meeting of the Midwest Political Science Association, Chicago, Illinois, April 14–16.

Achen Christopher H. 1986. *Statistical Analysis of Quasi-Experiments*. Berkeley: University of California Press.

Achen, Christopher H. 1983. "Toward Theories of Data: The State of Political Methodology," in Ada W. Finifter, *Political Science: The State of the Discipline*. Washington, D.C.: American Political Science Association.

Achen, Christopher H. 1979. "The Bias in Normal Vote Estimates," *Political Methodology* 6, 3: 343–56.

Aldrich, John H. and Forrest D. Nelson. 1984. *Linear Probability, Logit, and Probit Models*. Beverly Hills: Sage.

Alker, Hayward R., Jr. 1975. "Polimetrics: Its Descriptive Foundations," in F. Greenstein and N. Polshy, eds., *Handbook of Political Science*, Vol. 7. Reading, MA: Addison-Wesley.

Allison, Paul D. 1987. "Introducing a Disturbance into Logit and Probit Regression Models," *Sociological Methods and Research*. 15,4 (May): 335–74.

Almon, S. 1965. "The Distributed Lag Between Capital Appropriations and Expenditures," *Econometrica*, 33: 178–96.

Alt, James E. 1987. "Non-Linear Time Series Analysis of the British Political Economy." Prepared for the annual convention of the American Political Science Association, Chicago, September 3–6.

Alwin, Duane F. and David J. Jackson. 1980. "Measurement Models for Response Errors in Surveys: Issues and Applications," *Sociological Methodology*. San Francisco: Jossey-Bass.

Amemiya, Takeshi. 1985a. *Advanced Econometrics*. Cambridge, MA: Harvard University Press.

Amemiya, Takeshi. 1985b. "The Estimation of a Simultaneous Equation Generalized Probit Model," *Econometrica*. 46: 1193–1205.

Amemiya, Takeshi. 1981. "Qualitative Response Models: A Survey," *Journal of Economic Literature*. 19 (4): 483–536.

Armstrong, J. Scott. 1967. "Derivation of Theory by Means of Factor Analysis or Tom Swift and His Electric Factor Analysis Machine," *The American Statistician*. (December): 17–21.

Ashley, Richard A., Douglas M. Patterson, and Melvin J. Hinich. 1985. "A Diagnostic Test for Nonlinear Serial Dependence in Time Series Fitting Errors," *Journal of Time Series Analysis*. 7, 3: 165–178.

Axelrod, Robert. 1984. *The Evolution of Cooperation*. New York: Basic.

Axelrod, Robert and Robert O. Keohane. 1985. "Achieving Cooperation Under Anarchy: Strategies and Institutions," *World Politics*. 38,1 (October): 226–54.

Azar, Edward E. 1982. *The Codebook of the Conflict and Peace Data Bank (COP-DAB)*. Center for International Development, University of Maryland.

Azar, Edward E. and Thomas J. Sloan. 1975. *Dimensions of Interaction*. Pittsburgh: International Studies Association, Occasional Paper No. 8.

Bahadur, R. R. 1958. "Examples of Inconsistency of Maximum Likelihood Estimates," *Sankhā*, 20: 207–10.

Bahry, Donna and Brian D. Silver. 1987. "Intimidation and the Symbolic Uses of Terror in the USSR," *American Political Science Review*. 81,4 (December): 1065–98.

Bain, Lee J. and Max Engelhardt. 1987. *Introduction to Probability and Mathematical Statistics*. Boston: Duxbury.

Banchoff, Thomas F. 1987. "Using Computer Graphics to Explore the Generation of Surfaces in Four Dimensional Space," published by Prime Computer, Natick, Massachusetts.

Barnett, Vic. 1982. *Comparative Statistical Inference*, 2nd ed. New York: Wiley.

Bartels, Larry. 1988. "Imputing Political Interests," unpublished paper. Department of Political Science, University of Rochester.

Bartels, R. 1977. "On the Use of Limit Theorem Arguments in Economic Statistics," *American Statistician*. 31: 85–7.

Beck, Nathaniel. 1987a. "Alternative Dynamic Specifications of Popularity Functions." Paper presented to the annual meeting of the Political Methodology Group, Durham, North Carolina, August 6–9.

Beck, Nathaniel. 1987b. "Estimating State Space Models with Kalman Filtering." Paper presented to the annual meeting of the Political Methodology Group, Durham, North Carolina, August 6–9, forthcoming *Political Analysis*.

Beck, Nathaniel. 1986. "Estimating Dynamic Models is Not Merely a Matter of Technique," *Political Methodology*. 11, 1–2: 71–90.

Beck, Nathaniel. 1983. "Time-varying Parameter Regression Models," *American Journal of Political Science*. 27: 557–600.

Becker, Howard S. 1984. *Writing for Social Scientists*. Chicago: University of Chicago Press.

Bender, Edward A. 1978. *An Introduction to Mathematical Modeling*. New York: Wiley-Interscience.

Benjamin, Gerald. 1982. *The Communications Revolution in Politics*. Proceedings of the Academy of Political Science 34,4.

Berger, James O. and Robert L. Wolpert. 1984. *The Likelihood Principle*. Hayward, CA: Institute of Mathematical Statistics.

Berkson, Joseph 1980. "Minimum Chi-Square, Not Maximum Likelihood!" *The Annals of Statistics*. 8,3: 457–87.

Bishop, Yvonne M. M., Stephen E. Fienberg, and Paul W. Holland. 1975. *Discrete Multivariate Analysis*. Cambridge, Mass.: MIT Press.

Blalock, Hubert M. 1979. *Social Statistics*, revised 2nd ed. New York: McGraw Hill.

Blalock, Hubert M. 1972. *Social Statistics*. New York: McGraw Hill.

Bloom, David E. and Mark Killingsworth. 1985. "Correcting For Truncation Bias Caused by a Latent Truncation Variable," *Journal of Econometrics*. 27: 131–5.

Box, George E. P. and Norman R. Draper. 1987. *Empirical Model Building and Response Surfaces*. New York: Wiley.

Box, George E. P. and G. M. Jenkins. 1976. *Time Series Analysis: Forecasting and Control*, revised edition. San Francisco: Holden Day.

Brady, Henry. 1985. "Statistical Consistency and Hypothesis Testing for Nonmetric Multidimensional Scaling," *Psychometrika*. 50,4 (December): 509–37.

Brady, Henry and Stephen Ansolabehere. 1988. "The Existence of Utility Functions in Mass Publics," *American Political Science Review*. Forthcoming, December.

Bronowski, J. 1958. "The Creative Process," *Scientific American* (September), reprinted in *Scientific Genius and Creativity*. New York: Freeman.

Bross, I. D. J. 1971. "Comment on Good," in V. P. Godambe and D. A. Sprott, eds., *Foundations of Statistical Inference*. Toronto: Holt, Rinehart, and Winston of Canada.

Burt, Ronald S. 1973. "Confirmatory Factor-Analytic Structures and the Theory Construction Process," *Sociological Methods and Research*. 2,2 (November): 131–190.

Cameron, A. Colin and Pravin K. Trivedi. 1986. "Econometric Models Based on Count Data: Comparisons and Applications of Some Estimators and Tests," *Journal of Applied Econometrics*. 1: 29–53.

Ceci, Stephen and Elaine Walker. 1983. "Private Archives and Public Needs," *American Psychologist*. 38 (April): 414–23.

Cohen, A. C. 1960. "Estimation in the Truncated Poisson Distribution When the Zeros and Some Ones are Missing," *Journal of the American Statistical Association*. 55: 342–8.

Coleman, James S. 1981. *Longitudinal Data Analysis*. New York: Basic.

Cox, D. R. 1970. *The Analysis of Binary Data*. London: Methuen.

Cramer, J. S. 1986. *Econometric Applications of Maximum Likelihood Methods*. New York: Cambridge University Press.

Croxton, Frederick E. and Dudley J. Cowden. 1946. *Applied General Statistics*. New York: Prentice-Hall.

Crunchfield, James, J. Dayne Farmer, Norman H. Packard, and Robert S. Shaw. 1986. "Chaos," *Scientific American*. 255,6 (December): 88–101.

Davidian, M. and R. J. Carroll. 1987. "Variance Function Estimation," *Journal of the American Statistical Association*. 82, 400 (December): 1079–91.

Davidson, J., D. Hendry, F. Srba, and S. Yeo. 1978. "Econometric Modeling of the Aggregate Time-Series Relationship Between Consumers' Expenditure and Income in the United Kingdom." *Economic Journal*. 88:661–92.

DeFinetti, B. 1975. *Theory of Probability*, vol. 2. New York: Wiley.

DeFinetti, B. 1974. *Theory of Probability*, vol. 1. New York: Wiley.

DeGroot, Morris H. 1986. *Probability and Statistics*, 2nd edition. Reading, MA: Addison-Wesley.

DeGroot, Morris H., Stephen E. Fienberg, and Joseph B. Kadane. 1986. *Statistics and The Law*. New York: Wiley.

Dewald, William G., Jerry G. Thursby, and Richard G. Anderson. 1986. "Replication in Empirical Economics: The *Journal of Money, Credit and Banking Project*," *American Economic Review*. 76,4 (September): 587–603.

Dhrymes, P. J. 1974. *Econometrics, Statistical Foundations, and Applications*. New York: Springer-Verlag.

Dhrymes, P. J. 1971. *Distributed Lags: Problems of Formulation and Estimation*. San Francisco: Holden-Day.

Duncan, Otis Dudley. 1979. "How Destination Depends on Origin in the Occupational Mobility Table," *American Journal of Sociology*. 84,4: 793–803.

Edwards, A.W.F. 1972. *Likelihood*. Cambridge: Cambridge University Press.

Efron, Bradley. 1986. "Why Isn't Everyone a Bayesian?" with comments and rejoinder, *The American Statistician*. 40,1 (February): 1–10.

Efron, Bradley. 1982. "Maximum Likelihood and Decision Theory," *The Annals of Statistics*, 10,2: 340–56.

Efron, Bradley. 1981. "Nonparametric Estimates of Standard Error: The Jackknife, the Bootstrap, and Other Methods," *Biometrika*. 68: 589–99.

Efron, Bradley. 1978. "Controversies in the Foundations of Statistics," *American Mathematics Monthly*. 85: 231–44.

Efron, Bradley. 1975. "Defining the Curvature of a Statistical Problem (With Applications to Second Order Efficiency)," *The Annals of Statistics*. 3,6: 1189–1242.

El-Sayyad, G. M. 1973. "Bayesian and Classical Analysis of Poisson Regression," *Journal of the Royal Statistical Association, Series B*. 35,3 (Methodological): 445–51.

Enelow, James and Melvin Hinich. 1984. *The Spatial Theory of Voting: An Introduction*. New York: Cambridge University Press.

Engle, R. F. 1984. "Wald, Likelihood Ratio, and Lagrange Multiplier Tests in Econometrics," in Zvi Griliches and Michael D. Intriligator, eds., *Handbook of Econometrics*. Amsterdam: North-Holland, 775–826.

Engle, R. F. 1982. "Autoregressive Conditional Heteroscedasticity with Estimates of the Variance of United Kingdom Inflation," *Econometrica*. 50: 987–1007.

Feller, William. 1968. *An Introduction to Probability Theory and Its Application*, Volume I, 3rd ed. New York: Wiley.

Ferguson, Thomas S. 1967. *Mathematical Statistics: A Decision Theoretic Approach*. New York: Academic Press.

Fienberg, Stephen E. 1980. *The Analysis of Cross-Classified Categorical Data*, 2nd edition. Cambridge, Mass.: MIT Press.

Fienberg, Stephen E. 1970a. "An Iterative Procedure for Estimation in Contingency Tables," *Annals of Mathematical Statistics*. 41: 907–17.

Fienberg, Stephen E. 1970b. "Quasi-Independence and Maximum Likelihood Estimation in Incomplete Contingency Tables," *Journal of the American Statistical Association*. 65: 1610–16.

Fisher, Ronald A. 1930. "Inverse Probability," *Proceedings of the Cambridge Philosophical Society*. 36, 4: 528–35.

Fisher, Ronald A. 1925. "Theory of Statistical Estimation," *Proceedings of the Cambridge Philosophical Society*. 22: 700–25.

Fisher, Ronald A. 1922. "On the Mathematical Foundations of Theoretical Statistics," *Philosophical Transactions of the Royal Statistical Society of London A*. 222: 309–60.

Franklin, Charles. In press. "Estimation Across Datasets: Two-Stage Auxiliary Instrumental Variables Estimation (2SAIV)," *Political Analysis*, Fall, 1989.

Freeman, John. 1983. "Granger Causality and Time Series Analysis of Political Relationships," *American Journal of Political Science*. 27: 327–58.

Freeman, John, John Williams, and Tse-Min Lin. 1986. "Modeling Macro Political Processes." Paper presented at the annual meeting of the Political Methodology Group, Cambridge Massachusetts, forthcoming *American Journal of Political Science*.

Fuller, Wayne A. 1976. *Introduction to Statistical Time Series*. New York: Wiley.

Gallant, Ronald A. 1986. *Nonlinear Statistical Models*. New York: Wiley.

Geweke, John. 1984. "Inference And Causality in Economic Time Series Models," in Zvi Griliches and M. D. Intriligator, eds, *Handbook of Econometrics*. New York: North-Holland.

Glass, D. V., ed. 1954. *Social Mobility in Britain*. London: Routledge and Kegan Paul.

Gleick, James. 1987. *Chaos: Making a New Science*. New York: Viking.

Goldberger, Arthur S. 1971. "Econometrics and Psychometrics: A Survey of Communalities," *Psychometrika*. 36 (June): 83–107.

Goldberger, Arthur S. 1964. *Econometric Theory*. New York: Wiley.

Goldstein, Joshua and John R. Freeman. 1988. "Reciprocity in U.S.-Soviet-Chinese Relation." Presented at the annual meeting of the American Political Science Association, Washington, D.C., 2 September.

Goodman, Leo A. 1978. *Analyzing Qualitative/Categorical Data: Log-Linear Models and Latent Structure Analysis*. Cambridge, MA: Abt.

Goodman, Leo A. 1975. "The Relationship between the Modified and the More Usual Multiple-Regression Approach to the Analysis of Dichotomous Variables," in David R. Heise, ed., *Sociological Methodology 1976*. San Francisco: Jossey-Bass.

Goodman, Leo A. 1972. "A General Model for the Analysis of Surveys," *American Journal of Sociology*. 77 (May): 1035–86.

Goodman, Leo A. 1968. "The Analysis of Cross-Classified Data: Independence, Quasi-Independence, and Interaction in Contingency Tables With or Without Missing Cells," *Journal of The American Statistical Association*. 63: 1091–131.

Gourieroux, C., A. Monfort, and A. Trognon. 1984a. "Pseudo Maximum Likelihood Methods: Theory," *Econometrica*. 52: 681–700.

Gourieroux, C., A. Monfort, and A. Trognon. 1984b. "Pseudo Maximum Likelihood Methods: Applications to Poisson Models," *Econometrica*. 52: 701–20.

Granger, Clive W. and Paul Newbold. 1986. *Forecasting Economic Time Series*, 2nd edition, Orlando: Academic Press.

Granger, Clive W., R. P. Robins, and R. F. Engle. 1985. "Wholesale and Retail Prices: Bivariate Time Series Modeling with Forecastable Error Variances," in E. Kuh and R. Belsley, eds., *Model Reliability*. Cambridge: MIT Press.

Greenwood, M. and G. U. Yule. 1920. "An Enquiry into the Nature of Frequency Distributions of Multiple Happenings, with Particular Reference to the Occurrence of Multiple Attacks of Disease or Repeated Accidents," *Journal of the Royal Statistical Society A*. 83: 255–79.

Griliches, Zvi. 1967. "Distributed Lags: A Survey," *Econometrica*. 35: 16–49.

Grizzle, James, E., C. Frank Starmer, and Gary C. Koch. 1969. "Analysis of Categorical Data by Linear Models," *Biometrics*. 25: 489–504.

Grogger, Jeffrey T. and Richard T. Carson. 1988. "Models for Counts from Choice Based Samples." Discussion Paper 88-9, Department of Economics, University of California, San Diego.

Gudgin, G. and P. J. Taylor. 1979. *Seats, Votes, and the Spatial Organization of Elections*. London: Pion.

Haight, F. 1967. *Handbook of the Poisson Distribution*. New York: Wiley.

Hampel, Frank R., Peter J. Rousseeuw, Elvezio M. Ronchetti, and Werner A. Stahel. 1986. *Robust Statistics: The Approach Based on Influence Functions*. New York: Wiley.

Hannan, E. J. 1970. *Multiple Time Series*. New York: Wiley.

Hanushek, Eric A. and John E. Jackson. 1977. *Statistical Methods for Social Scientists*. New York: Academic.

Harman, Harry H. 1976. *Modern Factor Analysis*, 3rd Edition, reissued. Chicago: University of Chicago Press.

Harvey, A. C. 1981a. *The Econometric Analysis of Time Series*. Oxford: Philip Allan.

Harvey, A. C. 1981b. *Time Series Models*. Oxford: Philip Allan.

Haseman, J. K. and L. J. Kupper. 1979. "Analysis of Dichotomous Response Data From Certain Toxicological Experiments," *Biometrics*. 35: 281–93.

Hausman, Jerry. 1978. "Specification Tests in Econometrics," *Econometrica*. 46: 1251–72.

Hausman, Jerry, Bronwyn H. Hall, and Zvi Griliches. 1984. "Econometrics Models for Count Data with An Application to the Patents-R&D Relationship," *Econometrica*. 52:4 (July): 909–38.

Heckman, James J. and Robert J. Willis. 1977. "A Beta-Logistic Model for the Analysis of Sequential Labor Force Participation by Married Women," *Journal of Political Economy*. 85,1: 27–58.

Hendry, David F. 1976. "The Structure of Simultaneous Equations Estimators," *Journal of Econometrics*. 4: 51–88.

Hendry, David and G. Mizon. 1978. "Serial Correlation as a Convenient Simplification, Not a Nuisance: A Comment on a Study of the Demand for Money by the Bank of England," *Economic Journal*. 88: 549–63.

Hendry, David, Adrian R. Pagan, and J. Denis Sargan. 1984. "Dynamic Specification," Chapter 18 in Zvi Griliches and M. D. Intriligator, eds., *Handbook of Econometrics, Volume II*. New York: North-Holland.

Hendry, David and J. F. Richard. 1983. "The Econometric Analysis of Time Series (with Discussion)," *International Statistical Review*. 51: 111–63.

Hildebrand, D. K., J. D. Laing, and H. Rosenthal. 1977. *Prediction Analysis of Cross-Classification*. New York: Wiley.

Hinich, Melvin J. and Douglas M. Patterson. 1985. "Evidence of Nonlinearity in Daily Stock Returns," *Journal of Business Economics and Statistics*. 3,1 (January): 69–77.

Hodges, James S. 1987. "Uncertainty, Policy Analysis, and Statistics," with comments and rejoinder, *Statistical Science*. 2, 3 (August): 259–91.

Holden, Robert T. 1987. "Time Series Analysis of a Contagious Process," *Journal of the American Statistical Association*. 82, 400 (December): 1019–26.

Holgate, P. 1964. "Estimation for the Bivariate Poisson Distribution," *Biometrika*. 51: 241–5.

Holland, Paul W. 1986. "Statistics and Causal Inference," with comments by Donald B. Rubin, D. R. Cox, Clark Glymour, and Clive Granger, and rejoinder. *Journal of the American Statistical Association* 81, 396 (December): 945–70.

Hout, Michael. 1983. *Mobility Tables*. Beverly Hills: Sage Publications.

Hsu, P. L. 1939. "A New Proof of the Joint Product Moment Distribution," *Proceedings of the Cambridge Philosophical Society*. 35: 336–8.

Huber, P. 1981. *Robust Statistics*. New York: Wiley.

Huber, P. 1967. "The Behavior of Maximum Likelihood Estimates under Nonstandard Conditions," *Fifth Berkeley Symposium on Mathematical Statistics and Probability I*. Berkeley: University of California Press.

Hubert, Lawrence. 1974. "Approximate Evaluation Techniques for Single Link and Complete-Link Hierarchical Clustering Procedures," *Journal of the American Statistical Association*. 69,347 (September): 698–704.

Hubert, Lawrence. 1973. "Min and Max Hierarchical Clustering Using Asymmetric Similarity Measures," *Psychometrika*. 38, 1 (March): 63–72.

Hufbauer, Gary Clyde and Jeffrey J. Schott. 1983. *Economic Sanctions in Support of Foreign Policy Goals*. Washington, D.C.: Institute for International Economics.

Johnson, Norman L. and Samuel Kotz. 1972. *Distributions in Statistics: Continuous Multivariate Distributions*. New York: Wiley.

Johnson, Norman L. and Samuel Kotz. 1970a. *Distributions in Statistics: Continuous Univariate Distributions I*. New York: Wiley.

Johnson, Norman L. and Samuel Kotz. 1970b. *Distributions in Statistics: Continuous Univariate Distributions II*. New York: Wiley.

Johnson, Norman L. and Samuel Kotz. 1969. *Distributions in Statistics: Discrete Distributions*. New York: Wiley.

Johnson, Thomas H., Robert O. Slater, and Pat McGowan. 1984. "Explaining African Military Coups d'Etat, 1960–1982," *American Political Science Review*. 78,3 (September): 622–40.

Johnston, J. 1984. *Econometrics Methods*, 3rd ed. New York: McGraw-Hill.

Jöreskog, Karl G. 1971. "Simultaneous Factor Analysis in Several Populations," *Psychometrika*. 36, 4 (December): 409–26.

Jöreskog, Karl G. 1969. "A General Approach to Confirmatory Maximum Likelihood Factor Analysis," *Psychometrika*. 34,2: 183–202.

Jöreskog, Karl G. and Dag Sörbom. 1979. *Advances in Factor Analysis and Structural Equation Models*, edited by Jay Magidson. New York: University Press of America.

Jorgenson, D. W. 1966. "Rational Distributed Lag Functions," *Econometrica*. 34: 135–49.

Judge, George G., W. E. Griffiths, R. Carther Hill, Helmut Lütkepohl, and Tsoung-Chao Lee. 1985. *The Theory and Practice of Econometrics*, 2nd ed. New York: Wiley.

Kalman, R. 1960. "A New Approach to Linear Filtering and Prediction Problems," *Journal of Basic Engineering*, 82: 34–45.

Katz, Leo. 1965. "Unified Treatment of a Broad Class of Discrete Probability Distributions," in Ganapati P. Patil, ed., *Classical and Contagious Discrete Distributions*. Calcutta: Statistical Publishing Society.

Keohane, Robert O. 1986. "Reciprocity in International Relations," *International Organization*, 40,1 (Winter): 1–29.

King, Gary. In press-a. "Variance Specification in Event Count Models: From Restrictive Assumptions to a Generalized Estimator," *American Journal of Political Science*. Forthcoming.

King, Gary. In press-b. "A Seemingly Unrelated Poisson Regression Model," *Sociological Methods and Research*. Forthcoming.

King, Gary. In press-c. "Event Count Models for International Relations: Generalizations and Applications," *International Studies Quarterly*, forthcoming.

King, Gary. In press-d. "Fair Representation Through Legislative Redistricting: A Stochastic Model," *American Journal of Political Science*, forthcoming.

King, Gary. 1988a. "Statistical Models for Political Science Event Counts: Bias in Conventional Procedures and Evidence for The Exponential Poisson Regression Model," *American Journal of Political Science*. 32, 3 (August): 838–63.

King, Gary. 1987a. "Presidential Appointments to the Supreme Court: Adding Systematic Explanation to Probabilistic Description," *American Politics Quarterly*. 15, 3 (July): 373–86.

King, Gary. 1986a. "How Not to Lie with Statistics: Avoiding Common Mistakes in Quantitative Political Science," *American Journal of Political Science*. 30, 3 (August): 666–87.

King, Gary. 1986b. "The Significance of Roll Calls in Voting Bodies: A Model and Statistical Estimation," *Social Science Research*. 15 (June): 135–52.

King, Gary and Gerald Benjamin. 1985. "The Stability of Party Identification Among U.S. Senators and Representatives: 1789–1984," delivered at the annual meeting of the American Political Science Association, New Orleans, August 29–September 1.

King, Gary and Robert X. Browning. 1987. "Democratic Representation and Partisan Bias in Congressional Elections," *American Political Science Review*. 81, 4 (December): 125–73.

King, Gary and Andrew Gelman. 1988. "Systemic Consequences of Incumbency Advantage in Congressional Elections," photocopy.

King, Gary and Lyn Ragsdale. 1988. *The Elusive Executive: Discovering Statistical Patterns in the Presidency*. Washington, D.C.: Congressional Quarterly Press.

Kleinman, Joel C. 1973. "Proportions with Extraneous Variance: Single and Independent Samples," *Journal of the American Statistical Association*. 68,3 (March): 46–53.

Kmenta, Jan. 1986. *Elements of Econometrics*, 2nd ed. New York: Macmillan.

Knoke, David and Peter J. Burke. 1980. *Log-Linear Models*. Beverly Hills: Sage.

Knoke, David and James H. Kuklinski. 1982. *Network Analysis*. Beverly Hills: Sage.

Koenker, Roger. 1988. "Asymptotic Theory and Econometric Practice," *Journal of Applied Econometrics*, 3: 139–47.

Koenker, Roger. 1982. "Robust Methods in Econometrics," *Econometric Reviews*. 1: 213–90.

Koyck, L. M. 1954. *Distributed Lags and Investment Analysis*. Amsterdam: North-Holland.

Kritzer, Herbert M. 1978a. "An Introduction to Multivariate Contingency Table Analysis," *American Journal of Political Science*. 21: 187–226.

Kritzer, Herbert M. 1978b. "Analyzing Contingency Tables by Weighted Least Squares: An Alternative to the Goodman Approach," *Political Methodology*. 5,4: 277–326.

Lawley, D. N. and A. E. Maxwell. 1971. *Factor Analysis as a Statistical Method*. London: Butterworths.

Leamer, Edward E. 1978. *Specification Searches: Ad Hoc Inference With Nonexperimental Data*. New York: Wiley.

Lee, Lung-Fei. 1986. "Specification Test for Poisson Regression Models," *International Economic Review*. 27,3 (October): 689–706.

Lindley, Dennis V. 1987. "The Probability Approach to the Treatment of Uncertainty in Artificial Intelligence and Expert Systems," with comments and rejoinders, *Statistical Science*. 2,1 (February): 17–24, et passim.

Lindley, Dennis V. 1965. *Introduction to Probability and Statistics from a Bayesian Viewpoint, Parts 1 and 2*. Cambridge: Cambridge University Press.

Lindley, Dennis V. 1947. "Regression Lines and the Linear Functional Relationship," *Supplement to the Journal of the Royal Statistical Society*: 218–44.

Ling, Robert F. 1973. "A Probability Theory of Cluster Analysis," *Journal of the American Statistical Association*. 68, 341 (March): 159–64.

Little, Roderick J. A. and Donald B. Rubin. 1987. *Statistical Analysis with Missing Data*. New York: Wiley.

Lütkepohl, H. 1981. "A Model for Non-Negative and Non-Positive Distributed Lag Functions," *Journal of Econometrics*. 16: 211–19.

Maddala, G. S. 1983. *Limited-Dependent and Qualitative Variables in Econometrics*. New York: Cambridge University Press.

Maddala, G. S. 1977. *Econometrics*. New York: McGraw-Hill.

Manski, Charles and Daniel McFadden, eds. 1982. *Structural Analysis of Discrete Data*. Cambridge, Mass.: MIT Press.

Martin, Lisa. In progress. "Explaining Multilateral Economic Sanctions." Ph.D. Dissertation, Department of Government, Harvard University.

McCullagh, P. and J. A. Nelder. 1983. *Generalized Linear Models*. London: Chapman and Hall.

McDonald, H. Brooke and Richard Rosecrance. 1985. "Alliance and Structural Balance in the International System," *Journal of Conflict Resolution*. 29, 1 (March): 57–82.

McDonald, John F. and Robert A. Moffitt. 1980. "The Uses of Tobit Analysis," *Review of Economics and Statistics*. 72, 2 (May): 318–21.

McFadden, Daniel. 1984. "Econometric Analysis of Qualitative Response Models," in Zvi Griliches and Michael Intriligator, eds., *Handbook of Econometrics*. New York: North-Holland.

McFadden, Daniel. 1981. "Econometric Analysis of Probabilistic Choice," in Charles

264    **References**

Manski and Daniel McFadden, eds., *Structural Analysis of Discrete Data with Econometric Applications.* Cambridge, Mass.: MIT Press, pp. 198–272.

McFadden, Daniel. 1974. "Conditional Logit Analysis of Qualitative Choice Behavior," in P. Zarembka, ed., *Frontiers in Econometrics.* New York: Academic, pp. 105–42.

McGowan, Patrick J. and Robert M. Rood. 1975. "Alliance Behavior in Balance of Power Systems: Applying a Poisson Model to Nineteenth-Century Europe," *American Political Science Review.* 69: 859–70.

McKelvey, R. and W. Zavoina. 1975. "A Statistical Model for the Analysis of Ordinal Level Dependent Variables," *Journal of Mathematical Sociology.* 4: 103–20.

Merelman, Richard M. and Gary King. 1986. "The Development of Political Activists: A Model of Early Learning," *Social Science Quarterly.* 67, 3 (September): 473–90.

Merton, Robert. 1980. "On Estimating the Expected Return on the Market: An Exploratory Investigation," *Journal of Financial Economics.* 8: 323–61.

Miller, S. M. 1960. "Comparative Social Mobility." *Current Sociology.* 9(1): 1–89.

Mosteller, Frederick, Andrew F. Sigel, Edward Trapido, and Cleo Youtz. 1981. "Eye Fitting Straight Lines," *The American Statistician.* 35, 3 (August): 150–2.

Mulaik, S. D. 1972. *The Foundations of Factor Analysis.* New York: McGraw-Hill.

Mullahy, John. 1986. "Specification and Testing of Some Modified Count Data Models," *Journal of Econometrics.* 33: 341–65.

Muthén, Bengt. 1984. "A General Structural Equation Model With Dichotomous, Ordered Categorical and Continuous Latent Variable Indicators," *Psychometrika.* 49,1 (March): 115–32.

Muthén, Bengt. 1983. "Latent Variable Structural Equation Modeling With Categorical Data," *Journal of Econometrics.* 22: 43–65.

Nelson, Charles R. 1973. *Applied Time Series Analysis: For Managerial Forecasting.* San Francisco: Holden-Day.

Newbold, P. and Clive W. J. Granger. 1974. "Experience with Forecasting Univariate Time Series and the Combination of Forecasts," *Journal of the Royal Statistical Society A.* 137: 131–46.

Neyman, Jerzy. 1965. "Certain Chance Mechanisms Involving Discrete Distributions," in Ganapati P. Patil, ed., *Classical and Contagious Discrete Distributions.* Calcutta: Statistical Publishing Society.

Neyman, Jerzy and E. L. Scott. 1948. "Consistent Estimates Based on Partially Consistent Observations," *Econometrica.* 16, 1: 1–32.

Norden, R. H. 1973. "A Survey of Maximum Likelihood Estimation, Part 2," *International Statistical Revue.* 41,1: 39–58.

Norden, R. H. 1972. "A Survey of Maximum Likelihood Estimation," *International Statistical Revue.* 40,3: 329–54.

Oakes, Michael. 1968. *Statistical Inference: A Commentary for the Social and Behavioral Sciences.* New York: Wiley.

Pitkin, Hanna Fenichel. 1967. *The Concept of Representation.* Berkeley: University of California Press.

Pollock, D. S. G. 1979. *The Algebra of Econometrics.* New York: Wiley.

Pratt, John W. 1976. "F. Y. Edgeworth and R. A. Fisher on the Efficiency of Maximum Likelihood Estimation," *The Annals of Statistics*. 4,3: 501–14.

Prentice, R. L. 1986. "Binary Regression Using an Extended Beta-Binomial Distribution, with Discussion of Correlation Induced by Covariate Measurement Errors," *Journal of the American Statistical Association, Applications*. 81,394: 321–7.

Press, William H., Brian P. Flannery, Saul A. Teukolsky, and William T. Vetterling. 1986. *Numerical Recipes: The Art of Scientific Computing*. New York: Cambridge University Press.

Priestly, M. B. 1981. *Spectral Analysis and Time Series*. New York: Academic.

Priestly, M. B. 1980. "State-Dependent Models: A General Approach to Nonlinear Time Series Analysis," *Journal of Time Series Analysis*. 1, 1: 47–71.

Quandt, Richard E. 1988. *The Econometrics of Disequilibrium*. New York: Basil Blackwell.

Ragsdale, Lyn. 1984. "The Politics of Presidential Speechmaking, 1949–1980," *American Political Science Review*. 78, 4 (December): 971–84.

Riker, William H. 1959. "A Method for Determining the Significance of Roll Call Votes in Voting Bodies," in J. C. Wahlke and H. Eulau, eds., *Legislative Behavior: A Reader in Theory and Research*. Glencoe, IL.: Free Press.

Rivers, Douglas. In press. "Microeconomics and Macropolitics: A Solution to the Kramer Problem," *American Political Science Review*.

Rivers, Douglas and Quang H. Vuong. 1988. "Limited Information Estimators and Exogeneity Tests for Simultaneous Probit Models." *Journal of Econometrics* (November).

Rosenstone, Steven J. 1983. *Forecasting Presidential Elections*. New Haven, CT: Yale University Press.

Rothschild, V. and N. Logothetis. 1987. *Probability Distributions*. New York: Wiley.

Rubin, Donald B. 1987. *Multiple Imputation for Nonresponse in Surveys*. New York: Wiley.

Rucker, Rudy. 1984. *The Fourth Dimension: Toward a Geometry of Higher Reality*. Boston: Houghton Mifflin.

Schoenberg, Ronald. 1985. "Latent Variables in the Analysis of Limited Dependent Variables," in Nancy B. Tuma, ed., *Sociological Methodology 1985*. San Francisco: Jossey-Bass.

Shapiro, A. 1982. "Rank-Reducibility of a Symmetric Matrix and Sampling Theory of Minimum Trace Factor Analysis," *Psychometrika*. 47: 187–99.

Shapiro, Samuel S. and Alan J. Gross. 1981. *Statistical Modeling Techniques*. New York: Marcel Dekker, Inc.

Sheps, M. C. and J. J. Menken. 1973. *Mathematical Models of Conception and Birth*. Chicago: University of Chicago Press.

Silverman, B. W. 1986. *Density Estimation for Statistics and Data Analysis*. London: Chapman and Hall.

Sims, Christopher. 1988. "Uncertainty Across Models," *American Economic Review*. 78, 2 (May): 163–7.

Sims, Christopher. 1980. "Macroeconomics and Reality," *Econometrica*. 48,1: 1–48.

Singer, J. David and Melvin Small. 1972. *Wages of War: 1816–1965, A Statistical Handbook*. New York: Wiley.

Singer, J. David and Melvin Small. 1969. "Formal Alliances, 1816–65: an Extension of the Basic Data," *Journal of Peace Research*. 3: 256–82.

Singer, J. David and Melvin Small. 1968. "Alliance Aggregation and Onset of War, 1815–1945," in J. D. Singer, ed., *Qualitative International Politics: Insights and Evidence*. New York: Free Press.

Singer, J. David and Melvin Small. 1966. "Formal Alliances, 1815–1939: A Quantitative Description," *Journal of Peace Research*. 1: 1–31.

Siverson, Randolph M. and Michael R. Tennefoss. 1984. "Power, Alliance, and the Escalation of International Conflict, 1815–1965," *American Political Science Review*. 78, 4: 1057–69.

Spanos, Aris. 1986. *Statistical Foundations of Econometric Modeling*. Cambridge: Cambridge University Press.

Speed, T. P. 1987. "What is an Analysis of Variance?" with discussions and rejoinder, *The Annals of Statistics*. 15,3 (September): 885–941.

Stigler, Stephen. 1986. *The History of Statistics*. Cambridge: Harvard University Press.

Stimpson, James A. 1985. "Regression in Space and Time: A Statistical Essay," *American Journal of Political Science* 29, 4 (November): 914–47.

Suppes, Patrick. 1984. *Probabilistic Metaphysics*. New York: Basil Blackwell.

Tardiff, Robert M. 1981. "L'Hospital's Rule and The Central Limit Theorem," *The American Statistician*. 35, 1 (February): 43.

TenHouten, Warren, John Stern, and Diana TenHouten. 1979. "Political Leadership in Poor Communities: Applications of Two Sampling Methodologies," in Peter Orleans and William Russell Ellis, Jr., eds., *Race, Change, and Urban Society, Volume 5, Urban Affairs Annual Reviews*. Beverly Hills: Sage.

Thompson, H. R. 1954. "A Note on Contagious Distributions," *Biometrika*. 41: 268–71.

Tobin, James. 1958. "Estimation of Relationships for Limited Dependent Variables," *Econometrica*. 26 (January): 24–36.

Trivedi, Pravin K. 1984. "Uncertain Prior Information and Distributed Lag Analysis," in David F. Hendry and Kenneth F. Wallis, eds., *Econometrics and Quantitative Economics*. Oxford: Basil Blackwell.

Tsurumi, H. 1971. "A Note on Gamma Distributed Lags," *International Economic Review*. 12: 317–23.

Tucker, L. R. and C. Lewis. 1973. "A Reliability Coefficient for Maximum Likelihood Factor Analysis," *Psychometrika*. 38: 1–10.

Tufte, Edward R. 1983. *The Visual Display of Quantitative Information*. Cheshire, CT: Graphics Press.

Tufte, Edward R. 1977. "Political Statistics for the United States: Observations on Some Major Data Sources," *American Political Science Review*. 71 (March): 305–14.

Tukey, John W. 1977. *Exploratory Data Analysis*. Reading, MA: Addison-Wesley.

Tukey, John W. 1960. "A Survey of Sampling from Contaminated Distributions," in I. Olkin, ed., *Contributions to Probability and Statistics*. Stanford: Stanford University Press.

Vasquez, John. 1987. "The Steps to War," *World Politics* 40, 1 (October): 108–45.

Wald, A. 1943. "Tests of Statistical Hypotheses Concerning Several Parameters When the Number of Observations Is Large," *Transatlantic American Mathematical Society*. 54: 426–82.

Wallace, Michael D. 1973. "Alliance Polarization, Cross-Cutting, and International War, 1815–1964: A Measurement Procedure and Some Preliminary Evidence," *Journal of Conflict Resolution*. 17, 4 (December): 575–604.

Walt, Stephen M. 1985. "Alliance Formation and the Balance of World Power," *International Security*. 9, 4: 3–43.

Waltz, Kenneth. 1979. *Theory of International Politics*. New York: Random House.

Ward, Michael Don. 1984. "Differential Paths to Parity: A Study of the Contemporary Arms Race," *American Political Science Review*. 78, 2 (June): 297–317.

White, Halbert. 1982. "Maximum Likelihood Estimation of Misspecified Models," *Econometrica*. 50: 1–25.

White, Halbert. 1980. "A Heteroscedasticity-Consistent Covariance Matrix Estimator and a Direct Test for Heteroscedasticity," *Econometrica*. 48: 817–38.

Williams, D. A. 1982. "Extra-binomial Variation in Logistic Linear Models," *Applied Statistics*. 31,2: 144–8.

Wishart, J. 1928. "The Generalized Product Moment Distribution in Samples from a Normal Multivariate Population," *Biometrika*. 20A: 32–52.

Wismer, David A. and R. Chattergy. 1978. *Introduction to Nonlinear Optimization*. New York: North-Holland.

Wold, H. 1954. *A Study in the Analysis of Stationary Time Series,* 2nd ed. Stockholm Almquist and Wiksell.

Zellner, Arnold. 1984. *Basic Issues in Econometrics*. Chicago: University of Chicago Press.

Zellner, Arnold. 1971. *An Introduction to Bayesian Inference in Econometrics*. New York: Wiley.

Zellner, Arnold. 1962. "An Efficient Method of Estimating Seemingly Unrelated Regressions and Tests of Aggregation Bias," *Journal of the American Statistical Association*. 57: 348–68.

Zellner, Arnold and T. Lee. 1965. "Joint Estimation of Relationships Involving Discrete Random Variables," *Econometrica*. 33: 383–94.

# Index

272    **Index**